Patterns of Soviet Politics

THE DORSEY SERIES IN POLITICAL SCIENCE

EDITOR NORTON E. LONG *Brandeis University*

Patterns of
Soviet Politics

By RICHARD C. GRIPP

San Diego State College

Revised Edition • 1967

THE DORSEY PRESS

Homewood, Illinois

Revised Edition

First Printing, July, 1967

1002625423

T

Library of Congress Catalog Card No. 67–21009

to Helen, Jim, and Joyce

Preface

THIS SECOND EDITION constitutes a reorganization of material and chapters under several broad headings: the political environment, rule-making, and rule-administering and adjudicating. An introduction has been added to establish a framework for the study, and a new chapter on political environment is included to help fill in the framework. There is an additional chapter on the Communist Party. The rewritten and expanded concluding chapter seeks to highlight the patterns of Soviet politics and discuss the question of trends. New information has been added to all but the historical chapters, although these too, hopefully, have been improved.

In translating Russian words I have relied on fairly normal usage, but with slight variations. The designation for the soft sign has been dropped, while the Russian plural endings have been preserved. The Russian й and ы are transliterated as *y*, and the Russian у and ю are transliterated as *u*.

Several people have offered valuable suggestions for this edition, including the helpful critiques of Professors William B. Ballis and Robert A. Rupen, and the occasional but freely offered advice of a former colleague, Robert A. Lewis. Among my fellow departmental members at San Diego State College, Charles Andrain contributed useful suggestions for the chapter on political environment, and Vincent Padgett and Ivo Feierabend measurably assisted me over a long period of time by their insights into the field of comparative politics. Mr. Wallace Millson helped compile data on the plenary sessions of the Central Committee and on elections to the Supreme Soviet. My wife's typing of the manuscript, checking numerous details and editorial suggestions are appreciated. As for the book's flaws, they are attributable to me alone.

July, 1967   RICHARD C. GRIPP

Table of Contents

ix

Introduction

THERE ARE several different though related problems which make difficult the study of Soviet politics. In the first place, there exists an official secrecy about the USSR which, while diminishing measurably since the paranoiac Stalinist era, can be seen in such matters as the withholding of certain data about Soviet society—for example, crime statistics. The Soviet leadership has assumed that disclosure of such "sensitive" information would only be misused by anticommunist enemies, both domestic and foreign. Equally significant, too, is the fact that the USSR simply is not an open society. Information relating to the operation of the political system has not in the past been made available by its rulers merely to satisfy public and scholarly desires for information. The highly controversial nature of socialism, communism, Stalinism and totalitarianism-statism has given rise to some very strong Western feelings (especially is this true in the United States) of antipathy toward the USSR. This problem is further aggravated for American students by the openly and vigorously anticommunist and, for many years, anti-Soviet direction of United States foreign policy since World War II. For all of these reasons the study of Soviet politics, if it is to be both serious and fruitful, must be undertaken with unusual care. Strong prejudices about Soviet Communism, uncompensated for by deep knowledge of the subject, can only serve as a barrier to understanding the Soviet political system. The task, of course, is not impossible, but first one must attack some prevailing misconceptions about the subject in general.

Among the numerous myths which are popularly held concerning Soviet politics and which have frequently circulated in the West is the one ascribing mysterious and inexplicable "enigmas" and "dialectics" to them, the comprehension of which requires certain "keys," or special insights to their unraveling. Another widely held myth is that Soviet politics are manipulated by scheming rulers who harbor the worst of possible motives, for example, the desire to enslave mankind. Still another myth is that a communist political system, because it is communist, must inevitably result in gross inefficiencies and weaknesses of a fatal nature. This last myth struggles with a countermyth which ascribes to communist leaders all manner of success in winning new victories around the world. This book, in opposition to these and similar misconceptions, is written on the assumption that Soviet politics, basically, are a unique application of certain goal-oriented procedures to the universally common features of political systems. Consequently, serious students can, with some effort,

1

grasp the essentials of Soviet politics in both their theory and their practice.

The analysis of political systems has now reached the point at which we can discuss a given national polity somewhat within a common framework. We can begin to look at the Soviet Union in terms of input functions of popular demands—say for better and more abundant consumer goods—demands that are being articulated and aggregated chiefly, but not exclusively, by the Communist Party. The conversion mechanism of the Communist Party and the governmental apparatus translates, or converts, a number of these demands into authoritative outputs of the political system—rule-making, rule-administering, and rule-adjudicating functions. These outputs, the Soviet leaders confidently anticipate, will continue giving rise to feedback in the form of renewed support for the system. The political system, any political system, then, is the authoritative order-maintaining system for a society, held together as a rational system by the thread of legitimate force. Differences that do exist between political systems come more from the manner in which the common functions are carried out, that is, the unique patterns of given polities.

For the Soviet system, the Communist Party has labored mightily to win acceptance as *the* sole legitimate molder, director, and guide of Soviet society. The system's leaders, particularly since Stalin's time, occasionally leave the impression that their legitimacy as the proper inheritors of Marxism-Leninism is being challenged by various interest groups, if not by the citizenry in general. This is not so unique, however, from politics in Western systems. Soviet politics, then, can be viewed as ruling politics, not wholly different from ruling politics in other countries. In all systems, there are the common functions to be performed. What is different is how Soviet politics carries out these functions in ways different from, say, the British or American styles. What we are looking for here are the particular patterns of Soviet politics.

The Soviet political system might be analyzed also within a framework of a developing system—beginning in 1917 from a fairly underdeveloped, only partially-industrialized, and largely rural society. Perhaps political development can be depicted, as Fagen does,[1] by four generalized criteria:

1. Increased structural differentiation in the political system.
2. Movement away from ascription criteria and toward achievement criteria in political recruitment and evaluation.
3. Widening of the effective scope of political activity.
4. Increased secularization and "rationalization" in the performance of political functions.

---

[1] Richard R. Fagen, *Politics and Communication* (Boston: Little, Brown, 1966), p. 130.

Whether or not these criteria are wholly valid, Soviet political trends since 1917 bear a resemblance to this format. Two other terms which might be conveniently brought in at this point, relating to the developing nature of Soviet politics, are those of the mass mobilization society and a modernizing system. All communist state systems, in whatever country they have been introduced, are deeply involved in mobilization of the masses. The current Soviet and Chinese societies typify this movement. The drive toward modernity, if this includes mobilization, industrialization, growing attentiveness to popular demands, and rather efficient use of sophisticated instruments and techniques of political rule, also can be applied to the USSR.

One of the patterns of Soviet politics that we normally are aware of is that of Marxism-Leninism, or *communism*. This ideology is humanitarian, at least in its theoretical goal. Here, the Soviet leadership seeks to bring about a type of economic and social egalitarianism through which mankind will be better off than it would have been otherwise. The Soviet political system is thus very much ideal goal-directed. It has, in the view of its rulers, a grandiose objective, a purpose behind it all. Marxist-Leninist ideology also gives to Soviet politics the aura of a scientific, rationalistic flavor. Socialism, as the operating stage of Marxism-Leninism, constitutes an ethic for a system of political discipline emphasizing science. It offers a set of development goals that stress roles that are functional to modernization and the achievement of a rational society.[2] This approach is highlighted, for example, by national economic planning in which the Soviet leadership anticipates that all problems will be logically laid out for analysis and, as a result, solved. Perhaps the term "bureaucratic socialism" might better apply to a large nation such as the USSR engaged in a reasoned, planned endeavor to achieve the socialist-communist millennium.

In addition to Marxian-humanitarianism and bureaucratic socialism, the Soviet system might be depicted in terms of *elitist, party-state* politics. From its origin in 1917 under Lenin, the Soviet state has exemplified rule by an elite of the Communist Party. This rule goes a long way toward explaining the dynamic functioning of Soviet politics. The term party-state also helps point up the rule-administering and adjudicating roles of the state apparatus as it carries out and enforces the policies decided upon by high party leaders.

The foregoing discussion has attempted to introduce, in very brief compass, several threads which might help join together what can be

---

[2] David E. Apter, *The Politics of Modernization* (Chicago: University of Chicago Press, 1965), p. 329.

termed the main features of Soviet politics. The next step is to outline the historical and contemporary Soviet political environment, the climate as it were, within which Soviet politics are conducted. Much of the remainder of the book will take up in more detail and try to illustrate with examples the history, theory, and practical operation of Soviet politics. The final chapter will attempt to draw together certain conclusions which might be derived from the various ideas and information presented in order to outline the patterns of the Soviet political system.

PART ONE

The Political Environment

CHAPTER I

The Tsarist Heritage

THE OCTOBER REVOLUTION of 1917 brought into being a new political system in Russia based on a new ideology and, to some extent, employing a new methodology. Although the antecedents of Soviet Communism are to be found in Marxism, many of its roots can be uncovered in the Russia of earlier years. Russian history prior to 1917 has particular bearing not only on communist ideology but also on political institutions of the Soviet period. Governmental autocracy, economic underdevelopment, Great Russian predominance within the empire, even the peasant's unhappy existence were all Russian problems of long standing which carried over into the communist era. Important elements of this history relating to the nation's political traditions have been shaped by its land and its people.

NATURE AND NATIONALITY

In Russia as much as in any other country, geography, natural resources, diversity of races, and historical peculiarities have measurably influenced governmental practices, both tsarist and communist. Russian geography can be viewed as omnipresent, perverse, even dramatic; it constitutes a vital force in the makeup of "Mother Russia." The statement that the Soviet Union is a vast expanse of territory containing one sixth of the land surface of the world is by now a trite expression. It is vast, of course, and there exist within the country several important regions. The northern tundra, comprising some 10 percent of the total land area, is cold, barren, almost permanently frozen and mostly useless (except as a reserve for fur-bearing animals). South of the tundra, millions of acres of extensive forest constitute 21 percent of the world's timber resources. The wide and famous steppe, original home of the Cossack, with its level treeless plain takes in sizable portions of the Ukraine, Don, and Volga regions. Included in the steppe is the black soil (*chernozem*) strip, that extremely rich farming land of some 250 million acres.   There are, finally, approximately one million acres of desert and semidesert in the southern and central parts of the country.   With more than 75,000 miles of waterways, a great deal of which is navigable, the river system includes four of the world's longest rivers (Yenisei, Ob, Amur, Lena).   Because much of the Soviet Union is separated from other nations by seas, mountains, and deserts, the country enjoys an unusual degree of geographic insularity.

The climate, having great variety, is far from ideal for agricultural purposes; millions of square miles receive too little rainfall and are too hot or too cold for many months of the year.   Some temperatures illustrative of the climatic variations are the following:[1]

	January (in Fahr.)		July (in Fahr.)	
	Mean	*Minimum*	*Mean*	*Maximum*
Moscow	13	−43	64	100
Odessa	26	15	73	95
Tashkent	32	−19	81	109
Yakutsk	−46	−84	66	102
Verkhoyansk	−58	−90	60	95

With its abundant natural resources, the Soviet Union potentially is one of the richest nations in the world.   A few of her major resources include a trillion and a half tons of coal in addition to enormous oil reserves, immense hydroelectric potential, huge deposits of iron ore, and a million square miles of commercial timber.   There also are deposits of manganese, copper, lead, zinc, gold, platinum, aluminum, and nickel in varying amounts.   All of these factors of geography, climate and natural resources have had in one way or another a bearing on the development of communism in the USSR.

Some authors have attributed the moods and personality characteristics of Russians to their physical surroundings.   The vast steppes, for example, with their rugged life supposedly have bred a strong measure of resourcefulness among the people, while cold, dense forests have taught patience and Spartan frugality; long, navigable rivers, which have stimulated trade, encouraged a sense of hospitality and peacefulness.   The steppe, also, is said to have aroused in the Russians a "cosmic consciousness," along with a sense of toughness which is both fatalistic and tolerant, a flexibility of mind and spirit, acceptance of absolute authority, in addition to unlimited boldness of thought and action.[2]

[1] George B. Cressey, *Asia's Lands and Peoples* (2d ed.; New York: McGraw-Hill Book Co., Inc., 1951), p. 257.

[2] See Bernard Pares, *A History of Russia* (definitive edition; New York: Alfred A. Knopf, Inc., 1953), pp. 7–8; Edward Crankshaw, *Russia and the Russians* (New York:

The Soviet Union embraces more than 150 ethnic groups, with Slavs accounting for three fourths of the total population of more than 233 million by mid-1966. European types predominate, with Great Russians forming more than half of the total population. The 1959 census gave the following figures for the more numerous nationalities as follows:[3]

Nationality	Population
Slavs:	
Russians	114,588,000
Ukrainians	36,981,000
Belorussians	7,829,000
Other Europeans:	
Lithuanians	2,326,000
Jews	2,268,000
Moldavians	2,214,000
Germans	1,619,000
Poles	1,380,000
Caucasus groups:	
Azerbaijani	2,929,000
Armenians	2,787,000
Georgians	2,650,000
Central Asians:	
Uzbeks	6,004,000
Tatars	4,969,000
Kazakhs	3,581,000
Tadzhiks	1,397,000

The census counted 108 national groups plus some 17,000 additional people which it listed as "other nationalities." In response to a query in the census as to native language, 114,400,000 Russians named Russian as their native tongue, as did 10,200,000 people from the non-Russian national groups.

HIGHLIGHTS OF RUSSIAN HISTORY

The Slavs, ancestors of the Russians, were an Indo-European people who originated in the northern Carpathians in the fifth century and inhabited parts of what is now eastern Europe and western Russia. In these early centuries the Slavs migrated west (to become Poles, Czechs, and Slovaks), south (Serbs and Bulgarians), and east (Russians). In the east, the founding of the Russian nation and its first rudimentary political unification came perhaps as early as 862 when the Varangian Rurik

---

The Viking Press, Inc., 1949) pp. 21–30. For a very extensive discussion of the makeup and historical influences on the Russian character, see Anatole Leroy-Beaulieu, *The Empire of the Tsars and the Russians*, trans. Z. A. Ragozin (New York, G. P. Putnam's Sons, 1893), Part I, pp. 138–223.

[3] *Pravda*, February 4, 1960.

established himself as Prince of Novgorod. One of Rurik's successors (Olég) located his capital in Kiev and controlled the other important trading centers of Novgorod and Smolensk. Thus, the period of Kievan Russia was begun (ninth century) and was to be ruled over by princes of the Rurik dynasty until the thirteenth century. Early in the Kievan period the Church exerted considerable influence over both government and society. From Byzantium the Russians adopted Christianity (through Vladimir I in 988–990) with its religious sanctification of the state; this doctrine later set forth the tsar autocrat as heaven's anointed ruler. Other notable effects of the Church's early impact in Russia were to embrace the local language (which was similar to Church Slavonic) rather than Greek and to contribute to a behavior pattern of extreme formalism and no small measure of corruption both in the Church and in the government. Much of the Kievan period, however, was marked by internal fights for rule among contesting princes. After the death of Yaroslav the Wise (1054), the budding state was divided into a number of rival principalities. This, in turn, contributed to the later division of the Russian peoples into three main groups: the Little Russians (in the Ukraine), the White Russians (in the Baltic area), and the Great Russians (in the northeast). With the decline of Kiev, the way was opened for successive invasions of Russia by nomads, Letts and Lithuanians from the Baltic, Swedes from the northwest, Hungarians from the southwest, and, finally, from the east the Tatars in 1223.[4]

The Tatar empire eventually stretched from Asia (China) to eastern Europe (Hungary and Poland) and included all the important cities in Russia. With European headquarters of the empire in Sarai, near what is now Volgograd, the Tatars were to remain for some two and a half centuries (until 1480). The effects of Tatar rule, both direct and indirect, were of great consequence for Russian history. There was a shift in the economic, political, and ecclesiastical center of Russia to Moscow, a breakup of close ties between Russia and the European West, a marked decline in Russian civilization—all of which resulted in something of a religious, cultural, and political decline, as well as consolidation of a firm autocracy.

Ivan the Great (1462–1505) is given credit for throwing off Tatar rule, though the Tatar influence had begun to collapse much earlier; he also tripled Moscow's ruling domain. Ivan Grozny (the "Terrible"), who ruled from 1533–84, added more territories and started the eastward migration of Russians into Siberia. More significantly, the reign of Ivan

---

[4] Although the word Tatar is used historically to include "Mongols," more precisely, the Tatars were but one of several Mongol tribes.

Grozny reorganized Russian government, improved central and local administration, and revised the law code, but it also reduced the power of the council of the nobility and brought the autocracy to a peak of despotism and terror.

The period of 1604–13 was known as the "Time of Troubles" because of its weak tsars, involved court intrigue, a state of near anarchy, and the Polish invasion of Moscow. Finally, in 1612 an assembly (*sobor*) was called. This assembly elected Michael Romanov to the throne (1613–45). Thus began the 300-year reign of the Romanovs which was to continue until the fateful year of 1917.

The first three Romanovs (1613–82) ruled during a century in which Russia remained economically and morally bankrupt. Still, several accomplishments of the period can be recorded: a consolidation of the empire, development of the army, a revision of the law code (1649), and a weakening of Polish influence in Russia which resulted in a treaty signed between the two nations in 1686. During these 69 years a number of popular revolts broke out in protest against scarcity of food, high prices and high taxes, governmental corruption, and worsening conditions of serfdom—such as the sale of serfs without their land.

Peter the Great's rule (1682–1725), which historically separates ancient from modern Russia, made a lasting imprint on the country both for the tsarist and the Soviet periods. Among Peter's many achievements are included a drastic reorganization and secularization of the government, reform of the army, growth of a merchant and artisan class, and transfer of the capital from Moscow to the new city of St. Petersburg. In the process, he inflicted severe hardships on the people, including forced labor and long-term military conscription. As usually happens in Russian history, the peasant class suffered most under his merciless policies. Rightly or wrongly, by his determination to modernize and westernize Russia, Peter brought his country full-scale into European diplomacy, and by his military acquisitions (e.g., Livonia, the remainder of the Ukraine, Baltic and Caspian Sea ports) he made Russia into a great European power. Another such strong ruler was not to appear until Catherine II.

The reign of Catherine II (Catherine the Great, 1762–96) saw extensive territorial achievements which gained parts of the Black Sea coast, the Crimea, and two thirds of Poland (chiefly the Russian provinces). Pugachev's revolt (1772–74) against the government, with Cossacks constituting the main force, was a protest against both the nobility's undue influence with the tsar and against the harshness of peasant life. More significantly, under Catherine the worst evils of serfdom were seriously aggravated, becoming the *cause célèbre* for future decades of peasant revolt.

Alexander I (1801–25) achieved for his country no small amount of influence in European affairs by incorporating Finland into Russia, helping to defeat Napoleon in (1812–13), and gaining more Polish territory, in addition to the areas of Bessarabia and Baku. In December, 1825, shortly after the Tsar's death, some of the nobility, the Guard, and younger army officers infused with liberal-revolutionary sympathies, and aided by some of the literati, carried out the so-called Decembrist Uprising. This revolt, though weak and largely ineffective, sought such liberal reforms as a constitution which would embrace the idea of representation and would include the abolition of serfdom. The main effect of the uprising (Nicholas I did provide for an extensive codification of law in "response" to demands for reform) was to establish for Russia a revolutionary tradition.[5]

With clarity of purpose, rigidly authoritarian in his methods, vindictive, suspicious, a master of intrigue and cruel despotism, Nicholas I (1825–55) was the old Russian prototype for the twentieth century's Joseph Stalin. Nicholas adopted certain police state methods and, somewhat like Stalin, demanded elaborate confessions from his victims; he also required political obedience from all of his subjects. In foreign policy Nicholas considered himself the policeman of Europe; he helped both to curb revolt and to hinder reform movements throughout western Europe.

In the Treaty of Paris (1856) the main European powers, after having prevented a Russian victory in the Crimean War, aligned against Russia to deny her access to the Near East. Humiliated abroad, faced with increasing unrest at home, the new tsar, Alexander II (1855–81), inaugurated a series of internal reforms. These included formal abolition of serfdom in 1861, creation of elected local councils (*zemstva*), and a reform of the law courts in 1864 based on the concept of equality before the law and trial by jury, the reform of municipal government in 1870, the conscription law of 1874 (regularizing and lightening the duty of military service), and a relaxation of censorship as well as an expansion in the local school system. No wonder that Alexander II became known as the "Reforming Tsar." On the other hand, some of his improvements (such as the "Emancipation") proved to be more illusory than real.

With the accession to the throne of Alexander III (1881–94), following his father's assassination, a return to full autocratic rule was the mode; hopes for an expansion in the liberalizations of Alexander II were permanently dimmed. Although an attempt was made to alleviate the peasant's misery (for example, establishment of a Peasant's Bank and abolition

---

[5] Anatole G. Mazour, *The First Russian Revolution, 1825: the Decembrist Movement* (Berkeley, Calif.: University of California Press, 1937), pp. 261ff.

of the poll tax), the bitter distress of rural life was basically unrelieved. Censorship, curbs on freedom in the university, russification of minority nationalities, persecution of Jews, and introduction into the localities of agents of the minister of the interior—all constituted a climate hospitable to the growth of revolutionary feeling.

The last of Russia's tsars ascended the great imperial throne of Peter the Great, and Catherine II, in 1894. The ancestors of Nicholas II (1894–1917) bequeathed to him a functioning autocracy, an historic imperial system. Nicholas inherited much more, of course. He was left with many very difficult national problems and with a form of rule which no longer was sufficiently autocratic to command much obedience nor was it representative enough to withstand revolution. Nicholas II and his feeble attempts to rule through the outmoded, schizophrenic governmental system is the history of Russia from 1894 to 1917.

GOVERNMENT UNDER THE TSARS

Modern Soviet government is derived from Leninism and Stalinism. It is more than that; it is a government with roots feeding back into ancient Russia. One might argue, indeed, that several features of modern Soviet government are but present-day versions of earlier forms of tsarist government. A high degree of centralization, an inflated bureaucracy, controls over industry, dictatorship—with all of its ramifications, such as a secret police and infallibility of the rulers in all matters of dogma—even governmental censorship, are typical of Russian government, both old and new. Under the nineteenth century tsars, for example, a recurring administrative problem resulted from independent and arbitrary actions of governmental ministers. Instead of upholding the interests of the bureaucracy as a whole, these ministers competed with one another for the tsar's favors by representing opposing interests and cliques. Within this milieu, the tsar was known to play one minister off against another, by-passing his own prime minister in the process.[6] This identical ministerial problem, including the arbitrary actions of the autocrat, also occurred during the latter period of Stalin's reign and was one cause for the widespread governmental reorganization carried out by Khrushchev in 1957. At that time, in fact, Khrushchev referred to the ministers in Moscow as little gods. Analogies between the two systems of government can be carried too far, of course. It should be sufficient to point out some of the main features of government under the tsars and the ruling heritage which they left.

---

[6] Leroy-Beaulieu, *op. cit.*, Part II, pp. 80–82.

Although early traditions of monarchy and aristocracy can be traced to Kievan Russia, it is in the Tatar period of rule (1240–1480) that elements of the heritage of a strong autocracy can be found. From that time on, governmental despotism, be it that of Ivan the Terrible, Peter the Great, or Stalin, developed its own patterns, but the origins probably still rested in Tatar rule. In addition, the Tatars left remnants of their bureaucratic system. During this period, too, the princes of Muscovy, particularly Ivan I ("Grand Prince of Vladimir and all Rus"), established themselves and their city of Moscow as the preponderant influence among the Russians. Ivan III (Ivan the Great) in the fifteenth century freed himself and his principality of Muscovy from Tatar rule and became known as the "Sovereign of all Russia." He also took the title of tsar.[7] Ivan IV, who was crowned as tsar in 1547, established a body to advise him which he called the "Land Assembly" (*Zemsky Sobor*).[8] He also laid the groundwork for the marriage between the tsarist autocracy and the Orthodox Church. Henceforth, the tsars of Russia were to guard the true faith in return for the Church's blessing of divine rule. Peter the Great substituted the title of emperor for that of tsar (though the term tsar was still widely used), changed the designation "Grand States of the Russian Tsardom" to that of "Empire of all the Russias," moved the capital from Moscow to the new city of St. Petersburg, and reorganized the bureaucracy—all in an attempt to modernize and westernize the backward, eastern country of Russia. Peter's bureaucracy, later elaborated by Catherine the Great, set the framework and even the pattern for Russian administration which lasted until the end of the empire. Russian bureaucracy went on to gain international fame for its corruption and venality. Frequently operating beyond the normal restraints of legality, the bureaucracy functioned in an arbitrary and irresponsible manner; its lifeblood was widespread bribery.

Under Grand Prince Yaroslav (1019–54), an embryonic body of law was compiled, known as the Russian Law (*Russkaya Pravda*); its enforcement became the responsibility of contesting parties, the Church, and the state. There were later attempts to develop the law, such as those of Tsar Alexis

---

[7] "Tsar" may have been adapted from the word *Caesar*. At Russia's entrance into World War I, an official manifesto referred to the tsar as "Nicholas II, Emperor and Autocrat of All Russia, Tsar of Poland, Grand Duke of Finland ..." Frank Alfred Golder, *Documents of Russian History, 1914–1917*, trans. Emanuel Aronsberg (New York: Century Co., 1927), p. 29.

[8] The *Zemsky Sobor*, which later was to elect Michael Romanov to the throne, had the trappings of a representative assembly, a number of whose members were elected. It met several times a year to deliberate on such governmental matters as war and fiscal needs. After Michael's reign, the assembly declined in importance, and last met in 1698.

in the sixteenth century, also the famous "Instruction" (*Nakaz*) of Catherine the Great in the eighteenth century (a part of which was taken from Montesquieu's works), and the compilation and partial codification by Speransky of all known Russian laws in 45 volumes with an index, under the direction of Nicholas I. More progress was achieved under Alexander II when, among other reforms, judges were given something of a professional status, all persons were declared equal before the law, trial by jury was instituted, and a more standardized procedure for appeal was adopted. Unfortunately for the future codification of Russian law, ordinances were heaped upon ordinances, regulations upon regulations, decrees upon decrees—all in a huge incomprehensible proliferation of uneven, minute, and frequently contradictory statutes. The main difficulty lay in the fact that each tsar was an absolute sovereign who promulgated numerous laws, frequently with little if any thought or concern for what previously had been enacted. The sovereign in Russia was the fountainhead of all law, which flowed solely from his will. Equity, justice, impartiality, and legality were concepts empty of meaning and without substance, unless by chance they conformed to the mood of the tsar at the time. Even then, the bureaucracy was always on hand to deny the people any solid rights such as legal equality, except, of course, in return for a bribe.

The tsars were assisted in their administration by several institutions—the Chancellery, the Governing Senate, and the State Council. The tsar's personal Chancellery (created in 1812) contained several sections, including the infamous "Third Section" which was in charge of the political police. The Senate, founded by Peter the Great in 1711, was to supervise the entire central administration, though it appears in practice to have been little more than a high court of appeal. Members of the Senate, normally aristocrats appointed by the tsar, could do no more than recommend legislation. More important was the State Council (*Gosudarstvenny Sovet*), founded by Alexander I in 1810. Although not a true legislative body, the State Council did draw up and examine legislation for the tsar's pleasure as well as prepare the budget. Members of the Council, never more than 70 or 80, were past and present high functionaries who were, however, often too ignorant, incapable, or infirm to check or alleviate in any way the capricious acts of the tsars. Another quasi-legislative organ was the State Duma, which performed the role of a representative body duly elected by various social classes but which possessed virtually no actual power to influence governmental policy.

A number of ministerial "colleges," precursors of the later ministries, were organized by Peter to supervise specific branches of the central government; for example, there were colleges of foreign affairs, navy, justice, interior, and finance. Although the colleges were involved in some administration, only the tsar could coordinate the varied activities and independent claims of the several ministers, because there was no prime minister. When the tsar was incapable of enforcing such coordination (e.g., Nicholas II), administrative chaos became the normal rule. The ineffectual "Committee of Ministers" (transformed into the Council of Ministers in 1905) was utterly inept in meeting the problems arising from ministerial anarchy.

Governmental structure and administration below the national level were developed only in skeletal form under the tsars. Directly subordinate to the central government were approximately 50 provinces (*gubernii*) in European Russia, each headed by a governor (*gubernator*), and each embracing subordinate offices, such as those for taxation, communication, prisons, and public welfare.[9] The main purpose of this provincial administration was to enforce decrees of the central ministries, especially those of the Ministry of Interior. Each province was further divided into a number of districts (*uyezdy*), and each district was headed by a police official or "corrector" (*ispravnik*). Finally, provision was made for a system of local town councils (*gorodskye dumy*); these usually existed only on paper and at any rate were possessed of limited powers and financial resources. These several levels of administration accomplished virtually nothing of real value; their notoriety all too often resulted from their role as centers of local depotism.

Alexander II, the "Reforming Tsar," established a more elaborate scheme for local government in 1864: the *zemstvo* was organized on both district and provincial levels. Elected for a term of three years, the *zemstvo* chose from among its members a permanent governing board. The presiding officer, with a veto over the council's actions, was either a marshall of the nobility (elected by the nobility) or appointed by the government. As for the electoral process, heads of families formed communal assemblies to nominate rural district assemblies (*volosti*) which, in turn, appointed electors to the district *zemstvo*. Finally, the various district *zemstva* elected higher provincial *zemstva* (assemblies of 60 to 100 delegates). *Zemstvo* achievements included the establishment of some primary schools and hospitals, raising the level of literacy, some road building, and improvements in farming techniques.

---

[9] Pares, *op. cit.*, p. 257; Leroy-Beaulieu, *op. cit.*, Part II, p. 90. For a more extensive discussion of central and local government under the tsars, see Maxime Kovalevsky, *Russian Political Institutions* (Chicago: University of Chicago Press, 1902), pp. 169–222.

In 1895, however, when the *zemstva* asked Nicholas II to acknowledge a need for representative government, the Tsar replied that their hopes for anything but a continuation of unlimited autocracy were "senseless dreams." From this time on, the government's harassment of the *zemstva* focused on arrests of their employees and interference with their elections. The *zemstvo* movement nevertheless can be credited with two results (one negative and one positive) which were particularly meaningful for later Russian history: the first was a rather limited and eventually unfruitful experiment in local self-government; the second was a successful planting of the seeds of future political liberalism.[10] One notable achievement of tsarist government, both central and local, however, was the establishment of a rather well-developed police organization and a system of elaborate censorship.

If the administrative bureaucracy under the tsars was corrupt and burdensome, the police organization was almost stifling. To prevent a recurrence of the Decembrist Uprising in 1825, Nicholas I organized a special ("Third") police division the following year which was answerable directly to himself. This division was incorporated in the Ministry of the Interior in 1880. Moreover, regular police, subject to provincial governors and leading town officials, existed alongside of a loosely formed, centrally controlled *gendarmerie*, organized by regional commands throughout the empire. Among the functions of these several echelons of police were supervision of the internal passport system, collection of state taxes, general administration, public prosecution, censorship, and public health.

The most odious feature of the tsarist police was the infamous "Third Section" with its political espionage. A contemporary writer described this section as a power in itself within the government, "independent, privileged, placed outside of and above the normal sphere of action of all other authorities, outside of and above the laws...."[11] The political police were employed so frequently to hunt down conspirators and secret societies, to ferret out all opposition to the tsars, both real and imagined, that protection of citizens against normal criminal elements too often was neglected in the process. Thousands of *gendarmerie* spread throughout the country frequently became local tyrants, acting as extortioners and privateers rather than defenders of the public safety. An interesting precedent for the arbitrary and malignant procedures of the secret police

---

[10] Richard Charques, *The Twilight of Imperial Russia* (New Jersey: Essential Books, 1959), pp. 26, 86. Cf. Michael T. Florinsky, *The End of the Russian Empire* (New Haven, Conn.: Yale University Press, 1931), pp. 8 ff., who gives more weight of influence to the Duma and to local government under Nicholas II.

[11] Leroy-Beaulieu, *op. cit.*, Part II, p. 133.

that later were to blossom under the Soviet regime was the duty of the tsarist secret police to maintain a force of agents and informers to keep the government advised of all that was done, spoken, or even thought by Russians.   Leroy-Beaulieu, writing in 1898, mentioned the oppressive cloud which seemed to hover over the tsar's subjects even when abroad. "Last winter in Monaco," he reports "...I was talking with a landholder of the Don about his country. We were alone. Suddenly, a stranger came towards us. My friend immediately changed the subject...he thought he recognized a countryman."[12]   The secret police of Stalin's time gained international notoriety for its cruelty carried out with great finesse; it can be said, however, that Stalin was conducting his regime in a manner not unknown in old Russia.

The history of governmental control of the press is an uneven record of sporadic indulgence, contrasted with periods of extensive control and even suppression.   Press censorship was carefully prescribed in a series of decrees issued by Alexander II which placed general policy in the Committee of Ministers, with execution of that policy vested in the Ministry of the Interior and in the St. Petersburg Censorship Committee.   In one five-year period, 1865–70, the government issued 167 "warnings" and suspended 52 of the papers outright.   During other periods, such as the one just prior to 1914, a certain measure of freedom was accorded to the press.   Despite official intimidation, antigovernment views were still expressed at times in some of the largest and best-known newspapers. Russian government under the tsars, then, was typified by peremptory, vacillating, and tyrannical rule.   At all times, Russia was governed as one vast personal domain of the tsar; the sole aim of tsarism was tsarism, ruling for the sake of ruling (to use Herzen's words).

SOCIAL CLASSES

A class structure, sharply differentiated, has been a marked feature of Russian history.   In Kievan times freemen (churchmen, boyars, tradesmen) were set apart from semifreemen (debtors) who, in turn, were not the same as slaves.   By the middle of the seventeenth century, various classes had evolved around a feudal core of mutual service and obligation. Basically, the several classes were the clergy, soldier-gentry, merchants, and the peasants.   Class lines were quite rigid, for example, in matters of residence and marriage.   This arrangement fitted admirably the desires of the higher classes, adding to their status.   Unfortunately, in Kluchevsky's words, "the amenities of life enjoyed by the upper strata of the community

---

[12] *Ibid.*, p. 144.

entailed the legal debasement of the lower."[13] This upper strata constituted only a small minority of the total population.

The nobility, composed of princes, boyars (army officials and rich landowners), and service (nonhereditary) nobility, ranked close to the top of the class hierarchy, immediately below the crown. Princes and boyars considered themselves superior to the service nobility, the latter constituting the greater number. To the nobility as a whole fell the task of administration, leading the military forces, and serving as landlords; after Peter the Great, however, the tsars excluded the nobility from a meaningful sharing in the fruits of political power. The golden age of the nobility was reached in the second half of the eighteenth century. Having recently been freed from obligations to the state and holding their serfs in firm control, the prosperity and license of the nobility were at their zenith. It was, however, precisely this relief from obligatory service granted the nobles (in 1762), thereby affording them preferential treatment, which contributed to a further widening of the gulf between the classes.

Serfs were of two main categories, state and proprietary peasants. The latter group made payments to the landlord of two general types: rent (*obrok*), which was cash or payment in kind, and compulsory labor (*barshchina*). Just prior to the "Emancipation," there were some 60 million peasants under serfdom. Serf-owning landlords, totaling some 250,000, owned varying numbers of serfs, from a low of only a few to a high of 300,000 in one case (Count Sheremetev).

Despite the official abolition of serfdom in 1861, the latter half of the nineteenth century saw a continuance of class lines in tune with reactionary governmental policies of the time. The regime, in a move to enhance the economic position of the upper class, created a Nobles' Land Bank in 1885 to provide credit on favorable terms for the purpose of helping the nobility preserve their estates.

Tightened control over peasant institutions by the government and nobility was achieved through establishment in 1889 of a "land chief" (*zemsky nachalnik*) in each group of villages. Although the land chief, chosen by and responsible to the Minister of the Interior, was assigned judicial and administrative control over peasant organizations, he was all too frequently a corrupt, petty tyrant rather than a judicious administrator of local government. Furthermore, after 1890 a new electoral law gave to the nobility a greater proportion of representatives in the *zemstvo*, and, at the same time, provincial governors received greater authority to regulate *zemstvo* activities. The peasant (*muzhik*) lived in a different world from the member of the upper class (*barin*); the two groups were separated by

---

[13] V. O. Kluchevsky, *A History of Russia*, trans. C. J. Hogarth (New York: E. P. Dutton & Co., 1911–26), Vol. I, p. 187.

numerous barriers—legal, social, even linguistic. There were, moreover, other reasons for increasing conflicts between classes. Persecution of national and religious minorities continued while a decent standard of living for most of the population (peasants and workers) was all too noticeably absent. Finally, the Orthodox Church made little if any attempt to become a unifying element for society as a whole, in contrast with Catholic and Protestant experience in the West.[14]

The official census of 1897 disclosed that only 13 percent (16,785,000) of the population were urbanites. In the occupational breakdown, agriculture comprised approximately 75 percent of the working force, industry almost 10 percent, commerce some 5.8 percent, transport 1.6 percent, state service 1.4 percent, and private employment just under 5 percent. There was, in addition, a legal class breakdown which listed the peasants at just over 77 percent of the population, the nobility at 1.5 percent, and the clergy at .5 percent. These figures indicate only slightly the gulf of mistrust which worked to further separate the various classes.

THE ORTHODOX CHURCH

The Russians are still characterized as a religious people despite more than 40 years of officially inspired atheism. Communism has not yet succeeded in stamping out all religious influences in the country. Under the tsars, the Orthodox Church was supported and blessed by the government, although for different purposes at different times. The Church, in its "association" with the rulers, exerted a rather direct, occasionally vital, effect on the imperial system.

Christianity came to Russia by way of the conversion of Grand Prince Vladimir of Kiev in 988. At first the Church served as a powerful religious force in the lives of many Russians; it was more concerned with spiritual than with political matters—at least prior to the Tatar invasions. Following the Tatar period, the Church entered into its long and eventually disastrous marriage with the autocracy. Ivan III even recruited candidates for the bureaucracy from ecclesiastical schools. The rise of governmental absolutism, wars with the Tatars, schisms between the Church on the one hand and Rome and Constantinople on the other (leading to a separation in 1589), a general enfeeblement of the priesthood, and a seeking after greater social, material, and political power by Church officials all contributed to the weakening and decay of the Church as a wholesome, nonpartisan, spiritual leader in society.

---

[14] Michael T. Florinsky, *Russia: A History and an Interpretation* (New York: The Macmillan Co., 1953), Vol. II, pp. 1256–57.

The Church placed the full weight of its authority behind the monarchy for the convenience of both institutions, on the rationale that rule by the tsars was ordained of God. In return, the tsars gave the Church secular support, which included state subsidies running into millions of rubles. In a further downgrading of the Church, Peter the Great abolished its highest office, the Patriarchate, and made the Church subordinate to a governmentally sponsored body, the Holy Synod. The Synod, in turn, was headed by a senior procurator, appointed as the tsar's official "eye" over Church matters. Tsar Paul later declared himself to be head of the Church and the marriage between Church and state was at last consummated. The Holy Synod administered the Church bureaucracy mainly through the economic and education divisions; even in these organizations, headed by priests, many of the employees were lay bureaucrats. Priests, in actual practice, were often considered as virtual employees of the government, acting as police informants and using their churches as communication outlets for the regime.

THE PEASANTRY

Certainly one of the main streams of Russian history as well as a primary cause in the decline of the tsarist system was the steadily developing feeling of bitterness toward the regime on the part of the peasants. An important part of this history was covered in the period of serfdom extending from early in the seventeenth century (it became formalized as a state institution in 1649) until its official abolition in 1861. Under serfdom there were mutual rights and duties, though the rights seemed to belong exclusively to the landlords and the duties to the peasant serfs. In return for the serf's labor the "lord" was to feed him in periods of famine and contribute seed in the event of crop failure. The awesome power of the landlords over serfs included the right to confiscate a peasant's movable goods, restrict the peasant's freedom when he was not on the estate, command or prevent a marriage, sell a peasant to another landlord, and exercise general judicial control over peasants, including sentences of flogging and of forced labor exile to Siberia. The role of the government in this scheme seemed always to support the landlord, but only if the landlord made certain that peasants paid their taxes and that there were recruits readily available for military service.

Among the causes for the official ending of serfdom, known as the "Emancipation," several deserve mention. The general reform movement of Tsar Alexander II dealt in large measure with the problems and dissatisfactions of the peasants, all of which served to highlight the evils of serfdom.

There was also the factor that large southern landowners were entering international trade and discovering, in the process, the greater efficiency of wage labor over that of serfs. Most important, however, appeared to be the growing incidence of peasant uprisings, a reflection of the harsh realities of serfdom. With the oft-quoted warning of Alexander II, "Better to abolish serfdom from above than to wait till it begins to abolish itself from below," the ground was laid for dissolution of that odious institution so hated by the peasants. The act of abolition was carried out in 1861 by the Tsar's order of "This I desire, I demand, I command."

The Emancipation satisfied perhaps only the former landlords who charged peasants inordinately high prices for land in the north and who retained for themselves unreasonable amounts of choice land in the south. From the Emancipation the peasant received greater legal rights, but he still possessed only limited freedoms; he was burdened with enormous obligations, and he was left with insufficient property. He was, in fact, placed in the unenviable position of having the right to purchase perhaps half the amount of land he formerly cultivated at a price which he would rarely, if ever, be able to afford. The Emancipation, then, authorized legal rights for the peasant but did not guarantee them, did little to free him from the penalties and restrictions attached to his lowly class, and eliminated neither the poll tax nor the humiliating corporal punishment to which he was still subject. The peasant, in brief, failed to gain from the ending of serfdom that which he needed most—an improved economic and social status. In the process, he was bound closer than ever to his historic commune. The pre-Emancipation village commune, or *mir*, was a local authority which collected taxes and even had some judicial powers. The members of the *mir* elected their own officials.

Relinquishing his servitude to the landlord, the peasant became the servant of the commune, the traditional peasant community association. The communes inherited from the landlords the role of tax collector and overall farm manager. To the commune the peasant owed both duty and accountability. Communes controlled three types of land: individual house and garden allotments, fields under cultivation, and forests and pastures. Thus, land taken over by the peasants was administered for them by communes. Organizationally, a number of households made up a commune, and a number of communes formed an administrative subdivision of a *volost*, whose members, in turn, elected representatives, judges, other officials, and a village "elder" (*starosta*)[15] or at times a Council of

---

[15] Gerold T. Robinson, *Rural Russia under the Old Regime* (New York: The Macmillan Co., 1949), p. 79. Kovalevsky, *op. cit.*, p. 85 refers to the *starosta* as an elected district judge.

Village Elders. A number of peasants began to leave the commune, which was breaking up, by the early years of the twentieth century.

Other forces worked to the disadvantage of the peasants. For example, Finance Minister Witte (under Nicholas II) kept the price of bread low, which had the effect of encouraging peasant migration to the cities and thereby ensured a steady supply of inexpensive labor for industrial development. As a consequence, administered low grain prices worked a special hardship on small, landowning peasants. Serfdom had ended but poverty remained, with great numbers of peasants existing on an all too narrow margin between mere subsistence and starvation.

In 1851 the famous writer, Herzen, self-exiled to western Europe, described the life of the Russian peasant as being outside the law; neither the law, nor the government, nor its agents offered the peasant anything but discrimination and exploitation. "The Russian peasant...has never believed either in the authority of his lord, or in the justice of the courts, or in the equity of the administration... his whole life has been one long, dumb, passive opposition to the existing order of things: he has endured oppression, he has groaned under it...."[16] The peasant's life of misery continued, except for brief periods of only partial relief, for example in the establishment of the Peasant's Bank to provide credit for land purchases and in Prime Minister Stolypin's agrarian reforms. The latter aided the growth of individual peasant households and hopefully would hold off revolution. Basically, however, the lot of the peasant was unimproved prior to the revolutions of the twentieth century. All the seeds for revolt were there in the poor peasant, so long victimized and abused by the government and by higher social classes; he was condemned all too frequently to a hopeless, grinding poverty.

EARLY INDUSTRIALIZATION

The expansion of Russian industry in the latter half of the nineteenth century was aided by deliberate governmental policy. Through a rather wide application of protective tariffs, loans and subsidies, encouragement of foreign capital, and direct investments, the state contributed measurably to overall industrial development. Where once the government practiced nonintervention in private business, after 1880 the pattern more and more became one of assistance, and later of outright interference. By this technique the regime hoped to modernize the military machine and to obtain political advantages from increased industrial prosperity. Govern-

---

[16] Alexander Herzen, *From the Other Shore, and the Russian People and Socialism, an Open Letter to Jules Michelet* (New York: George Braziller, Inc., 1956), p. 180.

ment assistance and intervention in the economy has been a hallmark of both Russian and Soviet history ever since. Count Witte, Finance Minister at the turn of the century, stimulated the growth of state capitalism, planning for a rapid industrialization to lead Russia into modernity.

Additional railroad lines were under state construction at the same time that existing railways were being purchased by the government. Inheritance and gift taxes, and a tax on capital income (securities and interest-bearing deposits) had been imposed in the 1880's.[17] Despite a marked rise in general manufacturing capacity, Russia remained economically underdeveloped. Moreover, its working force was just beginning to emerge from its embryonic stage of development.

The rise in the numbers of the industrial proletariat stemmed, in part, from former serfs leaving the land. Accompanying this migration were the government's conscious efforts to force industrialization.[18] The growing number of workers stimulated greater demands for improved working conditions, some of which the government attempted to provide. A law of 1882, for example, prohibited employment of children under twelve and limited to eight working hours those in the age group twelve to fifteen. Other legislation just prior to the turn of the century prevented juvenile work on Sundays and holidays, restricted night work in textile mills to men aged seventeen and over, regulated and improved employment contracts and methods of paying workers, provided for school attendance for child workers, set the maximum day for all workers at eleven and one half hours and established a factory inspection system. To administer the latter, factory offices were organized, made up of factory "inspectors," members from the municipalities, *zemstva*, judiciary, and government officials; their task was to supervise worker-employee relationships. The agents of the factory offices, the inspectors, although expected to enforce plant rules, had as their ostensible function the protection of the rights of the workers. Unfortunately, these inspectors too often lacked sufficient enthusiasm for carrying out their role as spokesmen for the workers.[19]

---

[17] The output of manufacturing rose nearly four times between 1879 and 1899. The output of pig iron amounted to more than four million tons and that of iron-steel almost four million tons annually. In one four-year period (1909–13) pig iron production increased 59 percent, iron and steel 50 percent, coal some 40 percent, and coke 60 percent. Sidney Harcave, *Russia, A History* (3d ed.; New York: J. B. Lippincott Co., 1956), p. 399.

[18] By 1900 a total of roughly three million industrial workers included, among other categories, an estimated employment in textile production of 550,000, in metallurgy 500,000, and on the railroads 400,000. Hugh Seton-Watson, *The Decline of Imperial Russia, 1855–1914* (London: Methuen and Co., 1952), p. 123.

[19] The multifarious tasks of the overworked inspectors included that of being the "eyes, ears, and tongues of the Ministry of Finance." Theodore H. Von Laue, "Factory Inspection Under the 'Witte System': 1892–1903," *The American Slavic and East European Review*, Vol. XIX (October, 1960), p. 352.

Apart from those inspectors who aided management, the elaborate set of laws to provide for workers' rights frequently were superseded by contradictory legislation providing loopholes for employers, such as laws permitting night work for women and children in certain cases. Employers could maintain special police forces and there were penalties imposed on workers (all enforced by the government) for refusing to work, for striking, or for instigating strikes.

By the law of 1874 outlawing trade unions, sentences of prison or exile were provided for anyone found guilty of organizing an association which "stimulated hatred between employers and workers."[20]   Although in the early twentieth century official leniency toward unions helped them flourish to such an extent that by 1906 there were some 44 unions in St. Petersburg and over 40 in Moscow, this era of relative freedom was short-lived. Government suppression was brought back, once again, forcing the trade unions and the revolutionary political movements closer together in a tighter working partnership.   The numerous strikes which occurred in these years first broke out in the cotton mills of St. Petersburg in 1879 as a protest against the lowering of wages.   These workers demanded an increase in wages and improved working conditions, such as more sympathetic foremen and shorter working hours.   In the early 1900's large-scale strikes, though brief, started in a number of cities such as Baku, Tiflis, Kiev, and Odessa.   Marxist organizers supported the strikers in these years in the hope of stimulating labor discontent.   As could be expected, governmental measures to accommodate the rapidly expanding needs of both industrialists and workers were biased, vacillating, unplanned, and too often insincere.

REVOLUTIONARY SEEDS

In the latter years of the nineteenth century both Russians and foreigners predicted the approach of revolution.   In the 1880's the writer Constantine Leontiev foretold of a coming revolution that would be tyrannical, bloody, inhumane, and communist.   This dire forecast was to be partially fulfilled in 1917, but was realized earlier in the form of a rehearsal.   The atmosphere in Russia in 1898 has been depicted in terms of moral and intellectual anarchy, and densely ignorant masses clinging to the tsar in blind trust; above these, a few young liberals vainly attempting

---

[20] Seton-Watson, *op. cit.*, p. 127.   Government suppression of unions (some 80 unions had been dissolved by the government in less than a year, 1907–8) only aggravated worker's movements and resulted in more serious labor dissatisfaction, which in turn led to a growth in the number of secret labor organizations.   One union, a "police union," was established under government sponsorship and used to spy on trade union activities.

to get the people to take by force what it insisted on awaiting from the sovereign's benevolence.[21]

Among the forces contributing to the Revolution of 1905 one should cite numerous and widespread strikes, particularly the one in St. Petersburg in 1896. This strike was instigated by workers influenced by Marxist groups, such as the "Union of Struggle for the Liberation of the Working Class," whose members were protesting chiefly against low wages. Student disorders and demonstrations in the 1890's began in St. Petersburg University and spread to other universities in the country. Nationalistic pressures from such minorities as the Jews, Finns, Poles, and Lithuanians, particularly in the border regions of the nation, added to the general unrest.

By this time, the liberalism of the intelligentsia was becoming more apparent, and more revolutionary too. Liberal forces gained hope from the reforms of Alexander II in the 1860's which saw the Emancipation, judicial reform, and creation of the *zemstva*. Hope, unappeased, however, was transformed into growing distrust of the regime. The reactionary atmosphere of unrestricted and irresponsible autocracy which followed, so much a normal feature of the regimes of Alexander III and Nicholas II, blunted early liberal enthusiasm for the regime. Pogroms (organized attacks) against Jews in Russia at this time stimulated the intelligentsia to become both more socialist and more revolutionary. And there existed always the misery of the peasant whose patient tolerance and long suffering without violent upheaval were not to endure for many more years.

The government, of course, was not altogether unaware of this rise in revolutionary zeal. It was becoming obvious to many, if not always to the short-sighted Tsar, that a social eruption was imminent. Although Minister of the Interior Plehve argued for a "small victorious war" to hold back the forces of revolution, the war was as much if not more an impulsive and irresponsible adventure of the Tsar himself. The Far East was picked as the area and Japan as the intended victim in what, unfortunately, resulted in a war (1904–5) that was neither small nor victorious. A half-century earlier Russia's defeat in the Crimean War gave rise to popular disillusionment with the ruling monarchy. The reforms of the 1860's stemmed, in part, from this defeat. Now, overwhelming defeat of Russia in the Far East by a supposedly inferior Asian nation was the last insult which many of the Tsar's subjects were willing to suffer from an obviously incompetent regime.[22] Economic distress and peasant hardship, underlined

---

[21] Leroy-Beaulieu, *op. cit.*, Part II, pp. 507, 525–26.

[22] The defeat opened the door to fundamental social changes which the regime was totally incapable of handling. Donald W. Treadgold, *Lenin and His Rivals* (New York: Frederick A. Praeger, Inc., 1955), p. 15.

by the blind policies of a vacillating government which had been in-gloriously defeated in a frivolous war were simply too much. Revolution was more than probable, it was inevitable.

By early 1905 the *zemstvo* liberals were demanding, in addition to other improvements, a constituent assembly. This desire for an elected repre-sentative assembly which would modify the harshness of tsarism was a long sought for achievement—indeed the main one—in the hopes and expectations of Russian liberalism. On a Sunday late in January a large number of petitioners marched to the Tsar's Winter Palace in St. Peters-burg, humbly requesting a number of civil liberties, a separation of Church and state, political amnesty, a constituent assembly, and correction of certain other backward conditions. One account of subsequent events draws a vivid sketch. "Near the Winter Palace the throng grew . . . the troops fired, bringing down little boys perched on the trees . . . killing and wounding many men and women . . . the troops again fired. Again killed and wounded, again groans and cries, and a terror-stricken scattering crowd spreading indignation throughout the city."[23] Perhaps this event, more than any other during the reign, undermined the allegiance of the common people to the throne and shattered the image of Nicholas as the father of his people. In the spring a rash of sporadic protest strikes broke out. Some police and governmental officials were murdered (including the Tsar's uncle, who was governor general of Moscow). There was an increase, also, in peasant outbreaks which included dispossessing some estate owners, arson, and occasionally even murder.

The crucial month of the year was October. On October 13, the workers set up a committee in St. Petersburg, giving it the name of Council (Soviet) of Workers' Deputies. Similar organizations had been established, others soon were to be, in various parts of the country, but none was to be more famous than the Petersburg Soviet, one of whose leaders was Leon Trotsky. A number of strikes occurred, chief among them being the Moscow railway workers' strike of October 7 which launched the famous general strike. By mid-October varieties of strikes, carried out by working, trade, and pro-fessional people, paralyzed the capital. "By day mobs were in possession of the streets, red flags flew from the housetops, processions formed. . . . Police were powerless to intervene, urban life had come to a halt."[24] Effective government, practically speaking, was nonexistent. In November and December mutiny broke out in the armed forces resulting in the death of thousands and the wounding of many thousands more.

---

[23] Harold Whitmore Williams, *Russia of the Russians* (New York: Charles Scribner's Sons, 1915), pp. 64–65.

[24] Charques, *op. cit.*, pp. 124–25.

Even the irresolute Tsar was now convinced that he must at least make a pretense at reform. His reply to the Revolution, issued on October 30, was expressed in the October Manifesto. It promised freedom of speech, assembly, conscience, universal suffrage, as well as freedom from arbitrary arrest, and it promised the much-hoped-for representative assembly—a legislative duma. Two days later the Committee of Ministers was transformed into the Council of Ministers. The result of these measures, transforming the autocracy into a constitutional monarchy of sorts, was to win for the government a short breathing spell. Although the liberal and radical parties either opposed or failed to show enthusiasm for the government's proposals, mainly because they neglected to go far enough, the monarchy was saved from immediate collapse. In the process the opposition groups became somewhat confused, splitting into various factions. By mid-1907 the revolutionary movement was virtually exhausted. It had risen to notable heights in the drama of 1905, then had shuddered and collapsed. The government, though temporarily victorious, was shaken, altered (remaining an autocracy in spirit but a constitutional monarchy in form), and was revealing for the first time the signs of a fatal malignancy. The step taken by the regime towards a constitutional system, though limited and not in good faith, nevertheless was an irrevocable and fatalistic move away from the tsarist autocracy. It gave added hope, if not promise, to the liberals.

Moderate liberalism of the period centered around the *zemstvo* movement which had enjoyed some success in stimulating local government. Moreover, political power after 1905, heretofore the exclusive prerogative of the tsar and his bureaucracy, was shared with elements of the landed gentry, the business classes, and the more wealthy peasants. It was at this time, also, that political parties freely participated in the campaigns for election to the first Duma.

The "Octobrists," who took their name from the Tsar's October Manifesto, were opposed to the government, at least theoretically. Adhering to their belief in constitutional monarchy, the Octobrists favored the development of civil liberties and a representative system; beyond that they remained essentially conservative. To the right of the Octobrists was a group known as the "Union of the Russian People" whose program simply favored a return to the old tsarist autocracy. In the middle of the political spectrum stood the Kadets (Constitutional Democrats), the inheritors of *zemstvo* liberalism. The Kadets advocated a parliamentary system after the British pattern, championed both economic and social reforms and called for a breakup and distribution among peasants of the large landed estates. To the left was the Socialist Revolutionary Party

("SR's"), advocating, among other programs, socialization of the land. This party argued for peasant control of the land (which would be socially owned) and called for a system of producer's cooperatives for industry. After the Revolution of 1905 the SR's became more outright revolutionary, following the specific program of action of their leader Victor Chernov. Finally, the Social Democrats (Russian Social Democratic Labor Party, or "SD's"), avowedly Marxist, were not interested in parliamentary systems and (as with the SR's) boycotted the first Duma elections, though some among its Menshevik and Bolshevik adherents favored giving at least mild support to the Duma.

The history of the quasi-legislature in pre-1917 Russia is a record first of hope, then of frustration, and finally disappointment for the liberal movement. From the Russian word "to think" (*dumat*) comes the word Duma, which had been a consultative body, Boyar's Council, attached to the tsar in the fifteenth century. The electoral law for the Duma of 1906 provided for manhood suffrage at age twenty-five, but with a tax-paying qualification. The franchise, which divided voters into three classes— peasants, urban workers, and landowners, was rigged so that peasants would be highly represented; the government assumed that peasants would constitute a stable, conservative element in the assembly. Of 478 delegates to the first Duma (May–July, 1906), however, peasants constituted less than half, the majority of seats being won by the liberal Kadets. The Duma was clearly in opposition to the government. Its program called for extension of the franchise, abolition of the death penalty, amnesty for political prisoners, breakup of the large estates, reforms in administrative and procedural matters—including making the ministry responsible to the Duma—and an end to the government's "upper house," the State Council. The Duma debated leading problems of the times, and even published its debates. As for the government's response to all this, it merely waited for a plausible excuse to dissolve the Duma, which it did after 73 days of the Duma's existence.

After refusing to participate in the first Duma, both the SR's and the SD's took part in elections to the second. Unable to control the political makeup of the first Duma, the government more assiduously prepared the groundwork for the second. In this election campaign the Ministry of the Interior declared all parties to the left of the conservative Octobrists illegal and thus unqualified to distribute campaign literature. The government carried out other measures to intimidate opposition groups, including murder, but to little avail. The second Duma was still an oppositionist one, although the relatively cohesive middle element was considerably weaker (only 92 Kadets) than was the case with its predecessor. The extreme right was strengthened, partly because of government pressure; it contained some 95 more or less conservative to reactionary delegates. On the left were some 200 delegates, among them the Labor Group, SR's, and SD's (including 12 Bolsheviks). The second Duma, March to June, 1907, ineffectual as the first and even more unstable, was never in a position to affect policies of the government. It was dissolved by the Tsar after a brief life of three and half months.

By even more carefully rigging the next elections, government persistence eventually was rewarded in obtaining in the third Duma (1907–12) a body more to its liking. Giving up all hope for gaining the support of the peasants, the new electoral law retained the old system of indirect election, but progovernment landowners now were given $50\frac{1}{2}$ percent of the representation, with $22\frac{1}{2}$ percent going to the peasants and only 2 percent to industrial workers. National minorities were severely restricted and Central Asia was allowed no representatives at all. The elections upheld the government's confidence in the new electoral law. The largest party was the Octobrists (now progovernment) with 154 delegates. The Kadets were reduced to 54, and the forces of the left to 33. In addition there were 45 priests (following considerable governmental pressure on the Church for its support), 32 of whom were on the right, 9 of them Octobrists, and 4 Kadets. Serving as a simple ratifying instrument for official actions of the regime and lacking any truly effective opposition to the government, the third Duma was permitted to sit for its full five-year term. It did accomplish something during its period of existence, though. It examined the budget, forced the government's ministers to at least consider the Duma as something of a force, criticized the government's policies and gained a measure of respect both inside and outside of Russia. A fourth Duma was elected in 1912 and continued sitting until the revolution in 1917. Differing from that of the third Duma, the position of the moderate elements slipped as more rightists and leftists (including six Bolsheviks—one of whom was a police spy) gained seats.

It had not been difficult in 1881 for the new tsar (Alexander III) to return to the concept of absolute autocracy. The reforming zeal of his father was but a temporary interlude, an aberration, in the otherwise traditional dogma of perverse absolutism. Strong and forceful, a ruler with both purpose and direction, Alexander was supported and encouraged by his clever advisor, the arch-reactionary Constantine Pobedonostsev, Chief Procurator of the Holy Synod. Pobedonostsev, court philosopher of autocracy and reaction, was the unqualified enemy of all that Western liberalism stood for: rationalism, parliamentarism, civil liberties, constitutions, and a free press. He supplied to the regime the rationale for opposition to both the *zemstvo* movement and the Dumas. Pobedonostsev was the tutor and later advisor of Alexander's son, Nicholas II, whom he continued to influence until Nicholas dismissed him in 1905. Under Alexander's reign censorship was rigidly applied, freedom of the press and of the universities was severely restricted, courts were strictly circumscribed, and police brutalities were not infrequent.

The last of the Romanov dynasty, Nicholas II (1894–1917), possessed a fairly uncomplicated personality. Although numerous descriptions of him have appeared in history, several qualities of his character must be noted. In the first place, Nicholas was willful and capricious in dealing with members of his government—particularly with the chairmen of his Council of Ministers. In the initiation and promotion of clearcut policies— or, more accurately, in their absence—he was vacillating and unimaginative.[25] As for his ability to read the signs of the times and to provide constructive leadership for his people, he was woefully incompetent, suffering from a lack of realism and from extreme shortsightedness. Nicholas was much more comfortable in reviewing troops and writing in his diary the cryptic trivialities for which he is known than he was in overseeing matters of state. By any meaningful criterion, Nicholas II was one of the most ineffective of all the tsars, and the worst possible choice of destiny to have fallen upon him the final responsibility for trying to save the monarchy.

What caused this return to the past, this governmental reaction following the Revolution of 1905 and the period of the first three Dumas? People generally were tiring of revolutionary arguments and recurring uprisings. They longed for the former "normalcy" in which life, though harsh, was less disturbed. There was by 1907, also, a collapse of the revolutionary movement, partly as a result of irresponsibility among the membership of the revolutionary parties; in their great determination to carry out revolutionary actions against the regime, these parties failed to achieve any significant degree of cooperation among themselves. There were, too, successful repressive measures instituted by the government, such as imprisonment and exile for revolutionaries. One famous revolutionary leader, Azev, was discovered to have been for some time a police spy. This discovery alone demoralized revolutionary élan. The primary cause for growing reaction, perhaps, was in the general breakdown of Russian liberalism itself, a liberalism which unfortunately had no substantial middle class on which to rely for support. The failure of the liberals to coordinate their mutual desires and actions, their overambitious

---

[25] As for his relationship to the Dumas, he "sulked through the period of parliamentarism . . ." Treadgold, *op. cit.*, p. 19.

demands on the autocracy, continual infighting among themselves, and the lack of a consistent, well-thought-out program which might have some chance of gaining acceptance, all contributed to the demise of liberalism. The liberal leaders were enthusiastic and zealous, but they were neither politic nor clever, and, consequently, they missed an opportunity they might otherwise have had to make significant gains under the imperial system.   They were not to get another chance to achieve power until 1917.

CHAPTER II

The Bolshevik Revolution

FOR SOVIET COMMUNISM, the Bolshevik Revolution of 1917 has a deep and special significance, possessing virtually an aura of mystery about it. It is relied upon by the political elite to legitimize its rule, and it plays an important role in the process of political socialization. In Soviet schools, in books, articles, press, and speeches, the Revolution is continually referred to as a national inspiration, as the true beginning of the Soviet political system.

There were two revolutions in Russia in 1917. In February the first revolution overthrew the centuries-old tsarist system.[1] Almost from its origins Russia had been a monarchy; now, in February, it was suddenly and irrevocably ended. For Russian liberals the revolution meant a chance to usher in a new Western-type, parliamentary system; for peasants, workers, and soldiers the revolution promised a popular form of a socialistic democracy; for the Bolsheviks it meant an opportunity to close the gap in preparation for the anticipated true Marxist proletarian revolution to follow.

For the next eight months, until late October, Russia stumbled along under a Provisional Government which embodied a crude attempt both to harmonize the extremely divergent political forces in society and to provide at least a measure of stability in the country at a time when anarchy prevailed more often than order. The October, or Bolshevik, Revolution was the result not only of the previous eight chaotic months, but of earlier developments and events occurring in the eighteenth and nineteenth centuries.

---

[1] Dates in this chapter follow the Julian, or Old Style, calendar used in Russia at the time. It was 13 days behind that of the West in 1917.

DOWNFALL OF THE MONARCHY

On the eve of the February Revolution, the British Ambassador to Moscow stepped out of his official diplomatic role and candidly advised Tsar Nicholas II, "You have, sire, come to the parting of the ways, and you have now to choose between two paths. The one will lead you to victory and a glorious peace, the other to revolution and disaster."[2] That Nicholas neither appreciated nor understood the ambassador's warning is but a reflection of the fatal weakness of the regime. The warning illustrates the foreboding which many people felt about the political climate of the time.

By 1917 the monarchy was widely discredited due, in part, to the influence of the Empress and Rasputin in running the government. Rasputin passed himself off as a holy man who, in the process, exerted inordinate influence over the religiously mystical Empress. Consider two samples of the correspondence from the Empress to the Emperor, who was at the front in 1916:

> ...He [Rasputin] begs we should not yet strongly advance in the north....He says this is an advise. Our Friend [Rasputin] says Sturmer can remain still some time as President of the Council of Ministers as that one does not reproach him so much....He [Rasputin] implores either he [Sturmer] should go on leave for a month or at once to name another man in his place as Minister of Foreign Affairs....[3]

This outrageous interference in the normal functions of government and in the direction of the war with Germany by the degenerate Rasputin and the hysterical Empress was an open secret in Russia in 1916. No wonder the irresolute Tsar was confused in his administrative leadership and that many people concluded that the government was rotten to the core.

There were more important reasons for the monarchy's downfall. Chief among these was the practical defeat of Russia by Germany, by 1917, in World War I. The defeat caused widespread demoralization among both troops and the public. Another serious consequence was economic prostration. Added to these reasons were those of continued peasant distress and growing resentment stemming from hardships suffered by industrial workers.

---

[2] William Henry Chamberlin, *The Russian Revolution: 1917–1921* (New York: The Macmillan Co., 1935), Vol. I, p. 70. At this late date in the dynasty, Trotsky argues, the Emperor's choice, if indeed he had a choice, was only between different roads to ruin. Leon Trotsky, *The History of the Russian Revolution*, trans. Max Eastman (New York: Simon and Schuster, Inc., 1932), Vol. I, p. 98.

[3] Quoted in Frank Alfred Golder, *Documents of Russian History, 1914–1917*, trans. Emanuel Aronsberg (New York: Century Co., 1927), pp. 114n., 218. The Empress wrote her correspondence in English, however incorrectly.

Through it all reigned Nicholas, timid and undecided. Even when the final government crisis at long last became painfully apparent to the Ruler of all the Russias, he passively awaited the blow of destiny with a bemused, yet stoical resignation. Since his inauguration in 1894, in fact, Nicholas displayed neither a capability nor a willingness to comprehend the numerous forces of protest swirling up about him. It should not have been unexpected that he would be unable to see a revolution on the horizon. But then neither did the liberals nor the "revolutionaries" for that matter.

Few, if any, in Petrograd saw in the sporadic bread riots occurring in February, 1917, the potential collapse of the regime itself. And yet, there were officials in the government who had feared and even suspected some form of rebellion. Early in 1917 a force of 12,000 police and military troops was alerted in the capital, and a carefully worked out plan of defense which divided the city into six police districts was drawn up. What upset these careful preparations were the spreading, persistent riots and the unreliability of the Petrograd military troops. The troops, after firing first on the demonstrators in the streets, soon changed their minds and refused to execute the Tsar's order to put down the revolt. From that point on, the Tsar's government was doomed.

The first riots, taking place in late February, quickly spread throughout the city of Petrograd. By February 24 the striking workers switched their cries for "bread" to that of "down with the autocracy." In a telegram to the Tsar at his military headquarters on February 27, the President of the State Duma (Rodzyanko) stated, "The Capital is in a state of anarchy. The government is paralyzed; the transport service is broken down; the food and fuel supplies are completely disorganized. Discontent is general and on the increase. There is wild shooting on the streets; troops are firing at each other."[4] Some of the troops mutinied, eventually going over to the people. The leaderless Revolution, in which some 1,315 were killed and wounded, took place only in Petrograd, representing but a minute portion of the country's population. As for the rest of the country, they only heard about the Revolution. In all, the Revolution was not particularly violent; instead it was typified by intermittent firing from rooftops, much shouting, occasional police retaliation which was only half-hearted at best, and a great deal of aimless rushing about on the part of students, soldiers, and workers. Tsarism was a house of cards which shuddered and collapsed before the relatively light winds of physical opposition. The spontaneous and unexpected outbreak quickly swept out the old regime and swept in something new, though no one quite knew what at the time.

---

[4] *Ibid.*, p. 278.

"Nicholas was still free and calling himself Tsar," wrote a contemporary, "but where was Tsarism? It was gone. It had crumbled away in an instant. Three centuries to build it up, and three days for it to vanish."[5] Nicholas was prevailed upon to abdicate in favor of his brother, Grand Duke Michael. The timid (or realistic) brother quickly declined the honor, however, and the mantle of official state power fell upon a new Provisional Government. Nicholas II, who signed the document which foreclosed on the centuries-old monarchy, with his characteristic penchant for the inane and irrelevant, wrote in his personal diary the day following his abdication that he had enjoyed a long sleep. He noted, also that there was sunshine and frost and that he had read much of Julius Caesar. Once his mind had been made up, Nicholas shed the throne easily and fatalistically, with no more seeming concern than the manner in which he had worn the cloak throughout his 23-year reign. Just how the state was to exercise power and by whom, however, was not readily apparent.

THE PROVISIONAL GOVERNMENT

The collapse of the monarchy left the fourth Duma as the only official body remaining which possessed any semblance of governmental authority. A call to citizens to restore order, signed by Rodzyanko as head of the Duma, announced that the Committee of the State Duma and the Petrograd Soviet took upon themselves the task of establishing order and governing the country. On February 26, the Duma assigned to its Council of Elders the task of selecting a representative 12-member Temporary Committee; this committee included the Georgian Menshevik leader Chkheidze and Alexander Kerensky. The Mensheviks were the anti-Bolsheviks of the Russian Social Democratic Labor Party—the leading Marxist party in Russia. On March 1, ministers were appointed by the Duma, and the Provisional Government was established on March 2, the day Nicholas signed the formal order of abdication. Prince G. E. Lvov, a leader of the *zemstvo* movement, became Prime Minister; Paul Milyukov, a famous liberal leader of the Kadet party, was named Foreign Minister; and Alexander Kerensky, a lawyer and a member of the Socialist Revolutionary (SR) party, who was both a member of the Duma and a vice-president of the Petrograd Soviet, was designated Minister of Justice. Actually, Kerensky "designated" himself Minister of Justice by "agreeing" to accept the not-yet-proffered post in a dramatic, impromptu speech to the

---

[5] N. N. Sukhanov, *The Russian Revolution 1917, A Personal Record*, edited, abridged, and trans. by Joel Carmichael from *Zapiski O Revolutsii* (New York: Oxford University Press, 1955), p. 99.

Petrograd Soviet. Kerensky viewed himself as the natural and popular bridge between the bourgeois Provisional Government and the popular "Democracy" (Soviet). The following day the Petrograd Soviet, reconstituted in 1917 after its demise at the hands of tsarist officials in 1905, gave reluctant approval to the new government.[6]

The Provisional Government spoke for the more conservative leaders of society in advocating continued prosecution of the war, adaptation of a parliamentary system, and continuance of the alliance between the new regime and propertied elements of society. By tacit agreement between the main contracting parties, government and Soviet, the Provisional Government was to be officially sponsored as the holder of state authority, while the Soviet (wielding more actual political power) was to be the spokesman for the revolutionary forces in the capital (workers, peasants, soldiers). Orders of the government were carried out only with the concurrence of the Soviet, for the latter possessed power over troops, railroads, and the postal and telegraph services.

With a membership of almost 3,000 the Soviet represented some 160,000 soldiers and 400,000 workers in the capital. To provide leadership as well as to manage its affairs, the Soviet elected an All-Russian Central Executive Committee ("VTsIK") of eight members, including the ruling Presidium of the Soviet and representatives of the socialist parties (one of whom was Kerensky). The decisions of the Petrograd Soviet's Executive Committee were intended to bind all other soviets in intervals between the congresses. Yet, even this Executive Committee soon became large and unwieldy so that in April the Soviet created a smaller, inner bureau of 24 members which was to provide central leadership for the Soviet.

Ostensibly the new government was in control, but it held office with a shaky and unsure grasp. The Soviet, on the other hand, was not quite certain either as to the measure of its own strength, or just what to do with it. The weaknesses of the government were manifold; it lacked virtually all of the requirements for success. It did not have a bureaucracy with managerial experience. It had not yet won the loyalty of the army, while the police had been discredited as the despised instrument of tsarist autocracy and thereby rendered impotent. Even more important, the Provisional Government's philosophy of leadership, which included sympathy for Western parliamentarism, was coldly received by soldiers,

---

[6] This Soviet was a re-creation of the short-lived Petersburg Soviet first organized in 1905. The new version, like the old, was a nonparty group elected by factory workers, with representation coming from SR's, Mensheviks, and Bolsheviks. Other large cities soon had their soviets and, in early 1917, an all-Russian conference of soviets was called. See Edward Hallett Carr, *The Bolshevik Revolution, 1917–1923* (New York: The Macmillan Co., 1951), Vol. I, pp. 70–71.

workers, and by the peasant masses. Added to these handicaps was that of
open duplicity on the part of the Foreign Minister. In order to pacify the
Soviet, he had agreed to announce Russia's opposition to "imperialistic"
annexations, but at the same time he confidentially reassured the allies of
Russia's desire for "sanctions" and "guarantees" (in reality, her desire to
annex some territory). The Soviet and its supporters, desiring peace
above all else, consequently felt betrayed by the government. A solution
to the vexing problem of conflicting policies (government versus Soviet)
was attempted by reorganizing the Provisional Government into more of a
workable coalition in May, 1917. The coalition was made possible by the
Soviet's agreement to continue supporting the government in return for
the government's adoption of the Soviet's foreign and domestic policies.
In the new cabinet, Kerensky left his old post as Minister of Justice to
become Minister of War and Navy.

THE FIRST AND SECOND COALITION GOVERNMENTS

The simple program of the first coalition called for a "general" peace
without indemnities or annexations, a strengthened army, and plans to
convene the long-hoped-for constituent assembly. The coalition, by late
spring and early summer, was repeatedly demonstrating its incapacity to
govern. Yet, to hold down the rising forces of protest and anarchy at
that time might have proven too difficult even for a strong government.
Soldiers, having had their tight reins lifted by Order No. I of March 1,[7]
began to desert their posts at the front and to engage in various forms of
violent outbreaks—reflecting in part their disillusionment with continuing
the war. Moreover, the July offensive of the Russian troops turned
quickly into a disorderly rout at the hands of the Germans, with pillage,
outrages, and a complete breakdown of discipline on the Russian side
being the order of the day. In one night there were 12,000 army deserters
on the outskirts of Volochisk. On April 16, General Alekseev reported to
the Minister of War that the northern front was in complete disarray, and
that the soldiers willfully disobeyed orders of the officers.

Workers, following Bolshevik agitation, were seizing control of factories
and organizing committees to rule themselves. At this time, the
Bolsheviks, intermittently following Lenin's lead, were calling for abandon-

---

[7] Issued by the Petrograd Soviet on March 3, the main substance of which granted
more equality to troops in their relation to officers and provided for committees to
be elected in each military unit by the soldiers and sailors. These committees were
to have final say in control over arms as well as jurisdiction over disputes between
officers and men.

ment of the government and for "all power to the soviets."[8] This slogan proved to be popular and helped weaken support for the coalition.

Peasants were beginning to resort to violence—for example, in burning country estates. The peasants at this time were discouraged at the forced retirement of their favorite spokesman, Victor Chernov, from his position as Minister of Agriculture. As for popular feeling, Sukhanov reports, "The capital was seething. The temper of the masses and the desire for decisive action was growing daily."[9] Simultaneously, the Bolsheviks, under Lenin's skilled direction, were growing more bold.

Just prior to their publication, Lenin introduced the main points of his famous "April Theses" in a series of speeches. The Theses called for abandonment of the Provisional Government, replacing it with a workers' dictatorship, and for immediate seizure of the landed estates by peasants; they attacked all socialists save Lenin-type socialists, and called for a change in the name of the Bolshevik-dominated Russian Social Democratic Labor Party to that of the Communist Party. In addition, they called for abolition of the army, the bureaucracy, and the police and for establishment of model farms, one central bank, and a revolutionary international. At first the Theses were not supported by any other Bolsheviks, and when they appeared in *Pravda* the editors of this Bolshevik paper referred to parts of the Theses as unacceptable. Although this was not the first occasion on which the Bolsheviks failed to support Lenin, yet within a month after their publication, the Theses became part of the official platform of the Bolsheviks. Lenin's consistently logical programs and policies, in this era of general confusion, glowed brightly among other disorganized, less consistent revolutionaries. But it was becoming increasingly necessary for both the theoretical underpinning as well as the more practical superstructure of the Bolsheviks, in their drive to gain political power, to acquire greater support from industrial workers. To this potent source of power the Bolsheviks now turned their attention.

In the first two months of 1917, more than 500,000 workers took part in strikes. In these early months workers appeared to be not so much in favor of the Bolsheviks as simply in support of the various soviets. Many Russian workers and intellectuals had returned from emigration to Western countries and now contributed to the Russian workers' movement a large dose of additional radicalism. It was during the spring when in most factories quasi-administrative committees elected by the workers were organized; these committees maintained direct communication with

---

[8] By summer, Lenin had pretty much discarded his desire for all power to the soviets, preferring instead, all power to the "proletariat," i.e., Bolsheviks.

[9] Sukhanov, *op. cit.*, p. 419.

the Petrograd Soviet.   The factory committees, rapidly increasing in power, were now influenced more and more by the Bolsheviks who seemed to be active in virtually every factory.   Like so many other features of Russian life at this juncture, the rather sudden success of the factory committees augured ill for the continued existence of the government.   It was not long until the mass of workers, encouraged by skillful propaganda which championed their cause, leaned more and more toward Lenin's movement.   The impatient workers demanded immediate demonstrations, an end to the war, and the downfall of the Provisional Government. After an abortive attempt at a mass street demonstration which was announced for June 10 in Petrograd, a pro-Bolshevik demonstration by workers and soldiers was held on June 18.

Unfortunately for the health of the first ruling coalition, the earlier divergence between Soviet and Provisional Government (the "dual power") was carried over into a similar split within the Soviet itself.   The largest party in the coalition (SR's) was seriously divided into left, right, and moderate factions.   There was, furthermore, internal cabinet dissension, such as the conflict over agrarian policies, which contributed to the general collapse of the first coalition.   The July uprising, a spontaneous but relatively peaceful mass outburst signaled the breakdown of the first coalition.

The second coalition government was formed in July as a caretaker cabinet to hold together the threads of formal power until a stronger, more conservative government could be found which would be able to regain popular support for continuing the war.   The new administration constituted a shift to the right, but in the name of the left.   The cabinet, after all, was a *soviet* government, for its leader Kerensky (who now became Prime Minister as well as Minister of War and Navy) was a member of the Petrograd Soviet's Central Executive Committee.   Moreover, Kerensky promptly announced that the government would be guided by the instructions of the Congress of Soviets.   But this was no more than practical politics because the largely autonomous soviets were the sole repositories of actual power throughout the country.   And yet, whatever the government would, or in point of fact could, accomplish would depend in no small measure on the fortunes of the Bolsheviks.

The "July Days" (as the uprising in July came to be known), however, temporarily slowed down the expansion of Bolshevik influence.   Early in the month, the Bolsheviks reluctantly, because they doubted that the time was ripe for a successful *coup*, allowed themselves to be made the leaders of the armed demonstrations of workers and soldiers in which 20,000 Kronstadt sailors participated and some 400 people were killed and wounded. The revolt was premature and the government eventually restored a semblance of order. The Bolsheviks, by this time accused by their enemies of all manner of evil including that of being paid German agents, were for the present discredited in the eyes of many people. All Bolsheviks were subject to imprisonment, but only the leaders were known to the government and these seemed quite able to escape detection; Lenin remained in hiding from the government and from disenchanted Bolsheviks until the eve of the October Revolution. But if immediate threat from the left had subsided, the government was now beseiged by forces from the right.

General Kornilov, commander-in-chief of all Russian armies, in August demanded of Kerensky that all civil and military power be turned over to himself. His purpose was to establish a conservative military dictatorship. To forestall the *coup*, Kerensky sought help from other groups—including the Bolsheviks—by establishing a "Committee for Struggle with Counter-revolution" composed of representatives from the Petrograd Soviet, the All-Russian Central Executive Committee, Socialist Revolutionaries, Mensheviks, and Bolsheviks. In Kornilov's challenge, which further revealed the weakness of the coalition government, the Bolsheviks saw an opportunity to strengthen their hand. The Bolsheviks soon won the Committee's support for an armed worker's militia which, in reality, was but a resurrection and rearming of the Bolsheviks' former Red Guard. Perhaps these three developments (Kornilov's conservative revolt, Kerensky's forced alliance with the Bolsheviks, and re-creation of the Red Guard) more than any others cleared the ground for the October Revolution. To all these events, as causes of the Revolution, must be added the general debilitating effects of the war and the weakened and demoralized military forces, the unrelieved peasant distress, and the vacillating policies of the government.

The effects of World War I on Russian society had a direct bearing not only on the February Revolution, but even more so on the one in October. In the first place, Russia suffered perhaps 8 million casualties. There were other disasters, such as severe shortages of food, matériel, weapons and ammunition. The army's officer class was mediocre at best, lacking overall competence, resourcefullness, and courage. Trotsky considered the high command to be ignorant, corrupt, unheroic, and uninspired. To this indictment must be added weak central leadership which stemmed directly from the collapse of the monarchy and its replacement by the irresolute Provisional Government. Even had these difficulties not been present, however, there were other problems equally serious which limited Russian military successes.

Having mobilized more than 15 million men during the course of the war, Russia's troops in 1917 were for the most part young, raw recruits direct from the farms. These poor, illiterate peasants were put in uniform, denied adequate supplies and equipment, and thrust into the front to do battle with seasoned German forces. The Russian soldiers, with virtually no comprehension of the issues at stake, were considerably less than enthusiastic for continuing a war they could neither win nor understand. The breakdown of military discipline shifted control over the troops from officers to that of company and batallion committees elected by the soldiers. The resulting chaos, from the standpoint of military science, can be readily imagined. Finally, Kerensky lost the support of the troops for his conservative policies, such as those which backed the hated General Kornilov and the reimposition of the death penalty for erring soldiers at the front. But there were still other dilemmas faced by the government.

The agrarian problems were still unsolved. The peasant had not received his "due" share of the land as he had anticipated since 1861 and, in cases reminiscent of serfdom, some peasants were still having to pay high rent to landlords. Peasants had suffered more than any other class from the war; for example, the government commandeered some 10 million peasants and 2 million horses for the war effort. By early autumn anarchy was sweeping the rural areas with much burning and sacking of the landlord's estates. Other peasants, as delegates to the soviets, flocked to the cities with their demands for land and justice. In all this, the peasant soldiers effectively backstopped their rural brothers. The *muzhik*, in Trotsky's words, obviously had no trust in his province and district Kerenskys.[10]

In the face of the numerous other difficulties, among them transportation breakdowns and severe food shortages, Kerensky's second coalition rapidly was falling apart. With growing antipathy on the part of many SR's toward the government's prowar policy, in addition to complete loss of what little support it once had from workers, soldiers, and peasants, not to mention the heightened effectiveness of the Bolsheviks, the second coalition became a forlorn stepchild, unloved and unwanted. As for Kerensky himself, he only added to the government's problems.

In every important respect Kerensky, like the ill-fated Nicholas II before him, was out of step with the times. Kerensky never really understood either the meaning and significance of the February Revolution or the explosive forces in Russian society which demanded satisfaction. In the normal tsarist tradition, Kerensky avoided any positive program; he

---

[10] Trotsky, *op. cit.*, p. 394.

assumed instead that his popularity alone would sustain him in office.[11] Yet, it was not that Kerensky had failed to propagandize widely for his policies. He did by assigning commissars to each army unit for the purpose of raising morale and encouraging the troops to fight with renewed strength. Kerensky himself could be found at the front from time to time wildly flitting about like an enraged mosquito, as was his fashion, haranguing the soldiers on the great necessity for winning the war. The popularly elected soldiers' committes, too, were brought under a degree of government control. The chief failure of all of these efforts, of course, was that the cause of the Provisional Government, no matter how vociferously defended, was simply the wrong cause. The Russians were uninterested in Kerensky's desire to continue the war. Moreover, they were somewhat antagonistic toward Western ways which the Provisional Government seemed to reflect. But, despite all this Kerensky visualized himself as the man of the hour, not yet ready to surrender.

DOWNFALL OF THE PROVISIONAL GOVERNMENT

A third coalition cabinet was formed late in September, though hardly more effective than its predecessors; this cabinet was distinguished by the sterling mediocrity of its membership. The third coalition, by its very nature, was guaranteed not to succeed; it had inherited all the old problems, but enjoyed neither enlightened leadership nor forward-looking policies. As a harbinger of its doom, the day the new coalition was formed, the Petrograd Soviet set up a new Executive Committee, this time with Bolsheviks in the majority. Still Kerensky frantically reorganized in further vain efforts to save the situation.

Under governmental auspices a Democratic Conference was held in the capital on September 14 which 1,200 delegates attended, some of whom represented soviets, local legislative bodies, cooperatives, and trade unions. In rapid succession now, yet another group was formed which was named the Provisional Council of the Russian Republic. More popularly, this latter organization was dubbed the "Pre-Parliament," for its function was to deliberate until a genuine constituent assembly could be convened. More conservative than its predecessor the Democratic Conference, the Pre-Parliament represented chiefly propertied and nonsocialist factions.

---

[11] In Kerensky's defense, however, he was not accorded much support in his various efforts by his own majority SR Party. Kerensky, naturally enough, vehemently rationalizes his every action during 1917. See Alexander Kerensky, *The Catastrophe: Kerensky's Own Story of the Russian Revolution* (New York: D. Appleton and Co., 1927). For a defense of Kerensky's positive programs, see Alexander Kerensky, *Russia and History's Turning Point* (New York: Duell, Sloan, & Pearce, Inc., 1965), pp. 223–26.

Of the 550 delegates, some 180 had been members of the Democratic Conference and 156 were referred to as nonsocialists. The "democratic" majority (representatives of the soviets) of some 300 was made up of 60 Mensheviks, 66 Bolsheviks, 120 SR's, and sundry other groups such as the Martov-Sukhanov faction called Menshevik-Internationalists. Once again the Bolshevik party disregarded Lenin's wishes by voting to participate in the Pre-Parliament. But, shortly coming around to Lenin's view, the Bolsheviks noisily walked out on the opening day of the Pre-Parliament after bitterly attacking the government for continuing the war. The Pre-Parliament debated continuing the war while the Bolsheviks stepped up their revolutionary agitation which called for immediate peace, land to the people, and all power to the soviets.

After the abortive Kornilov revolt in August, the strength and influence of the Bolsheviks grew almost without interruption. Various elections held throughout the country give dramatic evidence of the shift to Bolshevism. In June, for example, the Bolsheviks received 12 percent of the vote in the Moscow city election; in a similar election in the same city in September they received 51 percent of the vote. From this point on, the soviets in the various parts of western Russia lined up behind Bolshevik leadership. On September 1, the Petrograd Soviet, though still nominally headed by the Menshevik Chkheidze, voted for a Bolshevik resolution calling for a government of workers and peasants, immediate peace negotiations, confiscation of large estates, and workers' control over industry. On September 9 the Bolsheviks won control of the Petrograd Soviet and on September 26 Trotsky replaced Chkheidze as president of that body. In other soviets too, the Bolsheviks were rapidly becoming the dominant influence.

Basically, Bolshevik propaganda exploited the keen desire of the people for peace, land, and socialism.[12] With respect to the war, the Provisional Government was denounced as an irresponsible supporter of the reactionary General Kornilov who, it was alleged, would continue the war and might even surrender Petrograd to the Germans. Reports were circulated, apparently valid, that the government was contemplating evacuation of Petrograd for the choice of Moscow, and the reports cautioned war-weary troops to be suspicious of any moves by the high command to transfer them—which might mean return of the troops to the front! To the peasants, who already were seizing some estates on their own, the

---

[12] Although Bolshevik publications numbered 41, with a circulation of 320,000 up to the July uprising, at the end of August only 50,000 copies of their publications were being printed. Yet, these relatively few copies were widely read in contrast to the millions of unread copies of the "bourgeois" press, according to Trotsky. See Trotsky, *op. cit.*, Vol. II, pp. 304–5.

Bolsheviks encouraged their revolts and aggravated their discontent. Finally, the Bolsheviks pitted the growing attraction of the soviets against the declining appeal of the government. The government was pictured as speaking for the reactionary bourgeoisie, while the soviets championed the true, socialist revolution. In this contest, history was on the side of the Bolsheviks in appealing to the people's religious-messianic tradition, to their innate distrust of propertied classes, and to their sympathy for native Russian collectivism. The Bolsheviks, led by Lenin, promised the people immediately what other voices ignored, or at best asked them to wait for. The Bolshevik promises might be sweeping, even unrealistic, but they were accepted by the workers, soldiers, and peasants and that is all that really mattered, in the final analysis, in October, 1917.

The necessary ingredients for Bolshevik success were at hand in October, then, if only they could be blended in the proper amounts. To accomplish this would require not only a large element of luck but a degree of careful planning and even more skillful leadership. On October 10 the Bolshevik's Central Committee adopted Lenin's resolution (voting 10–2 in favor) calling for armed insurrection. Seizure of power, in Lenin's view, was for the "proletariat" (Bolsheviks, Red Guard, its factory committees, and organizations in the army). At the same time Trotsky was arguing that the seizure of power was democratic, i.e., in the name of the Soviets. From then on, the party pursued a clear plan of action.[13]

Lenin's leadership of the Revolution was fortunate for in his personality were combined all essential qualtities of a great revolutionary leader. He was a militant activist with an all-consuming dogmatic faith, which was complemented by a very shrewd common sense. From the tactical standpoint, he had a lively imagination with an excellent sense of timing. Lenin also had a flagrant contempt for tradition and rules—even his own. Thus, when he insisted upon the iron discipline of the party to be binding on all of its members, he excepted himself from any such humiliation. Even majority decisions of the Bolshevik leadership were ignored by Lenin when he did not agree with them. But this is just what was so typical and consistent about Lenin. He was not, nor did he ever claim to be, a democrat, guided by the majority, limited by the niceties of parliamentary procedures which he so detested and criticized in Western systems of government. Rather, his was a higher destiny, as he saw it. He was to

---

[13] Trotsky, *op. cit.*, Vol. III, p. 92. An American journalist on the scene during October states that Lenin called for insurrection to be carried out on October 25 after rejecting October 24 as too early and October 26 as too late. John Reed, *Ten Days That Shook the World* (New York: International Publishers, 1919), p. 56. Trotsky contends that Reed is in error, because Lenin had been calling for immediate revolution since September. See Trotsky, *op. cit.*, Vol. III, p. 358.

lead a great, elemental upheaval which would usher in a worldwide system of enlightened and equitable government. Lenin's cause was that of proletarian justice; he championed peasant virtue and the untarnished simplicity of the soldier. The common enemy to be defeated was the evil inheritor of the old imperial system—the Provisional Government.

No other revolutionary leaders in Russia at the time were of the mold of Lenin, although he had some very able assistants such as Trotsky. The chief role of Trotsky in the October Revolution was head of the Bolshevik military staff. His influence, according to Sukhanov, was overwhelming, "the central figure of those days and the principal hero. . . ."[14] And it was Trotsky who by October dominated the Petrograd Soviet. On the other hand, few writers assign to Stalin any significant part either in the planning or execution of the insurrection. Trotsky, for understandable reasons, practically ignores Stalin in his account of the Revolution. Sukhanov states that Stalin left the impression of a grey blur, "looming up now and then dimly and not leaving any trace."[15] Successful revolutionary leadership, however, depends in no small measure upon loyal revolutionary followership, and it was the proletarian class, after all, in whose name the Revolution was to be baptized.

Reporting to the Sixth Congress of the Russian Social-Democratic Labor Party (RSDLP) in late July, 1917, Volodarsky stated that Bolsheviks have a great influence in factories.[16] This influence had been achieved as a result of exhaustive efforts of the Bolsheviks to win sympathy and support from the workers. This was accomplished chiefly by unending propaganda, both written and verbal, at factory benches and in the barracks, wherever there were workers to be found. Now, however, the Bolsheviks faced a dilemma. Although they labored for years to stir up proletarian support, in mid-1917 the workers were practically leading the Bolsheviks down the road to upheaval. Almost feverishly the Bolsheviks, after this point, worked to restrain workers and soldiers from violence which, though condoned in principle, might be premature and thereby run the risk of wrecking chances for a successful overthrow of the government. Workers were not only politically active in the capital as well as in other cities by now, but they assiduously preached to and converted peasants by taking the Bolshevik crusade to the villages. For, despite their Marxist doctrines,

---

[14] Sukhanov, *op. cit.*, p. 578.

[15] *Ibid.*, p. 230. Schapiro notes that Stalin, after accepting Lenin's leadership by mid-1917, was Lenin's faithful supporter in both the verbal and written word. Leonard Schapiro, *The Origin of the Communist Autocracy* (Cambridge, Mass.: Harvard University Press, 1956), pp. 39ff.

[16] Trotsky, *op. cit.*, Vol. II, p. 264. The congresses date from the founding in 1898 of the Russian Social-Democratic Labor Party, the predecessor of the Communist Party.

Lenin and his supporters were forced to carry out a proletarian revolution in what was, in fact, a peasant country.

The Bolshevik leaders seemed quite willing to exploit peasant unrest as a starting point for the insurrection. In addition to workers calling for revolt even before the Bolshevik high command felt sure of itself, the peasants had been plundering, looting, and rebelling since late spring. By autumn the peasants were not to be appeased by mere promises of "regulation of rural relations" or by vague statements to the effect that improvements would be brought about at some future time; what they did understand, as Lenin was well aware, was the cry for land—now. In light of peasant outbreaks, added to other fortunate circumstances, Lenin concluded that no more favorable conditions for revolution could be hoped for. Yet, there remained one more hurdle before the revolution. Once the Bolsheviks could be assured of adequate military support, they could, without further hesitation, jump to the lead of the rebellious workers, soldiers, and peasants.

On October 9, the Mensheviks in the Petrograd Soviet moved to create, as a part of that body, a Committee of Revolutionary Defense (later renamed the Military Revolutionary Committee) to take part in the defense of the capital against rebellion or invasion. The Bolsheviks agreed and the Committee was formed on October 20 with a majority of Bolsheviks. Trotsky was its president. The Soviet was now committed to defend the capital, in other words, the government. But the power to defend, in Bolshevik eyes, implied also the power to control—even to attack the government. On October 21, the capital's military garrison acknowledged not the government, but the Petrograd Soviet as the sole representative of authoritative power, and the Military Revolutionary Committee as its spokesman. The garrison then practically placed itself under Bolshevik jurisdiction. On the 23d, the Baltic Fleet wired Bolshevik headquarters (now located in Smolny Palace) of its pledge of support. Finally, at most factories organized workers were forming the Red Guard. "Companies of the Red Guard.... The worker with a rifle, the bayonet above hat or cap, the rifle-belt over a civilian coat—that is the essential image of the 25th of October."[17] And now the Bolshevik's final remaining task was to overthrow the Provisional Government.

The government, which never doubted that it could suppress any sporadic Bolshevik uprising, reacted to the common knowledge that the Bolsheviks were preparing an insurrection with a self-assured, yet per-

---

[17] *Ibid.*, p. 237. On first seeing the Red Guard on the steps of Smolny, Reed records "a huddled group of boys in workmen's clothes, carrying guns with bayonets, talking nervously together." Reed, *op. cit.*, p. 73.

plexed, manner.   No cause for panic, so long as Kerensky confidently assumed that the troops both at the front and in Petrograd were loyal to the government.   Yet, Kerensky's behavior, though confident, was frequently irrational.   At one time, upon hearing some shots fired, a not unusual occurrence in the nervous capital in late October, Kerensky rushed to the window and shouted "Stations everyone! Defend the Duma! Listen to me—I, Kerensky, am speaking to you, Kerensky is speaking to you! Defend your freedom and the revolution, defend the Duma! Stations everyone...!" According to his own account, Sukhanov then walked over to Kerensky to calm him saying, "Everything's all right.... Why create a worse panic than the shots?"[18]   Kerensky's faith, in the last analysis, resided in his belief that come what may, the Cossack forces would always support him. When the Bolshevik Red Guard finally began their open attacks on the government, it was to the loyal Cossacks that Kerensky turned for assistance. A telephone message from the government to three Don Cossack regiments ordered them to attack the insurgents. This was *the* critical moment. The Cossacks did not attack.

OCTOBER REVOLUTION

It was the Military Revolutionary Committee, along with the capital's garrison and certain other military units, which carried out the revolution. Orders now flowed smoothly from Bolshevik headquarters at Smolny, instantly obeyed by the soldiers.   The actual revolution occupied something less than three weeks time, roughly from the decision to set up the Military Revolutionary Committee to the capture of the Winter Palace on October 26.   In the last 24 hours, from approximately 2:00 A.M. on the 25th until 2:00 A.M. on the 26th, there were not more than 25,000 to 30,000 forces involved.   At about 2:00 A.M. on the 26th, the Bolshevik's field general of the insurrection, Antonov-Ovseenko, burst into a room of the Winter Palace in which were sitting the ministers of the Provisional Government and arrested them in the name of the Military Revolutionary Committee.   The Provisional Government was not overthrown so much as it was, like its tsarist predecessor eight months earlier, simply pushed over after it already had begun to crumble.   Those who pushed were the peasants, workers, soldiers, and sailors, all led by the Bolsheviks.   In Trotsky's words, "The party led the uprising; the principal motive force was the proletariat; the armed detachments of workers were the fist of the insurrection; but the heavy-weight peasant garrison decided the outcome

---

[18] Sukhanov, *op. cit.*, p. 94.

of the struggle."[19]   The Bolsheviks had finally brought communism into power, but it was highly questionable at the time whether they could keep it there in view of the many serious ruling problems which faced them.

On October 25, after two earlier postponements, the Second Congress of Soviets was opened by the Menshevik leader Dan (Il. F. Gurvich); it proceeded to elect a ruling presidium of 14 Bolsheviks, 7 SR's, 3 Mensheviks, and 1 Internationalist.   In addition, a new Central Executive Committee of the Petrograd Soviet was elected in which the Bolsheviks received 67 of the 116 seats.   This Central Executive Committee in turn, on Lenin's motion, elected a new government for the country made up exclusively of Bolsheviks.   The new government was designated—at Trotsky's suggestion—Council of People's Commissars (*Soviet Narodniykh Komissarov*) to avoid use of the discredited bourgeois word "minister." The Council was headed by Lenin; Trotsky was Commissar of Foreign Affairs, and Stalin was head of the Nationalities Commission.   And now Lenin addressed the Congress of Soviets.   He stood quietly, holding on to the reading stand, "letting his little winking eyes travel over the crowd as he stood there waiting, apparently oblivious to the long-rolling ovation. . . . When it finished, he said simply 'We shall now proceed to construct the Socialist order.' "[20]

In November a Cossack delegation called on Lenin and Trotsky to ask if the new Soviet government would divide up the great Cossack estates among the working Cossacks.   Lenin replied that by forming Cossack soviets and taking part in the Central Executive Committee, they themselves could rule on the division of Cossack lands.   This action seemed to win the powerful Cossack movement over to the point, at least, of not opposing for the moment the new Bolshevik government.   Two other events measurably helped launch the new government.

On November 19, after undergoing an extensive propaganda barrage from the Bolshevik party, the military garrison of Moghilev (western field headquarters of the Russian Army) took control of the city and arrested the chief of the headquarter's staff.   The garrison was now loyal to the Soviet government.   Finally, the Petrograd City Duma was dissolved by the Council of Commissars in November and replaced by a Bolshevik Duma.

The SR's withdrew their support from the new government when Lenin's proposal to curb the bourgeois press was adopted.   As a result of this vote in the Soviet's Executive Committee which favored Lenin, the SR's

---

[19] Trotsky, *op. cit.*, Vol. III, p. 290.   "At the decisive moment, he [Lenin] saw power go begging, he was able to grasp it—because he was permitted to do so."   Boris Souvarine "The Cult of Lenin," in Julien Steinberg (ed.), *Verdict of Three Decades* (New York: Duell, Sloan & Pearce, Inc., 1960), p. 174.

[20] Reed, *op. cit.*, p. 126.

withdrew from the Military Revolutionary Committee, five members of the Council of Commissars resigned from that body, and several noted Bolsheviks left the Central Committee of the Bolshevik party (Kamenev, Rykov, Zinoviev). The new government seemed rapidly to be losing support not only from its opponents (SR's), but also from the Bolshevik party itself. The government's support was to decline even more, however. Another tough problem which now faced the new leadership was what to do about the constituent assembly for which so many people had for so long fought. The assembly, in the popular view, was to be the final inheritor of all legal governmental authority in Russia.

The Bolsheviks, now in power, obviously were not keen on holding elections to a popular assembly which might well turn out to be anti-Bolshevik and which, in any case, would have legal claim to political power. Yet, great numbers of the urban populace had for years placed their hopes for an enlightened regime in just such a popularly elected assembly. The majority of Bolsheviks, then, in order to retain what little support they had left, were obliged to agree to calling the assembly, especially since the Bolsheviks themselves earlier had criticized the Provisional Government for postponing convocation of the assembly. Despite Lenin's objections, the Bolsheviks permitted the free election, based on universal suffrage, to be held.

The election began on November 12, continued beyond that date in some parts of the country; it confirmed Lenin's fears of the existence of a considerable anti-Bolshevik feeling. According to available, but incomplete, data, the following votes for delegates to the Constituent Assembly were compiled by Radkey:[21]

SR	15,848,004
SD (Bolshevik)	9,844,637
SD (Menshevik)	1,364,826
Kadets	1,986,601
Other	12,642,808
Total	41,686,876

The Bolsheviks received less than one quarter of the total vote in Russia's first and last election involving universal suffrage and a vigorous contest between competing political parties. This election could hardly have been considered a popular vote of confidence in the Bolshevik government. Still, the long-time professional revolutionary, Lenin, was not greatly worried. The Bolsheviks did win majorities in just those districts which counted from the standpoint of military force—Petrograd, Moscow, the Baltic

---

[21] Oliver Henry Radkey, *The Election to the Constituent Assembly of 1917* (Cambridge, Mass.: Harvard University Press, 1950), pp. 16–17.

Fleet, and in some of the nearby military fronts. Now, what remained was to nullify in some way the results of the election.

The Constituent Assembly was permitted by the Bolsheviks to meet just once, on the 5th of January, 1918; then it was dissolved by decree of the Central Executive Committee of the Petrograd Soviet—backed up by armed soldiers and sailors. The Bolshevik government could not and would not share power with any such assembly nor would it allow its dominance to be challenged—even though the challenge in this case came from a legally constituted, popularly elected assembly. The Constituent Assembly was neither missed nor long mourned; Russia, it seems, was not prepared by history, either psychologically or from the standpoint of experience, for any Western version of a parliamentary system.

The Provisional Government fell apart in October when challenged by a serious, planned attack from the Bolsheviks. It fell because of many reasons similar to those which spelled the end of the tsarist regime in February. As with its tsarist predecessor too, the Provisional Government collapsed as much as it was beaten. The wonder is not that the government could stay on its feet for eight shaky months, but that it could remain in existence for three months after it had been widely discredited in the July uprising. Causes of its downfall are readily apparent and involved all areas of Russian society.

The war resulted in economic collapse and a military catastrophe. Severe food and equipment shortages aided in the demoralization of the illiterate peasant troops and contributed to general apathy on the home front. A notable absence of skillful wartime propaganda on the government's part was no help in alleviating the widespread breakdown in military discipline, all of which was further aggravated by the incompetent military leadership. And when the government most needed the loyal support of its troops, they defected to the Bolsheviks—or at the least, remained neutral and refused to defend the government against attacks from the Red Guard. From everywhere Kerensky expected reinforcements, but none appeared. Industrial workers, too, suffered from low wages, in part the result of unenlightened management. The industrial strikes and rebellious marches throughout 1917 testify to the considerable worker dissatisfaction. Any attempt to solve the numerous problems of the peasants (Russia, after all, was a peasant country), difficult enough in peacetime, was simply postponed during the war. The most numerous class of Russia's citizens was given no hearing in the Provisional Government.

The failure of Russian liberalism, too, operated to defeat the government. Liberalism, in 1917, was a minority cause, trying to grow with neither popular understanding nor sympathy. It was, by and large, an alien doctrine planted in undernourished soil. As a political philosophy, liberalism lacked a widespread Russian tradition. Moreover, the liberals in 1917 were not enlightened, constructive leaders. They clung to vague ideas and even more vague slogans concerning social reform, right for right's sake. But where were their positive, concrete suggestions? What, specifically, did they propose to do about land reform, industrial working conditions, the need to conclude a peace with Germany? The liberals condemned themselves by their silence. The SR Party, in which much hope for liberal leadership rested, was, according to Radkey, a party in name only, "a conglomerate of discordant elements...."[22] The "democracy," as the popular soviets and their supporters referred to their movement, never gained any significant measure of faith in the bourgeois makeup of the Provisional Government—the spokesman for and defender of propertied elements in the country. Finally, the weak, immature sapling of liberalism was no match for the nation-shaking crises which so frequently blew across Russia in 1917. Though communism probably was not required by the times, what was required in October, 1917, was firm, dedicated, popularly based leadership. This, the Bolsheviks could lay some claim to.

The Bolsheviks developed a genius for revolution. At least Lenin did, and he attracted to his banner a number of dedicated and skillful assistants. Bolshevik leadership, although at times diverse, once it solidified behind Lenin was clear as to its goals, courageous and daring in its actions, and certainly clever in its political appeals. Its propaganda was superb in its simplicity, direct and popular in its approach. Where the Provisional Government was vague and uncertain, both in its pronouncements and its actions, the Bolsheviks appeared simple and easily understood. With these qualifications, added to their opponents limitations, they won the contest.

The history of tsarist rule and the short period of nominal authority exercised by the Provisional Government in 1917 point up several lessons for the maintenance of political systems. These governments did not aggregate peasant demands for land reform, workers' demands for increased wages, or demands of the citizenry in general for peace. Organizations, facilities, and channels for such aggregation never were adequately constructed in old Russia. The conversion mechanism, which turns inputs (demands, supports) into outputs (authoritative decisions) had been faulty for several reasons.

---

[22] Oliver H. Radkey, *The Agrarian Foes of Bolshevism; Promise and Default of the Russian Socialist Revolutionaries, February to October, 1917* (New York: Columbia University Press, 1958), p. 455.

The rulers relied on poor intelligence about their society, and they made very few moves to improve their sources of information. Political communication was poorly developed, and no concrete efforts were made to improve the process. Popular feelings, wishes, and desires were rarely, if ever, understood either by the tsars or their successors. Consequently, demand pressures were not translated, except in rare cases, into authoritative outputs. Those outputs that did result, almost exclusively, were cast in the image of the rulers' own desires. In almost all respects, the old Russian political system was too unstable to continue without drastic changes and, as it turned out, was unable to forestall a revolution.

CHAPTER III

Marxist-Leninist Theory

KARL MARX is considered the father and patron saint both of Marxism and communism. In Marx's ideas we have the main source for modern communism, and it is to him that communists pay homage as the founder of their movement. And so he was. And yet, Marx did not invent all of the ideas later attributed to him. In fact, Marx originated neither communism nor socialism.

Even before the birth of Marx, one Francois Babeuf advocated the overthrow of capitalist government and its replacement with a communist regime. Socialist predecessors of Marx, such as Saint-Simon and Louis Blanc, wrote of the necessity for the state to control private industry; Saint-Simon thought the whole world could be organized scientifically as a simple industrial phenomenon. Even the famous and still-used communist slogan "from each according to his ability, to each according to his need," was authored by the French anarchist, Proudhon. Nevertheless, Marxism as a body of theoretical statements and as an analysis of society emerges from the writings of Marx. All communist movements have been strongly influenced and guided by the teachings of Marx.

MARX AND MARXISM

Marx received inspiration for some of his philosophical constructs from the German schools of philosophy in which he was trained; he was especially influenced by Hegel (dialectical method) and Feuerbach (materialism). As for some of the more apparent features of Marxian economics, such as his labor theory of value, they stem chiefly from the classical school of English economics. There were other contributing movements, and personalities too, which influenced Marx and Marxism.

Liberalism provided Marxism with a humanitarian, democratic, and egalitarian goal for society. It was accompanied by a belief in the all-encompassing, benevolent powers of industrialization which forms part of the legacy of liberalism to Marxism.[1] Although Marx firmly believed in the inevitability and necessity of industrialization, he was also, on the other hand, a follower of early nineteenth century romanticism which, among other movements, thought that the Industrial Revolution, with its accompanying evils (such as child labor in dirty factories), had many unfortunate results. The great evil, as Marx saw it, was capitalism rather than industrialization per se. Capitalistic industrialization alienated man from his earlier wholesome, happy, and relaxed societal associations. Under capitalism all of man's creative energies were turned toward profit-making, toward simple accumulation of money which polluted everything it touched. And yet, if Marx and his movement lacked originality in specifics, his overall, general interpretation of history and his analysis of capitalism as well as his prognosis for a future worker's society are certainly novel; they single out Marx as one of the world's most influential men. His more important contributions, whether borrowed *in toto* or reshaped by him to fit his own purposes, include several main doctrines.

Communism necessarily grows out of capitalism, according to the analysis of Marx. Communism cannot, then, develop from its own foundations, but rather it emerges from a mature capitalistic society after going through a transitional period called socialism. This evolutionary interpretation by Marx had roots in the dialectical method first set forth by the philosopher Hegel. Where Hegel, however, stressed the "idea" as the essence of the real world in his dialectics, Marx reversed or, as he said, uprighted Hegel by arguing that the "ideal" is but the reflection by the mind of the material or real world.[2]

To the capitalistic parenthood of communism, then, Marx added dialectical materialism to construct his theory of economic determinism. In this, Marx viewed total human society as engaged in a class struggle to produce the necessities of life; the economic endeavors of man constitute the chief factor in history's progress.[3] Economic determinism argues that history in its main developments is influenced, shaped, and directed by the single most important catalyst in society—economics. Communism, then, is inevitable in Marx's thought because society evolves, naturally,

[1] Adam B. Ulam, *The Unfinished Revolution, An Essay on the Sources of Influence of Marxism and Communism* (New York: Random House, 1960), p. 96.

[2] Karl Marx, *Capital: A Critique of Political Economy*, ed. Frederick Engels; trans. E. Untermann, S. Moore, E. Aveling (Chicago: Charles H. Kerr and Co., 1909), Vol. I, p. 25.

[3] Alfred G. Meyer, *Marxism: the Unity of Theory and Practice: A Critical Essay* (Cambridge, Mass.: Harvard University Press, 1954), pp. 30–31.

through successive stages: primitive communal life, slavery, feudalism, primitive capitalism, advanced capitalism, socialism, and finally communism. This, for Marx, was the iron law of society and the invariable trend of history; the outcome of this historical transformation is completely predictable. Even more of a contribution, stemming from his economic interpretation of history, was Marx's observation that the economic organization of a given society determines that society's political-governmental system. Economic organization, in fact, determines the social, even cultural features of a given society as well.

Marx's economic analysis, which was concerned in some specifics with the means of production, dealt in particular with the role of the worker in this capitalistic, industrialized society. The evil force in man's life, for Marx, was capitalism. This plague on the worker's life created a deep gulf between the capitalist owners (bourgeoisie) and the dispossessed workers (proletariat). The ensuing class struggle was fought between the two great protagonists—those who owned all industry and consequently ruled the state, and the landless, propertyless worker who was the long-suffering victim of ruthless exploitation by the capitalists. This simple picture of evil versus good, of wrong versus right, was Marx's interpretation of all government, all economics, in fact, of all society. Although he argued that labor is not the source of *all* wealth, he considered it to be the necessary ingredient for making much of wealth useful. As workers pay for (reproduce) their own value through their labor under capitalism, they also produce some value over and above their simple wage cost to their employer. It is through this surplus value, for which the workers are unrewarded, that capitalist employers enrich themselves. Under this capitalistic exploitation, then, workers become increasingly poorer, more miserable, and exploited as the capitalistic thirst for profits increases and workers are driven ever more mercilessly. The steady impoverishment of the workers existing on a mere subsistence wage became, as it were, a law of nature for Marx. Eventually, the workers would rebel against their masters and overthrow the capitalist system. The groundwork would now be laid, in Marx's theory, for ushering in the new state, to be run for and by the workers—the dictatorship of the proletariat.

Although Marx was vague as to the precise form which this worker's dictatorship would take, Marx's partner Engels believed in 1891 that the workers would rule by way of a democratic republic which, in its makeup, would include a representative assembly.[4] As for the coming worker's revolution itself, Marx stated in 1872 that it would vary with the needs

---

[4] Karl Kautsky, *Social Democracy versus Communism*, ed. and trans. David Shub and Joseph Shaplen (New York: The Rand School Press, 1946), p. 39.

of the times. In some countries the revolution, because of the obstinacy of the capitalist class, would have to be violent. On the other hand, in certain countries (England and America were singled out as two examples) the workers probably would take power by peaceful means. For Marx and Engels, capitalistic society would go through a revolutionary upheaval because it would be radically pulled up by the roots. Whether this upheaval could be accomplished violently or peacefully were points of little concern. What was important to these communist theorists was that capitalism would be abolished and a new order would replace it throughout the world.

Marx made other contributions to social theory, such as his analysis of the real evils existent in mid-nineteenth century English capitalism. He was one of the first social scientists, in his approach to leading social problems and in his use of model building as an analytical tool. Whatever the contributions of Marx, however, over which there long has been disagreement, his purpose was clear. He sought to emancipate workers from what he viewed as their near slave-like conditions. Marx, for himself and his followers, was the savior of the working class, come to enthrone it upon its proper place as the lawful and rightful ruler of society.

As for interpretations of the Marxian system, two main views are current. The first, and older one, is that Marx to a considerable degree added the scientific method to earlier, utopian socialism. Here, Marx dissected capitalism, ferreted out its essence and examined its processes, cited its weaknesses and evils, and offered a prognosis for its future. Marx simulated a neat, well-ordered investigation which enjoyed, at least for the practitioners of Marxism, a precise scope and predictable results. As a result, Marxism was termed by many socialists as "scientific" socialism. Engels had argued that with the two great discoveries of Marx—the materialistic conception of history and the secret of capitalist production—socialism becomes a science. By this form of economic analysis, Marx introduced a measure of logic to his study and provided both an interpretation and a methodology not only for communists who were to follow later but also for socialist parties the world over. Socialism and communism for years after Marx were strongly influenced and shaped by Marxian thought. To a certain degree, they still are.

The other leading interpretation of Marx views the man as an inescapable victim of his environment. In its original form, then, the Marxism of Karl Marx is a mixture of old-fashioned Judaism, eighteenth century Rousseauism, and early nineteenth century utopianism.[5] Tucker interprets

---

[5] Edmund Wilson, *To the Finland Station* (Garden City, N. Y.: Doubleday & Company, Inc., Anchor Books, 1940), p. 475.

communism, in its fundamental conception, to be philosophical, even religious. Instead of being a social scientist, Marx was in reality a scientist turned myth-maker.[6] He was a moralist who learned the jargon of political economy and attempted to apply it to history. Marx ran into trouble, as Cole puts it, when he stopped writing history and plunged into theoretical economics. His difficulty lay in making deductions and generalizations from an abstract, unverifiable set of assumptions which had been set forth earlier by the classical economists.[7]

One difficulty facing those who attempt to interpret communism in the light of Marxism is that the latter, in its essential features, is not about communism as a future political system. Marx wrote vaguely of some millenium which he and his followers refer to as communism, but this in itself was not highlighted in his writings. Instead, the Marxism of Karl Marx constituted in the main an analysis of capitalism, its origins, growth, and evilness, and a prognosis of its eventual demise. As a result, Marxism as a guide or blueprint for a communist society simply is inappropriate; it is inadequate for this purpose. Nevertheless, Marxism *has* been used by communists as their theoretical guide, at least, and it is in this connection that it is studied as an ideological base for communism. Finally, whether Marxism is reasonable and scientific or not, inappropriate or not, it was trimmed and fitted to apply to a unique political-economic enviroment, that of post-tsarist Russia. Consequently, whatever form this Western-oriented movement of Marxism was to assume in 1917, it was compelled to adjust to the peculiarities and to the demands of the social and political scene of old Russia.

RUSSIAN POLITICAL THOUGHT

The first glimmerings of reformism arose in Russia following the revolt of December, 1825. The rebels, labeled "Decembrists," opposed the government's many inefficiencies as well as its policy of serfdom, sought a constitution with some form of representative government, and called for administrative and judicial reforms. By the mid-nineteenth century then, Russia was developing a native liberal movement, though it was led by and restricted to the intelligentsia. The persons contributing to the movement, liberal to radical in their sympathies, had divided into two main groups by 1850—those oriented toward Western intellectual patterns ("Westernizers") and those who focused on a native radicalism and who

---

[6] Robert C. Tucker, *Philosophy and Myth in Karl Marx* (London: Cambridge University Press, 1961), pp. 151, 227, 233.

[7] G. D. H. Cole, *A History of Socialist Thought* (London: Macmillan & Co., Ltd., 1953-60), Vol. II, p. 314.

were enamored of Slav literature ("Slavophils"). At first, the demands of these two groups were modest enough: a desire for an all-embracing philosophy and opposition to serfdom.

The Westernizers sought to Europeanize Russia after the political forms of the West; they hoped to move toward parliamentary systems and to achieve some civil rights. They were enamored of Hegel, leaned toward socialism, and sought progressive, democratic reforms. A leading spokesman for the Westernizers was Belinsky, who dealt with such ideas as the bourgeoisie, proletarianization of the masses, and class differentiations. The Westernizers, in seeking political reform of a type foreign to Russia, eventually became frustrated because of the many practical obstacles they met and, consequently, became more radical and revolutionary.

The ideological opponents of the Westernizers were the more conservative Slavophils who, instead of advocating political reforms, stressed abstract moral and religious improvements. The Slavophils sought a mild, halfway house between autocracy and constitutional monarchy which would rest on a foundation of religious faith and love. The outcome of Slavophilism was a grandiose "religious-nationalistic messianism."[8] Slavophil discussion circles in the 1840's, however, were the only forums where Russia's social problems were discussed. The program which Slavophilism did offer was that of an idealized peasant anarchism functioning under a benevolent tsar, or at least that of a romantic version of the old *Zemsky Sobor*. In any event, the schemes recommended by the Slavophils failed to inspire the liberal movement which by now was looking for more practical and concrete solutions to the problems arising out of tsarism.[9]

These early liberal, democratic stirrings arose at first not as movements to aid the masses, but rather as a self-reflection on the part of the intelligentsia who built upon and translated the concept of their own dignity to that of the higher dignity of all men. But the more moderate reformers, such as the Slavophils, while cooperating, still mistrusted those advocating sweeping changes, such as the Westernizers. The unbridgeable gulf which arose between moderate and extremist liberals, consequently, was to plague and hamstring the liberal movement in Russia from that time on.

The most well-known of the liberal-radical movements arising in Russia in the latter half of the nineteenth century was that of Populism (*Narodnichestvo*). The members of this group were known as Populists

---

[8] Martin Malia, *Alexander Herzen and the Birth of Russian Socialism, 1812–1855* (Cambridge, Mass.: Harvard University Press, 1961), p. 389.

[9] Richard Wortman, "Koshelev, Samarin, and Cherkassky and the Fate of Liberal Slavophilism," *Slavic Review*, Vol. XXI (June 1962), p. 263.

(*Narodniks*). Emerging in the late 1860's, Populism expressed a faith in human progress, Christian idealism, and moderation toward reform, as championed by its most popular spokesman, Mikhailovsky. Populism was a form of humanitarian socialism, rooted both in the regilious idealism and messianism of Russia as well as in the more secular socialism of the West. In 1874 Populism fostered a mass movement, the "Movement to the People" (*khozhdenie v narod*) through which more than 3,000 young intellectuals left their homes and studies to go into every European province of Russia "preaching socialism and progress."[10] Two events which occurred after the 1860's had a lasting effect not only on the whole Populist movement but on the future of Russian Marxism as well. First, the Populists were persecuted by the government for their beliefs and actions; these actions sometimes being no more radical than promoting simple cultural activities. Second, those Populists of the intelligentsia became disappointed with the natural lethargy and the unenlightened viewpoint of the peasants. The humble, trusting peasant, though often disgruntled, still had too much respect for the tsar to feel great sympathy for Populist socialism. Government harassment of the movement, coupled with disillusionment on the part of the intelligentsia, contributed to the transformation of Populism from a communal, socialistic theory into a more revolutionary, Marxist doctrine.

By the time of his death in 1894, Alexander III rather effectively had put down the Populist revolt, but not before it split into two main groups: the moderate Populists, and the revolutionary Populists, the latter dubbed "Land and Freedom" (*Zemlya i Volya*). Land and Freedom, in turn, broke up into a terrorist faction referred to as the "Will of the People" (*Narodnaya Volya*) and those of more moderate persuasion under Plekhanov—the "Black Redistribution" (*Cherny Peredel*). The *Narodnaya Volya* were terrorists advocating overthrow of the tsar and a popularly elected government. The *Cherny Peredel* carried out socialist propaganda, chiefly among peasants.

There were other minor, radical organizations such as the Fourierist Petrashevski circle in the 1840's and the Party of the People's Right (*Narodnoe Pravo*) in the 1890's. Several themes influencing if not dominating these liberal and radical groups in Russia in the nineteenth century all centered around socialism and its prospects for Russia.

There developed, too, a recurring native socialism influenced by leading Russian socialists such as Herzen, Belinsky, Bakunin, and Mikhailovsky. Socialism for the Russian intelligentsia, particularly in the latter half of

---

[10] James H. Billington, *Mikhailovsky and Russian Populism* (London: Oxford University Press, 1958), pp. 53, 79.

the nineteenth century, implied a new order, a sweeping away of the evils
of tsarist autocracy and its replacement by a just and humane society.
This tendency toward socialism was part of Russian liberalism. Western
ideas of the sanctity of private property had never been widely accepted
in Russia, and peasants had long thought it wrong that nobles should own
great parcels of land; a version of native agrarian socialism had always
been an accepted principle of Russian peasants.[11] Berdyaev distinguishes
three periods of socialism in old Russia: (1) utopian socialism as influenced
by Saint-Simon and Fourier, (2) Populist, or *Narodnik*, socialism, the most
Russian of all, but adopting some of Proudhon's ideas, and (3) Marxist,
or scientific socialism.[12] In addition to socialism per se, reform groups of
the nineteenth century sought improvements in governmental administration and justice, advocated opposition to the tyranny of the autocracy,
and expressed sympathy for the values and inherent worth of the common
man. But all these groups, sooner or later, ran up against autocratic
tsarism.

The autocratic tradition, ever a part of Russian political thought, has
origins which are not always clear. Conrad once depicted the autocracy
of the tsars as having neither Asian nor European parentage, nor any
apparent roots in earthly institutions. Rather, "What strikes one with a
sort of awe," Conrad notes, "is the inhumanness of its character." "It is
like a visitation, like a curse from Heaven, falling in the darkness of ages
upon the immense plains of forest and steppe lying dumbly on the confines
of two continents: a true desert harbouring no Spirit either of the East
or of the West."[13] More definite reasons, such as foreign invasions,
backwardness and illiteracy of much of the population provided a
hospitable soil for the growth of a strong autocracy. The Tatar and
Byzantine periods of rule in Russia contributed to the autocratic framework which, in turn, was energetically supported by Church, nobility, and
bureaucracy.

Russia's history always has lacked a sense of relative balance. Much
of its political thought has been positivist, dogmatic, and maximalist.
Western philosophical objectivity and a rigid logical method had never
formed a significant part of Russian traditions. Instead, Russian theory
longed for a wholeness, seemingly hesitant to reconcile itself either to
intellectual compromise or to a delicate balancing between extremes. As a
result, tsarist autocracy found it natural to ignore the feeble supplications

---

[11] Nicolas Berdyaev, *The Origin of Russian Communism* (London: Geoffrey Bles,
1948), p. 17.

[12] Nicolas Berdyaev, *The Russian Idea* (New York: The Macmillan Co., 1948), p. 100.

[13] Joseph Conrad, *Notes on Life and Letters* (Garden City, N. Y.: Doubleday, Page
and Co., 1921), p. 98.

for liberal reforms.   Liberalism, clearly, was not a part of the imperial
lexicon, but autocracy was.   Moreover, the Renaissance and Reformation
in Europe had not traveled far enough eastward to influence the non-
Western cast of Russian thought.

A logical concomitant to the failure of liberal movements to reform the
autocracy is the rise of a revolutionary tradition.   From the Decembrist
Uprising of 1825, sometimes referred to as the first Russian revolution,
through the radical movements after mid-century which promoted
terrorism, and finally the Revolution of 1905, all added to the growth in
Russia of a genuinely native revolutionary tradition.   In the 30-year period
of government repression ending with the death of Nicholas I in 1855, the
idea of revolt became the *ideal* of revolution, as Malia puts it, and the goal
no longer was but a political change of regime or of the citizen's legal
status.   The goal now was a more complete social and moral renovation of
the nation.[14]   The seeds of radical, revolutionary Marxism, coming from
the West, were sure to fall on receptive soil in Russia in the latter half of
the nineteenth century.

RUSSIAN MARXISM AND LENINIST THEORY

In the latter half of the century Marxism grew from a primitive doctrine
of two men into an international movement which inherited and dominated
all of the strains of socialism throughout Europe.   Where once there had
been small groups of sympathizers, now there were political parties.
Throughout the international socialist movement by this time, Marxism
clearly was the predominant tendency.[15]   By this time too, Marxism had
migrated east into Russia.

Although in 1868 Marx's *Das Kapital* was translated into Russian and
published in Russia, it is Georgiy Plekhanov who is considered to be the
father of Russian Marxism.   He was an ardent Populist in the 1870's who
had worked on the Russian journal *Annals* as a protege of Mikhailovsky.
While in Geneva in 1882 Plekhanov published a Russian translation of the
Communist Manifesto and founded the first Marxist party for the Russian
intelligentsia—the "Liberation of Labor."   This former Westernizer and
Populist helped establish Marxism as a rival contender to Populism in
trying to win support from the intelligentsia.   Marxism in Russia was an
expression of the westernizing tendencies of the liberal-revolutionary
groups.   Russian Marxism, in addition, because it was Marxism, required
a belief in the emancipation of Russia through the process of Western
industrialization.

---

[14] Malia, *op. cit.*, p. 416.
[15] Ulam, *op. cit.*, p. 135.

The grafting of Western Marxism onto the root of old Russia very significantly changed both Marxism and Russia. Early Russian Marxism quickly ran into obstacles, such as open opposition from the tsar's government. Although in some of the Western countries Marxism became respectable and academic, even parliamentarian, by necessity in Russia it grew into an outlaw movement which was narrow, concentrated, grim, and cruel.[16] It became an outlaw movement more out of necessity than choice because of its being forced underground as a result of the tsar's efficient police network. Marxism in Russia was introduced by Plekhanov and encouraged by other Russian radicals such as Martov, but it broke out into a successful rebel movement under the founder of Soviet Marxism, Vladimir Ilyich Ulyanov—Lenin. Lenin and Martov established an amalgam of Marxist groups called the "Union of Struggle for the Liberation of the Working Class" and organized the St. Petersburg Strike of 1896.

Lenin and Leninism

It might have been easy enough for Marx to write of communism in the abstract, picking and choosing examples and "evidence" for his conclusions from whatever country and from whatever period in history he thought suitable. Lenin and his colleagues, however, had to reshape Marxist theory to suit the particular situation with which they had to deal—Tsarist Russia. Although the observation is trite, nevertheless it is true that Lenin transformed a philosophy which was designed by its founder to fit a modern industrialized society such as England, Germany, or the United States into one which could work in precisely the opposite type of society, the backward, rural, economically underdeveloped Russia. Lenin, of course, realized this dilemma and, during the New Economic Policy (NEP), acknowledged that Russia needed temporarily a reinstitution of capitalism to both assist in industrialization and to stimulate the growth of a proletariat with a class consciousness. Lenin's "Marxism" highlighted revolution and class struggle, for these were more appropriate Marxian tenets for Russia than some of the other more abstract concepts. The points in Marxism that Lenin stressed, including the proletarian dictatorship and the revolutionary vanguard, were minor aspects of Marx's writings. Apart from the class struggle, these Leninist points of emphasis had not held Marx's attention nor concern for long.

In another way, too, Lenin departed from Marx's analysis. Marx argued that economics is supreme and that a nation's economic system would determine its political structure. Without disagreeing with this

---

[16] Wilson, *op. cit.*, p. 478.

Marxian doctrine openly, Lenin *acted* on the assumption that politics (if one held political power) could well determine a nation's economic system. So, if Lenin could overthrow the Tsar's government and take power, he had no doubt that he could also establish a Marxian-economic structure.

Soviet Marxism, in its early years, was almost wholly based on Lenin's interpretation of Marx's writings. Communism actually became, as the Soviet Communists continually point out, Marxism-Leninism. Lenin placed great weight on the imperialist era of capitalist development, as set down in Marx's theory. Stalin, at one time, in fact, defined Leninism as Marxism in the era of imperialism and of the proletarian revolution. It is also, he continued, the theory and tactics of the dictatorship of the proletariat.[17]

Marxist theory, for Lenin, was both a philosophy of explanation and a necessary tool. He certainly was a believer in Marxism, but he also was an effective employer of carefully chosen instruments and weapons to achieve his ends. Marxism, as he proved, was an excellent weapon. Lenin used Marxist theory to "rationalize strategies previously adopted," in Meyer's words. Lenin combined the doctrinaire rigidity of an orthodox Marxist with the flexibility of pragmatism.[18]

Lenin cannot be treated as a believer in democracy in either its theoretical or practical versions. He consistently refused to be bound by majority decision—even when such was a decision of his own party. In theory too, Lenin revealed his antidemocratic bias. It seems almost as though he felt obliged to pay lip-service to democracy, however, when he said that democracy cannot be imagined without representative institutions, or when he advocated democracy for the majority of people. Here he seems to be following Marx's lead. At other and more frequent times, though, he derided "parliamentarism" and observed that the destruction of the state (a Marxist goal) means also the destruction of democracy. The withering away of the state too, means the withering away of democracy since democracy is but one of the varieties of the state.[19]

If he had little and but fleeting sympathy for democracy as such, he did invent and rely upon the doctrine of democratic centralism. A Soviet interpretation of this doctrine is that democratic centralism means dual subordination; any one organization is subordinate both to the next higher echelon in the chain of command and to the appropriate local unit of

---

[17] Joseph Stalin, *Foundations of Leninism* (New York: International Publishers, 1939), p. 10.

[18] Alfred G. Meyer, *Leninism* (Cambridge, Mass.: Harvard University Press, 1957), pp. 235, 252.

[19] V. I. Lenin, *State and Revolution* (New York: International Publishers, 1932), pp. 41, 62, 73, 82.

government.[20] This partly explains it, but more accurately, democratic centralism in Lenin's conception and use of the term means internal party discussion and a measure of relatively free debate, at least in the highest party circles and election of the party's leaders (democratic), coupled with a disciplined obedience of all party members to the agreed upon decisions of the higher party apparatus (centralism). Thus, the making and executing of party decisions is a synthesis of "democracy and organization, of freedom and order, of dissent and unanimity."[21]

Imperialism was described by Lenin as capitalism in its monopoly stage. Monopoly capitalism would lead to an end of competition within the capitalist world which then would see all life commercialized, where everyone would be a small cog in the giant machinery of capitalism, and where a small number of capitalist-monopolists exploit almost the entire society. The instrument for such exploitation, for Lenin as well as for Marx, was the state. In this imperialist stage, capitalist nations would fight among themselves over the few remaining colonies available for exploitation.

Following the Marxian interpretation that the state is simply the instrument for exploitation by the ruling class, Lenin argued for an eventual end even to the proletarian state. It will begin to wither away immediately following a communist victory because there will be no further class antagonisms under communism and hence no further need for this instrument of suppression—the state. Of course, temporarily the victorious proletariat will need state power to crush the exploiting capitalist class *and* also to guide the masses of the population in organizing socialism.[22] Here we have a significant modification in the theory of Marx and Engels, that the state not only is an instrument for exploitation, but it is also a guide to point the way toward and to instruct the people in the ways of socialism. Lenin now provides the theoretical rationale for later Soviet leaders to continue the communist state indefinitely, so long as it is still the guide for the people, lighting their way to the millenium.

One of Lenin's most notable contributions was in formulating the plans for and carrying out a revolution. He was a revolutionist *par excellence*. Replacement of the capitalist by the proletariat state is impossible, Lenin argued simply and directly, without violent revolution. Here, it seems, Lenin was following more the traditional Russian anti-tsarist, revolutionary tradition than the tenets of Marx, who considered revolution as one, but

---

[20] V. A. Vlasov, *Osnovy Sovetskogo Gosudarstvennogo Upravleniya* (Moscow: Gosurizdat, 1954), p. 13.

[21] Meyer, *Leninism*, p. 93.

[22] Lenin, *op. cit.*, pp. 23, 25, 37.

not the only, means for the proletariat to come to power. Lenin accented the revolutionary side of Marxism simply because the Russian scene required it. Revolution would be the only way to free Russia of tsarism, and it would constitute a prelude for a larger, worldwide proletarian revolution. And yet, in his revolutionary program, Lenin was not at all an anarchist, nor was he a revolutionist simply for the sake of revolution. He was a "revolutionary with a bureaucratic mind" who relied upon a rather high degree of order and rationality; for him, revolution was not an end in itself but simply a means (the *only* means open to him and the Bolsheviks) to establish the dictatorship of the proletariat in Russia. Finally, a successful revolution for Lenin could, in fact must, be led by the worker's vanguard; it also must be carried out by a considerable majority of the whole people.

Lenin is noted particularly for his formation of the worker's vanguard, the Communist Party. For Lenin, a successful revolution against the Tsar and a full-fledged socialist state leading the Russian people to socialism all require a highly motivated, rigidly self-disciplined and well-coordinated party core. This was a departure too from Marx's view of the proletariat as a large, elemental, dynamic, and revolutionary force which did not at all call for, nor need, a vanguard elite group. For better or for worse, the Soviet Communist Party was to a very considerable extent the creation of Lenin. He was both its father and first nursemaid. But how could such a creation, so sincerely motivated and well-intentioned as was the party of the old, self-sacrificing Bolsheviks, be transformed after Lenin's death into a finely tuned instrument of personal dictatorship (as occurred under Stalin)? The trouble lay, it would seem, in Lenin's heritage. Instead of bequeathing to his heirs in the party hierarchy a semidemocratic school for socialism-communism, all Lenin really left was a half-developed system of centralized control which revolved around the all-important central figure of himself. Regular, impersonal, objective procedures of decision-making had not developed under Lenin the revolutionist, and democratic centralism was a meaningless formula.[23]

Leninism was the first serious attempt to adapt the abstract and incomplete philosophy of Marxism to a concrete political situation. Two questions immediately present themselves. Was "pure" Marxism rational and practical enough to have worked satisfactorily in some country at some specific time? Were the Leninist alterations necessary in order to make Marxism work—at least in Russia? We might speculate on answers to these questions, but they really are moot points. In our judgments of

---

[23] Meyer, *Leninism*, p. 100.

"practical" Marxism, we must simply accept the fact that Leninism was the changed form that Marxism took in Russia in the twentieth century, for better or for worse, for success or failure. If Marxism in its original form is a viable and workable political, economic, and social scheme, it is verified by Lenin and his supporters who brought it into being in Russia. If, on the other hand, Marxism is not workable, is too visionary, unrealistic, and abstract for real life, then Leninism with all of its adaptations and alterations of the doctrine tends to prove the point.

CHAPTER IV

Leninism into Stalinism

LENIN ORIGINATED a disciplined, monolithic, centralized political party with which the October Revolution was won. Moreover, he ruled the new Soviet government in its first critical years. On closer examination, however, the party and its leaders can be seen to be not nearly so single-minded and well-coordinated as those early victories imply. Instead, the communists in Lenin's day were split over personnel assignments, tactics, even principles. Before the Revolution Lenin fought the Mensheviks, Socialist Revolutionaries, even some fellow Bolsheviks (such as Zinoviev). After the Revolution Lenin argued for peace with Germany over the protests of the so-called "Left Communists" who sought to ignite a world revolution. Following the Civil War Lenin continued to emphasize a rigidly centralized party dictatorship in defiance of the more democratically minded "Left Opposition" and the Democratic Centralists within his party. At the Ninth Party Conference in 1920 Lenin and his supporters were openly attacked for past failures in personnel management, weak organizational structure, and shortcomings in directing educational and economic establishments. This attack was, in Daniels' words, the high point of democratic opposition within the party. It was, in a way, the climax of communist liberalism.[1]

Despite these and other problems involved in working out a party dictatorship, the period of rule known as "Leninism" was that of building the foundation for the modern Communist Party as well as a period of consolidating and strengthening Communist political power within Russia. Stalinism, by contrast, was the period of completing and perfecting the structure which Lenin began. From the October Revolution in 1917 until 1953, Soviet history is a history of Leninism and Stalinism, but chiefly that

---

[1] Robert V. Daniels, *The Conscience of the Revolution: Communist Opposition in Soviet Russia* (Cambridge, Mass.: Harvard University Press, 1960), pp. 116–17.

of the latter. Of the numerous events taking place during these two decades, several are worthy of being singled out for special attention. There were, in this 36-year period, five significant crises which the Communist regime went through. The outcome of each was to mark indelibly the Communist system from then on. To no small degree, our interpretations of communism even today hark back to the notable events of this time. These crises for early communism were the Civil War, the New Economic Policy, the problem of political succession following Lenin's death, industrialization and collectivization, and the Great Purge.

CIVIL WAR

There were several contributing factors in the war's start, but opposition to the new Communist government was the most important. Many problems arose around which opposition to the new regime could and did arise. Communist policies, such as the abolition of private trading, the signing of a humiliating peace treaty with Germany, confiscation of peasants' grain, the harsh—at times terroristic—methods of political domination, the compounding of worker dissatisfactions, all contributed to a rise in anti-Bolshevism during a period of severe rule which came to be known as that of "War Communism." There remained, too, those political groups which had opposed the Bolsheviks before, during, and after the Revolution, such as the Kadets and most of the Socialist Revolutionaries; other groups sought a return of the monarchy, or of the Provisional Government. This latter government, of course, had been replaced by the Bolshevik *coup d'etat*. Russians had not overwhelmingly endorsed either the spirit of Bolshevism or its leaders. Growing nationalist movements of various peoples, such as the Ukrainians, added to the general disharmony by seeking independence or autonomy from Great Russian dominance. As the incoming government, too, the Communists inherited a weakened and largely devastated country which had suffered from at least a century of misrule, capped by a destructive social, economic, and personal dislocation in World War I. Any programs offered by the new leadership, in light of such governing handicaps, at best could be only halfway attempts at solutions to these problems and were bound to be met with disappointment if not outright disgust from large numbers of citizens. To all these forces were added the open antipathy toward the new regime of a number of non-Communist military officers such as Kornilov and Denikin and by foreign nations which opposed Communist pronouncements and ideals both at home and abroad. In the face of this wide front of protest to the new Communist government, a war seemed inevitable.

Opposed to the Reds (Communists) in the war were the so-called Whites, all anti-Communist. The war continued for some three years, finally being won decisively by the Red Army. In large measure, the very fact that there was considerable diverse opposition to the Communists from so many sides became eventually a source of strength for the Communists and actually contributed to their winning the war. Disagreements among the various factions of the Whites and confusion as to precisely what they were fighting for, the reactionary nature of some of their leaders and policies, as well as overall lack of coordination of their efforts seriously weakened the White armies. Very limited participation of anti-Communist foreign troops in the war, and their too early withdrawal from the scene of conflict (which they viewed as a hopeless undertaking) in the long run aided more than harmed the Communists.

The White armies were not without their assets, of course, especially in the early part of the war. They were aided by large Cossack contingents, by limited British, French, Czechoslovakian, Italian, and U.S. troops in the west and by rather sizable Japanese forces in the east. This conglomerate international army did gain considerable territory and at times endangered the very existence of the Communist regime. Following some White military successes, anti-Communist governments were established, chiefly by Socialist Revolutionaries, in several areas throughout the country. The early successes of the White forces, nevertheless, were piecemeal and not solidly based. The anti-Communists were too much the victims of their own weaknesses and of the relentless Communist propaganda. In addition, they were seriously weakened by the blows rained on them from the Red Army, after this army finally became an organized, effective fighting unit.

The Communists offered a positive program of economic, social and political reform. Reminiscent of their skillful propaganda campaign carried out during 1917, the Communists in the Civil War pinpointed the weaknesses of their opponents. The Whites' cause, the Communists argued, advocated a return of the discredited monarchy, or at the least only another version of Kerensky's ineffectual Provisional Government. The Communists attempted to persuade the allied armies in their country that they were supporting the wrong cause which, at any event, was widely unpopular and was doomed to defeat. To the non-Russian minority groups in the country who sought independence and autonomy, the Communists stated that the Whites wanted a return of Great Russian imperialism after the fashion of the tsars. To all of these groups, and especially to the people of Great Russian origin, the Communists argued that the Red Army was protecting Mother Russia from invasion by foreign nations. To these propaganda achievements, the Red Army added some solid military victories. The Communists won over an opposing force that too often was reactionary, poorly directed, confused, quarrelsome, and internally divided and which lacked any meaningful program or mission. The Communists won the Civil War, as they had won the Revolution earlier, partly because of the weaknesses of their enemies, but more importantly because of their own strengths.

The long-range political significance of the Civil War was that it added to the strength of the Communist foundation in Russia. The regime wrapped itself in the garb of protector of the new young socialist system as well as of Mother Russia against all enemies at home and abroad. The steel of Soviet Communism, forged in the Revolution, was hardened in the victorious Civil War. At least, Communists viewed it this way. The war, then, added luster to communism's heroic idealism, an important contribution to party morale. Moreover, the war demonstrably prejudiced Communist leaders and their successors against the allies who had invaded Russia and who had contributed men and material aimed at clipping off the budding communist system. In line with Marxist and Leninist theory, which purported to reveal the evils of capitalism, the Civil War proved in a very practical manner to the new Soviet leaders that their historic enemy was the capitalist West. Communist leaders were not soon to forget this bitter lesson, and Soviet foreign policy toward the West has been influenced ever since by that event.[2]

Victory for the Communists over their enemies in 1921, however, only opened the door to other problems for the new regime, problems that were not to be solved easily and satisfactorily. The first of these domestic problems arose from the unfavorable reaction within the country to the new Communist policies and procedures.

THE NEW ECONOMIC POLICY

By 1921 the Civil War had ended. Left in its wake was severe internal distress. The economy was at a virtual standstill with industry completely disrupted; general industrial production was one seventh of the prewar figure. Pig iron output in 1921 was only 3 percent of the prewar level; stocks of metal, industrial products, food, consumer's goods, and fuel had

---

[2] Souvarine contends that another effect of the Civil War was to outlive traditional Bolshevism which, he states, could not outlive the "psychosis of systematised murder. At the war's end, the principles, practices, institutions and customs of Bolshevism were turned by the weight of the calamities it had endured. It was its misfortune rather than its fault." Boris Souvarine, *Stalin: A Critical Survey of Bolshevism* (New York: Longmans, Green and Co., 1939), pp. 254–55.

been exhausted. Most factories were idle and many mines had been destroyed. The nation's transport was almost worn out, inflation became uncontrollable, and famine had begun to reach sizeable proportions. To these difficulties were added the novel Communist programs which were directed at radically transforming the economy through nationalization of industry and of wiping out private business as well as individual farming. "War Communism," that severe forced-draft economic exploitation ruthlessly carried out by the Communists in the 1918–21 period when the new government was fighting for its life, had left a black mark on the regime in the eyes of many people. More and more citizens, such as workers, sailors, and non-Bolsheviks, were becoming increasingly disappointed in Communist rule which, all too frequently, was arbitrary, cruel, and vicious toward its opponents.

Important groups of individuals opposed, with increasing bitterness, Lenin's regime because it curbed other political parties which had become spokesmen for workers, because the regime subordinated trade unions to central party control, and, above all, because it suppressed democratic liberties—the goal of all socialists. These opposing forces included Socialist Revolutionaries, Mensheviks, and worker's organizations.

Early in 1921 increasing strikes by workers broke out as a result of their dissatisfactions with governmental policies, which included a cut in their food rations. Then, as if to cap it all, sailors of the Baltic Fleet who were stationed at the Kronstadt Fortress revolted against the weaknesses, abuses, and tyranny of the Communist government. Ironically these sailors, joined by many Petrograd workers, were the same revolutionists who earlier had helped the Bolsheviks come to power. Now, they opposed Communist tyranny in the name of all Russians who sought freedom and the opportunity to determine their own fate. The slogan of the Kronstadt rebels was—Soviet power, but without the Communists. The Kronstadt Revolt expressed a growing anti-Communist feeling when the Communists had been in power only three years. To the peaceful requests and demands of the Kronstadt sailors, who contended that they did not want to shed any blood, the Communist government declared war. The Communists now attacked (and conquered) their own former supporters—sailors, workers, and members of the Petrograd Soviet. The Kronstadt defenders were defeated, some of those remaining alive were executed, others imprisoned and exiled. Clearly the regime was in danger, and drastic ameliorative action was now called for. Lenin's solution, over which a number of Communists strongly disagreed, was the NEP.

Basically, the NEP was a temporary retreat from too much communism too fast. It sought to give the regime a breathing spell by permitting a partial withdrawal into older, more familiar capitalism. Lenin, in discussing the necessity for the NEP, noted that one of Russia's economic difficulties stemmed from the rural makeup of the majority of Russian society. Socialism needed capitalism, Lenin argued, first to stimulate the growth of economic consciousness, then to teach the Communists how to construct, manufacture, and trade in the modern world. The NEP, in Lenin's words, was a retreat to state capitalism.[3] Stalin referred to the NEP as a special policy of permitting capitalism while yet retaining the "commanding positions" (heavy industry, transportation, foreign trade, banking) in the hands of the state for the purpose of effecting a transition from capitalism to socialism.[4]

The NEP reestablished the right, to a limited degree, of private ownership, including retail (but not wholesale or foreign) trade and private mutual benefit societies. Small industry and crafts were freed from state control, but the "commanding positions" were to remain the function of the government. Even in the private sector, however, the small entrepreneur was discriminated against politically, educationally, and in his army and government service. And free enterprise was more free if one happened to be a party supporter. One communist observer of the NEP at the time later wrote: "The NEP has become a racket.... One year's sheepbreeding in the south has produced Soviet millionaires of a strange kind, former Red Partisans, whose daughters live in the most beautiful hotels in the Crimea and whose sons gamble for large stakes at the casinos."[5] Restrictions on peasants were eased so they could sell part of their produce on the open market, lease land and, by 1925, even hire labor. Confiscation of the peasant's grain by the hated government procurement "armies" was replaced by a more acceptable grain tax. Finally, foreign capital was again welcomed into the country and curbs on foreign trade agreements were eased.

Even so, the NEP was not much of a return to capitalism. The denationalized handicraft and small workshops comprised, in 1923, only 12½ percent of the country's total enterprises. Although in the first year or two under this program the private trader (*Nepman*) furnished perhaps half of the immediate market for products of the industrial firms, by 1928 the *Nepman* handled not more than one fourth of total trade.[6]

---

[3] V. I. Lenin, *Selected Works* (New York: International Publishers, 1937), Vol. 9, p. 286.

[4] J. Stalin, *Works* (Moscow: Foreign Languages Publishing House, 1954), Vol. 7, p. 374.

[5] Victor Serge, "Vignettes of NEP," in Julien Steinberg (ed.), *Verdict of Three Decades* (New York: Duell, Sloan and Pearce, 1950), p. 145.

[6] Maurice Dobb, *Soviet Economic Development Since 1917* (London: Routledge & Kegan Paul, Ltd., 1948), pp. 142–44.

The NEP was a qualified economic success; it was a definite political success in saving the Communist regime. Although other factors contributed to economic rehabilitation (such as a welcomed respite of peace), the NEP did manage to facilitate industrial production and agricultural output, increase domestic trade, strengthen the nation's finances, and improve the lot of the peasants. Despite some internal opposition from "leftist" party leaders (those fearing that any concessions to capitalism would be ruinous for the future of communism), the NEP had a larger meaning than simply a temporary emergency measure to forestall further economic regression. In a way, the NEP retreat gave testimony to a realistic side of communism. For Lenin, as was his bent (for example, his willingness to forego talk of world revolution in order to gain peace with the Germans), retreats, concessions, apparent contradictions—all were justified in order to continue his party in power. This is not to say that Lenin was shallow or insincere in his Marxist beliefs, for he certainly was not that. What it does say is that Lenin was quite willing to compromise and bend the Communist system when and where necessary to meet practical problems of the day; chief among them was keeping the Communists in power. In this sense the NEP was a landmark event which set the tone for a very practical type of communism which ever since has been followed by Lenin's successors. Now, with Lenin's death, the third great crisis arose. Who and what were to follow after the death of the creator and main sustainer of early Soviet Communism?

THE SUCCESSION STRUGGLE

All through the early years of the Soviet regime there had been a jockeying for power and a beginning of the contests over who would get Lenin's favor. With Lenin's intermittent, at times serious illnesses from 1922 onward, the struggle over his succession was well under way by the time he died in January, 1924. Lenin had not singled out anyone as his successor, although he did describe Trotsky as the most able member of the Central Committee. Yet, he also felt that Trotsky was too self-confident. Of Stalin, Lenin recommended that he should be replaced as party general secretary because he was "too rude" and lacked "caution." Schapiro speculates that if Lenin began to have misgivings about Stalin in 1922, it already was too late. Lenin "had conjured up a monster which he no longer had the strength to control."[7] After Lenin's death, three of the ruling Political Bureau (Politburo) members—Stalin, Zinoviev, and

---

[7] Leonard Schapiro, *The Origin of the Communist Autocracy* (Cambridge, Mass.: Harvard University Press, 1956), p. 342.

Kamenev—temporarily assumed the mantle of power as a guiding triumvirate for the party's Central Committee.

Leon Trotsky evidently assumed, as did many other party members, that he would replace Lenin as head of the party and government. Trotsky was the intellectual superior of his colleagues in the party leadership. He had been an early co-worker and supporter of Lenin and a well-known Marxist and revolutionary pamphleteer. He was the military leader of the Bolsheviks in both the Revolution and the Civil War, and an early member of the Politburo. He was Commissar of War when Lenin died. And yet at times he opposed Lenin, occasionally bitterly, and was tainted slightly by a previous Menshevik background. Trotsky exhibited one fatal weakness: he refused to actively combat his enemies within the party. Stalin won over Trotsky in large measure because Trotsky would not and could not fight for personal power, according to Eastman. Trotsky could win support for his ideas and ideals, but not for himself. He had a genius for losing friends and alienating people. He was, perhaps, one of the world's worst politicians. He simply laid down and let Stalin first kick him out of the leadership circle and then out of the party itself.[8] The posture which Trotsky adopted in his fight with Stalin was not defensive, it was suicidal.

Joseph Stalin, old Bolshevik of Georgian background, was a longtime Marxist and revolutionary, though not a very distinguished one. A member of the first Politburo, he became commissar of nationalities in the first Communist government. He had two other posts of importance within the party structure, that of a member of the Organization Bureau (Orgburo) and, in 1922, general secretary of the party, which placed him at the head of the party Secretariat. After April, 1917, differing from other top party officials, he followed closely Lenin's lead in all policy matters. Stalin's key posts in the Politburo, Orgburo, and Secretariat gave him access to policy-making; he directed the party's organizational work, and most important, controlled almost all party appointments. From this position of strength Stalin later would launch his bid for supreme power.

Two other famous old Bolsheviks were Gregory Zinoviev and L. B. Kamenev. An early confidant of Lenin, Zinoviev had been with him in Switzerland before the Revolution and was one of the members of the first Politburo. He was a member also of the 1921 Politburo and was chairman of the Third International in the early 1920's in addition to being leader of the powerful Leningrad organization of the Communist Party. Kamenev, an editor of *Pravda* before the Revolution, was another of the first Politburo

---

[8] Max Eastman, "The Character and Fate of Leon Trotsky," in Steinberg, *op. cit.*, pp. 186–88.

members and holder of several important posts in the government. He
also held power in the Moscow party organization. Both of these two old
Bolsheviks shared something in common by having opposed Lenin's call to
seize power in October, 1917, as well as expressing opposition to some of
Lenin's early programs.

There were others who figured prominently in the post-Lenin power
struggle. Among these were A. I. Rykov, first Commissar of the Interior
and formal head of the government following Lenin's death; M. P. Tomsky,
head of the trade union organization; Nikolai Bukharin, famous Marxist
theorist, a leader of the more world revolutionary-minded "left" Communist faction in the party, and editor of *Pravda*.

By way of careful planning and clever scheming, Stalin in 1924 sided
with Zinoviev and Kamenev against Trotsky, whom they all opposed
because he was the logical heir of Lenin. Then, gaining support from other
quarters (the more conservative "right" Communists) Stalin in 1928
attacked Zinoviev and Kamenev; the latter two belatedly then joined
Trotsky in opposing Stalin. Still later, Stalin turned on the right faction
(such as Rykov and Tomsky) and had them removed from their posts. By
the late 1920's Stalin's serious opposition among the old Bolsheviks had
been eliminated, and by late 1930 the Politburo had become completely
Stalinist controlled.

Stalin was helped in his victory too, because his side was the more
popular among rank-and-file party members. Trotsky downgraded the
emphasis on building up a single nation, Soviet Russia; instead, he advocated concentrating party efforts on igniting the long-hoped-for and
long-expected world revolution—his doctrine of "permanent revolution."
Stalin, more in the practical Leninist tradition and more in keeping with
the interests of regional party secretaries throughout the Soviet Union, was
the champion of the doctrine "socialism in one country." He advocated
building a solid base for the new system in Russia first, *then* proceeding
abroad with the world revolution at some later, more convenient time.
Here again, Trotsky and at times Zinoviev, Kamenev, and Bukharin were
the Marxist idealists. Stalin, on the contrary, was the more realistic
leader. The majority of party members during the succession struggle
were more inclined toward the cautious, practical plans of Stalin than they
were to the more visionary international schemes of his opponents. Having
at least for the time won the succession struggle, Stalin could now move to
the next great problems of his regime—how to industrialize the economy
and collectivize agriculture.

The post-Lenin power struggle taught that the succession process in a
Communist system is likely to be bitter and hard-fought and its outcome

unpredictable. The succession struggle also pointed to another tendency in a Communist regime—that to gain and hold power is the highest objective of competing party leaders. But, then, this aspect of Stalinism— that the primary goal is personal power—is not too different from Leninism, nor even so different from other political systems throughout the world for that matter.

INDUSTRIALIZATION AND COLLECTIVIZATION

In 1928 the first Five-Year Plan was launched. Basically, the plan sought to organize natural resource exploitation, industrial production, and distribution for the achievement of overall national goals, as determined by the party hierarchy. The goals were socialization, industrialization, and modernization of agricultural, backward Russia; at that time rural areas amounted to about 82 percent of the country. The enormous undertaking of putting together a plan for the nation's economy for a period of five years was begun in 1925. One of the early Soviet planning officials pointed out that the plan's "control" figures assigned to each important branch of industry certain concrete goals to achieve in investment, transactions, production, imports and exports, income and expenditures, and prices.[9]

Industrialization

Broadly, the accomplishments aimed for by the first Five-Year Plan were to eliminate private industry, radically increase industrial production (which was scheduled to rise over 200 percent in the plan period), strengthen other areas of the economy which concentrated on producer's (instead of consumer's) goods, and to begin collectivizing agriculture. The plan also was intended to win sacrifices and renewed dedication from the people—all directed toward molding a planned economic system. There were several problems connected with formulating the plan, though. What organizational structure would be required (the State Planning Committee, *Gosplan*, was the instrument chosen); what would be the adequacy and reliability of information received by *Gosplan;* how precise an estimate was possible of Soviet productive capacity; and was the plan to be a directive, guide, or pious hope? The Soviet regime from 1928 up to the present has, in many respects, been trying with greater precision to answer just these questions.

The first Five-Year Plan was "fulfilled," according to Soviet testimony,

---

[9] G. T. Grinko, *The Five-Year Plan of the Soviet Union: A Political Interpretation* (New York: International Publishers, 1930), p. 22.

in four and a half years. Despite the fact that the plan "failed" in that a
number of its goals were unachieved, it did markedly increase industrial
production (almost a fourfold increase), and it raised the level of output in
such commodities as coal, oil, pig iron, and electric power. As a result, the
Soviet Union was well on the road to becoming a modern industrial nation.
In another sense the plan was a very definite success. Politically it continued and greatly elaborated earlier sporadic efforts at national planning
(such as the first, primitive State Commission for the Electrification of
Russia, *Goelro*) and set the trend and established an organizational framework for what was to become a permanent feature of the Soviet economic-
governmental system; this is national economic planning guided by the few
party leaders at the top and carried out by the hordes of party and
government bureaucrats throughout the country. From the time of the
first Five-Year Plan, friend and foe would praise or damn the Soviet
Communist system in large part because of its habit of widespread,
nationwide economic planning.

The second Five-Year Plan, 1933–37, differed in emphasis from the first
by stressing the necessity for filling in specific gaps in production (such as
in nonferrous metals), rather than striving for sheer magnitude of output.
The second Five-Year Plan included a high rate of investment. Slightly
more attention was paid to light industrial construction. The limitations
of national planning and the weaknesses of the plans themselves were
especially apparent as they began to be implemented. Nevertheless, the
first two Five-Year Plans marked an important watershed between the
state capitalism of the early and middle 1920's and the predominantly
collectivist or socialist economy that emerged by the later 1930's.[10]

Collectivization

At the Fifteenth Party Congress in 1927, known as the "Congress of
the Five-Year Plan," the decision was announced to collectivize agriculture.
The first plan called for one quarter of the peasant farms and 15 percent
of the nation's cultivated area to be collectivized by 1933. Prior to this
drive to reorganize farming there were 24,500,000 peasant farms in the
country; among them were 8,500,000 "poor" peasant farms, 15,000,000
"middle" peasant farms, and 1,000,000 belonging to the more affluent
peasants, the *kulaky*.[11]

The ideal goal for farm organization in the minds of the leaders remained
the state farm (*sovkhoz*), in which all peasants would be employed, as an

[10] Dobb, *op. cit.*, p. 281.

[11] Andrew Rothstein (ed.), *History of the Communist Party of the Soviet Union*
(Moscow: Foreign Languages Publishing House, 1960), p. 442.

agricultural proletariat, in a number of wholly state-owned and operated enterprises. Realistically, though, the regime was forced to settle for something much less. The "temporary" collective farm (*kolkhoz*) system provided at first for three types of organization. In the first, the commune, members worked land in common and shared tools and equipment as well as some features of communal living. This plan was the closest to the *sovkhoz* ideal and least popular with peasants. The second form, one of joint land cultivation, was the farthest from the *sovhoz;* it was a production cooperative with peasants retaining title to land, equipment, and livestock, but dividing the crop on the basis of the size of each member's holding. This type, as one might anticipate, was the peasant's favorite. The third, and most widespread form of *kolkhoz* (because it was promoted by the government), was the *artel*, in which members pooled land and machinery, worked collectively, but retained separate homes, livestock, and small garden plots. Early failure in production goals of a number of *sovkhozy*, coupled with strong peasant resistance to collectivization in general forced the regime to accept for the time being the *artel* as the most feasible type of government-organized farm system.

During the period of forced collectivization in the late 1920's and early 1930's, party and government bureaucracies were aligned against the peasant in the battle over which way agriculture would go. The nation's leadership wanted more *sovkhozy* and *kolkhozy* and an end to private peasant holdings and individual farming. Most of the peasants wanted just the reverse. The government imposed heavy, even crushing taxation to overcome peasant resistance, withdrew the peasant's right to rent land and hire labor, and abolished the peasant's village commune (*mir*). Starting in 1928, but concentrated in the winter of 1929–30, the government carried out a vicious policy to wipe out the *kulak* class of peasants. Local government and party officials confiscated the *kulak* land, barns, livestock, equipment and supplies, and even their personal property. Occasionally *kulaky* were murdered in the process. Many peasants retaliated by refusing to work in the common fields, hiding their food, burning their crops, breaking their implements, slaughtering millions of the cattle, sheep, goats, and horses rather than giving them up to the *kolkhozy*. At times the peasants actively fought the representatives of party and state. A number of government agents were assassinated by peasants, and the government retaliated with peasant executions (reaching a number of 40 a day in February, 1930).[12] All peasant resistance was heavily penalized by the government's armed forces; *kulaky* and

---

[12] Bernard Pares, *A History of Russia* (definitive edition, New York: Alfred A. Knopf, Inc., 1953), p. 528.

suspected *kulaky* were deported to the northern and eastern parts of the country.

Early in 1930, Stalin called for a temporary retreat and for an easing in the collectivization drive in order to end the chaotic scene of disrupted rural life and in a further attempt to gain his objectives, which physical force was only partially successful in achieving. Collectivization was now to be voluntary on the part of peasants. One result of this breathing spell was a large-scale peasant exodus from collectives.

The government now emphasized inducement to peasants to join the collectives. The peasants, retaining the confiscated land of the *kulaky*, were promised preferences in receiving new land, machinery, seed grain, and tax credits. Meanwhile, pressures such as heavy taxation continued to burden private peasants. Collectives also had access to more modern farm machinery from the government-operated machine-tractor stations (MTS) which had been initiated in 1928. Finally, peasants were allowed to retain their houses, garden plots, family livestock, and small tools outside of the collectives. As a result, collectivization increased in the 1930's so that 52.7 percent of the peasant households formed 211,100 farms by 1931, a figure which grew to 93.5 percent by 1938.[13]

Results of the first years of collectivization were mixed. In Dobb's words, the "birth-pangs were sharp; the attendant midwifery was rough."[14] That peasant suffering was widespread is a modest enough evaluation; in many cases the hardships created were nothing short of disastrous. Several million peasants died of famine and malnutrition during 1932–33 as an indirect result of forced collectivization. Many others were exiled and imprisoned. Almost all lost their land save for the small garden plots. Private agriculture in the Soviet Union had been wiped out. There were other shortcomings which were not resolved by the new system. Peasants, once in collectives, were not necessarily enthusiastic and, consequently, tended to neglect the collective acreage in favor of cultivating their own private plots. Mechanization all through the 1930's, too, lagged behind the needs of the collectives. Crop failures in 1931 and 1932 could not be prevented or alleviated simply by formally reorganizing the structure of agriculture.

From the regime's standpoint there were, on the other hand, solid achievements arising from collectivization. Agricultural life within the nation was placed under government-party control and peasants were now subject to the political and propaganda influence of the party. The

---

[13] Jesse D. Clarkson, *A History of Russia* (New York: Random House, Inc., 1961), p. 595. Rothstein, *op. cit.*, p. 471.

[14] Dobb, *op. cit.*, p. 229.

historically independent and stubborn peasant would find it increasingly difficult if not virtually impossible henceforth to remain in opposition to the Communist Party and its programs. Even more important, the Soviet leadership now was in a much more favorable position to marshall the nation's agricultural resources in fulfillment of its plans along the lines toward which it was directing industry. It hoped, thereby, to achieve a dramatic increase in the output of agricultural commodities. In the process, collectivization of Soviet agriculture became a model for other communist nations to follow as a necessary mark of a communist system. And, as with national planning, collectivization was destined to form a part of the broader definition of modern communism.

THE GREAT PURGE

From the Russian word *chistit* (to clean) comes the word *chistka*, or purge. Political purges under the Communists could extend from mere removal from office with no further penalties attached, to actual execution in some cases. From 1917 on, the party leadership, or a fraction thereof, has purged various individuals and groups from active participation in Soviet life. Even prior to the Revolution, of course, Lenin sought to eliminate his opponents, such as the Mensheviks, from positions of influence within the RSDLP. Stalin removed those who stood in the way of his succession to power, such as Trotsky, and those groups who frustrated his programs, for example the *kulaky*. In 1918 the Bolsheviks purged a number of their opponents. In the process they relied upon various methods, not excluding terrorism and assassination, even massacres. In 1921, there were 156,931 party members expelled out of a total membership of 585,000.[15] Purges within the party apparatus in 1933–34 were aimed at weak-willed or ignorant party members and at those who were in the party for mere expediency's sake—"careerists" and "degenerates."[16] In 1933 Ukrainian nationalist tendencies were purged when 28,000 members were expelled from the party and 237 party secretaries were dismissed from their posts.[17] Apart from these early efforts, the high point of political "cleansing" in the Soviet Union was reached in the Great Purge of the mid-30's.

Extending roughly from early 1935 until late 1938, the Great Purge

---

[15] Zbigniew K. Brzezinski, *The Permanent Purge* (Cambridge, Mass.: Harvard University Press, 1956), p. 50.

[16] John A. Armstrong, *The Politics of Totalitarianism: The Communist Party of the Soviet Union from 1934 to the Present* (New York: Random House, Inc., 1961), p. 10.

[17] Georg Von Rauch, *A History of Soviet Russia*, trans. Peter and Annette Jacobsohn (New York: Frederick A. Preager, Inc., 1957), p. 223.

executed, imprisoned, or exiled all members of the old Lenin Politburo (except Stalin, of course)—a former chairman of the government (Rykov), two former heads of the Communist International (Zinoviev and Bukharin), a former head of the central trade union organization (Tomsky), a former chief of the general staff (Marshall Tukhachevsky), two of the former topmost secret police officials (Yagoda and Yezhov), the chairmen of the governments of Belorussia, Ukraine, Uzbek, and Tadzhik, heads of the Commissariats of Finance and Agriculture, hundreds of factory managers, 70 percent of the 1934 Central Committee, and millions of ordinary Soviet citizens.[18]   In the years 1936–38, Brzezinski estimates 850,000, or about 36 percent of total party membership, were purged in one 18-month period.[19]   According to Khrushchev's secret speech to the Twentieth Party Congress in 1956, 70 percent of the 139 members and candidate members of the party's Central Committee were purged, as were 1,108 out of 1,966 elected delegates to the Seventeenth Party Congress.[20]   Well-known personalities as well as unknown, nameless victims, millions of citizens in all, were purged during the 1930's in what at times amounted to very widespread, extremely vicious, and inhumane terrorism.   The question we now raise is, why was the Great Purge carried out at such a cost to the nation?

There are numerous speculations and several educated guesses as to the why of the purges, and especially of the Great Purge.   The key figure in the picture, of course, was Stalin, but he never revealed his true motives. Several plausible explanations are possible, though.   The purges seemed intended to shake up and terrorize the population in order to prepare them for any necessary personal sacrifices that might be required in the future. Desperate measures may have been needed by the regime to keep peoples' support, if not loyalty.   Associated with these reasons is the "scapegoat" theory.   Instead of holding the Communist leadership and the communist system to blame for early failures, these failures instead were attributed conveniently to "spies" and "wreckers."   Under Communist theory (and practice) the regime, the leader, and the party are infallible; always and at all times they are right on all matters whatsoever.   How is it then that mistakes have been made in the Soviet Union and shortcomings have existed all along?   The Great Purge offered a simple rationalization—traitors in our midst.

---

[18] Donald W. Treadgold, *Twentieth Century Russia* (Chicago: Rand McNally & Co., 1959), p. 280.   Louis Fischer, "The Moscow Trials and Confessions" in Steinberg, *op. cit.*, pp. 333–34.

[19] Brzezinski, *op. cit.*, p. 99.

[20] Bertram D. Wolfe, *Khrushchev and Stalin's Ghost* (New York: Frederick A. Praeger, 1957), p. 124.

Persons accused in public trials during the Purge confessed to all sorts of crimes as demanded by their accusers, no doubt in hopes of having their lives spared in most cases. Were shoddy goods produced in Soviet factories? We did it deliberately to alienate the people from communism, replied the defendants in the trials. Thus the public could blame the "traitors," not the regime, for the poor grade of products. There were shortages of bread in the collectives. Who was responsible? "I was," replied defendant Grinko, who had served as deputy chief of the *Gosplan*. Tractors serving collective farms broke down frequently. Agricultural Commissar Chernov said he, working with Trotsky, was responsible so that peasants would be dissatisfied with the regime.[21] So the ills and shortcomings of communism were personified, rationalized, and explained away.

The most prevalent single explanation, and the most logical, is that Stalin relied upon the purge as one of his main techniques in gaining full dictatorial power. Stalin's position was not secure as long as the old Bolsheviks and other key leaders such as Red Army officials were around to plot against him or to join a "Trotskyite" anti-Stalin clique. It was necessary for Stalin to remove from the scene all opposition to his personal rule be it opposition that was past, present, or future, real or imaginary. Only in this way could he satisfy his paranoiac personality that he had reached an unassailable position. Of course, Stalin did not carry out the purges by himself; he simply presided over them. Thousands of zealous police officials, ambitious junior party hopefuls, fear-ridden government employees, and disgruntled vindictive neighbors and relatives joined in accusing other people, a great many of whom were innocent, of being anti-regime and anti-Communist. The purge, like a great conflagration, spread in part by its own impetus to engulf large segments of the Soviet population on all levels of society.

One other factor might be pertinent, too—that of the economic value to the country from what amounted to a slave labor system. Millions of those arrested were assigned to the penal slave labor camps. Here virtually unpaid work on canals, timber cutting, and so forth, provided the regime with abundant, although very inefficient labor. In this the police agency (NKVD and later, the MVD) acted as manager of the vast prisoner-staffed economic enterprise. No doubt, the several causes listed above all played some part in initiating and carrying out the purges.

The effects of the purges of the 1920's and 1930's, particularly of the Great Purge, were serious and long-lasting. Stalin has written of the

---

[21] Fischer, *op. cit.*, p. 350.

1933–36 purge that through it the party weeded out undesirables, although there were, he concedes, grave mistakes committed in the process. Nevertheless, he argued that the purge was unavoidable and its results were beneficial. "Our Party," he continued in a masterpiece of understatement, "is now somewhat smaller in membership." On the other hand, he noted, "it is better in quality."[22] Other effects were not so "beneficial." The military forces probably were weakened by extensive purging of the high officer class. This could have adversely affected Soviet fortunes in the early days of World War II.[23]

The purges seriously altered the composition and the procedures of the Communist Party. The old Bolsheviks, especially those who had aided Lenin in the Revolution and the Civil War and who hung on through the difficult 1920's, were practically wiped out by the Great Purge. Many other key party leaders also fell by the wayside. Not only did the old Leninist concept of the party change in the process by the Communist Party itself might, as Meyer contends, have been destroyed; that is, the party as the manager, operator, and owner of Soviet society working in the name of the proletariat. This Leninist idea now was replaced by a Communist Party which became but an instrument, among several, of Stalin's personal dictatorship.[24] From this point on, the party apparatus, central and regional, was to be the main support of the dictator and his ruling wand of the moment.

The purges terrorized the Soviet population and pointed up for all citizens to see that one side of the regime was stark, extremely harsh, and absolutely ruthless. Opposition to either the communist system or to its current rulers could and, in many cases, did result in swift and severe punishment, even death for many. A number of Western writers have thus characterized Soviet Communism as a political system oriented toward the promoting of mass, wide-scale terror.

The purges solidified Stalin's personal iron rule of Soviet governmental, political, economic, and social life. From 1938 on Stalin was widely recognized and proclaimed as *the* undisputed leader and boss of the USSR. His rule, henceforth, was to go unchallenged and his every whim, no matter how arbitrary or contradictory, was enforced throughout virtually the

---

[22] J. Stalin, *Problems of Leninism* (Moscow: Foreign Languages Publishing House, 1940), p. 649.

[23] Armstrong argues, on the contrary, that because of the large numbers of untrained, older military commanders left in the 1930's, their replacement by younger bettertrained officers during the purges may, in fact, have raised the quality of the officer corps prior to World War II. See Armstrong, *op. cit.*, p. 64.

[24] Alfred G. Meyer, *Communism* (New York: Random House, Inc., Studies in Political Science, 1960), p. 82.

whole country. The Soviet Union was completely caught up in the "cult of personality."

COMMUNIST THEORY SINCE LENIN

After Lenin passed from the scene, those communist leaders who remained, such as Trotsky, Zinoviev, Kamenev, and Stalin, faced additional and equally serious problems of political rule compared to those with which Lenin wrestled. These leaders disagreed over a number of practical governmental matters, sometimes forming opposing factions within the party apparatus in the process. To a lesser degree, they fell out over theoretical interpretations of Marxism and Leninism. In this respect, several developments occurred which measurably affected Marxist theory in the Soviet Union and abroad.

The triumph of Bolshevism-communism in Russia, in the name of Marxism, added to the nationalistic breakup of international socialism as a result of World War I, split the socialist movement in Europe. Some of the parties joined the Russian controlled Third (Communist) International and eagerly supported the Bolsheviks. These groups became the communist parties in various countries, such as the Communist Party, USA (CPUSA). Most of the European socialists, however, including the American Socialist Party, rejected Soviet Communism rather completely, yet at the same time they considered themselves to be the followers and spiritual heirs of Marxism.

The Soviet Union, in its first years, declared itself to be in the transitional period between "capitalism" and communism, that is, in the interim phase of socialism about which Marx wrote. For more than four decades after the Revolution, what the Soviet Communists did they did in the name of "socialism," via the instrument of the dictatorship of the proletariat. No matter that these Soviet theories and practices were disowned by European and American socialists who argued that Soviet Communism was adulterated socialism; for many people in the West, what they saw in the Soviet Union they interpreted as "socialism" in action. Western socialists have advocated, for example, public ownership of industry, transportation, and natural resources. They have not desired, as in "socialism" in the USSR, such Soviet accomplishments as dictatorship, totalitarianism, one-party rule and police-state methods. Marxism, too, in part by default and in part by the theoretical aggressiveness of the Soviet Communists, became less and less an international liberation movement of workers, as envisaged by Marx and Engels. Now it was more and more a tightly disciplined international organization devoted to the advancement of and controlled by a single nationalist state—the Soviet Union. International Marxism was rapidly becoming national communism.

The most important post-Lenin event for the growth of communist theory was the rise to a position of dominance, not only in the Soviet Union, but throughout the communist world, of Joseph Stalin. For a little more than two decades after Lenin, communism was what Stalin was, or what he said it was, which amounted to the same thing. Until his death, virtually the entire international communist movement, with only such exceptions as the Yugoslav and Chinese Communist parties, paid Stalin homage as the true theoretical heir of Marxism-Leninism. Throughout the communist world the doctrine had now become Marxism-Leninism-Stalinism.

Stalinism

Was it unadulterated hypocrisy which changed the enthusiasm of revolutionary messianic Leninism into the cold, harsh dictatorship of Stalin? Ulam claims that, instead, it was ideological self-deception that allowed the transformation. Neither Lenin nor his colleagues could bring themselves to believe that immutable Marxism-Leninism could mean something different from what it meant at the time of the Revolution.[25] One significant change in Marxism-Leninism resulted from Stalin's victory over Trotsky.

Contrary to the view of Trotsky and some other old Bolsheviks, Stalin pushed through to acceptance by the Soviet Communist Party his social-ism-in-one-country doctrine. Trotsky, following a more "purified" Marxism, championed the doctrine of immediate worldwide, or at least Europewide, revolution on the part of workers in all countries, in collaboration with Russian Bolsheviks. For Trotsky, Russia was more the instrument rather than the goal of communist endeavors. For Stalin, however, Russia came first, and he concentrated economic power on the building of socialism-communism within the Soviet Union.

Following Lenin's lead, Stalin announced a prolongation of the transition time between the communists' assumption of power and the eventual withering away of the state, a time during which the state would continue in force. This transition period must not be regarded as "fleeting," Stalin wrote. Instead, it would cover an entire historical era including civil wars, external conflicts, much organizational work and economic building, all accompanied by advances, retreats, victories, and defeats. In defining

---

[25] Adam B. Ulam, *The Unfinished Revolution* (New York: Random House, 1960), p. 209.

this period during which the dictatorship of the proletariat would rule, Stalin listed several characteristic features. These would include: (1) violence, unrestricted by law with respect to capitalists and landlords, (2) leadership of the peasants by the proletariat, and (3) building of socialism for the whole society.[26] Under Stalin, Soviet citizens were to await the withering away of the state at some future, more propitious, and undetermined time.

Personally dominating the Communist Party during his life, Lenin intellectually stimulated it to become a force for enthusiastic support on the part of a great many of its adherents. But Stalin was no Lenin and the intellectual talents of the teacher far outshone those of the pupil. Stalin viewed the party somewhat differently. He considered it to be an instrument through which he could rule. From the standpoint purely of theory, he simply rehashed Lenin's doctrines. He held the party to be the vanguard of the proletariat, its leader and guide. The party, he said, is the "organized detachment of the working class." The proletariat needs the party first to serve as its general staff in seizing power. Then, the party is needed to maintain the dictatorship.[27]

Stalin added little to the theory of Marxism-Leninism. He was not the philosophical type, as were Marx and Lenin before him. Stalin was more concerned with daily political management and with bolstering and ensuring his dictatorship than he was with original theoretical analyses of society. Not that he did not enunciate new interpretations of Marxism-Leninism, but he did so rather ineptly and with a lack of sophistication. His "theories," much more so than was the case with Lenin, were more justifications of his arbitrary actions rather than philosophical deductions arrived at through rigorous mental effort.[28]

Post-Stalin Communist Theory

The former Communist theorist Djilas has written that Lenin's revolutionary communism gave way to Stalin's dogmatic communism which, after Stalin, was followed by a nondogmatic communism of the so-called collective leadership.[29] Where Stalin had been less interested in basic

---

[26] Stalin, *Works*, p. 189.

[27] J. Stalin, *Foundations of Leninism* (New York: International Publishers, 1939), pp. 112, 118.

[28] Milovan Djilas, *The New Class* (New York: Frederick A. Praeger, Inc., 1957), pp. 52–53.

[29] As Horowitz puts it, "The Soviet assertion and insistence on the monolithic appearance of socialist politics, particularly as this developed under Stalin, was a response to the absence of genuine theory, an inability to make useful generalizations concerning strategies for social development. Irving Louis Horowitz, *Three Worlds of Development* (New York: Oxford University Press, 1966), p. 135.

theory than Lenin, so the post-Stalin Soviet leaders have followed the Stalin mode of practical, day-by-day rule with, if anything, even less concern for complex theoretical interpretations and innovations. Pronouncements on the philosophy of communism since Stalin's death have sought to accomplish no more than to reaffirm periodically the general Marxist-Leninist party line (for example, during party congresses) and to meet new international or domestic problems as they arise.

In a mild, noncontroversial statement on socialism, a Soviet source in 1954 described that doctrine as based on public ownership of the means of production either by state operation or by cooperative-collective farming; it is a system in which exploitation of man is nonexistent, and planning guides the national economy. And, in a reiteration of simple Marxism, the economic laws of socialism (like those of other systems) function independently of the will of the people; they have their own unchangeable "objective" character. While socialism lays the "material-production" base for communism, the latter is deemed to include a higher, more abundant life than is the case with socialism. Under communism there will be no classes and thus no class differences and all means of production will become public property.[30]

The Soviet Union has, since 1954, been drawing steadily closer to communism, according to theoretical pronouncements of its leadership. In 1957 Khrushchev said communism's "bright edifice" now appears more clearly on the horizon. In 1959 Khrushchev stated that the transition from socialism to communism "proceeds continuously" and the door to communist society is already opening. And, according to Khrushchev, the Twenty-first Party Congress in 1959 marked the beginning of "wide-scale construction of communist society," with the new Seven-Year Plan marking the first stage in this historic period.[31] In 1961 Khrushchev told the Twenty-second Party Congress that socialism "has been consolidated" within the framework of the worldwide socialist commonwealth and that the Soviet Union had begun the comprehensive, all-out building of communism, which means, to continue Khrushchev's vague description, setting up the material and technical basis of communism.[32] The 1961 party program stated that by 1980 "a communist society will on the whole be built in the USSR."[33]

---

[30] *Politicheskaya Ekonomiya* (Moscow: Gosizpolit Akademiya Nauk, SSSR, 1954), pp. 366, 373, 403.

[31] Moscow Radio Broadcast, November 6, 1957, January 28, 1959, and January 14, 1960.

[32] *Pravda*, October 18, 1961.

[33] The complete text can be found in Jan F. Triska (ed.), *Soviet Communism: Programs and Rules* (San Francisco: Chandler Publishing Co., 1962).

Official Soviet theory, as of 1962, then, has indicated that the long transitional period of socialism (which Stalin said would not be "fleeting") that was to usher in communism may be nearing completion in the Soviet Union. The Soviet system is now in the period of full-scale development of communism. But, one may ask, how long will it take to *achieve* communism, now that its "full-scale" construction has begun? At the Twenty-second Party Congress Khrushchev stated frankly that the job could not be done in less than 20 years. Communism, then, in Soviet words, has finally been "ushered" in; it has been delivered to the door, but apparently it is going to take some time to unwrap the package.

Two post-Stalin developments, perhaps, motivated Soviet leaders to suggest that the transitional socialist period may be nearing an end and that the communist era is rapidly approaching for their country. Growing dissatisfaction of Soviet citizens over continual shortages of even poor-quality consumer's goods might be allayed by a more definite promise than had yet been made of the arrival of the communist golden age. It may have been, too, that Chinese Communist claims in the 1950's that they already had evolved a more advanced system of communism than had the Russians goaded Soviet leaders into setting out some positive Russian milestones along the road to communism. As for the future communist society itself and the form it would take, this too was mentioned in passing at the Twenty-second Party Congress in 1961.

In the 1961 statement, the classless society of full equality and the abundant life for all formed a part of the rather undramatic definition of communism. Other ingredients in the definition include a highly organized and centralized pattern of industrial production, national economic planning, and a division of labor. Under communism, a new form of government, called social self-government, is to replace the present form. Moreover, this communist society, as described in the party program, will be built, *in the main*, in 20 years.[34] In referring to "social self-government," Soviet leaders may have felt conscience-stricken; they announced, finally, that the withering away of the state in the Soviet Union actually had begun. In 1960 a Soviet writer referred to the state withering away when he wrote that state functions gradually will lose their "political character," passing into self-governing institutions.[35] The 1961 party

---

[34] Khrushchev's speech to the Twenty-second Party Congress, in *Pravda*, October 19, 1961. See Chapter VI for a discussion of the trend toward "self-government."

[35] Georgi Shakhnazarov, "When the State Has Withered Away," *The Soviet Review*, Vol. I (November, 1960), pp. 58–59. To this, Romashkin adds that as the elements of coercion gradually disappear from the state the population as a whole will become involved in the "public organization." P. Romashkin, "Sotsialisticheskoe gosudarstvo i kommunisticheskoe samoupravlenie," *Partiynaya Zhizn*, No. 9 (May 1961), p. 13.

program called for handing over in a few years to nonstate, "public" organizations the management of places of entertainment, clubs, libraries, and other cultural establishments. Of course, the state still is needed, in the Soviet view, so long as there is a continuing military threat from abroad.

At the Twenty-second Congress, Khrushchev stated that the conditions which necessitated the dictatorship of the proletariat have disappeared, and, consequently, in the Soviet Union the dictatorship has been transformed into the "all-people's state." So, with a mere verbal stroke of his hand, Khrushchev sweeps away the dictatorship. But, Khrushchev cautions, the state does not become weaker. Rather, it actually increases in strength as an "instrument" of the will of the people. The state will remain long after the first phase of communism has been completed because it has other tasks to perform. The state will wither away only following a developed communist society in the USSR *and on condition* of the victory of "socialism" in the international field.[36] Taking these statements at face value, Soviet Communists appear to be arguing that the state is beginning to wither while yet increasing in strength. In any event, the Soviet state will not really wither, in the sense of atrophying. It will do that, supposedly, only when communism has fully arrived in the Soviet Union and when "socialism" is victorious internationally. All in all, no measurable light has been shed on the question by recent Soviet pronouncements, and we can fully expect the Soviet state to continue in force for the foreseeable future in more or less its present form and strength. Perhaps the Communists are serious about the state withering away at some undertermined time in the future. They certainly are not seriously doing anything about it for the present.

At the Twentieth Party Congress in 1956 Khrushchev told the delegates that communists do not regard violence and civil war as the only way to remake society. In a number of capitalist and former colonial countries the winning of a stable parliamentary majority, backed by a mass revolutionary movement of the proletariat, can secure for the people fundamental social changes.[37] In this theoretical statement, Khrushchev is bypassing the confirmed revolutionist Lenin, and returning to the original views of Marx on the possibility of workers peacefully dispossessing capitalists in their rise to power. In the 1961 program of the Communist Party too, the export of revolution was held to be impossible. Instead, workers in capitalist countries must themselves revolt against their system when conditions are ripe for that event. And, the revolt may be a peaceful,

---

[36] *Pravda*, October 19, 1961.

[37] Khrushchev's report to the Twentieth Party Congress. Moscow, TASS, February 14, 1956.

nonviolent one, if the ruling bourgeoisie will give up power peacefully to the workers' movement.[38]

In several respects Marxism, as an economic theory oriented toward Western, industrialized society, should not have been tried out first in a non-Western, nonindustrialized nation. That it was introduced there and that it succeeded (at least a version of it did) suggests the viability and attractiveness of communism to some people. That Soviet Communism is not pure Marxism, of course, has been obvious for years.

Lenin's most important contribution to Marxism was in reshaping Marxist theory to fit old Russian political philosophy and in applying it to an economically underdeveloped and largely peasant country, fitting all of this into a unique political situation. Lenin's basic purpose, in the broadest sense, was that of Marx: to bring into being a new, rational, and humanitarian system for the majority of citizens, chiefly the workers. In a number of important ways, however, Lenin's ideological goals did not match his more practical and arbitrary actions.

Soviet Communism in the 1960's bears the very marked imprint of Stalin's period of rule. Lenin originated and inaugurated the Communist Party as a leading, vanguard core of the workers. Stalin prostituted it into a vehicle for his personal dictatorship. In addition to the party, Stalin fashioned other organs, such as the police and the bureaucracy, into supporting pillars for his massive totalitarian edifice. Stalin also contributed to the "nationalization" of Marxism-Leninism, in defiance of the international flavor of pure Marxism. Although even here, he was following Lenin's lead.

Soviet Communist theory in the 1960's still is based on Marxism as well as on a complete acceptance of Leninism. As for Stalinism, its doctrines of collectivization, industrialization, and militarization remain as points of current communist doctrine, while the more odious and harsh features of Stalinism have been disowned by his successors.

Modern Soviet theory continues the Leninist-Stalinist practice of freely altering Marxism when needed. It may well be, in fact, that the extensive modifications to Marxism as carried out in the Soviet Union since the philosophy was introduced outweigh the original "corpus Marximus." Ulam summarizes the chief theoretical problem of modern Soviet Communism when he asks, where does Marxism lead the Soviet Union next?[39] The question is not without meaning for Marxist theory and for the future of Soviet ideology. For Soviet leaders, however, the question is probably without a great deal of significance so long as their main everyday problems

---

[38] *Pravda*, July 30, 1961.
[39] Ulam, *op. cit.*, p. 254.

of political rule, both foreign and domestic, are solved with a reasonable degree of satisfaction. The general Marxist framework may serve today only the purpose of a language of communication in the Soviet Union. The integrating function of Soviet ideological myths has been largely achieved, so that modern theory is not so necessary as before and is taken for granted, with only an occasional refreshening of it to keep it alive.[40] Heartfelt or not, Soviet leaders continue to stress historic Marxism-Leninism, though in amended form. The theory continues as a rallying point around which these leaders still hope to capture popular enthusiasm, or at the very least, to win tacit acceptance from the citizenry for both party programs and party leaders.

Theory can serve also to justify, on occasion even explain, actions of the regime. Within the ideologically oriented Soviet society in which everything and everyone is to be dedicated to the building of communism, who can disagree openly with the nation's political leadership if everything it does and advocates is done so in the name of Marxism-Leninism? The doctrines of theory, as translated by the Communist Party elite, constitute the ultimate authority, the unchallenged holy writ of their society. Moreover, the leadership at times is restricted to the confines of its own theoretical framework. It is committed, for example, to opposing the noncommunist West in much the same way the missionary by his dogma is committed to opposing the heathen. To understand past and present communist theory, then, for both Soviet citizens and Western students alike, is to be able to comprehend more fully current Soviet programs, policies, and maneuvers and to predict with a bit more confidence future Soviet actions both at home and abroad.

LENINISM INTO STALINISM

The organization and operation of the political and economic system which can be described as Leninism, including formation and orientation of the Communist Party, the NEP, and early efforts directed toward economic planning, evolved over the course of a decade and set the framework for what can be termed Stalinism. Although Lenin's accusations against all his opponents to the effect that they were counterrevolutionaries was knowingly a lie, he did, nevertheless, set an important mold. This for the Soviet Union was that the stability of the dictatorship is the supreme law for the party and for the nation. All other national problems, goals, and desires enjoy a lower priority. With this doctrine, as Schapiro puts it,

---

[40] Alfred G. Meyer, "USSR, Incorporated," *Slavic Review*, Vol. XX (October, 1961), p. 375.

Lenin equipped Stalin with his weapons.[41] Leninism laid the groundwork for Stalinism which, in turn, can be typified by four major aspects.

In the first one, Stalinism embraced a full-blown political dictatorship which was personally directed by the autocrat himself. Stalin exercised his power by way of three leading instruments, all of which were subordinate to and controlled by himself: the party apparatus, the police, and the governmental bureaucracy. One of the effects of the long years of personal dictatorship, be it of the relatively lighter Lenin variety or of the heavier Stalin type, was that no orderly procedure was established for the transfer of power from one top leader to another. Consequently, struggles over the succession to power became crises which were associated with accidental outcomes, and they might be harsh and ruthless.

In the second aspect or contribution of Stalinism, the Communist Party apparatus emerged as the most important organization within Soviet society. Perhaps the party as such under Stalin was not so exclusively powerful as under Lenin, but its apparatus was more so. It permeated all levels of Soviet life, and, although it shared power with the police and the bureaucracy, it was first among equals. The party was expanded, given increased experience in controlling society, and assigned philosophical and moral supremacy in addition to no small amount of control over other organs. These advantages enjoyed by the party were to be of considerable influence when the party apparatus was to do battle with the police and bureaucracy following Stalin's death.

A third contribution was the flowering of a complete totalitarian format which reached down into almost every nook and cranny of Soviet life. There evolved, for example, oppressive censorship of the press and very strict controls over cultural and educational matters. A police state arose in which the lives and fortunes of citizens were jeopardized by arbitrary actions of party and state officials. No political opposition to the official regime and its leader, however innocuous, was permitted to exist at all. The totalitarian system was *total*.

Finally, the heritage of Stalinism left, in addition to the above, a foundation for the modern communist state. Central economic planning had been established, and, by 1953, the fifth Five-Year Plan had been launched. Full "nationalization" and close central management of industry, trade, transport, and construction became an accomplished feature of the Soviet economy. Collectivization of agriculture was a normal pattern in the USSR by 1953.

Leninism and, more importantly, Stalinism had set the pattern for Soviet Communism, both in theory and practice. The successors to Lenin

[41] Schapiro, *op. cit.*, pp. 360–61.

and Stalin would, to a considerable degree, follow in the footsteps of their predecessors. They would, to be sure, alter Marxist-Communist theory to fit ever new situations. Even this technique, though, was very much in the tradition of Lenin's NEP and Stalin's foreign policies in which the latter joined working alliances with fascist and capitalist nations at varying times. In the process, one might question how Marxist, or even how revolutionary, is Soviet Communism.

A great many of the early Communist plans and programs were casually abandoned or contemptuously ignored. Thus, Bolshevik promises of a Constituent Assembly, an end to the death penalty, independence for all nationalities, an honorable "democratic" peace, land for peasants, bread for all, and an end to the police, standing army, and the bureaucracy were promises which Lenin and Stalin failed to carry out.[42] What Lenin and Stalin did accomplish was to hinder their successors in attempts to make the giant edifice both responsive and efficient.

---

[42] See the discussion in Souvarine, *op. cit.*, pp. 188–89.

CHAPTER V

The Soviet Political Environment

THE POLITICAL ENVIRONMENT, or climate, within a nation may be most easily depicted as the sum total of both popular and elite attitudes, opinions, customs, and practices which relate to political processes within the overall political system. It is the atmosphere within which politics, national and local, are conducted, and we might say it begins with the concept of political culture. Related to public opinion, political culture is made up of the subjective attitudes, the expressive symbols and shared values, the empirical beliefs which are held by the inhabitant-participants of political systems. Political culture reflects how the citizen views his individual role in the system and how he perceives its various parts, particularly how he fits into the scheme. What we are concerned with here is a "patterned set of orientations toward politics," in Verba's words,[1] in which certain norms and values are related.

Questions to be asked of any political culture include those of specific group or class attitudes, the interrelationship among these attitudes, and the shared values, particularly the dominant ones, resulting from them. More specifically, what are the popularly held attitudes toward candidates for office, policies, myths and ideologies, national goals? Individual identification with given units, organizations, or structures within a society reveals something of a given political culture.

In the USSR, political culture is tied up with ideology, more so than in many other political systems because of the strong theoretical determinants of modern Soviet communism. Its origins rest in historical Russian messianism, to which has been added the mission and rationale of Marxism-Leninism and the supposed legitimacy of Communist Party rule; all contribute toward considerable ideological militancy as a regime-sponsored

---

[1] See the discussion by Sidney Verba in "Comparative Political Culture," in Lucian W. Pye and Sidney Verba (eds.), *Political Culture and Political Development* (Princeton, N. J.: Princeton University Press, 1965).

value. Obviously, the degree of ideological commitment toward communism as a societal goal, however, varies widely among the collective farmer, worker, scientist, artist, government official, and Communist Party leader. The latter two categories more closely identify their personal roles in the Soviet political system with the ideological goals as proclaimed by the regime. The party and government officials who are keepers of the official creed, the full-time ideologists, as it were, interestingly enough may be the more conservative element of contemporary Soviet society. They are the most suspicious of challenges offered up by creative intellectuals such as artists and poets. The ideologists might well have been the most threatened by de-Stalinization and its implied erosion of strict ideological controls over society.[2]

On the other end of the scale, we might suggest that farmers are among the least ideologically oriented participants in the Soviet culture, chiefly because theoretical communist pronouncements over the decades since 1917 have not been translated into measurably higher standards of living for this class. If ideologies in modern societies are significant for only a relatively brief period of time, as Apter contends,[3] then we might suggest that Soviet ideology among some citizens, such as farmers and the more rebellious students, has not been very successful in becoming a widely shared value. And yet, the people generally accept the governing regime, Rush argues, because of an absence of alternatives. They do not, however, share fully in the party's fundamental goals.[4] Of course, it is rather spurious technique to assign ideological fidelity to entire classes. The more so since ideological commitment, or lack of it, is so much an individual matter as to almost defy class association with it.

Political Socialization

A main function of any political system is to perform a socialization role by indoctrinating young citizens into becoming sympathizers with and supporters of the system. The precise measure of success by the Soviet regime in this function is impossible to determine. Their citizens have not

---

[2] See the discussion in Priscilla Johnson (ed.), *Khrushchev and the Arts: The Politics of Soviet Culture, 1962–1964* (Cambridge, Mass.: M.I.T. Press, 1965), p. 88.

[3] *The Politics of Modernization* (Chicago: University of Chicago Press, 1965), p. 327. But Brzezinski argues that once ideology is embodied in a party bureaucracy with a vested interest in its power, it can continue exerting a transforming influence on society, even though the majority of professional party bureaucrats have lost their revolutionary fervor. Zbigniew Brzezinski and Samuel P. Huntington, *Political Power: USA/USSR* (New York: Viking Press, 1964), p. 68.

[4] Myron Rush, *Political Succession in the USSR* (New York: Columbia University Press, 1965), pp. 89–90.

openly revolted against the system, and they do participate in a number of regime-directed customs, such as mass turnout in voting for the local, regional, and national legislatures.   A firm case for enthusiastic and voluntary citizen support, which the Communist Party claims, however, cannot be based on such flimsy evidence.

Public opinion polls, which would tell us a great deal about political socialization, have only recently been attempted in the USSR and not on a very broad scale at that.   In 1960 in the USSR, the Young Communist League's newspaper, *Komsomolskaya Pravda* founded the Public Opinion Institute and subsequently published the results of its first poll, which related to matters of war and peace.   The second poll by this newspaper asked questions on living standards of Soviet citizens.   Of the respondents in this latter poll, 73.2 percent reported a rise in their personal living standards.[5]   A more controversial poll of Soviet youth was taken by *Komsomolskaya Pravda* in 1961.   This included 16,000 respondents, ranging in age from 15 to 30.   Although the overwhelming majority of answers were interpreted as favoring the regime, a few replied in a callous manner, suggesting that they have not gone along with political socialization.[6]   In 1963, 10,000 questionnaires were given out to respondents in the Estonian Republic; the results revealed "serious deficiencies" in the work and maintenance facilities of enterprises.[7]   In early 1964 a poll was published showing the responses of young workers (up to age 30) in twenty-five Leningrad enterprises.   The responses were as follows:[8]

	Number	Percent of Total
My work is completely satisfactory.......	427	16.0
My work is satisfactory.................	664	24.9
Those expressing only a vague opinion....	1153	43.3
My work is not satisfactory.............	297	11.1
My work is completely unsatisfactory.....	125	4.6
	2665	99.9

Public opinion polling in the USSR is too infrequent and the validity of their polling techniques has not yet been established to the satisfaction of Western scholars in order to permit much in the way of conclusions from the polls.   One thing most clear from a year's study in Moscow, according to Feifer, is the complete absence of a public or "community" apart from the party.   Public opinion simply is "party" opinion; the party's will, he

---

[5] *Komsomolskaya Pravda*, May 19, 1960; October 7, 1960.

[6] *Komsomolskaya Pravda*, January 11, January 26, 1961.

[7] R. A. Safarov in *Sovetskoe Gosudarstvo i Pravo*, No. 4 (April, 1964), p. 87.

[8] *Voprosy Filosofii*, No. 4 (April, 1964), p. 75.

claims, "is the single cohesive element within society."[9] What information
we do have about socialization from Soviet opinion polls and from other
sources, such as letters to the editors of the newspapers, is quite limited.
Nevertheless, in light of the above data, some people in the USSR are not
accepting socialization, although their numbers and influence throughout
the Soviet political system are unknown.

 .   Soviet citizens have revealed in numerous ways that they have in the
past, and in the future would again be, quite dissatisfied with the harsh
totalitarianism of Stalinism.   For the overwhelming majority of Soviet
citizens, Stalinism hopefully is dead and buried.   Other citizen complaints
have centered around the paucity and poor quality of consumer goods and
the widespread shortage of adequate housing. When, in 1962, the regime
sharply raised prices of meat and dairy products, rioting reportedly broke
out in Novocherkassk in front of party headquarters, a mob attacked and
plundered several major structures, and bloody clashes took place between
rioters and troops.[10]   These and other demonstrations, including workers'
strikes, support the observation by Brown that increasingly open protests
are being registered by people who are discontented, as expressed in the
hundreds of thousands of letters with complaints and suggestions being
received by the press, the party, government, trade unions, and other
agencies.[11]

 On the other hand, Soviet citizens appear satisfied with the goal and
direction of Soviet foreign policy and with the regime's attempts to improve measurably both the availability and quality of consumer goods
in recent years. A widespread citizen's pride exists in the promise of
Soviet "communism" as an idealistic, humanitarian goal for mankind.
Even Soviet refugees alienated from the system approved of the welfare
state in principle, state ownership of the main features of the economy,
and such specifics as socialized medicine.[12]

 Soviet regimes from Lenin on have worked assiduously and long on the
task of effective political socialization. Soviet internal propaganda, no
doubt unsurpassed among nations of the world, has utilized a wide range
of techniques and arguments in attempts to win over citizens of all classes,
ages, and occupations to accepting and supporting the Soviet political
system. As a mass mobilization society, all citizens eligible to vote for the

---

 [9] George Feifer, *Justice in Moscow* (New York: Simon and Schuster, 1964), p. 126.

 [10] See the commentary in Albert Boiter, "When the Kettle Boils Over," *Problems
of Communism*, Vol. XIII (January–February, 1964), p. 36.

 [11] Emily Clark Brown, *Soviet Trade Unions and Labor Relations* (Cambridge, Mass.:
Harvard University Press, 1966), p. 311.

 [12] Raymond A. Bauer, in Alex Inkeles (ed.), *Soviet Society, a Book of Readings*
(Boston: Houghton Mifflin Co., 1961), p. 236.

legislatures are encouraged, urged, and otherwise pressured into turning out to vote for the officially endorsed slate of candidates. In many other ways, from citizen participation in local government, to parading and demonstrating in support of the regime's foreign policies (even to the extent of occasionally throwing objects at the American Embassy in Moscow), and to enlisting millions of youths in Communist Party auxiliary organizations, the regime never rests in its efforts aimed at achieving widespread if not total political socialization of the citizenry.

Since Stalin's time regimes have promised much to the average person, catering to the growing popular demands for food, housing, consumer goods, higher wages, and more legal rights. The Soviet state now claims an extensive list of constitutional guarantees for the citizen, including personal income, personal property, education, pensions, medical benefits, inviolability of the person, assistance, freedom of speech and press as well as freedom for meetings and assembly, defense for those accused of crimes, and the right of every citizen to be elected to public office.[13] In a further claim of recent successes by Brezhnev for the five-year period ending in 1966, the following results were obtained:

National income up 33 percent.
Average worker and employee earnings up 19 percent.
Housing fund investments increased 10 billion rubles.
Retail trade turnover increased 34 percent.
Payments and benefits to the people from public funds increased by over 14 billion rubles.
Lowering of prices on a number of consumer goods.

The next five years, according to plan, will see a further expansion in the production of consumer goods, a considerable rise in real income per capita (30 percent), an increase in minimum wages, introduction of a five-day work week, and pensions for collective farmers.[14]

The point of the foregoing is not to evaluate the satisfactions of the average citizen with the Soviet welfare state but rather to give testimony to the regime's growing efforts to satisfy a number of popular demands and, in turn, to increase the supports for the system. One demand of the citizens about which the regime is very cautious is that of a widening of popular control over the mechanism of the political system. Political rule still is reserved for the Communist Party elite, of course, and no marked change in this mode has occurred since Stalin.

---

[13] See the optimistic type of discussion in V. A. Patulin, "Lichnost: ee prava i svobody v Sovetskom sotialisticheskom gosudarstve," *Sovetskoe Gosudarstvo i Pravo*, No. 2 (February, 1966), pp. 99–100.

[14] Speech of General Secretary Brezhnev to the Twenty-third Congress of the CPSU. *Pravda*, March 30, 1966.

Political Communication

How does the citizen communicate with his political system? How are citizen demands voiced and given weight and how is support for the system registered? More importantly for a dictatorship, how is necessary information made available to the citizens and how are instructions and commands transmitted downward to the populace? Finally, how does the regime receive the required information on the wide range of subjects which enables it to perform its roles successfully? These are some of the questions asked of communication within a political system. In the Soviet Union the questions are answered as befits both a dictatorship and a communist modernizing and mobilizing society.

The most well-known communications channel is that of the Communist Party. In 1966 the newspaper and journal circulations of the leading party organs were as follows:[15]

Pravda (main Communist Party newspaper)—7 million daily.
Komsomolskaya Pravda (Communist Party Youth newspaper)—6.4 million daily.
Selskaya Zhizn (Communist Party agriculture newspaper)—6.2 million daily.
Kommunist, Partiynaya Zhizn, Agitator, Political Self-Education (journals)—3.7 million copies per issue.

In Brezhnev's speech to the Twenty-third Communist Party Congress, he cited the following figures relative to other communications media, mostly for the year 1966:[16]

7,700 newspapers published in the USSR.
About 4,000 magazines published.
The combined newspaper and magazine circulation increased 60 percent (by 74 million) since 1961.
More than 1.25 billion copies of books and pamphlets published yearly.
More than 70 million radio receivers and plug-in sets and 120 TV centers.
According to the plan, there will be 40 million TV sets by 1970.

The point of the foregoing is not that all communications media in the USSR are organs of propaganda but that they are well developed and expanding. The Communist Party does use its own media, of course, such as *Pravda* and *Komsomolskaya Pravda*, as the most frequent propaganda outlets. Apart from the press itself, the Communist Party exercises considerable influence over public education and such cultural spheres as art and literature. Specific sections of the Communist Party's central and regional organs are charged with the responsibility of politically supervising these functions.

---

[15] *Pravda,* March 30, 1966.
[16] *Ibid.*

The government apparatus, too, working in conjunction with the Communist Party, has developed communications media, highlighted by the leading government newspaper, *Izvestiya*. In 1964 its editors received 482,000 letters from readers. This upward flow of popular feelings dealt mainly with complaints arising from minor frustrations.[17] For the same year *Pravda* received 322,000 letters and other correspondence from its readers.[18] The chairman of the local government's executive committee of Belgorod *Oblast* in one year received 7,815 letters, complaints, and statements. Of these, 3,707 were received through higher party and government organs and 1,561 were received directly from employees of local governments.[19] The government Ministry of Culture and its State Committee for the Press are directly concerned with political communication. The ministry is assigned the task of stimulating the development of culture and publishing; an equally important role is the censorship and "guardian" functions.

Perhaps the most serious single effort to achieve a complete political communication function, including downward flow of instructions and upward flow of information, or "feeling the pulse" of the citizenry, is that of legislatures on national, regional, and local levels of Soviet government. The legislatures increasingly are representing the voters and receive, through their deputies, requests, suggestions, and often complaints from their constituents. This channel is the one being relied upon more and more by Soviet citizens to transmit their demands into the political system. The regime is reciprocating, having established in 1966 additional standing commissions (legislative committees) in the legislature to open wider this channel for an upward flow of information.[20] On regular and local levels of government, too, the legislatures and councils serve similar functions of limited interest articulation. Soviet legislatures on the national, regional, and local levels have long been used by the regimes as channels of political communication intended to build firm support for the Communist Party, its leadership elite, and its plans, objectives, and goals. Five-year as well as annual plans and annual budgets are carefully, albeit mechanically, brought before the legislature for its stamp of approval.

---

[17] *Izvestiya*, January 5, 1965.

[18] *Pravda*, January 3, 1965.

[19] I. A. Azovkin, "O nekotorykh formakh neposredstvennoy svyazi rabotnikov sovetskogo apparata s massami," *Sovetskoe Gosudarstvo i Pravo*, No. 8 (August, 1960), p. 124.

[20] See Chapter IX for a listing of the new commissions. Reportedly 74 *oblast* and *kray* consumer co-ops have set up special departments to study consumer demands, even conducting surveys to this end. Also the Council of Ministers of the Russian Republic devoted some time to the problems "of how to full satisfy the growing demands of the consumer." *Sovetskaya Rossiya*, November 11 and November 16, 1966.

The regime uses the national legislature to bestow legitimacy on its rule. In turn, regime policies and leaders always are given formal approval by the elected national legislature, the Supreme Soviet.

In mass mobilization societies, of which communist systems are one type, political communication is a function which is given very serious attention. The Soviet Union illustrates the solicitous attention which a going mass-mobilization society can devote to the matter. Despite this we can ask if political communication is effective in the Soviet system. Does it air grievances from below, efficiently present demands of the citizens, provide accurate information on popular attitudes, and smoothly and competently transmit regime policies downward? Well-traveled avenues of political communication cannot in themselves guarantee popular acceptance of unpopular policies, such as harsh features of totalitarianism, arbitrary government censorship, or persistently illogical programs for collective farmers. Another limitation, perhaps inherent in political systems employing centralized decision making, is pointed out by Holt and Turner. This stems from the fact that channels of information narrow as they approach the center. Consequently, information which eventually reaches central decision makers tends to be only aggregate information. In the process, certain types of specific information more than likely are not available to these decision makers.[21] The problem raised here is whether any crucial information which might be vital to successful rule is not reaching the top decision makers. All modern leadership groups, of course, in whatever political system, face similar problems.

Inkeles argues that, with some exceptions, mass communication in the USSR has been extraordinarily effective in shaping patterns of thought about public issues among Soviet citizens.[22] Communism in the USSR does have limitations and weaknesses, but it does possess upward and downward flow patterns of information; Soviet decision makers do know a great deal about what goes on below, and citizens do have channels both for informing themselves and registering some complaints.

CLASS STRUCTURES

If political culture reflects attitudes held by the citizens toward the political system, then a brief discussion of attitudes that are held by Soviet citizens is in order. Although there obviously are differences in social

---

[21] See Robert T. Holt and John E. Turner, *The Political Basis of Economic Development* (Princeton, N. J.: D. Van Nostrand, Inc., 1966), p. 302.

[22] Inkeles, *op. cit.*, p. 227.

and political role playing and in satisfactions derived from the system, depending somewhat on one's social class, most citizens in modern societies have access to shared values regarding political ideology and societal goals. This is especially true in the USSR because of regime monopolization of historical interpretations, ideology, public policy, and the outputs of the political system. Another complicating factor in our attempt to dissect social classes is the changing structure of Soviet society, for example the rural to urban population shift characteristic of any society that has been rapidly modernizing.

The following breakdown shows some class changes, chiefly in population engaged in agriculture over a thirty-four-year period. The figures also show the rapid decline of private enterprise in the USSR.[23]

	Percent of Total Population			
	1928	*1937*	*1959*	*1962*
Workers and employees......	17.6	45.7	68.3	73.6
Collective farm peasants and artisans in cooperatives.....	2.9	48.8	31.4	26.3
Landowners, city bourgeoisie, merchants, and kulaks.....	4.6	—	—	—
Independent peasants and artisans not in cooperatives....	74.9	5.5	0.3	0.1

More significant questions can be raised, however, about various role perceptions which are held by the several classes in society. Certainly, farmers must view their roles within the political system somewhat differently from that of, say, scientists. The two classes are literally worlds apart from the standpoint of satisfaction of their separate demands. Following this, it is logical to conclude that voluntary support for the Soviet political system and its ruling elite differs measurably between farmers and scientists. Our evidence on this latter point is rather thin, however, and rests more in the category of conjecture.

For our purposes, we can separate several classes in the USSR based on occupation, as follows:[24]

1. Ruling elite.
2. Intelligentsia.
3. White-collar employees.
4. Workers.
5. Farmers.

---

[23] *Pravda*, December 6, 1964.

[24] Inkeles lists the following social classes in the USSR: Ruling elite, superior intelligentsia, general intelligentsia, white-collar, working class, peasantry (with several subbreakdowns within the working class and peasantry). Inkeles, *op. cit.*, p. 560.

Elite Class

The first class, and the easiest one to discuss, is that of the regime itself, or the political elite. It includes the leaders of the Communist Party and the national government, for example, the Communist Party Central Committee and its various organs (Politburo, Central Auditing Commission, Secretariat), the national Council of Ministers, leading members of the legislature, and the leaders of the communist parties and governments of the union republics. The demands of the elite, naturally, are very effectively articulated and aggregated (mainly through the Communist Party apparatus), and to a large degree they are satisfied, of course, because this class is in control of the political system. In his study of the Communist elite, Djilas includes those who have special privileges and economic preference because of the administrative monopoly they hold. The Communist Party makes the class, he continues, but the class grows in part because it uses the party as its base.[25] Miller argues that the crucial element in class differentiation is less in privileges themselves than in attitudes of the privileged toward the underprivileged and vice versa, as in general acceptance of wide distinctions between the elite and others in choice of theater seats, special waiting rooms, and such.[26] The elite class is not identical with the Communist Party because only the top echelons of the party are influential decision makers and thereby rulers of the Soviet political system, that is, in the elite.

The system, in large measure, is organized and disciplined in order to satisfy the demands of the political elite. Whether all of their demands, such as steadily increasing industrial production and agricultural output and even new foreign policy successes, will be met, however, frequently rests in a sphere of behavior beyond the control of the manipulators of the political system. This "command" system, though, is set up to satisfy elite demands. Attitudes of the political elite in the USSR, similar to attitudes in any other elite-type system, obviously, are strongly biased toward the system. A comparative study of American and Soviet elites (political, governmental, military, economic, labor, scientific, and cultural) was made for the five dimensions of:

Unitary or pluralistic society.
Integration or separation of political functions.
Nature of the political party system.
Relation of mass media to the government and to the people.
Control of primary and secondary education.

---

[25] Milovan Djilas, *The New Class* (New York: Frederick A. Praeger, Inc., 1957), pp. 39–40.

[26] Wright Miller, *Russians as People* (New York: E. P. Dutton, 1961), pp. 136–37.

Members of American elites were found to be equally unanimous in support of a pluralistic system as their counterpart Soviet elites were in support of a monolithic system.[27]

Intelligentsia Class

The second class to be described is that of the intelligentsia, which embraces a large and continuously expanding number of Soviet citizens. Referring to this class, one of the leading journals of the CPSU published the table below.[28]

GROWTH IN NUMBERS OF THE SOVIET INTELLIGENTSIA
BY DIVISIONAL GROUPS
(In Thousands)

	Number of Intelligentsia		Increase—in Number of Times
	1939	1959	
Leaders of enterprises and their subdivisions................	757	955	1.3
Engineers—technical workers...	1,656	4,205	2.5
Agronomists, zootechnicians, veterinary workers, foresters....	295	477	1.6
Medical workers, teachers, educators....................	1,553	2,835	1.8
Leaders of organs of state, administration, party, *Komsomol*, trade unions, cooperatives and other public organizations and their subdivisions...........	445	392	0.9

This class is difficult to define: the official Soviet view includes most "educated" people as well as those in responsible positions. In Haimson's view, recent decades have rapidly transformed the character of professional roles so that the meaning of the word "intelligentsia" has altered. Where once the term meant a selected few who were engaged in exploring new ideas and in criticizing existing ones, now it applies simply to all those engaged in occupations requiring intellectual and technical skill.[29] For our

[27] Robert C. Angell, "Content Analysis of Elite Media," *Journal of Conflict Resolution*, Vol. VIII (1964), p. 361.

[28] A. Golota and B. Korolev, "Sovetskaya Intelligentsiya v Period Razvernutogo Stroitelstva Kommunizma," *Kommunist*, No. 10 (July, 1962), p. 17. Boris Meissner estimates a 12.3 million member intelligentsia (technical, economic, scientific, and cultural) in 1959. See *Problems of Communism*, Vol. XV (November–December, 1966), p. 59.

[29] Leopold Haimson, "Three Generations of the Soviet Intelligentsia," *Foreign Affairs*, Vol. 37 (January, 1959), pp. 243–44.

purposes, the intelligentsia includes such people as leading Communist Party workers (*apparatchiki*); college-educated engineers and managerial personnel; educators, scholars, and journalists; scientists; key technicians such as agronomists, architects, and physicians; and artists, writers, musicians, and poets.   Common attributes of this class are education (usually higher education), "intellectual" work (versus manual labor) and an occupational position of some significance commanding both responsibility and respect within Soviet society.

The intelligentsia rather efficiently articulates its interests, which are at times similar—if not identical—to the interests of the political elite itself. Some of the interests of this class are aggregated via a particular interest group, say that of the managerial bureaucracy.   Other subclasses within the intelligentsia have a very poor record of interest aggregation, for example writers, musicians, and educators.   This record is apt to change rapidly, however.   Soviet writers, for one group, since approximately 1964 have articulated and aggregated their demands much more widely and effectively than had been the case at any time since World War II.

By and large, then, the demands of the intelligentsia are more likely than not to be met satisfactorily, increasingly so since the early 1960's. This stems in no small part from the fact that the members of the intelligentsia are broadly diffused throughout the political system.   Demand satisfaction of the intelligentsia class is curbed somewhat by the regime's ability to ignore demands which may differ from regime desires, such as those of artisits for abstract painting, or educators for studies in sociology. On the other hand, demands of scientists are more likely to be met simply because modern society requires such competent highly trained specialists as physicists, chemists, surgeons, and biologists.   Some noted Soviet scientists have enjoyed great economic success while persistently refusing, almost defiantly it would seem, to join the Communist Party.   Scientists in the USSR enjoy both high prestige and top incomes.

The intelligentsia is the main class from which new members of the political elite are recruited.   Higher education, positions of importance, and individual ability more and more are requirements for being co-opted into the ruling circles.   One author contends that the Soviet intelligentsia is largely hereditary, the children of the intelligentsia virtually monopolizing the better known universities and the more distinguished institutes.[30]

Certainly, the intelligentsia constitutes a main pillar of support for the political system, again in part because so many of these people constitute a vital ingredient within that system.   In return, this class receives num-

---

[30] David Burg in Richard Pipes (ed.), *The Russian Intelligentsia* (New York: Columbia University Press, 1961), p. 80.

erous benefits from the system in better education, higher incomes, and many other material rewards. As the class of intelligentsia continues to grow, the elite probably can anticipate a commensurate growth in its base of support.

Ironically, while the intelligentsia forms a broad support for the regime, it also is the class which on occasion gives rise to dissidence within the system. If this class gets much from the regime, it also has the ability to see more of what is potentially available to it. This class can make comparisons of foreign societies with theirs at home and thus determine more objectively what they deserve out of society. More importantly, the intelligentsia in post-Stalin USSR is coming around to the view that the political elite needs, in fact must have, the rather full support of this vitally important class. Inkeles suggests that any new programs aimed at social equalization could be accomplished only at the expense, and hence with the alienation, of those groups on whose support the regime rests.[31] The interest of the ruling elite in social stability as a foundation for its programs of internal and foreign expansion is such that it seems most unlikely that it would undertake a program designed to effect one phase of its ideological goals at the expense of the stability of the system as a whole. It may, in fact, be said that despite recurrent affirmations of the aim of achieving a classless society, this goal can no longer be realistically regarded as one towards which the present leadership is actively and effectively oriented. Indeed, there is no reason to assume that the present rate of social mobility, which probably equals that in the United States and possibly surpasses it, will be maintained. But if it is not, major consequences for the structure and functioning of Soviet society as now "traditionally" constituted may be expected.[32] As the intelligentsia class more accurately analyzes political life, and as it realizes the key position which it holds in such matters as shared values and collective, community-wide attitudes toward the ruling system, it can be expected to increase even more its demands on the elite class.

Several subclasses of the intelligentsia have softly and respectfully objected to some regime actions. Writers and poets have requested less regime censorship (Yevtushenko even mildly rebuked the Communist Party leader, Khrushchev, in 1962), economists and economic managers have urged reform of the weak organization and management of the economy, the law profession has pressed for additional improvements in the areas of law adjudication, and military leaders have fought for an improved defense posture against even Khrushchev's desires. All of this

[31] Inkeles, *op. cit.*, p. 572.
[32] *Ibid*, pp. 572–73.

adds up to a gentle opposition to the regime when in the view of the intelligentsia it continues to commit errors and fails to articulate demands adequately. This opposition, if that is what it can be called in such an embryonic stage of development, has effected a number of changes and improvements in the system since Stalin's time.

A more vigorous form of opposition to the regime has come from young people, a number of them university students. Disgust and very mild student rebellion occurred in 1956 at several Soviet universities when students openly ridiculed the official party line when it attempted to rationalize the use of Soviet troops in putting down the Hungarian Revolution. Burg, a former Soviet student who attended Moscow State University, estimates that during the political thaw in the USSR in 1956 from one fourth to one third of the Soviet students revealed some political discontent. Among history majors in Moscow University a group of ten to fifteen graduate students printed and distributed leaflets against Khrushchev and the party dictatorship in 1956–57 and called for a return to Soviet democracy and the "Leninist line."[33] An American who spent a year at Moscow State University contends that the average Russian student is apolitical, being either cautious or indifferent toward domestic affairs and relatively uninterested in foreign affairs.[34] If Burg's estimate of discontented students and Robert's estimate of student indifference are anywhere near accurate, then we may conclude that a sizable percentage of university students is not being effectively socialized into the Soviet political system.

Discussion of failures or shortcomings in political socialization raises the question of a potential open opposition, even outright rebellion, against the regime and against the system. From available information on the Soviet Union there is almost no indication that dissident citizens are planning, or indeed even expect, any such strong action. Rather, such opposition, as suggested above, takes the form of requests, articulated demands, disgust, even indifference, but not much if anything at all in the way of planned opposition. Soviet citizens, of course, are not used to thinking in terms of opposition as the Western citizen does. There are no opposition political parties, no opposition factions in the legislature, no opposition candidates nor political movements, no opposition press nor

---

[33] Burg, *op. cit.*, pp. 90–91.

[34] David Robert, "Moscow State University," *Survey*, No. 51 (April, 1964), p. 31. Somewhat different is the view of another American graduate student who studied for a year at the same university. His protrayal of a very able Soviet undergraduate was that "He was a passionate socialist...." Feifer, *op. cit.*, p. 163.

institutions around which active regime dissidence can easily form. "Rebellious" Soviet intellectuals react more in terms of apathy and skepticism than of political contention directed toward the regime, toward the Communist Party, toward communism, or toward the political system.

White-Collar Class

The class of white-collar employees might simply be referred to as the "bureaucracy." The most appropriate Russian term is *sluzhashchiy* (employee). These people staff the numerous office positions required to run a vast party-state apparatus. This class includes those white-collar, or non-manual, workers in party and government offices, in the admintrative staffs of industry, agriculture, transport, construction, and service industries. As such, it includes the large army of clerks, secretaries, bookkeepers, accountants, salespeople, lower echelon supervisory personnel and technicians who are neither manual workers nor those enjoying high prestige or managerial authority. These people are not, by profession, intellectuals and decision makers. Instead, they carry out the orders of policy makers, administering the system and serving the Soviet population in most of its "governmental-managerial" needs.

Somewhat similar to the two higher classes, the white-collar class can articulate its demands rather adequately, but aggregation of these demands is not high. Satisfaction of their demands appears to be not much better than in the case with workers. White-collar employees understand the workings of the system (in a way, they actually run it), but their potential power is not so easily focused and concentrated, partly because there are no established and freely operating opposition parties with which the regime could be pressured or threatened, and partly because these people do not occupy positions of importance. The class, then, does not hold in its hands much effective power, and its somewhat larger potential for power cannot easily be organized and aggregated.

The attitudes of the white-collar class toward the regime and communism are considerably less favorable than those of the two higher classes, simply because white-collar employees have a much smaller stake in the system and their personal rewards and benefits are considerably fewer than is the case with the intelligentsia and the elite. Here, too, there is a difference of attitude within the white-collar class itself. A minor functionary, for example, can be expected to be more highly socialized into the system than, say, a salesperson in a store, because of a higher degree of Communist Party indoctrination, but also because the functionary's potential rewards are greater than those of the salesperson. Generally, however, it should be assumed that the white-collar class normally supports, even actively, the regime and the system, because this class is in such intimate contact with running the system.

Working Class

Workers in Soviet society, those who engage in nonagricultural, manual labor, make up one of the most important of the classes, historically and ideologically. From Marx's time on, communism, supposedly to be constructed on a capitalist base, was to be a political system of, by, and for industrial workers. The very ideology of Marxism analyzes capitalism in preparation for the salvation of the workers. This ideology has both motivated Soviet leaders and embarrassed them over the decades since 1917. These leaders have, in brief, attempted to erect a workers' society, but without practical worker control. Communist theory in this respect does not at all match communist practice.

Workers, nevertheless, have been catered to by the regime in allowing them a voice in factory management for a short time after 1917, in authorizing trade unions to offer workers such benefits as insurance programs and rest home facilities, and in calling for workers' preference to seats in the legislature and openings in institutes and universities. Since Stalin's death, particularly in the past decade, the regime has concentrated on improving workers' benefits, such as more abundant housing, shorter working hours, and increased rates of pay.

Soviet regimes from Lenin's time on have, on the other hand, also discriminated against workers. Under Lenin the workers' rights to have a hand in factory management were soon curbed, and trade unions lost their ability to fight for workers. Under Stalinist terror the lives and welfare of workers (and almost all other classes) were tenuous and continually subject to the whims of the dictator. Workers arriving late to work under the worst years of Stalinism, for example, were criminally liable. Low wages, frequently harsh living standards, and few fringe benefits resulted in a lower level of political socialization for workers than for the three higher classes in Soviet society. Most importantly, workers were not permitted to rule in what was so loudly trumpeted as a workers' society. A survey taken in 1960 of 4,700 workers in 60 industrial enterprises in Krasnoyarsk (Siberia) revealed the causes listed in the table below for workers leaving their work voluntarily.[35]

---

[35] *Voprosy Ekonomiki*, No. 5 (May, 1962), p. 53.

BASIC CAUSES OF WORKERS LEAVING THEIR JOBS

Cause	Percent of Total
Dissatisfaction over wages	17.5
Dissatisfaction with character of work	13.9
Dissatisfaction with living conditions	11.2
Remoteness of housing from work and poor transport	4.2
Impossibility of placing children in nursery, etc.	4.0
Desire to return to one's relatives	17.5
Unsuitable climate	0.6
Health of the worker	4.9
Sickness of relatives	4.3
Desire for more education	5.2
Other causes	11.3
Cause not indicated	5.4
	100.0

Of the four main causes of quitting, wages and living conditions were two. In a 1963 poll of 70,000 workers who had recently left their jobs, the workers again emphasized low wages and poor living and working conditions.[36] These poll results follow:

Cause	Percent of Those Leaving
Low wages, poor living and/or working conditions	47.1
Locality of the job	25.4
Dismissed for reasons of automation or job reclassification	18.3
Family or marriage	9.2
	100.0

The articulation and aggregation of the demands of Soviet workers have never been rated high by Western analysts. In very recent years, however, all citizen demands, including those of workers, are being increasingly satisfied, although many (such as housing) are a long way from being adequately fulfilled. From the foregoing discussion, what can be said regarding the worker's views of the regime and what he expects from communist society, present and future? First, workers desire and anticipate more pay and more abundant consumer goods. Their expectations from the society are rising in response to a rise in demand satisfaction. The worker does not expect to take part in political rule; that sphere he has been taught to believe is reserved for the political elite. A 1965 survey of Soviet factory workers in the Ural car factory suggests that the more skilled the worker's classification and the more responsible position he holds, the more he takes part in so-called "public assignments" (those civic duties carried on after working hours).[37]

[36] *Problems of Communism*, Vol. XIII (January–February, 1964), p. 28.

[37] A. Krasilov, "Zavod: Zhizn, Trud, Dosyg Ludey," *Kommunist*, No. 12 (August, 1965), p. 50.

PUBLIC ASSIGNMENTS OF URAL CAR FACTORY WORKERS, 1965

	Shop Chiefs	Workers in Factory Adminis- tration	Fore- men	Engi- neers	Workers of 1–2 Cate- gories	Workers of 5–8 Cate- gories	Women Workers
Average number of public assignments for each participating group	1.4	1.6	1.2	2.1	1.0	1.5	0.9
Which part of the group has a public assignment (in percent)	100	92	80	100	64	68	52
Number of hours/day engaged in public work for each participating group	2.3	1.1	1.1	0.8	0.8	0.7	0.6
Part of the group which in its free time is occupied with public work (in %)	96	88	88	64	64	64	40
Number of public organizations (on an average), except KPSS, VLKSM, trade union, in which workers take part	4.5	2.8	4.4	4.3	1.9	2.2	1.2
Average number of meetings per week	4.0	2.1	1.1	1.4	0.9	0.7	0.7

The results of this survey clearly indicate that the less skilled the worker is (and, of course, the lower paid), the less interested he is in civic duties and the less socialized he is into the political system. It may well be that the worker holds attitudes only slightly more favorable toward the regime than that of the lowest Soviet class, the farmers. There have been vague reports of strikes by workers, slowdowns and vigorous arguments of workers with management over working conditions, pay rates, and sundry other problems.[38]

Peasant-Farmer Class

Somewhat akin to the industrial worker, the peasant-farmer class, of all classes, has the least access to information and shares least in the dominant values within the system, while being largely uninterested in the regime's goals. His empirical beliefs about the system differ greatly from those of the higher classes. Historically, the average peasant has never been socialized into the political system. His concept of law, government, and the state and how he views his own role within the political culture can best be protrayed by the term alienation. Partly because of the late emancipation from serfdom, followed by a low level of achievement up

---

[38] See Boiter, op. cit., pp. 37–42.

to the Revolution of 1917, Russian peasants have expected very little and received very little from Russian political rule. Communist Party rule has not been much better than that of the tsars for the peasants; forcing them into collectives accompanied by compulsory deliveries of agricultural commodities to the state caused them to resist on a mass scale in the late 1920's and early 1930's, so much so as to create widespread famine conditions. Moreover, Soviet policy of concentrating attention on industrialization to the virtual ignoring of agricultural problems has helped to keep peasant farmers politically alienated.

A few farmers, key members of the more successful collective farms, are somewhat better off than the average, ranking above the lower paid, unskilled workers in terms of remuneration and prestige. At one model collective farm in the Cossack areas the farmers are reluctant to leave a guaranteed minimum wage of $106 per month. This particular farm, although unusual, showed a profit in 1965 of more than $1 million.[39]

For the overwhelming majority of farmer-peasants, however, (approximately 60 percent of whom are women) discontent and an uncooperative attitude continue to be quite prevalent. The peasant's values are markedly different from those of higher classes, particularly the top three classes. Soviet regimes, however, have not attempted seriously to politically socialize peasants into the system. Even widescale propaganda as carried out by the Communist Party has often missed the peasants for reasons of poor channels of communication, high illiteracy rate, and low educational levels of rural citizens, all aggravated by a noticeable unconcern for these people on the part of the political elite. On the whole, peasant-farmers have received very little out of communism and probably are worse off, mainly because of the inefficiencies and illogic of collectivization, than they would have been without that system. In discussions with Soviet peasants, Mehnert was constantly aware that they regarded themselves as the poorest of the poor, as the lowest class on the social scale.[40]

As we might anticipate, peasant-farmers in the Soviet Union have been rather antagonistic toward the regime. Political socialization has been very low and political recruitment from this class almost nonexistent. Active support among this class for the regime and for communism has been noticeable by its absence. The goals and objectives of the regime, particularly, have won little if any sympathy from farmers. One might even portray the relation between the regime and the peasant classes as one of a tacit, undeclared war. At the least, farmers in the USSR have

---

[39] *New York Times*, June 19, 1966.

[40] Klaus Mehnert, *Soviet Man and His World* (New York: Frederick A. Praeger, Inc., 1962), p. 24.

done nothing to aid the growth and development of communism. The peasant-farmer simply has been unable to see anything for himself in the Soviet political system. This alienation might be in the process of change, however.

Since approximately the mid-1950's, and especially since the early 1960's, the Soviet regime has been much more seriously attending to the needs of the peasant-farmer class. In 1958 the abolition of the machine tractor stations (a useful tool with which to govern farmers) heralded one of several changes that were forthcoming. With increased party activity on the collective farms, a natural result was that local party officials became more interested in agricultural problems and, in turn, farmers began to express their demands through party channels. In 1966 the government drew up plans to guarantee collective farmers a minimum annual cash income. Despite these and other recent improvements which at least have been promised the farmers, they suffer from such low prestige and relatively low incomes as to suggest that the political elite will need a long time and much effort to win their willing support. One of the peasant's problems is that of a relatively low rate of upward mobility into a higher class.

Class Mobility

Class structure in the USSR, not surprisingly, has changed somewhat since 1917, partly in response to increasing urbanization, advances in literacy and education, and the growing technical nature of life in a modern industrialized nation. These changes are suggested in the table below.[41]

CLASS COMPOSITION OF POPULATION IN THE USSR
(In Percentage of Total Population including Nonworking Family Members)

	1913	1928	1939	1959	1964
Total population (including nonworking family members).....	100.0	100.0	100.0	100.0	100.0
Workers and employees........	17.0	17.6	50.2	68.3	75.1
Collective farm peasants and handicraftsmen in cooperatives.	—	2.9	47.2	31.4	24.8
Individual peasants and handicraftsmen not in cooperatives..	66.7	74.9	2.6	0.3	0.1
Bourgeoisie, landowners, traders and *Kulaks*................	16.3	4.6	—	—	—

The table is of very limited value, however, because those employed on state farms (hence part of the nation's farm population) and all government

---

[41] *Narodnoe Khozyaystvo SSSR v 1964 g.* (Moscow, 1965), p. 33.

and party workers and officials are carried under the designation "workers and employees." Another breakdown, which does separate collective from state farmers, points to the decline in farm populations from 1950 to 1964.[42]

AGRICULTURAL EMPLOYMENT, 1950–64
(In Millions)

	1950	*1960*	*1962*	*1963*	*1964*
Total agricultural employment..	30.7	29.0	27.7	27.3	27.3
Collective farms..............	27.6	22.3	20.0	19.4	19.2
State farms and agricultural enterprises.................	2.4	6.3	7.7	7.9	8.1

An accompanying growth in urban population is indicated by figures which show urban population as a percent of total population.[43]

	1913	*1940*	*1959*	*1965*
Population percent urban......	18.0	33.0	48.0	53.0

Shifting class structures raise the question of class mobility. Communism in both its theory and its practice has encouraged and stimulated class movement, which permits the USSR to be rated as a highly mobile society. One of the basic rationales of communism, in fact, is that there are no "class" lines and all positions theoretically are open to all people. This often has been the case through various periods of Soviet history. Inevitably, however, as a society modernizes, becomes more sophisticated and technical, upward mobility is slowed. Several factors serve as a damper on mobility, making it rather difficult to move up from the peasant, or working, class to that of the intelligentsia. These factors are:

1. Restricted access to higher education, particularly the general universities, as population growth exceeds that of higher educational institutions.
2. Favorable changes in the law on inheritance taxes, thus permitting upper classes to "take care" of their children.
3. School admittance favorable to one's class: sons of military officers selected for military academies; railroad training schools for sons of railroad men; high prestige universities catering to children of the elite and intelligentsia classes.
4. Important managerial jobs in party, government, and industry open to the more educated applicants.
5. Official emphasis on strengthening family relationships which helps the upper classes to provide more educational and training benefits for their children.

Class mobility in the USSR still is reasonably flexible, but increasingly the upper classes are in a more advantageous position to perpetuate themselves

---

[42] *Ibid.*, p. 419. Two of the figures total incorrectly, but are quoted accurately.
[43] *Ibid.*, p. 11.

and select their own successors. One study suggests the existence of only limited mobility in practice, particularly for those on the lower end of the social scale. In one Leningrad factory, for example, 73.7 percent of the workers were themselves children of workers. In a Sverdlovsk factory 57 percent of the workers were children of workers, while 75 percent of the specialists were children of specialists. Thus education, although tending to promote social mobility between functional groups, also erects a partial barrier against entrance into the elite class, as well as providing a floor below which a member of the elite cannot fall.[44]

The Average Soviet Citizen

Accompanying this new mobility, other concepts of political socialization, political recruitment, interest articulation, and aggregation and support for the system depend rather significantly on one's class, even his subclass. All of these concepts, as discussed in this chapter, run at a "higher" level (e.g., better socialization, more frequent recruitment) for the upper classes, mainly those of the elite and the intelligentsia. The concepts are less applicable, or "lower," for the white-collar workers and lowest of all for workers and peasants. Might it now be possible to construct something of an "average" citizen profile regarding these concepts? Although we lack adequate opinion polls of Soviet attitudes, what we do know of the feelings and beliefs of those who have left the USSR and of some who have remained might permit us to hazard this profile of an average citizen in the USSR today.

As a cross-section sample of all five social classes discussed above, the average Soviet citizen may be portrayed as reasonable well socialized into the political system, accepting its main goals and cooperating with its customs and procedures. He carries out his civic duties, perhaps not enthusiastically, but not rebelliously either. He might be akin to the average American with respect to political socialization; he reluctantly believes it is his duty to cooperate with the system, and he shares the dominant values of the culture.

Political recruitment is quite another matter. The average Soviet citizen cannot anticipate opportunities for important office equal to the expectation of his American counterpart. Across the board, we should rate the average Soviet citizen's chances in this sphere as rather low. The main Soviet versus American difference here is that the Soviet citizen must be an active Communist Party member of some years' good standing to

----

[44] "Education and Social Mobility in the USSR," *Soviet Studies*, Vol. XVIII (July, 1966), pp. 61, 65.

have a chance to be recruited into the ruling elite. His American counterpart has two parties to choose from and, on occasion, may be a latecomer in party membership.

Similarly, there are vast differences between the USSR and Western nations in interest articulation and aggregation. In the latter nations there are a number of different organized interest groups through which the citizen can articulate and aggregate his demands for presentation into the mechanism of his political system. The average Soviet citizen, however, has available to him only a very few interest groups, and the farmer has had almost none at all. The chief limitation is the monopolistic approach to political power as practiced by the Communist Party. If the Soviet citizen happens to have access to the Communist Party as an interest group, that is all he needs. If he does not, then any other groups can be of only marginal help to him. Moreover, the demands of the Communist Party and its leadership elite take precedence over all other demands. A result of this is that a number of potentially competing demands of Soviet citizens simply are not articulated and aggregated into the Soviet political system, whether for a lack of party interest, time, money, or facilities. As in political recruitment, the demands of the average Soviet citizens have a "low" rate of articulation and aggregation. This, however, is in process of change, rather rapid change at that, to be discussed in later chapters.

The subjective attitudes held by the average Soviet citizen toward communism generally and toward the regime specifically vary in accordance with the degree to which the citizen shares in societal values and the level of sophistication of his empirical beliefs. The goals of communism as announced by the Communist Party, for peace abroad and prosperity at home, for economic egalitarianism (at least to the extent that there are no very rich versus very poor people), for public (socialist) ownership of the more important means of production, and for promised improved communications, transport, and living conditions, are subscribed to by the average citizen. In addition, he is favorably disposed toward what might be labeled as "welfare communism": free medical and dental services, adequate education, the "right" to work, and the future expectation of an abundance of consumer goods. All of these benefits are not yet available to him, but he believes in them as part of the promise of communism.

The attitudes differ, however, with respect to the ruling elite. "Russians do not think their courts are an instrument of totalitarianism, police-state repression, terror ... because they do not think that way about Soviet rule ... 'The regime' means an apartment, a job, and a good education for one's children—as well as restrictions on travel abroad. It means spectacular progress as well as purges."[45]   The average citizen accepts, as mentioned above, many of the regime's goals.   Furthermore, he rather firmly believes his leaders are peace loving and sincerely trying to counteract what he is convinced is a belligerent and warlike stance of the U.S.   The regime's foreign policy wins his general acceptance.   That the Communist Party leaders rule him, also, is given tacit approval by him.   After all, the Soviet citizen is unaware of how a vigorous democracy works.   When his leaders tell him they operate a democratic system (and *they* believe they do), he has little if any counterinformation with which to disagree with them.   He also, obviously, is accustomed to the Communist Party leisurely making the major decisions for the political system.   This is normal procedure according to his own experience.   What the average citizen does disapprove of is the harsh dictatorship of the Stalinist variety.   The citizen does not like slave labor camps, secret police, Stalinist paranoia and the other severe accouterments of totalitarianism.   Of course, there are numerous personal frustrations of Soviet citizens, such as shortages of some goods or bureaucratic red tape, but it is questionable whether he blames the political elite and the political system for this.   Toward the elite, then, the citizen is willing to give his mild, if not complete, support, with the reservation that he does not want a return to Stalinism.

If the foregoing profile of the average citizen anywhere near resembles the "real" average Soviet citizen, then we can conclude that political socialization is as effective in the USSR as in the U.S. and that the Soviet citizens give as much support to their political system as is the case with, say, American, British, or French citizens.

Nationality Policies

Soviet nationality policies on occasion have been reminiscent of tsarist policies, while at the same time they try to reflect communist ideology. Under the tsars, Great Russians from the capitals at Moscow and St. Petersburg dominated the other ethnic groups within the empire.   In addition, anti-Semitism had official blessing during part of old Russian history.   Ethnically, nationally, even religiously, tsarism was characterized by unenlightened chauvinism, led and dominated by Great Russians. Under the Communists this practice was bound to change.

Marx's denial of the importance of nations and his belief that all workers, everywhere, were brothers under the skin set the foundation for communist ideology which has deemphasized national boundaries as well

---

[45] Feifer, *op. cit.*, pp. 341–42.

as racial and ethnic differences. Marx thought workers of the world should unite (a slogan still carried on the masthead of each day's issue of the two main Soviet newspapers, *Pravda* and *Izvestiya*) into a world brotherhood of workers. This belief formed the base of the Socialist and later Communist Internationals. This workers' brotherhood concept, in fact, is the kernel idea of an international, or worldwide, communist movement. Moreover, a number of early Marxists and Russian communists (beginning with Marx himself) were of Jewish ancestry. These factors must have contributed to communism's ideology, which opposes all forms of racial and ethnic discrimination. All nations, all races, all people are equal under the theory of communism.

Soviet practice under Lenin followed communist theory in these matters. It was Stalin, though, a member of one of the old Russian empire's minority groups (Georgian), who returned to tsarist policies. In the new Soviet government of 1917, Stalin's first position was that of Commissar of Nationalities. He already had written tracts on the subject and had become the party's expert on nationalities. Non-Russian Stalin, however, reinstituted Russification, for example in keeping the higher echelons of the Communist Party (and even, to an extent, the party organizations in various union republics) staffed with Russians. The notable exception to this policy was the case of Stalin's native Georgians, who exerted an inordinately weighty influence (for example, the notorious head of the national secret police, Beriya) in Soviet political circles. Anti-Semitism, too, while not officially endorsed by Stalin (unlike the climate under some of the tsars), was not greatly discouraged by him either. Stalin's anti-Semitism might have been carried into the Communist Party's Central Committee. This Committee had a greater proportion of Jews in 1939 (just when Stalin gained full power) than in later years when he had an opportunity to consolidate his authority. Stalin's last Party Congress in 1952 saw a percentage decline in Jews on the Central Committee by more than half since 1939.[46] One of the last acts of Stalin just prior to his death was to prepare for a new purge having anti-Semitic undertones.

Stalin's immediate successors, Malenkov and Khrushchev, meant Great Russians again led the nation, but Khrushchev, particularly, began to deemphasize Russification of the ethnic minorities. Local Communists of the particular nationality (Ukrainian, Belorussian, Armenian) began to replace Russians in the top party and government posts within their respective republics. Apparently a continuing policy, though, is to keep some Russians in relatively high positions within the various union

---

[46] See the table, p. 122.

republics. In the central committees of the Young Communist League (*Komsomol*) in the union republics, a Russian was the second secretary in nine of fourteen republics outside of the RSFSR in 1966. It long has been customary for most of the fourteen Communist parties in non-Russian republics to have a Russian as their number two party official, the second secretary, instead of one of the ethnic nationals of the particular republic. Seweryn Bialer lists these figures which reveal Russian dominance of the Communists Party's Central Committee.[47]

	1939 Percent of USSR Population	1939 Percent of Central Committee, CPSU	1952 Percent of Central Committee	1956 Percent of Central Committee	1959 Percent of Population	1961 Percent of Central Committee
Russians...	58.4	66.9	71.5	67.1	52.0	62.7

Thus, Russians have staffed the Central Committee in greater proportion than their population percentages warrant, the high point being reached after Stalin consolidated his power. After Stalin's death (1953) the proportion began changing a bit more in line with population distribution. On the national party level, Khrushchev began putting a few non-Russians on the Politburo (then, Presidium), of the Central Committee. The 1966 post-Khrushchev Politburo of fifteen (full and candidate members) contained several non-Russians.

Several reasons for this Russian dominance other than simple chauvinism, even in the case of Stalin, stem from the revolutionary features of communism, the requisites of national development and modernity, and the problems inherent in a large, multi-racial state. The drive for communism requires a drastic change in customs and old patterns of life, at least in the formative years, such as changing from private to collective and state farming and from capitalistic to socialistic management of the economy. Moreover, centralized Moscow rule of some peoples who had enjoyed elements of self-government (albeit briefly, as in the Ukraine) was bound to cause resentment among these peoples. A number of the national minorities have been no happier with Russian Communist dominance of their lives than they were under the Russian tsars. Georgians, Armenians, Ukrainians, and those of the Baltic republics (Latvia, Estoniya, Lithuania) all resisted, to some degree, Russian-Soviet rule. Somewhat understandably, the Moscow Communists felt obliged to

---

[47] Seweryn Bialer, "How Russians Rule Russia," *Problems of Communism*, (September–October, 1964), p. 46.

rely on Russians (hopefully more loyal) to carry out the novel, highly centralized administration required when communism is introduced. Secondly, the Soviet drive toward modernity, including equality of sex, industrialization, and mass education, also met resistance in various parts of the country, for example, feudal attitudes toward women, nepotism, kinship and family loyalties, and individualism in Central Asia. These old-fashioned attitudes plagued Soviet goals of social and cultural modernization. Modernity requires effective nationwide communications, beginning with a single national language. This accomplishment has been frustrated by lingering loyalties to native languages and customs, extending even into the mid-1960's. The Soviet leadership does not want to kill off local languages, yet it repeatedly points out the necessity for a common national language.

It is questionable just how successful the Russification and even communization (in its aspect of social modernity) of the peoples of Central Asia have been. One author observes that in fact Central Asian culture is being strengthened. Seclusion of women has spread to groups not previously following it (Kazaks and Kirghiz) and even to some party and governmental officials—seeing in it a mark of local prestige and personal attainments.[48] Linguistically, too, selected loan words are fitted into Central Asian phonetic and grammatical patterns, religious beliefs and practices continue strongly, and there is a lingering continuance of bride prices being paid and polygyny being practiced, although both are illegal. Even the collective farms in Central Asia have the form of tribal genealogical kin groups, and the most highly educated Central Asians appear to be the most skilled communicators of ethnic cultural values.[49] Active opposition to Russian, hence Soviet, political activity, however, seems absent, and ambitious Central Asians seeking national status and recognition and material benefits from Soviet society are the ones most likely to undergo ostensible self-Russification.[50]

Between 1926 and 1959 Russians formed increasing percentages of the population in most of the regional republics. The following table illustrates this growth, particularly in Central Asia, perhaps the least "Russian" of all the Soviet areas.[51]

---

[48] Elizabeth E. Bacon, *Central Asians under Russian Rule, A Study in Culture Change* (Ithaca, N. Y.: Cornell University Press, 1966), p. 205.

[49] *Ibid.*, pp. 204, 213.

[50] *Ibid.*, p. 156.

[51] I. A. Kinganov, *Natsii SSSR i Russkiy Vopros* (Frankfurt/Main: Druck, 1961), p. 49.

RUSSIANS AS A PERCENT OF TOTAL POPULATIONS

	1926	1959
RSFSR	78.6	83.2
Ukraine	9.2	17.7
Belorussia	7.2	9.1
Caucasus:		
Azerbaijan	9.5	13.9
Georgia	3.6	10.8
Armenia	2.2	3.2
Central Asia:		
Kazakhstan	19.7	43.1
Kirghiz	11.7	30.2
Uzbekistan	5.6	13.6
Tadzhikistan	6.8	13.3
Turkmenia	8.2	17.3

Thus, when the leadership attempts to solve problems typical of any large nation-state made up of such a mixed population, it might be only natural for the most abundant nationality (particularly if the leadership itself is composed mainly of Russians) to try to unify the country linguistically, culturally, and politically. Several other communist nations, such as Yugoslavia and Czechoslovakia, have not satisfactorily resolved similar problems. From the viewpoint of a Soviet leader in Moscow, then, there is some logic in Soviet nationality policy as it has been carried out.

In what might have been a limited resurgence of Stalin's anti-Semitism, the Khrushchev period saw a number of Jews convicted of violating such crimes as gold hoarding, fraud, and embezzlement; a number of those convicted were sentenced to death. Khrushchev himself was reported as having used derogatory language in referring to Soviet Jews who had been convicted of certain crimes. For the record, at least, both Khrushchev and his successors have denied that anti-Semitism is either a policy of the government or an existent problem within the country. Post-Khrushchev leaders have not commented on the fact that some recent Soviet criminals have been Jews; these leaders do quote Lenin, however, on the necessity to combat anti-Semitism. Bialer gives the following figures illustrating a decline in the number of Jews on the Communist Party's Central Committee. The number of Jews on the Committee is based on a relative figure of 100 for the year 1939:[52]

1939	1952	1956	1961
100	47	33	7

Perhaps Stalin began eliminating Jews from the Committee after he gained full dictatorial powers in the late 1930's. Stalin's successors, for whatever

---

[52] Bailer, op. cit., p. 48.

reasons, have continued the decline reflected in the 1952 figure. There are reasons, though, which might explain even if they do not justify the cautious attitude of Soviet Communist leadership toward Soviet Jews, if one wants to assume that these leaders are not anti-Semitic.

Being highly religious, Jews face the automatic mistrust and antagonism of the atheistic regime, whose policy clearly and explicitly is directed against any and all religions. In addition, some Jewish customs and traditions, as well as their languages, all were believed by the regime to be in opposition to Communist objectives to unify, nationalize, and mobilize the masses and transform them into a single type, Soviet Communist mold. Moreover, Zionism has worried Communist leaders, causing them to suspect the Soviet and Communist loyalty of Jews in the USSR. The Soviet political elite is nervous about any group (particularly a religious one) which seems to cultivate and promote social, cultural, or religious views which have not originated out of Soviet communism or which do not have the complete endorsement and understanding of the regime.

The nationality policy of the Soviet leadership seeks to win the enthusiastic support of ethnic minorities within the country for its goals of communism. This does not in itself mean Russification, even though it may appear so to some of these minorities. In the process, the leadership faces numerous nationalistic, cultural, and linguistic barriers to its goals and it has not to this date been overly successful in winning deep support.

PART TWO

Rule Making: The Communist Party

CHAPTER VI

The Ruling Elite

FUNCTIONALLY, the political elite in the Soviet Union is made up of the policy makers, who determine the major decisions for the Soviet political system. Just who and how many they are, however, is not easy to determine. Some Western scholars refer to them as the *apparatchik*, or party apparatus, the professional, full-time, paid workers of the Communist Party. Fainsod suggests there might have been 150,000 to 200,000 in the paid apparatus in 1962.[1] Schapiro in 1959 calculated the central, regional, and local party apparatus at 225,000 to 235,000.[2] Several sets of figures from Soviet sources, which are not mutually exclusive, however, might be considered.

Members and candidate members of the Communist Party central committees of union republics, *kray* and *oblast* party-committees.....................	27,000[3]
Paid party officials in primary party organizations and shop party organizations (7 percent of the total of 750,000 secretaries and party group organizers).....	52,500[4]
Staffs of *rayon*, city, *okrug*, *oblast*, and *kray* committees and auditing commissions of union republics.......	ca.328,000[5]
Elected party members to staffs of: party committees, bureaus of primary and shop party organizers; secretaries; deputy secretaries; party group organizers...	2,600,000[6]

---

[1] Merle Fainsod, *How Russia is Ruled* (rev. ed.; Cambridge, Mass., Harvard University Press, 1963), p. 206. The ruling elite, for Aspaturian, corresponds to the more than 4,600,000 party members who are drawn from the various categories of the intelligentsia. See his chapter in Roy C. Macridis and Robert E. Ward (eds.), *Modern Political Systems: Europe* (Englewood Cliffs, N. J.: Prentice-Hall, 1963), p. 497.

[2] Leonard Schapiro, *The Communist Party of the Soviet Union*, New York, Random House, 1960, p. 525.

[3] *Partiynaya Zhizn*, No. 15 (1963), p. 26.

[4] *Ibid.*, p. 26.

[5] *Kommunist*, No. 18 (December 1965), p. 39.

[6] "KPSS v tsifrakh, (1961–1964 godu)," *Partiynaya Zhizn*, No. 10 (May, 1965), p. 17.

It appears difficult to pin down the "apparatus," either in precise definition or approximate numbers. Available data simply are too scanty and noncomparable to permit a reasonable estimate.

Returning to a broad description, however, we can conclude that the party elite is made up of all people in the Soviet Union who actively and responsibly participate in leadership decision making. These must include top party leaders and high governmental officials on the central, regional, and local levels; the inner core of the military high command; upper-echelon economic managers; and such officials as directors of academic and scientific institutions. Of these, we might single out the top echelon of leaders for special treatment, the Central Committee of the CPSU and its Central Auditing Commission. The members of this group elected at the Twenty-third Congress in 1966 total 439, as follows:[7]

Regular Central Committee members........................ 195
Candidate Central Committee members..................... 165
Central Auditing Committee members...................... 79
                                                          ———
   Total... 439

These 439 Communist Party members, whom we shall refer to in this chapter as the Central Committee Group, constitute the inner core of the Soviet political elite. They are the most important 400 members of the Communist Party and, consequently, of the political system. All of the members and candidate members of the Central Committee's Politburo (19) and all national secretaries of the party (11) are members of this Central Committee Group. All but one of the eighty-four members of the national Council of Ministers and a number of officials in the leading echelons of the Supreme Soviet also are from this group. The table below illustrates the important positions held in the national government by many of these leaders as of mid-1966.[8]

CORRELATION OF CENTRAL COMMITTEE GROUP
WITH GOVERNMENTAL OFFICIALS

	Total Number of Officials in Organization	Number of Central Committee Group Members in Organization	Central Committee Group Members, as a Percent of Total Officials in Organization
Council of Ministers, USSR.	84	83	98.8
Presidium of Supreme Soviet, USSR..................	36	30	83.3
Chairmen of USSR Supreme Soviet Commissions......	20	12	60.0

[7] *Pravda*, April 9, 1966. For a breakdown of Central Committee members and delegates to the congresses of 1952, 1956, and 1961 as to their ages and the dates of

On the regional government level, the following figures are appropriate:

	Total Number of Officials	Number of Central Committee Group Members	Central Committee Members as a Percent of Regional Officials
First secretaries of communist parties of union republics...	14*	12†	85.7
Chairmen of councils of ministers (government) of union republics..................	15	15	100

* There is no separate Communist Party for the Russian Republic (RSFSR).

† The first secretary of the Latvian Communist Party was recently placed on the Politburo, CPSU, and his Latvian replacement had not appeared on the Central Committee Group by mid-1966.

These tables illustrate the dominance over the main organizations in the Soviet government, nationally and regionally, that is held by the members of the Central Committee Group. The figures on the central Soviet governmental organization, the Council of Ministers, illustrate the practical merger of high party with high governmental officials in the upper level of the government, testifying to the description of the USSR as a party-state system. At this level, the fitting together of the two parts (party and government) is extremely close, and it is not too meaningful to question whether the head of the government, the Chairman of the Council of Ministers (who also is a key party leader on the Politburo), is first a governmental official and secondly a party leader or vice versa. With a few exceptions (such as Malenkov vs. Khrushchev in the 1953–55 period), the distinction is not significant. If, to the above data, we add other party organizations, for example, the national and republican party secretariats with their respective offices and branches which help to supervise important features of Soviet society, then a picture emerges of Soviet political life as one of elite politics. The remainder of this and parts of later chapters in the book address themselves to the question of how elite politics work in the USSR.

POWERS AND RESPONSIBILITIES OF THE ELITE

The powers and responsibilities of the elite, as the fount of authoritative decision making within the Soviet political system, begin with setting

their entrance into the party, see John A. Armstrong, "Party Bifurcation and Elite Interests," *Soviet Studies*, Vol. XVII (April, 1966), p. 429.

8 Compiled from *Pravda*, April 9, 1966; *Izvestiya*, August 4, 5, 1966.

national policy. Much of the time and energy taken up by the elite, as noted in the previous chapter, is devoted to convincing the citizenry that its decisions are legitimate and authoritative. The range of subjects extends from broad, overall policy (five-year plans, annual budget, military expenditures) to rather detailed questions relating to policy implementation. The Council of Ministers recently, in recommending to the legislature the creation of new ministries, prefaced its statement with the words "guided by the decisions of the Central Committee plenum, the Council of Ministers USSR introduces for consideration by the Supreme Soviet USSR."[9] In this implementation the elite also provides administrative guidelines, again not only for party organizations but for other spheres of Soviet society as well, such as curriculum matters for public schools. The elite also sets the organizational framework for Soviet institutions, such as the abolition of the machine tractor stations in agriculture in 1958, drastic party reorganization (in 1962 and again in 1965), and the economic council reorganizations in 1957 and 1965 in industry. One of the themes or patterns of Soviet political life is an almost constant organization and reorganization of institutions; particularly is this so with respect to the economy.

Still another important task of the elite is to pick and train future candidates to replenish its own membership. The elite must be concerned with singling out promising young people who might be educated, indoctrinated, and trained sufficiently so that one day they will fill the numerous positions of control required by the Soviet system.

Rule making, both in its broad features and in some of its more detailed ones, is the main function performed by the Soviet political elite. This in itself does not differ greatly from rule making in other political systems, although ideologically it is unlike a dictatorship of the fascist variety and it differs in its outlook, mode, and customs from democratic political systems.

THE PARTY SECRETARY

If Soviet life in all of its main features is guided, shaped, and directed by the Communist Party and especially by its elite, the workaday cadres are the party secretaries. The first secretaries of the party, from the General Secretary of the CPSU down through the first secretaries of the regional and local committees and the secretaries of the primary party organizations, form some of the most influential leaders of the Communist Party and, consequently, of the Soviet political system.

---

[9] *Pravda*, October 2, 1965.

There could be some 3,700 important party secretaries, assuming each committee listed below is headed by a secretary.[10]

National party secretaries...................................	11
Secretaries of union republic party committees.................	14
Lower governmental units having party committees in 1965......	3728
Other units equal to *rayon* committees in 1965................	17
Total..	3770

In addition to these numbers, there are many secretaries who cannot be considered as important party officials. A Soviet source cites the figure of 750,000 for elected secretaries of primary and shop party organizations and party group organizers.[11]

With great understatement, one Soviet source notes that "much depends on the first secretary" of a party committee. The secretary, most of all, organizes the work of the committee and its apparatus and has the right of "collective" decision making in questions of leadership, although the secretary should consult others to preserve the concept of collective rule.[12] Added to their normal powers are additional governmental positions held by a number of secretaries. In the Kazakh Republic, for example, many secretaries of city party committees are also members of the city government's executive committee.[13]

To become a first secretary one obviously must be loyal, at least outwardly, to communism, to the Soviet regime, and to the current party leadership. There are other desirable qualifications which include great energy, devotion to one's tasks, a measure of sacrifice—especially regarding one's personal time— and preferably some knowledge of the particular area of society which the secretary is to supervise (agriculture, industry, culture). In the Belorussian Republic serveral years ago, however, only one third of the party secretaries in rural *rayony* were specialists in agriculture, while almost one half of the secretaries of city party committees were specialists in industry, transportation, culture, and other branches of the economy.[14]

Education of some measure is virtually a prerequisite to the position of secretary. In primary organizations approximately 60 percent of the secretaries by 1960 had a secondary or higher education. In rural *rayon* committees more than 90 percent of the secretaries had some higher educa-

---

[10] "KPSS v tsifrakh," 1965, p. 17.

[11] *Partiynaya Zhizn*, No. 21 (November, 1964), p. 23.

[12] A. Kravchenko, "Vysshiy printsep partiynogo rukovodstva," *Partiynaya Zhizn*, No. 17 (September, 1960), p. 43.

[13] G. V. Nechitaylo, *Organizatsionno-massovaya Rabota Gorodskikh Sovetov Kazakhstana* (Alma Ata, Kazakh: Akademia Nauk, 1957), p. 23. See, also, T. Akhunzyanov, *et. al.*, "Gorkom partii—organizator mass," *Kommunist*, No. 14 (September, 1960), p. 66.

[14] F. Surganov in *Kommunist*, No. 13 (September, 1959), p. 59.

tion; 92 percent of the secretaries in city party committees had some higher education and more than 95 percent of the secretaries in *oblast* and *kray* party committees and in union republic central committees had such education.[15] This is an unusually high percent of those having higher education compared with an overall average among party members of only 13 percent.

The secretary's key position within the political hierarchy is not permanently ensured, however. Inadequate qualification or inattention to his duties, not to mention illegal activities, are grounds for the secretary's removal. The party replaced more than one third of the secretaries of *kray* and *oblast* party committees in 1961 in the Russian Republic for being "weak" and for lacking proper education or specialist training.[16] The local secretary may also be removed for supporting the losing side in a power struggle in which he may be involved, even though indirectly. If, however, the secretary is clever, hardworking, faithful to the party line, and enjoying a certain amount of luck, he may continue for a long time as an important member of the nationwide ruling group.

In addition to the secretaries of the Central Committee, CPSU who serve on the ruling Politburo, a number of regional secretaries are elected to the national and regional legislatures. In the 1958 election for the Supreme Soviet, there were 153 governmental units represented from which deputies were elected (such as republics, cities, *oblasty*). In 134 of these units, the first secretary of the respective unit was among those deputies elected. This is illustrated for 1958 and succeeding elections by the following table:[17]

FIRST SECRETARIES OF REGIONAL-LOCAL PARTY COMMITTEES
ELECTED TO SUPREME SOVIET USSR

	Regional-Local Governmental Units	Regional-Local Units Electing the First Secretary of Their Respective Party Committees	Percentage of Governmental Units Represented by their First Secretaries
1958 election.....	145	139	95.8
1962 election.....	141	129	91.4
1966 election.....	144	135	93.0

The party secretary is a very important member of the nationwide ruling apparatus. At the topmost level is the General Secretary of the CPSU (First Secretary during Khrushchev's time), the single most powerful

[15] M. Polekhin and F. Yakovlev, "O nekotorykh voprosakh organizationnopartiynoy raboty," *Partiynaya Zhizn*, No. 13 (July, 1960), p. 13.

[16] G. Voronov in *Pravda*, October 21, 1961.

[17] Compiled from *Pravda*, March 29, 1958; *Izvestiya*, March 21, 1962; *Pravda*, June 15, 1966.

leader in the Soviet system. Assisting him are his lieutenants, the national secretaries of the Communist Party, CPSU (numbering ten at the Twenty-third Congress, five of whom are on the Politburo). Also important are the first secretaries of the union republics and of other large cities, territories, and districts. On each level in the hierarchy of the Soviet political system from top to bottom, in fact, the key official is the party first secretary.

Lenin guided and directed the Politburo, while Stalin (the party's first General Secretary) dominated it and subjected it to his arbitrary control. The most well-known party secretary since Stalin was First Secretary Khrushchev. A brief look into certain features of his secretaryship can serve to highlight leadership problems and challenges for the party secretaries.

Khrushchev in his period of rule from 1955 to October, 1964, attempted to revitalize party leadership and imbue it with a high degree of popularity, while at the same time he seriously (and quite vigorously, if not very successfully) attacked the nation's main problems. He had the party rules changed in 1961 (this change was canceled in 1966) to provide for a regular turnover of all party leaders so that new blood would be constantly forced into the leadership circles. He drastically reorganized party, governmental, and economic structures (many of these changes also were later voided) and repeatedly attempted novel approaches, both in domestic and foreign policies. His ruling techniques and policies often were highly innovative. Khrushchev's play for popularity saw higher quantity and quality of consumer goods, better housing, and generally improved living standards. In his own view he was the people's choice, and he acted somewhat in the stereotyped fashion of an American political leader. After an abortive *coup* in 1957, Khrushchev finally was forced out of his leadership position in 1964 as a result of pressures that had been building for some time.

Many of Khrushchev's policies failed to achieve any measurable degree of success: the Cuban missile crisis, the attempts to hold together the Soviet East European empire, domestic programs such as the Virgin Lands agricultural scheme, the creation of the *sovnarkhoz* system, and the drastic party reorganization in 1962. More importantly for our purposes, though, is an analysis of the leadership techniques which contributed to his downfall. Perhaps Khrushchev's policy failures would have been swallowed by his cohorts had he not violated a number of rule making customs, theoretical and procedural.[18]

---

[18] Excellent discussions on Khrushchev's leadership and causes for his downfall can be found in R. Lowenthal, "The Revolution Withers Away," and Merle Fainsod, "Khrushchevism in Retrospect," *Problems of Communism*, January–February, 1965; Z. Brzenzinski, "The Soviet Political System," *Problems of Communism*, January–February, 1966. *The New York Times* of October 24, 1964, purports to give, according to "reliable sources," a blow-by-blow account of Khrushchev's demise.

The Soviet regime, after Khrushchev's downfall, accused him, among other shortcomings, of subjectivism, "drift," infatuation with unworkable plans, hasty and unrealistic schemes, bragging, unwillingness to rely on practical and scientific experience, bad manners and rudeness, bourgeois sociology as opposed to historical determinism, and "voluntarism."[19] At least as important, if not more so, in Khrushchev's demise, were his one-man attacks against the established rule making procedures. In his change in the party rules in 1961 he forced some of the party *apparatchik* out of their positions, and he weakened unity of the apparatus as a whole when he split the regional and local party organizations into two groups in 1962. Most serious, as far as his own fate was concerned, he abused the Central Committee's oligarchical redoubt, the Presidium. To meetings of this select, inner body, he invited on occasion non-Presidium members, even some regional party officials. Khrushchev attempted to use the Presidium as his personal executive organ instead of respecting it as the policy-making body, and when the Presidium opposed his policies (or when he thought they would), he took to the hustings, by speeches, comments, and published notes. He fought the Presidium—as an institution—and it reacted to save itself. Against Khrushchev was aligned the "common front of the oligarchy in defense of institutional procedures."[20] When circumstances frowned on him, he attempted ever-new innovations, and when other party officials opposed him, he fought the party—its leaders and *apparatchiki* and its organizations. Not possessing the reputation and charismatic leadership qualities of Lenin nor the personal dictatorial power of Stalin, Khrushchev failed increasingly to hold his position against his opponents, who had strength of numbers, determination of motives, and the organization of the apparatus. Ironically, Khrushchev earlier was the one who restored the party to its former position of preeminence by discrediting Stalin's arbitrary emasculation of party rule, downgrading the police apparatus and eliminating its power to challenge the party; in his battle for control with Malenkov, he raised the party as an institution over that of the governmental-economic bureaucracy. After having restored the party to its former position of supremacy over Soviet society, he was first checkmated, then overthrown, because he tried to rule outside of the restored party institutions and apparatus. He failed, in a way, to pay respect to the very institutions which he was instrumental in strengthening.

It is popular to portray Khrushchev (and maybe not too inaccurately at that) as a transitional figure standing between Stalin's harsh dictator-

---

[19] *Pravda*, October 17, 1964; editorial in *Partiynaya Zhizn*, No. 20 (October, 1964), pp. 3–7; *Politicheskoye Samoobrazovaniye*, No. 1 (1966), pp. 89–91.

[20] Lowenthal, *op. cit.*, p. 14.

ship and a more enlightened oligarchy or, as the Russians depict it, "collective leadership." If he was, as Horowitz suggests, the "interim pope" between Soviet totalitarianism and Soviet authoritarianism,[21] his uneasy tenure resulted in a certain transformation of the ruling mode within the Soviet political system. Khrushchev "de-Stalinized" the system of most of the harsh features of totalitarianism and thereby made life easier and more pleasant than was the situation under Stalin. Khrushchev raised the party's position in Soviet society in line with Leninist theory and Leninist practice. As a result of this increase in party power, he paved the way for the growth (even against his will) of regularity in decision making which, in turn, bred both expectation of and appreciation for established rule making institutions among his colleagues.

Most significantly, perhaps, Khrushchev contributed to a rapid increase in desires for satisfaction of popular demands. His tenure saw a more open articulation of demands ranging from artistic and literary freedoms to a greater abundance of consumer goods. Khrushchev aided, even incited (at times aggregated) such popular demands as those for a more rational bureaucracy and for fewer police and governmental restrictions on citizen's lives. That many Soviet citizens more and more are demanding the abundant life—now—is in part attributable to Khrushchev unleashing these demands, by implying that communist abundance is right around the corner and by increasing the available quantities of consumer goods. As for his own rule, Khrushchev promised the Soviet people much more than he was able to deliver. For the process of rule making in the Soviet political system, Khrushchev's successors are faced with certain restrictions on the decision-making process—confining it within the established policy-making organs of the party and executing those decisions through regular party and government channels. The successors also must face the fact that personal, arbitrary whims of ruling (Cult of Personality) have been widely discredited within the system. Finally, Khrushchev's successors may be obliged to increase even more the satisfaction of popular demands, thereby limiting their options in the choice of alternative policies in the realm of economic investment. The dictatorship of Khrushchev was not nearly so severe as that of Stalin's; Khrushchev's successors may be forced into continuing to moderate even further the arbitrary and remaining dictatorial features of the Soviet political system.

———————

[21] Irving Louis Horowitz, *Three Worlds of Development* (New York: Oxford University Press, 1966), p. 156. For Linden, Khrushchev was on the reforming end of the political spectrum. Carl A. Linden, *Khrushchev and the Soviet Leadership, 1957–1964* (Baltimore: Johns Hopkins Press, 1966), p. 21.

TRAINING THE FUTURE ELITE

Current rule makers must provide for future rule makers to ensure the continuance of a viable and successful system. Soviet leaders devote an unusually high degree of energy and resources to this task, partly because the Communist Party handles a great deal of political socialization and all of the political recruitment for Soviet society.

Political recruitment is the function by which a political system renews itself and provides for young, energetic candidates to be groomed for future leadership roles. Recruitment in the USSR, in all its phases, is guided and directed by the elite of the Communist Party. This elite leaves very little to chance in what is one of the most serious functions of the leadership group of any communist system. The Soviet Union, of course, (as well as other communist states) is governed under a firm dictatorship of the Communist Party. Its leaders fully intend to keep it that way by prescribing the particular format and rules for political recruitment. Thus, at the Twenty-second Congress of the CPSU in 1961 the Communist Party's First Secretary, Khrushchev, had the party rules changed to provide for a regular turnover (at least one fourth of the members of the leading organs, from the Central Committee Presidium down, were to be changed at each regular election of the party). Khrushchev's belief was that this practice would invigorate leadership circles with a regular supply of new talent. The post-Khrushchev leadership abandoned this rule at the Twenty-third Congress in 1966.

Political recruitment into the leading echelons of the Communist Party is highly mobile for energetic, capable, experienced, and, above all, loyal Communist Party members. While any party member can seek high political office, the post-Stalin tendency has been to stress competence on top of a certain minimum level of education.

The process of political recruitment is fairly open, and successful candidates rise through a number of assignments, functional and regional, to successively more responsible positions. Perhaps they begin with a local district secretaryship, passing through the district and republic levels, possibly to an important position in the capitol. Although mobility upward through party leadership positions have several alternatives, similar to other occupations of importance in the Soviet Union, one of the most widely used channels is that of industrial management. This results in part from official emphasis on industrialization, and heavy industry at that, beginning with the origins of the Soviet Union. Without excluding the intelligentsia, the military, or agricultural channels, the party offices which have had some contact with and responsibility for industry, such as the first secretary of an important province, city, or district, provide greater opportunity for upward mobility within the leadership hierarchy. The other main channels for political recruitment, apart from strategic positions within the Communist Party itself, are government jobs and the economic, managerial bureaucracy.

Political recruitment in the USSR has successfully replenished the leadership ranks. Moreover, this recruitment over the years has helped retain the basic features of the Soviet political system. For the continuance of a socialist-communist framework, for keeping Communist Party dominance of the ruling and governing apparatus, and for the further development of economic planning as well as state and collective operation of agriculture, for all of these functions political recruitment meets the requirements as prescribed by the Soviet regime. In the five-year period (1961–66) between the last two party congresses, 32,300 party and governmental officials were trained in special party and government schools.[22] Much of the regime's attention in training is concentrated on the Communist youth organizations, chiefly the All-Union Leninist Communist League of Youth—the *Komsomol*. There are other party-sponsored youth organizations, the Octobrists (up to age 9) and the Young Pioneers (ages 9 through 14). It is the *Komsomol*, however, which throughout Soviet history has been the main instrument of party indoctrination and political recruitment of Soviet youth.

From its origin in 1918 the *Komsomol* has been influenced, guided, and controlled by the Communist Party. The party rules state, in fact, that the *Komsomol* conducts its activities under the guidance of the party. This interweaving of the two organizations by way of the *Komsomol* leadership only testifies to the main purpose of the youth organizations in the Soviet Union—the promotion of the interests of the party. In this way, the *Komsomol* serves as a pre-party, training and recruitment organization among youth.

The organization of the *Komsomol* is patterned after that of the Communist Party. At the top is a guiding central committee elected by a congress; the committee is directly subordinate to the Central Committee, CPSU. The *Komsomol* Central Committee in turn elects a Central Auditing Commission, a Secretariat, and a guiding Bureau with a first secretary at its head. The current First Secretary (S. P. Pavlov), reelected in 1966, has served in the post since 1959, is 36 years old and is a regular member of the Central Committee, CPSU. These facts further testify to the importance which the party attaches to the *Komsomol* and to the

---

[22] *Pravda*, March 30, 1966.

rigorous party control over that organization. At the union republic level (with the exception of the RSFSR), there also are congresses and central committees. On the local level conferences or general meetings elect guiding committees or bureaus. Finally, there are primary organizations of the *Komsomol* in factories, schools, and other institutions; there were 348,000 such organizations in 1966.[23] Each unit, from the topmost to that on the bottom rung, is headed by its appropriate first secretary.

Membership in the *Komsomol*, open to young people from age 14 to 28, with some exceptions,[24] has grown from a relatively few thousand to a figure which in 1966 totaled 23 million. Soviet figures covering a 40-year period are given in the following table.

Komsomol MEMBERSHIP[25]

1918	1927	1937	1947	1957	1963	1966
22,100.	2,089,951	4,282,309	7,700,951	18,347,499	ca.20,000,000	23,000,000

The figure in the table above for the year 1957 represents probably less than one half of the eligible youth at that time.[26] Since its birth in 1918, there have been more than 90 million *Komsomol* members.[27] A partial breakdown of the 3,821 elected delegates to the Fifteenth Congress of the *Komsomol* in 1966 is given below. In addition 2,306 delegates (58.5 percent) were members or candidate members of the Communist Party, 666 of whom are elected members of higher party organs.[28]

Workers (manual)	735
Collective and state farmers, agricultural specialists	789
Students of educational and teaching institutions	263
Workers from constitutional organizations	177
Foremen and brigadiers of industry, construction, and transportation	112
Shop chiefs and heads of shifts	202
Chairmen of collective farms and directors of state farms	35
Brigade leaders and managers of agricultural sections	132
Representatives of science	108
Department of national, regional, or local legislatures	524

---

[23] *Izvestiya*, May 18, 1966.

[24] If elected to a position of leadership in one of its organs, a *Komsomol* member may stay in the organization beyond the age of 28. *Ustav Vsesouznogo Leninskogo Kommunisticheskogo Souza Molodezhi* (Moscow: Tsk VLKSM, 1959), pp. 6–7.

[25] *Partiynaya Zhizn*, No. 20 (October, 1957), p. 95; *Pravda*, November 20, 1962; *Izvestiya*, May 18, 1966. Apart from the *Komsomol*, there are more than 20 million Pioneers (ages 10–14) and more than 14.5 million Octobrists (ages 7–9). See Allen Kassof, *The Soviet Youth Program, Regimentation and Rebellion* (Cambridge, Mass.: Harvard University Press, 1965), p. 1.

[26] The 1959 census lists more than 35 million in the age group, 16 to 24, inclusive. If one can estimate 3 million youths in each year of the age group 14 to 26 for 1957, in addition to those *Komsomol* members in the overage (above 26) category, the figure of 18 million plus may represent less than 40 percent of the eligible youth who are *Komsomol* members. For census breakdowns, see *Narodnoe Khozyaystvo SSSR v 1959*

In fulfillment of their task as a party support organization, *Komsomol* members have suffered along with regular party members the misfortunes and hardships which accompanied communism's growth in the Soviet Union. Through the uncertainties of the NEP period and the harsh and bitter experiences of forced industrialization, and the general deprivations of collectivization, the *Komsomol* members were required to sacrifice along with the general populace. Even the Great Purge reached down into the ranks of the *Komsomol* organization to eliminate a number of its leaders and members. As with party members, however, successful *Komsomol* leaders may well anticipate the rewards which come to those party members in the leadership circle.

Party rules assign to the *Komsomol* the role of active helper and future manpower reserve of the party. Furthermore, the organization is responsible for educating the nation's youth in the spirit of communism, with responsibility for indoctrination and supervision of the Young Pioneers, including the election of *Komsomol* senior classmen to councils of Pioneer units.[29] The *Komsomol* is to draw young people into the work of building their society and to train a rising generation for positions of leadership. In pursuit of these tasks, the *Komsomol* Press in 1966 published 132 newspapers and almost 70 youth journals.[30] Per-issue circulation of these youth newspapers and magazines is more than 47 million.[31] The purposes of this flood of party propaganda are to develop in young people a deep conviction in the creative ideals of communism and conscientious and creative attitudes toward labor and the public interest, as well as to oppose slackness, mismanagement, hostile ideology, demagoguery, hooliganism, and drunkenness.[32] The *Komsomol* is instrumental in the political socialization process.

Perhaps the most important continuing problem facing the *Komsomol* is that of maintaining the interest of youth in *Komsomol* and party activities. What is difficult under optimum conditions—capturing and holding youthful excitement and enthusiasm—no doubt is far from easy when all that may be offered young people in a tangible way is the opportunity to

---

Godu (Moscow: Gosstatizdat, 1960), p. 11. General Secretary Breznev complained at the Twenty-Third Party Congress that out of 2.5 million communists under age 30 only 270,000 work in the *Komsomol*. *Pravda*, March 30, 1966.

[27] *Pravda*, May 18, 1966.

[28] *Izvestiya*, May 20, 1966.

[29] *Komsomolskaya Pravda*, February 5, 1967.

[30] *Partiynaya Zhizn*, No. 9 (May, 1966), p. 17.

[31] In addition, the youth press publishes 32 million copies of books each year. *Komsomolskaya Pravda*, May 18, 1966.

[32] *Pravda*, June 16, 1965.

sacrifice in the building of a rather vague and indeterminate goal, that of "socialist construction," or a "communist society." Still another problem is that the type of young person who becomes an activist in the *Komsomol* often tends to be either the self-seeking, or the rather dull, conformist.

The *Komsomol* over the years, it must be assumed, has been rather successful in helping the party fight its wars, train its citizens, and build its communist system. If, in fact, the *Komsomol* succeeded in accomplishing only one task, that of serving as an indoctrination school for future party members, it would be considered worthwhile by the party's leadership.[33] From the viewpoint of the individual who participates in the movement, rewards for faithful *Komsomol* membership, apart from satisfaction of youthful *élan*, are those offered for membership in the parent Communist Party. These include a chance to help build a communist society and an opportunity to share in political power which accompany select party jobs in the Soviet Union.

---

[33] Fainsod states that the Communist Party membership is made up overwhelmingly of people who earlier had been in the Young Pioneer and the *Komsomol* groups. See Fainsod, *op. cit.*, p. 240.

CHAPTER VII

Organization and Membership

THE ORGANIZATIONAL FORMAT which the Soviet Communist Party was to assume became for Lenin at the turn of the century a problem of the utmost significance. The precise structure of the party, its orientation and its goals, even the degree of discipline and loyalty shared by the members, in Lenin's view, would spell victory or defeat for communism in Russia. At one and the same time Lenin thought the ideal party should reflect a small, hard-core, disciplined group of fellow conspirators in revolution making, but more than that it should be an instrument of large enough proportions and influence to lead the workers, educate the masses, and transform society. In his pamphlet, *What Is to Be Done*, written just prior to the Second Congress of the RSDLP in 1903, Lenin described this party: "A small, compact core, consisting of reliable, experienced and hardened workers, with responsible agents in the principal districts and connected by all the rule of strict secrecy with the organizations of revolutionaries...that the organization must consist chiefly of persons engaged in revolutionary activities as a profession..."[1] The assignment for the party, then, would be to organize and carry out a revolution against the Tsar, to assume political power in the name of the working class, to govern a large nation, and to usher in the Marxist system.

To meet these diverse and exacting requirements, Lenin first of all fought for control of the new RSDLP. At its Second Congress, held in Brussels and London in 1903, Lenin advocated restricting party membership to dedicated, professional revolutionists who would devote their whole energies to carrying out instructions of the party leadership. Temporarily in the majority at one point in the proceeding of the Congress, Lenin and his supporters assumed the mantle of "majorityites" (Bolshe-

---

[1] V. I. Lenin, *Selected Works*, ed. J. Fineberg (New York: International Publishers, 1938), Vol. 2, pp. 133, 139.

viks), while his opponents became known as "minorityites" (Mensheviks).
The two groups constituted rival factions within the RSDLP, fighting, for
the moment, over control of the party's journal, *Iskra*. Lenin won this
first battle, although it was to be some years later before the Bolsheviks
became clearly the dominant force within the RSDLP. In arranging for a
Third Congress of the party (held in 1905) Lenin narrowed his focus on
definite qualifications which would be required of party members. These
qualifications were those now found in the developing Bolshevik faction
of the RSDLP. They included disciplined, professional committeemen
grouped around a band of conspirators—all linked by personal allegiance
to their chief, Lenin. They would follow Lenin's leadership no matter how
adventurous so long as his leadership appeared sufficiently radical and
extreme.[2]

The party after the Revolution was to evolve under Lenin's insistent
and ever-present guidance into a tightly organized, homogeneous leadership clique—to be, in brief, the conscience of the revolutionary "spirit"
and the advance guard of the worker's movement. Goals, policy, strategy,
and tactics all were to emanate from the party leadership. The main
followers were the workers, peasants, soldiers, and sailors. The Leninist
party became far more than an elite of professional revolutionists, however.
It became an instrument for elite leadership of the masses, an educational-
training medium to teach the people about communism; it was to be both
the vanguard and the conscience for Soviet society.

CENTRAL ORGANIZATION

In establishing what was to become a dictatorship of the party, although
in the name of the proletariat, the emphasis first was on organization. To
achieve all that Lenin hoped for through such a party, it was necessary to
so structure the apparatus—particularly its central organization—that
both the timeless "will" as well as the daily instructions of its leadership
would flow smoothly downward, being accepted immediately and implemented thoroughly at all lower levels. To a rather surprising degree,
Lenin and his collaborators were successful in laying the foundation for
just such a centralized party.

The Party Congress

Party congresses, to be held at least once every four years, are referred
to in the party rules as the "supreme organ" of the Communist Party

---

[2] Leonard Schapiro, *The Communist Party of the Soviet Union* (New York: Random
House, Inc., 1960), p. 61.

(CPSU). Counting from the first, organizing "meeting" of the RSDLP in 1898, there have been 23 party congresses up to 1967. Six congresses were held prior to the Revolution. From 1918 through 1925 eight congresses were held—one a year. Only three congresses were held in the 1930's, none in the 1940's, three in the 1950's, and two in the 1960's, the most recent (the Twenty-third) in 1966.

Prior to Stalin's rise to full dictatorial power, party congresses were held more frequently; more often than not they were occasions for debate and resolution of high party matters concerning both leadership and policy. Even the Fourteenth Congress, as late as 1925, although controlled in its final decisions by Stalin, nevertheless saw an attempt by the opposition to oppose Stalin's growing domination of the party and government. After this last flurry of open opposition to Stalin, congresses were fewer, none being held from 1939 to 1952; they were decidedly less important too, and given over simply to ratifying the programs and plans of Stalin and his supporters. Party congresses since Stalin's death in 1953, if not exercising much in the way of independent authority, at least have been convened more regularly and have been the forum for launching most major policy decisions of the regime, both foreign and domestic.

Congresses are made up of elected delegates according to a ratio set by the Central Committee of the party. In both 1952 and 1956, at the Nineteenth and the Twentieth Congresses, one voting delegate represented 5,000 party members, and one nonvoting delegate represented 5,000 candidate members. At the Twenty-first Congress in 1959 the delegate representation was approximately one delegate per 6,000 party members; at the Twenty-second Congress the representation was one delegate per 2,000 members and at the Twenty-third Congress it was one delegate per 2,500 members. Although delegates formally are elected to the Congresses, Stalin and his collaborators prearranged much of the selecting process to achieve representation favorable to their side. In the absence of contrary information, we can assume this has been the procedure followed by Stalin's successors.

Who are the elected delegates to the Communist Party's "supreme organ"? The table below gives a partial breakdown of the delegates who were elected to the Twenty-third Congress, by occupation, sex, age, and years of party membership.[3]

---

[3] Compiled from *Pravda*, April 1, 1966. The categories in the occupational breakdown are not mutually exclusive because the categories listed in the original source number eleven, with total delegates adding up to 7,951.

DELEGATES TO THE TWENTY-THIRD CONGRESS OF THE CPSU

	Number of Delegates	*Percent of Total Delegates*
Total delegates....................	4,943	100
Occupational groups (estimated)		
Workers in industry, construction,		
transport, communications.....	1,577	31.9
Engineers, economists, technicians.	1,484	30.0
Party secretaries................	1,204	24.3
Other........................	678	13.7
Women delegates...................	1,154	23.3
Age of delegates:		
Up to age 30...................		8.0
31–40...................		32.2
41–50...................		34.3
51–60...................		21.7
61–		3.8
Period in which delegates joined the Party:		
Pre-Revolutionary..............		18 delegates
1917–30......................		4.8
1931–40......................		15.5
1941–45......................		24.7
1946–55......................		24.2
1956–		30.4

The congress elects a Central Auditing Commission for the purpose of management supervision of those business activities undertaken by the party's central bodies. The Commission also audits the accounts of the party treasury and of the various enterprises which serve directly the Central Committee. More important among the tasks of the congress, however, is electing a smaller, guiding Central Committee.

The Central Committee and Its Apparatus

At the first meeting of the RSDLP in 1898 there was elected a guiding Central Committee of three. It was short-lived, though, with two of its members quickly being arrested. At the Second Congress another Central Committee of three was elected, all three being loyal to Lenin during the early Bolshevik-Menshevik controversy. Although the end of 1903 saw a nine-member, Bolshevik dominated Central Committee, this Committee refused to follow all of Lenin's desires and, late in 1904, actually expelled Lenin from that body. The Third Congress in 1905 elected an all-Bolshevik Central Committee which became a focus within the party for a power struggle between the party's two main factions—Bolshevik and Menshevik. The Sixth Congress, meeting in the summer of 1917, elected an enlarged Central Committee (22 full members), most but not all of whom were controlled by Lenin. The Congress prescribed regular meetings of the

Committee (at least once each two months), and established smaller guiding organizations of the Central Committee—a Secretariat and a Political Bureau. Henceforth, both the organizational makeup of and dominance over the Central Committee were to be key questions over which contestants for power were to battle throughout Soviet history.

In the early 1920's the Central Committee was authorized an administrative apparatus which included a number of departments through which the Committee could exercise control over all national activity. During this period the Committee succeeded in bringing under its close supervision local party organizations throughout the country. By early 1921 the staff of the Committee's apparatus numbered 602 people.[4] This large staff was to become, as the Central Committee's Secretariat, the body concerned with the party's daily management of the economic, cultural, military, and social life of the nation. The Leninist Central Committee, with its Political Bureau (Politburo), Organizational Bureau (Orgburo), and Secretariat were later perfected into an efficient bureaucratic hierarchy by Stalin for achieving and maintaining strict authoritarian control over both the government and lower party organs.

Overall responsibility for general control over the nation's political activity still remains in the Central Committee which, according to party rules, calls congresses of the party and appoints its Politburo, Secretariat, special bureaus, and committees.

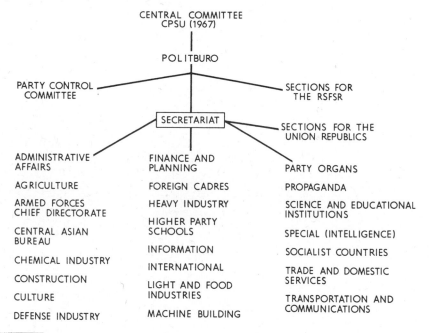

4 Schapiro, *op. cit.*, p. 246.

In the reorganization of the Central Committee in 1966, the Bureau for the RSFSR was abolished, and several minor changes were carried out. According to the rules, the Central Committee between party congresses directs all party activity, central and local, selects and places leading personnel of the party, directs the work of central state and public organizations of workers within their party groups, establishes various organs of the party and guides their work, designates editors of newspapers and journals working under its jurisdiction, and watches over expenditures from the party budget.

Policy guidelines set by the Central Committee usually are announced in its periodic plenary sessions which are held, supposedly, at least every six months. When in plenary session, the Committee assumes the function of discussing the "construction" and the "activities" of Soviet state organs.[5] Of the several organs which make up the Central Committee, the Politburo ranks as the most important. Comparing the legal powers of the Central Committee with its more perfunctory activities as seen in many of its plenary sessions, one can safely conclude that the Politburo and the Secretariat *in fact* exercise the real powers in the *name* of the Central Committee.

Politburo

The Politburo was first organized in 1917 to deal only with urgent measures; the original Politburo included Lenin, Trotsky, Kamenov, Zinoviev, Stalin, Bubnov, and Sokolnikov. Inactive from its origin, the Politburo was reconstituted and given new vitality in 1919. From then on it became, under the regimes of Lenin and Stalin, the single most influential power center within the Soviet political structure.

According to Khrushchev, the Politburo during Lenin's leadership was an instrument embodying majority rule and deciding important policy matters.[6] The Politburo, however, soon overshadowed even its parent— the Central Committee. Between April and November, 1919, for example, the Central Committee met 6 times (it was supposed to meet at least 16 times in that period) whereas the Politburo held 29 separate and 19 joint meetings (with the Orgburo).[7]

---

[5] A. I. Denisov and M. G. Kirichenko, *Sovetskoe Gosudarstvennoe Pravo* (Moscow: Gosurizdat, 1957), p. 157.

[6] From Khrushchev's secret speech to the Twentieth Party Congress. See Leo Gruliow (ed.), *Current Soviet Policies, II* (New York: Frederick A. Praeger, Inc., 1957), p. 175.

[7] Schapiro, *op. cit.*, p. 240.

In the years following Lenin's death the Politburo became an organization through which (along with the Orgburo and the Secretariat) Stalin's grab of absolute power was made easier. Although in the first post-Lenin years Stalin had difficulty in maintaining a sympathetic majority of the Politburo members, in time that body became completely dominated by Stalin; it was used by him to get official endorsement for most of his actions, both regular and arbitrary. In 1925 Stalin referred to the Politburo as "sovereign" and as being superior to all other organs of the Central Committee, except that of the Central Committee Plenum itself.[8] This Politburo under Stalin was divided into subcommittees, such as those for foreign affairs under Molotov, heavy industry under Kaganovich and trade under Mikoyan. In this division of responsibilities, each specialist acted as "a court of first instance" on those problems falling within his area of specialty. At regular Politburo meetings outside experts would be called in to give testimony on current problems.[9]

The membership of the Politburo during its first period of existence from 1917–52 ranged from a low of 5 full voting members (1919–21) to a high of 15 (1948). As for nonvoting, or candidate, members, there were none in the period 1917–19, only 2 during 1932 and 1938–41, and as many as 8 in 1926 and 1927–29.

As a decision-making body under Lenin and Stalin, the Politburo normally was guided by majority vote; this involved at least the concept of collective rule, even though in fact it was frequently influenced, if not dominated, first by Lenin, then by Stalin. At the peak of his rule, however, Stalin frequently disregarded the Politburo, calling it into session "only occasionally," according to Khrushchev. In other problem areas which by rule and custom were within the province of Politburo decision making, Stalin often ruled independently of that body.[10]

At the Nineteenth Party Congress in 1952 the Politburo (along with its junior partner the Orgburo) was abolished and in its place a larger Presidium (25 full and 10 candidate members) of the Central Committee was created. All of the full members of the old Politburo of late 1952 except 2 (Andreev and Kosygin) were reelected to the new Presidium. One reason given by Khrushchev for the changeover was that by this maneuver, Stalin evidently planned to get rid of the old Politburo members and replace them with newer supporters who would "extol" him in all ways.[11]

[8] J. Stalin, *Political Report of the Central Committee to the Fourteenth Congress of the C.P.S.U.(B)* (Moscow: Foreign Languages Publishing House, 1950), p. 170.

[9] Merle Fainsod, *How Russia Is Ruled* (Cambridge, Mass.: Harvard University Press, 1953), p. 282.

[10] Gruliow, *op. cit.*, pp. 176, 183, 187.

[11] *Ibid.*, p. 187.

In addition, there was set up at this same time a smaller, inner Bureau of the Presidium, composed probably of old Politburo members. In any event this Bureau of the Presidium was abolished five months later upon Stalin's death. The Presidium inherited all of the same high policy-making functions long enjoyed by the Politburo.

Khrushchev has referred to the Presidium as the executive organ of the Central Committee which introduces questions regarding party interests for the consideration of the Committee. Presidium meetings took place at least once a week and policy questions were settled by majority vote. Although disagreements were permitted, according to Khrushchev, decisions of the body usually were unanimous.[12] If a deadlock in the Presidium discussions occurred, another Presidium member has stated, the session was interrupted and by the next day a consensus was usually forthcoming.[13]

In June, 1957, a leadership crisis broke out in the Presidium when three of its members (Molotov, Malenkov, Kaganovich) led a move to unseat Khrushchev from his dominant position within the party and governmental hierarchy. The immediate crisis was precipitated six months earlier, however. By late 1956 Khrushchev, like Stalin before him in the 1920's, was having difficulty in holding together a working majority in the Presidium to support his programs. Continuing through the first half of 1957, the leadership struggle between the pro-Khrushchev and anti-Khrushchev forces came to the surface intermittently in Presidium sessions, in plenary meetings of the Central Committee, in the higher echelons of the governmental bureaucracy and in various party circles throughout the country. At the June, 1957, Presidium session, when two of Khrushchev's supporters on the Presidium were out of Moscow, the anti-Khrushchev forces proposed the removal of Khrushchev from his position as First Secretary of the party. At the voting on the question, a majority voted against Khrushchev. Instead of resigning his office, as his opponents no doubt expected, Khrushchev argued that his appointment as First Secretary came not from the membership of the Presidium, but from the whole Central Committee meeting in plenary session. Moreover, the Presidium session, which extended over a two-day period, was presented on the second day with a petition signed by 70 of the 133 regular members of the Khrushchev-dominated Central Committee; it demanded a plenary meeting of the latter body to resolve the crisis. A plenary meeting was held which then supported Khrushchev and voted his opponents out of the Presidium.

---

[12] *Pravda*, November 19, 1957; *New York Times*, July 5, 1956; May 11, 1957.
[13] According to Mikoyan, *New York Times*, June 14, 1957.

Khrushchev's relationship to the Presidium and Central Committee in 1957 could be compared with that of Stalin's in the late 1920's. In both cases, their positions were somewhat precarious, although they both won the final battles against their opposition. Even though the old Politburo made policy decisions in the 1920's (as was the case with the Presidium), controversial questions relating to power struggles were carried over to plenary meetings of the Central Committee chiefly because Stalin more often than not lacked a clear majority in the Politburo.[14]

At the June, 1957, Central Committee Plenum which fully endorsed Khrushchev, the revised Presidium, now minus the ringleaders of the anti-Khrushchev faction, was enlarged from 11 full and 7 candidate members to 15 full and 9 candidates. In the new Presidium those who held additional positions in the Secretariat (8 members) gained more influence. Not since early 1953 had all party secretaries simultaneously been voting members of the Presidium. By 1958, the number of full Presidium members was 14 and candidate members, 9. This number held steady up to the Twenty-second Congress in 1961, when the number was changed to 11 full and 5 candidate members. Between 1926–47 full members of the Politburo had averaged 11. These figures point out that, with a few exceptions based on unusual circumstances (such as in the death of Stalin), Soviet leaders have discovered that a working decision-making body as expressed in the Politburo-Presidium of from 10 to 15 members is of optimum size.

At the Twenty-third Congress in 1966 the name of Presidium was changed back to Politburo, which seemed more of an appropriate term in light of what the body does, according to General Secretary Brezhnev. This was the only notable change in the Party's highest decision-making body, however. The new 1966 Politburo was, with a very few changes in membership, almost identical with the Presidium of October, 1964. The numbers were similar, too, with the 1964 Presidium having 11 regular and 6 candidate members on it, and the Politburo of 1966 having 11 regular and 8 candidate members.

Secretariat

At the time the Orgburo and the reconstituted Politburo were established in 1919 there was also created within the Central Committee a personnel office for party cadres—the Secretariat. At first the Secretariat acted as a screening board for policy matters taken up by the Politburo and

---

[14] Schapiro, *op. cit.*, p. 314.

Orgburo. Even in its personnel function, though, the Secretariat was intended to be only an arm of the Orgburo. From that time on, the Orgburo, Politburo, Central Control Commission, and especially the Secretariat became more centralized (local control commissions, for example, were now more closely subordinated to the Central Control Commission) and were brought more under the omnipresent influence of Stalin. When he was made general secretary of the party in 1922 Stalin, by this time, was dominant in the Orgburo, the Central Control Commission, and the Secretariat. From 1922 until mid-1930's Stalin enlarged and restructured the Secretariat and its mushrooming apparatus so that all activity within the Soviet Union, be it industrial, agricultural, cultural, or whatever would fall at least indirectly under the supervision of one of the divisions of the party's Secretariat.[15]

By 1962 the Secretariat constituted a large administrative suborganization of the Central Committee. There are a number of departments (*otdely*) of the Secretariat broadly categorized by (1) administrative function (for example, the Administrative Affairs Department), (2) economic (such as Construction), (3) special functions relating to the party's overall mission (Propaganda) and (4) those activities concerned with the union republics. Membership on the Secretariat throughout its history has included simple functionaries; it has included also some of the party's most noted leaders. In 1961 all five of the secretaries, headed by Khrushchev, were national leaders and all were regular members of the Presidium. As of 1962, however, only four of the nine secretaries were regular Presidium members. By mid-1966, four of the eleven secretaries were regular Politburo members.

Other Central Organs

The Central Control Commission since the 1920's has had jurisdiction over local control commissions—the latter are responsible for investigating charges made against party members for indiscretions in their personal or public life. As one might anticipate from such an assignment as this, the control commissions usually were involved intimately in party squabbles and as a result were probably unable to conduct an objective, judicial-type investigation of any given conflict having national implications. In its use, or rather abuse, the Central Control Commission under Stalin's early reign became yet another device, like the Secretariat, for combating local resistance to central party direction and for enforcing central discipline on the local organs. An important Lenin-originated and Stalin-continued

---

[15] Fainsod, *op. cit.*, pp. 169–71.

decision-making apparatus in the 1920's was the joint Plenum of the Central Committee and the enlarged Central Control Commission.

The Central Control Commission went through two more internal reorganizations to become the Party Commission. Its assigned functions prior to the 1962 reorganization included watching over the discipline of party members and holding responsible all members who violate party programs, rules, and morals. The Commission also has served as an appeal board hearing discipline cases coming from lower party organs.

Some of the above activities were taken over by the joint Committee of Party-State Control established in 1962. This Committee was made subordinate both to the Central Committee and to the Council of Ministers. The purposes of the Control Committee were to maintain a regular check on the fulfillment of party and government directives, on production reserves, on measures to improve production and reduce costs. The Committee and its subordinate control committees on regional and local levels also guarded against such crimes as bribe-taking, embezzlement, and speculation.[16] In each of the union republics there was established a joint Committee of Party-State Control. In 1966 the Committee of Party-State Control was divided into a Committee of People's Control, under the Council of Ministers, to check on governmental decisions and regulations, and a Party Control Committee, under the Central Committee, to serve as the party's appellate and internal controlling organization, supervising party applications, acceptances, and exclusions and voiding party membership.

All of the union republics have a separate communist party with the exception of the Russian Republic. The latter's great size as well as its historical position of preeminence within the country make it a unique problem in party organization and control. The problem, if not solved, is at least managed by party activity in the Republic supervised directly through the national Central Committee.

The central organs of the Communist Party are aided and supported, in fact built upon, regional and local party bodies. The Soviet edifice rests to no small degree upon the successful organization and operation of its lower party structures.

REGIONAL PARTY ORGANIZATION

The second echelon of control and direction in the party structure, the union republic communist parties, follows very closely in organizational format the national party model. Thus, at the union republic level there is

---

[16] *Pravda*, November 20, 1962. Its assignment includes censuring party officials, for example, an institute director who violated discipline. "V Komitete Partiynogo Kontrolya pri TsK, KPSS," *Partiynaya Zhizn*, No. 6 (March, 1967), p. 41.

a party congress, legally the highest party organ in the republic. Ordinary congresses of the union republics are to be held once every two years; those union republics having *oblasty* (the RSFSR, Ukrainian, Belorussian, Kazakh, and Uzbek republics) may, if they so chose, hold a congress once every four years.

There are central committees of the union republics meeting in plenary session at least every four months, according to the rules. The inner, guiding body of a central committee is its bureau, composed of approximately a dozen members who are responsible for handling current work of the central committee and providing it with central direction. This bureau includes in its membership the secretaries of the republic's central committee. The organizational and operational format for these bureaus follows that of the Politburo of the Central Committee, CPSU. There are normal sections, such as those for propaganda and agitation, industry and transport, construction, trade and finance, and agriculture. Special sections of the committees may also be established to solve specific tasks. The Kazakh Central Committee, for example, organized a special Bureau for the Northern *Oblasty* which, in turn, has a Party Organs Section and an Agriculture Section. The Bureau is headed by one of the secretaries of the Kazakh Central Committee.[17]

Similar to the national model, in the regional party structure the key organs which exercise actual power are the small inner bodies, in this case the bureaus. The central committees and congresses serve the functions of ratifying and legalizing what the republic's party leaders, through their bureaus, decide. Regional party organs are the second echelon step in the party's hierarchical structure. They constitute, in a way, a rather important subadministrative layer for transmitting downward the programs, instructions, and orders of the central organs. The regional units do more, however; they watch over regional government, and they also closely guide and direct local party groups.

LOCAL PARTY ORGANIZATION

On the *kray* and *oblast* levels, the party conferences are the equivalent of the national and regional congresses. The conference elects a territorial or province committee (*kraykom* or *obkom*), an auditing commission, and other organizations as needed, including a small guiding bureau of not more than nine people. Again, as is the case with higher party units, the internal structure of the *kraykom* and *obkom* bureaus have subject-matter

---

[17] *Partiynaya Zhizn*, No. 16 (August, 1960), pp. 27–28.

sections for such functions as agriculture and local industry.

The 1962 reorganization provided for two distinct party committees (one for industry and one for agriculture) in each *kray* and *oblast*. After Khrushchev's removal in 1964, single party organizations were restored on all levels. And, despite these recurring organizational changes, there has been a remarkable stability among first secretaries of *oblast* party committees. This *oblast* level of party elite retains its basic characteristics of age of members, degree of education, even the familiar route to political power.[18]

On the city and district levels, party conferences are convened yearly (less frequently in a city with borough subdivisions) by the city committees (*gorkomy*) and district committees (*raykomy*). Meeting at least once every three months, according to the rules, *gorkomy* and *raykomy* elect their guiding bureaus of seven to nine members; these bureaus include the committee secretaries. One such bureau, meeting twice monthly, included in one day's agenda discussion of the March, 1965 Central Committee Plenum, admittance into the CPSU, confirmation of cadres and personnel matters.[19] *Raykomy* normally are divided into "instructional groups" for industry, construction, transport, schools, institutions, and local industry. In some cases, a *raykom* secretary directs the work of each instructional group. To improve party efficiency in the Tadzhik Republic all sections of the *gorkomy* and *raykomy* have been abolished. This has followed a nationwide trend in which *raykom* sections frequently have been abolished and replaced with party instructors. In some republics (Armenia, Belorussia, and parts of the RSFSR), however, *raykom* sections for agriculture and for propaganda-agitation were retained. In still other cases a few *gorkomy* and *raykomy* have been merged in the hope of gaining added efficiency, though this hope has not always been realized.[20]

The lowest level of the party pyramid, the primary party organizations (or cells), are established by *gorkomy* and *raykomy*. These organizations, in Soviet terminology, are the "basic" working units of the Communist Party. The primary organizations are formed at places where there are three or more party members—in factories, mills, state and collective farms, military units, villages, government offices, educational and cultural establishments. Primary organizations are required to meet monthly (a goal not always achieved) and to elect a guiding bureau—if the particular organization has at least fifteen members.

[18] See the discussion in Grey Hodnett, "The Obkom First Secretaries," *Slavic Review*, Vol. XXIV (December, 1965).

[19] "Buro raykoma," *Partiynaya Zhizn*, No. 2 (January, 1967), p. 36.

[20] "Selskiy raykom partii i ego apparat," *Partiynaya Zhizn*, No. 23 (December, 1957), pp. 4, 6; No. 13 (July, 1960), p. 10.

As of January, 1965 the number of primary party organizations in the nation were distributed as shown in the table below.[21]

	Number	Percent of Total
Enterprises of industry, transport, communications and construction................	77,838	25.0
State farms.............................	11,601	3.7
Collective farms........................	38,251	12.3
Trade and food enterprises...............	13,513	4.3
Educational and scientific institutions, hospitals, cultural-instructional institutions...	69,086	22.1
Economic organs and institutions, from central to local.......................	50,287	16.1
Others.................................	51,331	16.5
	311,907	100.0

Each party instructor in the local committees is assigned responsibility for supervising the operations of from 10 to 20 primary organizations.

Regional and local party organization, then, follows the format of the national party structure. There are congresses or conferences acting as representative "legislative" organs which, in turn, elect a committee. The committee, finally, selects a small, ruling bureau;

COMMUNIST PARTY ORGANIZATION
Central, Regional, Local

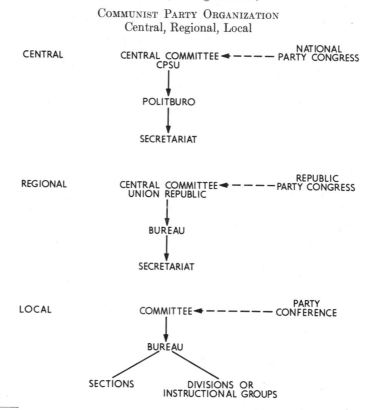

[21] "KPSS v tsifrakh, (1961–1964 godu)," *Partiynaya Zhizn*, No. 10 (May, 1965), p. 16.

the latter has its own apparatus resembling in microcosm the apparatus of the national Secretariat. Departures from the model do occur depending upon such factors as the size of the regional or local party organization, its location and its overall mission—such as economic or cultural.

The tasks of the bureau, in addition to leading the organization, are to assure that regular meetings of the organization are held, to present the most important topics of the day and to prepare for their discussion, and to "tactfully" listen to remarks and suggestions. The bureau also bears responsibility for assisting workers in learning good habits of administration and for educating people in the soul of communism.[22]

TRENDS IN REGIONAL AND LOCAL PARTY ORGANIZATION

As befits the Soviet administrative penchant there are almost periodic reorganizations of the party apparatus. Throughout Soviet history the leaders have attempted with varying degrees of success to resolve the complex yet obvious problem of dual control. On the one hand the governmental bureaucracy has been held responsible for administering the communist state system. Yet by the very nature of that system the party apparatus has been required to watch over all activity within the country—including that, and especially that, of the governmental bureaucracy. As a result, problems of overlapping and confused jurisdiction, duplicating functions of control, and contradictions in supervisorial areas between party and governmental bodies inevitably arose. In 1959, by decree of the Central Committee, CPSU provision was made for local party units to establish special party commissions for "controlling" administrative activity in industry and state farms. But what, specifically, were these commissions to control, and in what manner were they to exercise such control? The commissions have been empowered to "protest" against those illegal and "incorrect" administrative decisions which conflict with party and government decrees. One such commission at the Red October Factory in Volgograd studied a lag in the work of the gauge shop and discovered unequal loading wire-drawing assemblies. The commission then helped "adjust" the rhythm of work. Yet, occasionally the commissions have acted irresponsibly in taking the place of the normal administrative unit. This occurred in some state farms.[23] The perennial dilemma on state versus party apparatus in economic management has not yet been finally resolved simply by creating the party administrative control com-

[22] Editorial, "Buro pervichnoy partorganizatsii," *Partiynaya Zhizn*, No. 22 (November, 1964), pp. 7, 9.

[23] L. Kulichenko, "Partiynyy kontrol za proizvodstvom," *Partiynaya Zhizn*, No. 21 (November, 1959), p. 16. A. Konovalenko, "Partiynyy kontrol v sovkhozakh," *Partiynaya Zihzn*, No. 13 (July, 1960), p. 44.

missions. The 1962 reorganization, providing for even more proliferated administration (in each *kray* and *oblast* there will be *two* party committees, one for industry and one for agriculture) only aggravated the situation and added to the complexity of confused leadership and managerial supervision. Shortly after Khrushchev's removal in 1964, this particular reorganization of splitting up the units was "undone." After the removal, accounts in the Soviet press referred to Khrushchev's wild-eyed schemes.

Other developments have included the right given to central committees of union republics and to *kraykomy* and *obkomy* to set up new party committees where none previously had existed—chiefly in large organizations having one hundred or more communists. Primary party organizations were granted more authority to register, admit, and examine cases of party members. In 1961 there were established, in the greater Moscow area, sub-*rayon* party committees (*podraykomy*) of seven to nine members to improve communication among various party committees within the Moscow *Oblast*. Late in 1964, again after Khrushchev, a number of new rural *rayon* party committees were organized in a return to earlier, more customary patterns of local party organization.

Local party organs are created, allowed to exist, occasionally even abolished on the whim of higher party bodies. These local organs have no rights of their own apart from those granted from above. From central, down through regional, and finally settling on the local levels of organization, the Soviet Communist Party structure is strictly ruled and disciplined from above. There is no federalism in the system from top to bottom, only a highly centralized unitary dictatorship. All units within the system are fully expected to answer the helm from above, no matter what the signal— slow, full speed ahead, or reverse. Lenin's main organizational principle for the party, enunciated before the Revolution, has proved all he hoped it would be and has well stood the test of time. The party organizations may be numerous, duplicating even falling over each other, but they are disciplined.

PARTY MEMBERSHIP

An old Bolshevik contemporary of Lenin (Piatakov), later purged by Stalin, at one time described his undying loyalty to the Communist Party. For him, there could be no life outside the party, for his dedication to it was without reservation. If necessary, he would believe black to be white for the party's sake. To completely merge with the party he would fuse himself with it, even to the point of abandoning his own personality so that "no particle left inside him" would be at odds with and would not belong to the party.[24] What manner of party was it that could win such fervent support from at least some of its adherents? Part of the answer surely lay in the party's great cause as originally conceived in Marxism—the emancipation of the slave-like worker. Any sacrifice in this great worldwide mission, as Marxists saw it, would not be too high a price to pay on the part of its truly devoted followers.

Writing in the *Communist Manifesto*, Marx and Engels state that communists have only the proletariat as their interest. Always and everywhere, they continue, communists represent the interest of the working class movement as a whole. It was Lenin of course, following Marx and Engels, who was the creator and molder of the modern Soviet Communist Party. The Dictatorship of the Proletariat, of which Marx wrote, for Lenin was a dictatorship of the advance guard of the workers— the Bolshevik, or Communist Party. The small, hard-core party, for the Bolsheviks, was the only instrument capable of bringing about a "socialist" revolution and the only force able to organize and direct the new system. The party would be the teacher, guide, and leader of the new socialist- communist order. So convincingly dedicated was Lenin to this ideal and goal that Stalin later defined Leninism as the theory and tactics of the proletarian revolution in general, the theory and tactics of the dictatorship of the proletariat in particular.

The culmination of Marx's Dictatorship of the Proletariat and of Lenin's "vanguard" was Stalin's smooth-running, omnipresent, and virtually omnipotent machine. For Stalin, the high point of the party's development was reached when "not a single important political or organizational question is decided by any soviet or mass organization without guiding directions from the party."[25] This is party dictatorship *par excellence*. But to achieve such a party as Lenin and Stalin envisaged it would be necessary to guide the right people into the party's ranks. Membership, in terms of social classes, would be a question of paramount importance if the party was to meet the tasks its leaders set for it.

After gaining more or less effective governmental power in late 1917, the Bolshevik faction was now obliged to become a full-fledged party and not remain simply a band of rebels. To discredit and weaken existing government, to criticize all political groups and factions save your own conspiratorial one, to propagandize with grandiose promises, to enflame workers, peasants, soldiers, and sailors, in brief, to carry out a revolution was one thing. Now, suddenly, for this rebellious faction to become itself *the* government and *the* author and protector of internal peace, law and order

---

[24] Quoted in Schapiro, *op. cit.*, p. 381.

[25] J. Stalin, *Problems of Leninism* (New York: International Publishers, 1934), p. 135.

and, finally, to originate concrete proposals for governmental actions, was
quite another matter. One of the foremost problems to resolve, even more
so than in pre-revolutionary times, was that of party membership. What
should be the desirable optimum size of the party? What of recruitment
policies, membership requirements, organizational structure? Even the
social background of its members was important. This last point, in fact,
proved to be one of the more difficult problems to solve.

Membership Figures

Although fluctuating over the years, party membership has more or less
steadily increased. Soviet sources refer to 8,400 Bolsheviks in 1905 and
46,000 in 1907. By April, 1917, there were some 80,000 members of the
RSDLP, but by August of that same year, at the Sixth Party Congress,
there were an estimated 240,000 members. By the Ninth Party Congress
in 1920, the number had more than doubled, to over 600,000, although a
purge reduced the membership to approximately 400,000 by the Eleventh
Congress in 1922. A million members were counted by the time of the
Fourteenth Congress in 1925; by 1930 the figure had increased to almost
two million. Although there were 2,809,796 members in early 1934, by
the first part of 1941 there were only 2,477,666, a net decrease in the seven
years reflecting the hundreds of thousands of party members purged during
this period. The total number of members purged from 1932–38 probably
exceeded one million. One estimate is that 850,000 (36 percent of total
membership) were purged in the 1936–38 period alone.[26] Apart from the
purges, large numbers of party members were dropped because of incom-
petency or related reasons of unsuitability. Others voluntarily dropped
out during their period of candidacy. Still others were killed during World
War II and, of course, a number died of natural causes since 1917.

Recruitment, which occasionally reached mass proportions (following
Lenin's death, and during World War II) has far outpaced absolute
increases in total party membership. In the period 1925–29, there were
1,225,000 new candidates enrolled, but the party increased in membership
by only 876,000.[27] By 1946 well over one half of the members had entered
the party since 1941. Rigby's estimates for the percentages of members in
1953 who joined during six main periods are:[28]

---

[26] Zbigniew K. Brzezinski, *The Permanent Purge: Politics in Soviet Totalitarianism*
(Cambridge, Mass.: Harvard University Press, 1956), pp. 98–99.

[27] T. H. Rigby, "The Selection of Leading Personnel in the Soviet State and Communist Party" (Ph.D. dissertation, University of London, 1954), p. 54.

[28] *Ibid.*, p. 60.

Date of joining	Percent of Membership
Before 1921..	.8
1921–28...	2.3
1929–33...	7.0
1936 (November)–1941 (May).......................	16.0
1941 (June)–1945.................................	49.0
1946–53..	25.0

During World War II mass enlistments recorded 470,405 new candidates accepted in 1942 while in the second half of that year 701,674 new members were brought in. During the entire war period party membership grew from 3,908,000 to 5,760,000 (up to January 1945).[29] Following the sizable postwar recruitment drives, membership rapidly climbed to 6,013,259 regular and 868,886 candidates by the Nineteenth Congress in 1952. The Twenty-first Congress in 1959 listed 7,622,356 regular and 616,775 candidates.[30] At the Twenty-second Congress in 1961 the membership stood at 8,872,516 regulars and 843,489 candidates. Thus, total party membership of 9,716,000 in late 1961 approximated 4½ percent of the country's total population at that time. In January, 1965, party membership stood at 11,758,169, which was 5.13 percent of the total population at that time. If to these membership figures are added the various Communist youth organizations, then Communist Party and party-related organizational membership is considerably more than 5 percent of the population. At the Twenty-third Party Congress in 1966 the party membership was 12,471,000.[31]

Social Composition

A persistent and vexing problem for party leaders which existed even prior to the Revolution is that of the social composition of the party membership. How, in 1917 and immediately thereafter, could a dictatorship of and for workers be justified in a nation made up chiefly of peasants? The old Bolsheviks who carried out the Revolution and guided the new regime in its first years were, in the main, intellectuals, not laborers. Stalin discussed the problem in his report to the Fourteenth Party Congress in 1925 when he objected to the desire of some party members to enroll 90

---

[29] *Partiynaya Zhizn*, No. 20 (October, 1957), pp. 82–83. In these crucial years the leadership frantically sought the loyalty of the troops as well as of the general populace—a loyalty, though, which it did not always get.

[30] Figures are from A. Rothstein (ed.), *History of the Communist Party of the Soviet Union* (Moscow: Foreign Languages Publishing House, 1960), pp. 239ff. Figures on party membership are not too reliable, especially for the early years. Official Soviet accounts disagree on occasion. For a year-by-year breakdown from 1917 through 1952, see Fainsod, *op. cit.*, p. 212.

[31] *Pravda*, March 30, 1966.

percent of the country's working class in the party within a couple of years. Unreasonable, replied Stalin, since by October, 1925, only 8 percent of the total 7 million industrial and agricultural workers had joined the party. In the preceding years the ratio of workers in the party had been falling behind the general increase in total numbers of workers. As for the ratio of peasants in the party to total peasants, the problem was even more aggravated. In a rural population of more than 54 million in 1925, only 202,000 (0.37 percent of the peasants) were party members. The situation, Stalin continued, is "deplorable." As for overall ratios, in 1925 workers made up 58.6 percent of total party membership, with peasants totaling 23.8 percent and office employees and others, 17.6 percent.[32]

Over the years official recruitment policy for new members has stressed drawing into the party's ranks selected occupational groups. Rigby notes several main phases of recruitment, as follows:[33]

> Up to 1919. . . . . .All classes recruited
> During the Civil War. . . .Open recruitment
> 1919–33. . . . . .Emphasis on industrial workers over white
>   collar workers and intelligentsia
> 1938–World War II. . . . . .Mass enrollment of administrative employees
> During World War II. . . .Open recruitment
> Post-World War II. . . . . .Emphasis on peasants

By 1954 the occupational breakdown of the party was estimated at the following percentages:[34]

	Approximate Number	Approximate Percent of Total
Industry, mining, transport, etc.	2,600,000	36
(of whom junior foremen and rank-and-file workers).	(1,300,000)	(18)
Agriculture: collective and state farms and MTS.	1,400,000	19
(of whom junior foremen and rank-and-file workers).	(750,000)	(10)
Political and administrative hierarchies.	1,500,000	21
"Culture": education, medicine, scientific research.	700,000	10
Armed forces and police.	1,000,000	14
	7,200,000	100

Applying the above percentages to other estimates, one can hazard a guess that in 1955 approximately 9 percent of the nation's non-agricultural

---

[32] J. Stalin, *Works* (Moscow: Foreign Languages Publishing House, 1954), Vol. 7, pp. 353–57.

[33] Rigby, *op. cit.*, p. 69.

[34] T. H. Rigby, "Social Orientation of Recruitment and Distribution of Membership in the Communist Party of the Soviet Union," *American Slavic and East European Review*, Vol. XVI (October, 1957), pp. 289–90.

workers and approximately 5 percent of those employed in agriculture were party members.[35] These estimates, if representative, do not speak favorably for the desires of Stalin and his heirs to increase the proportion of workers in the party in the 30-year period, 1925–55. If these figures approximate the actual situation in 1955, then the percentage of party members employed in agriculture was a fraction higher than existed in 1925 (4 percent versus 3.7 percent). The nonagricultural party worker ratio changed not at all in the 30-year period; this segment of the population still accounted for only 8 percent of party membership.

A somewhat different breakdown of party membership for the years 1956 to 1965 is provided from official Soviet sources.[36]

OCCUPATIONS OF PARTY MEMBERS
(In Percent)

	1956	1961	1965
All Communists	100.0	100.0	100.0
1. Workers	32.0	34.5	37.3
2. Collective farmers	17.1	17.5	16.5
3. Employees in all branches	50.9	48.0	46.2
Breakdown of 3, above			
Leaders of organizations, institutions, enterprises, state farms, RTS	14.1	10.2	7.8
Engineer-technical workers, agricultural specialists, agronomists, architects	20.1	29.2	32.5
Scientific workers, educational and public health employees, literary and artistic people	18.8	21.5	23.3
Workers in trade and public catering	4.7	4.9	5.8
Workers in controlling, accounting, clerical	13.2	11.9	10.8
Others (communication, municipal economy, etc.)	29.1	22.3	19.8

These figures indicate shifts reflecting slightly increased percentages of workers, engineering-technical workers, and scientific, educational, and related groups, while leaders of organizations have shown a notable decrease since 1956. The percent of workers taken into the party in the first half of 1966 increased, following instructions from the Twenty-third Congress.[37]

The party leadership is proud of the members who are educated and, accordingly, notes with satisfaction the increasing numbers of members

---

[35] Party membership for 1955 is estimated at 7 million, including candidate members. Nonagricultural employment for 1955 is estimated at 38 million, agricultural employment at 37½ million. See Warren G. Nutter, "Employment in the Soviet Economy: an Interim solution to a Puzzle," *Soviet Studies*, Vol. XII (April, 1961), pp. 381–82.

[36] "KPSS v tsifrakh," 1962, p. 48, and "KPSS v tsifrakh," 1965, p. 11.

[37] *Partiynaya Zhizn*, No. 18 (September, 1966), p. 5.

who are getting an education. The following table shows this growth since 1922.[38]

FORMAL EDUCATION OF PARTY MEMBERS

Total Members (incl. candidates)	1922		1956		1961		1965	
	No.	%	No.	%	No.	%	No.	%
Total members....	387,313*	100.0	7,173,521	100.0	9,626,740	100.0	11,758,169	100.0
Higher..........	2,317	.6	801,384	11.2	1,283,548	13.3	1,763,262	15.0
Incomplete higher and middle.....	24,225	6.3	1,850,370	25.8	2,852,158	29.6	3,578,255	30.5
Incomplete middle.	*	....	2,127,862	29.6	2,755,652	28.6	3,277,024	27.9

* Incomplete figures for 1922.

This table shows that although formal education has been steadily increasing among party members, the nation's political leadership, as such, is reflected in general party membership and still suffers in 1965 from a very low level of formal education.

The following table shows the party members by nationality and by the number of party members within the respective union republics.[39] Those republics in which there are more total communists than communists of that particular nationality (such as Lithuania) tend to confirm the general knowledge that large numbers of Russian communists work in and help guide the activity of native communists of non-Russian republics. Omission of figures for the RSFSR is additional confirmation.

NUMBER OF PARTY MEMBERS BY NATIONALITY AND BY UNION REPUBLIC, 1965

	Communists of That Nationality	Total Communists in the Republic
Russians (RSFSR)............	7,335,200	not available
Ukraine...................	1,813,400	1,829,638
Belorussia.................	386,000	319,196
Uzbek....................	193,600	314,279
Kazakh...................	181,300	450,486
Georgia...................	194,300	248,375
Armenia...................	187,900	104,305
Azerbaijan.................	141,900	198,539
Lithuania.................	61,500	86,366
Latvia....................	44,300	95,742
Tadzhikistan	41,900	67,624
Kirghiz...................	35,000	84,721
Turkmenia	32,400	57,206
Moldavia..................	40,300	85,379
Estonia...................	33,900	54,836
Others....................	1,035,300	—
Total................	11,758,200	

[38] "KPSS v tsifrakh," 1962, p. 48, and "KPSS v tsifrakh," 1965, p. 11. *Partiynaya Zhizn*, No. 20 (October, 1957), p. 88.

[39] "KPSS v tsifrakh," 1965, p. 8.

Requirements and Rewards of Party Membership

The party rules provide for membership of any Soviet citizen who subscribes to the party's rules and programs, takes an active part in "building communism," works in one of the party organizations, fulfills party decisions, and pays the required dues. A person can join at age 18 if he can get the recommendation of three party members, each of whom is a regular member of at least five years' standing and has been acquainted with the applicant at his place of work for at least one year. Normally applicants under the age of 23 enter the party only by way of the *Komsomol*. In addition to these requirements an applicant must serve a year's candidacy prior to full membership. He then is formally admitted by his appropriate primary party organization, although even then his admittance must be ratified by the next higher party committee. A party member's status can be revoked through initiation by a primary organization, with ratification by the next higher committee.

A reading of the party rules discloses that membership carries with it numerous duties and some burdensome responsibilities, but few tangible rights. A party member is expected not only to support and defend the party programs, but actively to fight for them. Moreover, party members are to be examples of sobriety, to be hard and devoted workers, well-informed exponents of the party "line," schooled in the principles of Marxism-Leninism, and duty bound to direct state affairs. A party member, ideally, is the champion of the worker's interests, guardian of state property, preserver of party and state secrets, unrelenting critic of inefficiency—he is to be, in short, the eyes and ears as well as the right hand of the party high command. Such membership requirements involve no small amount of personal sacrifice. The member must pay a certain percentage of his monthly salary for dues (it can be as high as 3 percent in some cases.) His personal life after working hours is supposed to be given over to such activities as production meetings, election campaigns, and lectures on world affairs. He is precluded from practicing any open religious life and is expected to be a model of the law-abiding, upstanding citizen. More important, however, party members in positions of leadership are held accountable for the success or failure of the various economic activities within their area of supervision even though their personal responsibility for a given problem may be minimal. It is possible, also, to be expelled from the party.

For a three-year period slightly more than 200,000 members were expelled from the party, as revealed in the table below.[40]

---

[40] "KPSS v tsifrakh," 1965, p. 10. See the party rules, Section I (Appendix I) for these and other reasons for expulsion from the party.

LOSS OF PARTY MEMBERSHIP

	1962	1963	1964
Total expelled....................	65,163	69,454	68,770
Members......................	33,582	36,797	34,525
Candidate members..............	31,581	32,657	34,245
Reasons for expulsion:			
Various misdemeanors, incompatibility with the calling of communist......	31,370	34,045	30,763
Losing, forfeiting connections with party organizations (Rule 8)........	13,614	14,422	15,877
Relinquishing rights to membership (Rule 16)......................	20,179	20,987	22,130

There are, of course, some advantages to party membership. The rights include those of participation in party meetings and party organs on matters of policy, the right, at party meetings, to criticize errant members, to participate in discussions when one's own case is being heard, and to address statements and suggestions on any party matter up to the Central Committee and to require an answer to same. Party members have the right, also, to be elected to party organs. This last provision pinpoints a right of true substance. In effect, a Soviet citizen normally must be a Communist to enjoy the fruits of high office, to be a ruler of Soviet society. Membership is no guarantee of success, but without the party ticket a citizen will be denied the opportunity even to try for high positions of authority and responsibility. The party member, if able, intelligent, and lucky may one day be among the few very powerful rulers of the Soviet Union. The party member, after all, is a participant in an elite group; he is a part of the vanguard of the working class. However, instead of working toward a classless society, the Communist Party officialdom in the Soviet Union constitutes a very well-defined and tangible upper class in society.

THE PARTY AS AN ORGANIZED UNIT

The organizational structure of the Soviet Communist Party has always been of great importance to the party's leaders. Beginning with Lenin and continuing to the present time, these leaders believed that, to a considerable extent, their success in controlling the political and governmental system, even the victory of communism, would depend in part on how and in what manner the Communist Party is organized. From time to time the party's structure has been altered both on the central and on lower levels; some units of the party were amalgamated, others abolished outright, while yet new ones were created in hopes of achieving greater efficiency. In all of these changes, though, party control for the sake of party control has constantly recurred as the one all-pervading, dominant theme.

By 1952 the Soviet Communist Party, in Schapiro's analysis, was characterized by six main features. First, the party had become, though selective, a mass party which included the nation's elite from all occupations. Second, the party also was dominated by a numerically small apparatus of officials and secretaries. Third, the apparatus had been highly centralized in the Secretariat. Fourth, the ascendancy and personal domination of Stalin, of course, was another feature of the party by 1952. Fifth, the consequent decline in the influence of the party—as opposed to the rise of the secret police and the administrative bureaucracy of the government, for example—resulted directly from Stalin's personal dictatorship. Sixth, party members by this time had interpenetrated into all phases of national life.[41] In the years since Stalin's death, the six features distinguishing the party in 1952 have changed, but only to a small degree.

Although by 1962 Khrushchev had largely filled Stalin's old role as party boss, the general influence of the party which had declined under Stalin was reestablished to resume its former position of unquestioned primacy in comparison to other organizations such as the bureaucracy, the police, and the army. There has been also a shift more toward the use of unpaid party workers in the hope of reducing the high cost of the permanent apparatus. Since the early 1960's, too, the party high command has emphasized a greater turnover of party officials in key posts chiefly for the purpose of adding to the number of experienced leaders, but perhaps also to make a bit more viable democratic procedures within the party system. The 1961 party rules for the first time put limits to the length of service of Central Committee Presidium members—although allowing a slight loophole in this restriction for key leaders. In addition the membership of the Central Committee was to be renewed at least one fourth at each election. The membership of the party committees of union republics and their subordinate organs also were to be renewed in part at each election. Finally, secretaries of primary party organs were restricted to two consecutive terms. These Khrushchev-imposed restrictions on the number of terms and the requirement for regular turnover were eliminated in the rule changes approved at the Twenty-third Congress. In most other respects, such as dominance by the central apparatus and by the officials and secretaries, and the infusion into all

---

[41] Schapiro, *op. cit.*, pp. 547–50.

areas of life by party members, the basic features of the Communist Party as sketched in 1952 are unchanged.

There have remained, still, some unresolved organizational problems for the party high command. As with governmental institutions, so with party institutions, the search for the organizational ideal continues. Probably because of the philosophical confines of Marxism-Communism—that a final, determinate, all goods, all efficient system can be reached—party leaders delude themselves into thinking that their administrative-management system can become perfect if only the correct combination of organizational structures and efficient party secretaries can be dialed. Until the regime is convinced otherwise, and that possibility seems remote, repeated personnel shifts, occasionally of sizable proportions, and continual reorganizations will typify the Soviet Communist Party.

CHAPTER VIII

Leadership and Control

THE FUNCTIONS of the Soviet Communist Party are both varied and far-reaching. Indeed they are as broad and extensive as is the Soviet political, governmental, economic, cultural, and social system itself. The party defines the goals and tasks and exercises leadership of the state "in all fields of its activity." The policy of the party "is the basis of the activity of the Soviet state."[1] More than just the vanguard of the working class and the dictatorship of the proletariat, the Communist Party is the guiding compass as well as the bow-sprit for the conduct of virtually all organized activity in the USSR. The merging with, in effect taking over, of Soviet life on the part of the party is described by a famous Yugoslav Communist as a process in which the communist government constitutes, in practice, a party government; the communist army, a party army; and the state, a party state.[2]

The 1961 party program broadly outlined the functions of the Communist Party with these inspirational and grandiose phrases. "The Party is the brain, the honour and the conscience of our epoch, of the Soviet people. . . . It looks keenly into the future and shows the people scientifically motivated roads along which to advance, arouses titanic energy in the masses and leads them to the accomplishment of great tasks."[3] These then, generally, are the functions of the party.

More specifically, the activities of the party include the following:

Domestic: (1) Establish plans and broad policies for various aspects

---

[1] *Osnovy Sovetskogo Gosudarstvo i Prava* (Moscow: Gosurizdat, 1947), p. 24; and "Kommunisticheskaya partiya—rukovodyashchaya sila sovetskogo gosudarstva," *Sovetskoe Gosudarstvo i Pravo,* No. 8 (August, 1955), pp. 8–9.

[2] Milovan Djilas, *The New Class* (New York: Frederick A. Praeger, Inc., 1957), pp. 72–73.

[3] Jan Triska (ed.), *Soviet Communism: Programs and Rules* (San Francisco: Chandler Publishing Co., 1962), p. 125.

of Soviet life and to oversee their fulfillment; (2) Initiate most of the important governmental acts, decrees, reorganizations; (3) Supervise, at least indirectly, normal governmental functions (central-regional-local) throughout the nation; (4) Select the cadres for present and future officials in party government, industry, and agriculture; (5) Establish the structural framework and operational guidelines for education, cultural life, and for such tasks as scientific investigations.

Foreign: (1) Determine both the general outlines and specific actions in the area of foreign policy; (2) Set the policies for foreign trade and economic assistance programs in support of foreign policy; (3) Provide the guidemarks for the Soviet defense posture at home and abroad; (4) Carry out active working relationships with other communist governments in such fields as foreign policy, military defense, economic development, and trade; (5) Strive to guide and direct the international communist movement toward a unified policy.

CENTRAL FUNCTIONS

Pronouncements on party policies, though originating from decisions arrived at by the top leadership, normally are issued at various meetings of the party's leading organizations. The most important of such meetings are the congresses; 23 have been held counting from the first organizing meeting of the RSDLP in 1898.

Party Congresses and Conferences

The Second Congress of the RSDLP was held in Brussels and London in 1903, and four more were held prior to the Revolution. From 1918 there was one congress of the party held each year through 1927. The Sixteenth Congress was held in 1930, the Seventeenth in 1934, the Eighteenth in 1939, and 13½ years later, Stalin's last Congress, the Nineteenth, in 1952. The Twentieth, Twenty-first, and Twenty-second Congresses were in 1956, 1959, and 1961, respectively. The Twenty-third Congress was held in 1966. Party rules require the holding of at least one ordinary congress each four years and extraordinary congresses (such as the Twenty-first) on the call of the Central Committee, or on demand of at least one third of the party membership.

Congresses may formulate, elaborate, or interpret party rules; always the congresses give formal sanction to programs announced by the party's leadership. Other matters are dealt with in accordance with current questions, such as the role of the party in the State Duma (at the Fourth and Fifth Congresses), organization of trade unions (Ninth), propaganda and agitation in the press (Twelfth), internal party fights and the struggle for power (Fourteenth through Sixteenth), third Five-Year Plan (Eighteenth), international affairs (Nineteenth), de-Stalinization (Twentieth), the new Seven-Year Plan (Twenty-first), the struggle over control of the international communist movement (Twenty-second), and a new five-year plan as well as party rule changes and international affairs (Twenty-third). Apart from the congresses, there was yet another type of broad meeting labeled the party conference.

From 1905 until early 1941 the party conducted 18 party conferences; these were junior-type congresses. As with congresses, the conferences discussed important problems, such as the Polish question (Ninth Conference), the Anti-Trotsky campaign (Thirteenth), the Five-Year Plan (Sixteenth), and the role of party activities in industry and transport (Eighteenth). Conferences of this type have not been held since 1941. A 1966 change in the party rules authorizes calling of all-union party conferences between congresses, for the purpose of discussing urgent questions of party policy.

In the Soviet regime's early years the party congresses and conferences were deliberating bodies for much of what became official policy. They constituted forums where the party as a whole—as represented by its elected delegates—dealt with matters of rather considerable importance. After the Fourteenth Congress in 1922, however, the general tenor of these gatherings changed. No longer did they seriously debate party affairs. No longer were they to any measurable degree originators or even interpreters of party policy. Instead their purpose now was simply to endorse and approve policy previously set by the top leadership. Although some debate was still permitted, even opposition views aired, party congresses and conferences became more perfunctory because they were now attended by selected representatives of the apparatus who were chiefly loyal to the party Secretariat and to its general secretary—Stalin. After 1922, virtually unanimous approval was given to the programs of the leadership by its faithful followers in the congresses and conferences. As Stalin's rule became more entrenched, even these modest party sessions were held less and less frequently. Only one conference was held after 1932—the one in 1941. In violation of party rules which called for a congress to be held at least each four years, Stalin allowed five years to pass between the Seventeenth and the Eighteenth Congress, and the Nineteenth Congress was convened 13½ years after the Eighteenth. As congresses and conferences were allowed to atrophy under the latter part of Stalin's reign, so the same fate was suffered by the plenary sessions of the party's Central Committee. Since Stalin, congresses have been held with greater regularity to hear leaders discuss important issues of foreign and domestic policy and to hear of the many and glorious accomplishments of the party. Problems are likely to be aired at these meetings, but the elected delegates do not determine policy, nor do they even call into question actions or plans of the leadership. The delegates are there to give a semblance of democratic approval and to place the stamp of legitimacy on the policies of the party elite.

Central Committee Meetings

Almost as significant as the congresses and the conferences were the plenary meetings of the Central Committee; these have been held at infrequent intervals to deal with matters of current importance for the party. There have been more than seventy reported plenary meetings of the Central Committee since 1923, some nine of these having been joint meetings (between 1923 and 1933) with the Central Control Commission. These joint meetings were a deliberate arrangement by Stalin to enhance his power during the periods of the NEP and during his battle with the Left Opposition; the meetings initiated government policy in these years.[4] There are no officially reported plenary meetings of the Central Committee for the years 1917–23 (although some probably occurred), and only two were held between 1940 and 1953. Thus, for the years in which plenary meetings were officially reported, they averaged slightly more than two a year. Although six plenary meetings were held in 1924 and five in 1927, they became fewer in direct relation to the increasing efficiency of Stalin's dictatorship. As with party congresses and conferences, Stalin had less and less need for plenary meetings of the Central Committee during the latter period of his reign. Following Stalin's death, congresses have been held more frequently (three in eight years), and plenary meetings of the Central Committee have averaged more than two a year (six were held in 1958 alone).

Plenary sessions of the Central Committee are supposed to be held, according to party rules, at least every six months. Their purpose, as the party's officially elected central representatives, is to transact formal party business between sessions of the party congresses. The sessions handle major party matters, such as announcements of changes in key party personnel, approval of decisions and policies of the Politburo, and occasionally decisions on struggles for power (in 1957 and 1964 over

[4] Leonard Schapiro, *The Communist Party of the Soviet Union* (New York: Random House, Inc., 1960), pp. 318–19.

Khrushchev).   The following account of the plenary session of the Central Committee which removed Khrushchev from power in October, 1964, is cited in the *New York Times* from what is noted there, simply, as "reliable sources."[5]   It is probably close to the actual course of events.   When Khrushchev was vacationing in the resort of Sochi, a meeting of the Central Committee Presidium on October 12 and 13, 1964, voted unanimously to remove Khrushchev as First Secretary and convened a plenary session of the Central Committee for Tuesday night (October 13). Meanwhile, the Presidium members were persuading the Central Committee members to support the *coup*.   Khrushchev had arrived back in Moscow that afternoon.   The Central Committee session lasted through most of the night, with the party theoretician Suslov, a Secretary of the Communist Party and a Presidium member, speaking for some five hours. Khrushchev made an angry, aggressive, ineffectual defense of himself, even insulting the Central Committee members when he saw he was going to lose.   Early in the morning of the 14th, the formal vote was taken that removed him from party leadership.   The following day the Presidium of the Supreme Soviet removed him as Chairman of the Council of Ministers.   In this account, the salient point for our discussion here is that, from time to time, struggles for power are broached in the Presidium and, if they are of the greatest importance (challenging the leader of the party), they are brought to the Central Committee for decision.

The plenary sessions are opened by a speaker who covers the major topic for consideration; additional speakers usually take part and, finally, prepared resolutions or policies are approved.   On occasion policy is actually formulated at this time.   Normally, the plenary sessions merely ratify (in the name of the entire Communist Party) actions of the Politburo. The sessions average several each year, although Stalin sometimes neglected to convene them for a year or two at a time.   Since Stalin's death in 1953, the sessions have been more regularly held, some forty taking place from March, 1953, through December, 1966.   The yearly average of sessions for this period has been approximately three, and the average meeting time per session is slightly more than three days.   The main subject matters taken up at these forty sessions were general political, such as personnel changes; governmental, party, and economic reorganizations; plan and budget approval; power struggles (eighteen sessions); agriculture (twelve sessions); industry (nine); and labor problems (one).   At a few of the sessions more than one subject was discussed, such as agriculture and international affairs.   Increasingly in the post-Stalin

---

[5] *New York Times*, October 24, 1964.

years, and especially since Khrushchev's removal, the sessions have been airing problems and complaints, often pointing, at least indirectly, to very serious errors in economic and agricultural administration, in plans, and even in party supervision.[6] If this trend continues, it is conceivable that plenary sessions of the Central Committee will increasingly perform the function of articulating and filtering popular demands into the political system.

REGIONAL AND LOCAL FUNCTIONS

On the regional (union republic) level there are party congresses in addition to plenums of the central committees of these parties. The congresses study drafts of party programs and statutes, hear reports from the central committee and from the auditing commission, hold elections for the central committee and auditing commission, and deal with other topics such as capital investment in industry, matters of construction and improvements in collective farming.

The congresses in the republics are carbon-copy miniatures of national party congresses. On the republic level they apparently follow a rigid procedural format, no doubt prescribed by Moscow. In December, 1963, and January, 1964, for example, in congresses held by the communist parties of Moldavia, Tadzhikistan, Turkmenia, Latvia, Estonia, Lithuania, Kirghiz, Azerbaijan, and Georgia, the identical procedure was:

1. Report of the communist party's central committee.
2. Report of the auditing commission.
3. Elections to the central committee.
4. Elections to the auditing commission.

There are, in addition, special meetings called by the union republic central committees, such as the conference of first secretaries of *oblast* committees in the Ukraine that was held to discuss plenums of the Central Committee, CPSU, and of the Ukrainian Central Committee.[7] A five-day seminar was called for newly elected secretaries of *rayon* and city party committees and for chairmen of *rayon* governments in the Uzbek Republic. Among other topics, the seminar dealt with questions of democratic centralism, checking up on administration by primary party organizations, party leadership of local governments, furthering Soviet democracy, the work of trade unions, and "ideological work" of party organizations.[8]

---

[6] See the excellent discussion of the September, 1965, Plenum dealing with agricultural problems in Solomon Schwarz, "Agriculture: The Curtain Is Lifted," *Problems of Communism*, Vol. XV (March–April, 1966).

[7] *Pravda Ukrainy*, April 2, 1961.

[8] *Pravda Vostoka*, March 29, 1961.

Apart from party meetings as such, the republican central committees, following the national format, supervise virtually all activity of importance within the borders of their respective republics. Inadequate performance by local party officials may at any time call down upon them the wrath and punishment of the republican central committee, be it a matter of industry, agriculture, the arts, or virtually any subject which is not reserved to the national government (such as military and defense matters, or foreign policy).

Local party organs hold conferences and plenary meetings which serve purposes similar to those on the regional and national levels. The Samarkand *Obkom* in 1960 held a three-day seminar for secretaries of city and *rayon* party committees located within the territory of the *oblast*. The seminar heard lectures and reports on party organizational work, and on matters relating to the *Komsomol*, trade unions, and local governments. A three-day seminar in another *oblast* was held for secretaries and deputy secretaries of party committees from a number of collective farms. In this seminar new party members were discussed, the participants heard a talk on the "international situation" and they viewed films on agriculture.[9]

A plenum of the Tashkent *Gorkom* dealt with party and government decrees relating to municipal affairs and adopted measures aimed at improving the work of enterprises which produce construction materials.[10] One instructor of the Stalingrad *Gorkom* reported on monthly meetings of his committee. The committee discussed letters, complaints, and statements received by the committee, and the next month it dealt with carrying out decisions already reached.[11] This instructor spent most of his time assisting the secretaries of the subordinate primary organizations within the *rayon* in arranging for party meetings, examining complaints, and taking part in various conferences. One plenary meeting of the Stalinsk Party Committee, which took place in a worker's club at a construction site, criticized party work in construction affairs and decided to send 300 Communists and 700 *Komsomol* members out to work on solving certain problems in construction.[12] At each of a number of sessions of a rural *rayon* party committee, five to ten questions were discussed under these general headings:

1. Campaigns for sowing, harvesting, wintering cattle, etc.
2. Development of the economy for the quarter, half year, year.
3. Party-political work, and work with cadres.[13]

---

[9] *Ibid.*, August 2, 1960.

[10] *Ibid.*, June 3, 1960.

[11] "Bolshe initsiativy," *Partiynaya Zhizn*, No. 13 (July, 1961), p. 34.

[12] *Pravda*, March 20, 1961.

[13] V. Kulikov, "Selskiy raykom partii segodnya," *Kommunist*, No. 11 (July, 1965), p. 65.

The party has regular duties to carry out, then, based on its administrative divisions, union republic, *oblast, rayon,* and city. The party apparatus also assumes responsibilities for functions of a specific nature, such as industry and agriculture. Since the 1962 reorganization, the trend has been in this direction.

PARTY IN INDUSTRY

A recurring problem which has faced party leaders throughout most of Soviet history is that of controlling industry. In fact, at least since the late 1920's industry has been the area in which most party attention has been directed. To what extent should party officials—particularly on the lower organizational echelons—within reason interfere with economic administration? Should party representatives dictate to economic managers specific, technical decisions which are normally a part of professional administration? If so, what effects on industrial management will result from such technical decisions made, or at the least strongly influenced, by members of the "political" apparatus? Or, should economic administrators alone make economic decisions? In this case, however, the Communist Party might risk losing control over operational decision making in industry. If the standard operating rule that the party must control all phases of Soviet life is adhered to in practice as well as in theory, what price can safely be paid in lost efficiency in order to ensure continuous political dominance of economic affairs? Soviet leadership, since 1917, has never resolved the dilemma, even to its own satisfaction. Direct party control over industrial decision making has waxed and waned over the years in response to momentary evaluations and reevaluations by the leadership as to whether economic administration was suffering from such close interference or whether party controls needed to be strengthened to ensure managerial loyalty to the regime.

The party assignment in this respect is clear enough. It is to bind together management and workers in pursuit of identical basic interests. By joining in common effort the leading personnel of all organizations within society, it is hoped that the rise of special interests among varying groups will be prevented. The party stands as the overall integrating force in industrial management. In general, party representatives are admonished to "control," inspect, and to check up on economic administrators, to facilitate and speed up production as well as to ensure plan fulfillment, but not to "interfere" with nor take over the directing functions of the administrators themselves. On occasion ministries will be singled out for criticism, for example the Ministry of Light Industry, USSR, and the Ministry of Light Industry, RSFSR, were critized for giving insufficient attention to large textile enterprises and for falling down on providing adequate material and financial reserves for factory reconstruction and repair.[14] The burden of spelling out just what constitutes enough but not too much supervision, however, is left up to local party officials to resolve. If party supervision is successful (increasing production, for example) the local officials are praised. If it is unsuccessful, they may lose their jobs. At all events, these local officials must always bear personal responsibility for their decisions being "right" or "wrong."

Several broad tasks have been given to party organizations in industrial enterprises. These include helping to fulfill monthly production quotas, working to improve quality of output, using the reserves of production to maximum effect, "strengthening" labor discipline, striving for a smooth work flow within the enterprise, introducing new techniques of production and systematically controlling the "economic activity" of administrators.[15] In one case the bureau of an *Obkom* criticized a regional economic council for "inadmissible" practices because it did not pay attention to suggestions of workers and for other shortcomings.[16] One director, however, scorning the advice of his factory's party secretary, announced that he was uninterested in the party's "agitation points" and threatened to fire the secretary if the director's orders were not fulfilled.[17] In another *rayon*, the local party committee inadvisedly recommended one of its own party secretaries to be deputy director of a factory.[18] When a mechanic was reprimanded by his factory director, the mechanic (who was a deputy secretary of the factory's party organization) prevailed upon the local party bureau to cancel the reprimand. The bureau's action later was condemned as completely "inadmissible in our practice of party leadership of economic decisions."[19] These cases reveal a few of the shortcomings that arise in party-industry conflicts.

More normal is the situation where party and industrial leaders cooperate to carry out production assignments for which they are mutually responsible. A party bureau which recommended measures to increase

---

[14] "O rabote partiynogo komiteta Orekhovskogo Khlopchalobumazhnogo Kombinata imeni Nikolaevoy K.I." *Partiynaya Zhizn*, No. 23 (December, 1966), p. 19.

[15] D. Goginova, *Partiyniy Kontrol na Predpriyatie* (Moscow: Gosurizdat, 1949), pp. 8–9.

[16] F. Timov, "Rukovodstvo promyshlennostyu v novykh usloviyakh, "*Kommunist*, No. 1 (January, 1958), p. 62.

[17] M. Groshev, "K chemu vedet beskontrolnost?" *Partiynaya Zhizn*, No. 4 (February, 1955), pp. 65–66.

[18] *Partiynaya Zhizn*, No. 12 (June, 1965), p. 27.

[19] *Ibid.*, No. 23 (December, 1964), pp. 33–34.

mechanization within a factory is cited as a healthy example of expected party-industry cooperation.[20] There is the approach, too, that the party is the oilcan of industry. One Soviet source refers to this when he writes that occasionally an enterprise writes to its ministry and gets no answer. The enterprise then turns to local party organs for cooperation and mediation. As a result, party organs must appear before the ministry in their role of solicitors for their plants on economic matters. At the same time, the ministry tries to place responsibility for deciding economic tasks on the shoulders of the party organs.[21] There are other party tasks, such as transmitting downward the official party line.

The partial two-month diary of a party group organizer in a sheet rolling mill reveals an emphasis on propaganda as a main endeavor of this party group:

January 15th: The newspaper *Magnitogorsk Metal* began to print an article titled "Obscurantists without masks." The collective read and discussed it. All workers were present. The conversation was led by the agitator, Communist Kakutev.

January 21st: An open meeting of the party group was held. They discussed the question: mass political work in the brigade and the fulfillment of assignments for the first twenty days of January.

February 8th: We read materials from the newspaper on the international situation. Workers asked for a report on this theme. This request was transmitted to the party bureau. The report was promised.

February 12th: We heard a report on the international situation. The lecturer was sent by the party committee.

With Agitator Domoshirov we arranged for him to discuss a day in the Soviet Army.

February 17th: We read the answer of Comrad Mikoyan to the Cuban journalists.

Operator Pavlov has difficult living conditions. He was put on a list of those specifically needing living quarters.

February 19th: I agreed with the chief of the shift, Comrade Kakutev, on preparation for a party meeting of the group regarding the question of the speed of fulfillment of the production plan in February.

February 22nd: Today is political education. All communists came to the study.

February 24th: We heard a report from the chief of the shift, Comrade Kakutev, on the work of the brigade in February, and also an explanation by the old welder, Communist Suslov, as to why the furnace delays the work of the mill.

Our party group is friendly. All sixteen communists are found in very responsible sections. In the brigade there are fifty workers. The brigade has overfulfilled its task for the first year of the Seven-Year Plan. In this year already there was produced 120 tons of sheet-rolled materials.[22]

---

[20] *Pravda*, July 9, 1955.

[21] *Pravda*, July 29, 1966.

[22] A. Stepanov, in *Partiynaya Zhizn*, No. 7 (April, 1960), pp. 50–51. At the 13th Congress of Trade Unions in 1963, 60 percent of the delegates were Communist Party members. *Trud*, October 31, 1963.

Bringing the USSR to full industrialization and keeping it there has been and remains a task too important to be confined to mere economic administrators. Party officials from top to bottom have insisted upon guiding, at times even directing and interfering with, industrial management. The question which remains, both for students of the Soviet political system and for the leaders of that system themselves, is how effective has been party guidance of industry. Perhaps, the direction of Soviet industry would be greatly improved if the party ceased its function of supervision and allowed economic managers more of a free rein. And yet, given the nature of economic organization in the USSR, of the requisites of a command economy, of the demands in central planning and of specific regime-directed economic goals, some political oilcan for the administrative wheels of industry such as the party apparatus may be required. The Soviet leaders believe so, at least.

PARTY IN AGRICULTURE

As in industry so in agriculture, the party seeks and plans not only to set overall policy but to control and shape the important managerial decisions. Soviet agricultural administration must not only be party oriented; it must be party guided, directed, and influenced. To accomplish these objectives a rather widespread party apparatus was established in rural areas as a necessary precondition to providing for party hegemony over agriculture.

Party organization in the countryside early in Soviet history had been set up on the territorial principle. By mid-1930 there were 30,000 rural primary party organizations working with some 404,000 communists. Of this latter number, 263,000 communists belonged to territorial party groups, 115,000 to collective farm groups, and 26,000 to organizations in state farms and in the Machine Tractor Stations (MTS). In the winter of 1933 political departments were organized both in state farms and in the MTS. The party leadership at this time sent 17,000 experienced party workers to the political departments of the MTS and 8,000 to the state farms. The MTS were to become centers of political leadership over the collective farms. By the Seventeenth Party Congress in 1934 there were 790,000 communists working with 30,000 primary party organizations in the collective farms. Rural primary party organizations increased to more than 110,000 in 1947 and to 148,000 by 1950.[23] By this time, too, the organizational trend was toward establishing party groups on the "produc-

[23] Andrew Rothstein (ed.), *History of the Communist Party of the Soviet Union* (Moscow: Foreign Languages Publishing House, 1960), pp. 457, 486–87, 624.

tion" principle, that is in state and collective farms and on the MTS—as contrasted with the earlier "territorial" principle. With the abolition of the MTS in 1958, direct party control over agriculture probably was weakened. It was, at any rate, now more the responsibility of the streamlined *raykom* apparatus to be the party's shepherd over agricultural matters in the countryside, indirect as such control would be. Greater reliance for agricultural management now became the responsibility of local governmental bodies. That this move failed to satisfy the regime is attested by the 1962 reorganizations which stripped the *raykom* apparatus of many of its supervisory responsibilities over agriculture.

Similar to its function in industry, the party apparatus in agriculture seeks to insure Communist Party domination as well as to increase the output of farm commodities. Specifically, party officials watch over fulfillment of higher party directives, conduct educational and propaganda courses, try to increase production and introduce new farming techniques, supervise all phases of agricultural administration, and serve as the clearing house for appointment of agricultural officials.[24] At the party organization of one collective farm, the two-month plan for group discussion included the following:

January 15th: Organizing socialist competition and fulfilling responsibility of workers in pig farms; agitation at the farms; examination of the monthly plan for milk production and cattle raising; discussion of the December Plenum of the Central Committee.

January 20th: On fulfillment of the first yearly plan for selling meat to the state; examining work of the *Komsomol* in the collective farm.

February 5th: The decisions of the December Plenum of the Central Committee; graphic presentation of the collective farm's responsibility for 1960; preparation for election meetings of collective farm workers.

February 15th: Work of agitators in consolidating sections; on the fulfillment of socialist responsibility of workers in cattle raising.

February 20th: Listening to the report of the zootechnician of the collective farm on preparation of new feeding methods of pigs; work of communist labor at the farms.[25]

Lethargy among collective farm workers coupled with a lack of initiative on the part of party members works to limit the overall effectiveness of party groups. One party secretary complained that only half of the 864 pig farms in his *oblast* had active party groups.[26] In other cases there may be flurries of party meetings and conferences attended by most

---

[24] For an elaboration of these duties, see Roy D. Laird, *Collective Farming in Russia: A Political Study of the Soviet Kolkhozy* (Lawrence, Kan.: University of Kansas, 1958), pp. 85–87.

[25] A. Lishchenko, in *Partiynaya Zhizn*, No. 3 (February, 1960), p. 50.

[26] *Partiynaya Zhizn*, No. 11 (June, 1961), p. 45.

of the farm workers which may, however, have the adverse effect of interrupting rather than facilitating output. One *raykom*, in fact, held 10 different conferences within a 15-day period and, in the process, interfered with the sowing of grain.[27]

At other times, however, the party apparatus helps to raise output through its various efforts to stimulate agriculture. *Komsomol* members occasionally are sent to areas where agricultural production is lagging. Units of government and party committees from time to time are re-organized and key leaders including those on the management staffs of collective and state farms are shifted and changed in attempts to raise efficiency.

What assessments can we make about the role of the party in agriculture? The consensus among Western specialists on the Soviet system is that agriculture in the USSR has been a very weak part of their economy, if not actually a failure. One is tempted to ask if there is a communist way to grow potatoes (or to organize industry)? The Soviet leaders have believed in a unique communist form of agriculture, though some other communist leaders (Poland, Yugoslavia) doubt it. In the Soviet Union, at any rate, agriculture has been remarkably unsuccessful, and the party has not done much if anything to improve agricultural prospects. Even some Soviet spokesmen are calling attention to both general and specific failures in their agricultural sector. At the September, 1965, Plenum of the Central Committee, the head of the Latvian Communist Party (who also is a member of the Politburo) referred to general shortcomings when he said that "Literally all farm workers in every republic, in every *oblast*, in fact the entire Soviet people, have suffered greatly as a result of the errors made."[28]

Several causes for party ineffectiveness in agriculture can be highlighted. The party has not, over the years, been nearly so concerned with agricultural difficulties compared, say, to those of industry. As a result, the party apparatus in agriculture has been weak in both numbers and quality. The party also has forced on peasants the perennially unpopular collectivization of agriculture, and it has attempted other schemes of dubious value, such as the New Lands program. Finally, central plans simply may lack feasibility, in scope as well as in procedure. Thus the first secretary of an *obkom*, at the September, 1965, Central Committee Plenum, complained

---

[27] *Pravda Vostoka*, April 19, 1961. One agricultural party *buro* in a four-month period discussed more than eighty various questions, all superficially. *Pravda*, September 28, 1966.

[28] Cited in Schwarz, *op. cit.*, p. 13. The errors referred to are those of former party First Secretary Khrushchev.

that "All secretaries of *oblast* committees will remember being called every year to the agricultural section of the RSFSR Central Committee of the CPSU, where the cropping pattern was being determined, and how we were pressured to endorse it, and how it was then presented as originating from below, from the *oblast* party and executive committee levels."[29]

On balance, it can safely be concluded that for a number of reasons the party in agriculture has been unsuccessful either in satisfying general peasant demands or in measurably raising agricultural productivity. The post-Khrushchev party leadership is painfully aware of this, however, and since 1964 has concerned itself with questions of how to develop more rational plans for the improvement of agriculture.

THE PARTY IN ARTS AND EDUCATION

An important function of the Communist Party, and one which is carefully attended to, is that of setting guidelines and providing a framework for the cultural aspects of society. The significance of this function is that art, literature, and education have so much to do with the process of political socialization. If the party fails here, it fails to sell its own people on the desirability of adopting communism. The 1961 party program referred to Soviet literature and art as being "imbued with optimism and dynamic communist ideas" and stated that the Communist Party shows "solicitude" for their proper ideological and artistic standards.

Art and Literature

Since the early 1920's the Central Committee has had as one of its sections Agitation and Propaganda (*Agitprop*), or a version thereof. In 1966 this section was renamed the Propaganda Section. This section has subdivisions for newspapers, journals, radio and television, publishing houses and distribution, and for polygraphy. Party control over literature, for example censorship and editorial policies, begins in this section and extends downward through the Soviet Writer's Union and its various branches, and eventually to individual editorial boards of newspapers, journals, and state publishing houses.

Soviet history is an uneven record of periods of rather heavy party censorship of literature alternating with brief lapses of "thawing." Immediately after the Revolution Lenin shut down the anti-Bolshevik press in Russia, but by the early 1920's a relatively high degree of literary freedom existed. In these early years the degree of freedom that existed

---

[29] Schwarz, *op. cit.*, p. 20.

permitted criticism of the actions of both party and government. There were novels, plays, poems, and short stories in which the sympathetic treatment of opposition revealed its reality in Soviet life.[30] By late 1928 the party called for a mobilization of literature, theater, and movies to support communist viewpoints in culture. The year 1932 saw a last outbreak of literary protest against steadily increasing restrictions under Stalinism. In 1934 the Union of Soviet Writers was formed, and by 1941 all other literary groups but this one had been dissolved. Meanwhile, party influence grew more firm. Although literary controls, among many others, loosened during World War II the party tightened them up again immediately thereafter. In 1946 Politburo member Andrei Zhdanov took over concentrated and high-level control of all propaganda affairs. Zhdanov became the spokesman for an intensive effort to achieve ideological purity; this period is referred to as the Zhdanovshchina."[31]

After Stalin, the period from 1953 until the later 1950's marked one of the recurring thaws in rigid party censorship of literature. Writers and artists cautiously began to criticize Stalinist "formalism." Two of the country's most eminent composers, Shostakovich and Khachaturyan, called for greater freedom in music. Although party leaders continued to insist on setting literary standards and on requiring artistic fidelity to "socialist realism," artists were permitted more leeway, for example in choice of general themes and style.[32] In 1956 Khrushchev's denigration of Stalin and Stalinism raised hopes among some Soviet citizens for even more literary freedoms. This year also saw publication of the novel *Not by Bread Alone* by a promising young Soviet writer (Dudintsev); this work was a fictionalized though poignant criticism of some obvious weaknesses in party officialdom as these existed in the USSR.

After the Pasternak affair in 1958 (when his novel *Dr. Zhivago* had been published abroad and awarded a Nobel Prize), the Central Committee issued a ruling forbidding Soviet writers to publish abroad materials not previously cleared for publication in the USSR. Soviet censors earlier had returned to Pasternak his manuscript for *Dr. Zhivago* as being unacceptable. Just what is and what is not acceptable depends on the interpretation of editors and censors. Here, for example, are excerpts

---

[30] Alex Inkeles and Kent Geiger (eds.), *Soviet Society* (Boston: Houghton Mifflin Co., 1961), p. 476.

[31] The Central Committee Resolutions, elaborated in speeches by Zhdanov, set policies for literature for the next fifteen years. Harold Swayze, *Political Control of Literature in the USSR, 1946–1959.* (Cambridge, Mass.: Harvard University Press, 1962), p. 36.

[32] Ernest J. Simmons (ed.), *Through the Glass of Soviet Literature: Views of Russian Society* (New York: Columbia University Press, 1953), p. 26.

from a nine-page guide to "socialist realism" posted on a bulletin board of the Moscow Artists' Union in 1957. Its intent is to assist orthodox painters in their official form of art.

Portrait of Lenin: Show him as leader of the workers' party; as head of the Socialist state. Portraits should stress his humaneness, nobility, intelligence, and other sterling qualities of character.
Art: Show artists at the industrial site, at the plant; a writer and painter watching construction workers; musicians playing for the workers at a power station.[33]

Following the incident of Pasternak, another freeze set in by late 1962 and early 1963. In December, 1962, First Secretary Khrushchev attended a showing of abstract art in Moscow. His vitriolic comments on the artists' works are reflected in the following quotations.

This painting shouldn't have been hung in the exhibition. Pictures should arouse us to great deeds. They should inspire a person .... And if pictures like this appear, it means that we are not doing our work properly. This includes the Ministry of Culture and the Central Committee's Commission on Ideology....
What is hung there is simply anti-Soviet. It's amoral. Art should ennoble the individual and arouse him to action ....
Comrade Ilyichev [Communist Party Secretary in charge of culture and the arts], I am even more upset by the way your section [Central Committee Section on Culture] is doing its work. And how about the Ministry of Culture? Do you accept this? Are you afraid to criticize?[34]

By early 1963 the party's censorship apparatus criticized writings of Ehrenburg, poetry by Yevtushenko and others and abstract art in general. In March, 1963, Khrushchev and his party lieutenant in charge of culture, Ilyichev, addressed a large meeting of writers, artists and poets in the Kremlin. The purpose of the meeting was to give these intellectuals the party line on cultural activities and to inform them that party controls over such activities would be tightened. Ilyichev said the goal of the artistic community should be socialist realism which is, he noted, a quest for the new and artistically beautiful, "true to life, interpreted from the position of the Communist world view."[35] To these comments, Khrushchev added:

[33] Quoted in Ralph Blum, "Freeze and Thaw: The Artist in Russia—I," *The New Yorker*, August 28, 1965. In the party view, literary values are party values, an d literary goals, party goals. "The official ideology...requires that all pursuits be directed toward and evaluated in terms of that end." Swayze, *op. cit.*, p. 23.

[34] Quoted in Priscilla Johnson (ed.), *Khrushchev and the Arts: The Politics of Soviet Culture, 1962–1964* (Cambridge, Mass.: M.I.T. Press, 1965), pp. 102–5.

[35] *Pravda*, March 9, 1963. In 1963 two letter-petitions signed by a number of well-known artists and scientists were sent to Khrushchev, pleading for more tolerance of liberality in the arts. Priscilla Johnson, "The Regime and the Intellectuals," *Problems of Communism*, Special Supplement (Winter, 1962–Summer, 1963), p. iv.

Our party always stands for *partiynost,* in literature and in art. It welcomes all—old and young in literature and art, party and nonparty, but firmly stands on the positions of communist ideology in questions of artistic creativity. They are the support of the party, its reliable soldiers. . . .

The press and radio, literature, painting, music, movies, theater—they are a sharp ideological weapon of the party.[36]

In these and the preceding quotations, the point is clearly made that cultural activities and communications media are to serve the people in a manner determined by the party. They are instruments to be used by the party for party objectives—the attainment of communism. Art for art's sake is not permitted, not officially, at least.

Since the party line for the arts was so forcefully enunciated in 1963, the regime has allowed a bit of a thaw again. Taking heart from the poet Yevtushenko, who at one time talked back to the leader Khrushchev and got away with it, and from more novels being published which criticize the period of Stalinism, such as Solzhenitsyn's *One Day in the Life of Ivan Denisovich,* Soviet artists have increased their demands on the political system for more literary freedoms. And yet, literary freedom, as such, does not yet exist in the USSR.

In September, 1965, two Soviet writers (Daniel and Sinyavsky) were arrested and charged with publishing novels abroad under assumed names, novels which tended allegedly to discredit and defame the USSR, its people and political system. The defendants were tried, finally, in February, 1966, convicted and sentenced to imprisonment of five years for Daniel and seven years for Sinyavsky. Although a number of Soviet writers over the years have been harrassed, imprisoned, some even executed, the Daniel and Sinyavsky trial was, for the first time in the Soviet Union, one in which the principle evidence was the literary works of the defendants themselves. They were put on trial for what they had written. The trial was significant for several reasons, the most important being the "political crime" involved.

During the trial the defendants withdrew their earlier confessions of guilt, claiming their innocence up to the end. They obviously had published abroad, secretly, what they could not get published in the Soviet Union. In his testimony, Sinyavsky revealed that he had been persecuted earlier for what he had written "honestly." "I have received reprimands, I have been attacked in the press and at meetings. Apart from my salary," he thoughtfully observed, "I have enjoyed no particular

---

[36] *Pravda,* March 10, 1963. *Partiynost,* virtually untranslatable into English, refers to party spirit, party principle, to the *idea* of "partyness."

benefits."[37]   The defendants at times answered the prosecutor in a brusque, somewhat defiant manner, so untypical of the normally humble role of defendant in a Soviet trial.   These excerpts from the trial illustrate the point.

PROSECUTOR: But you knew that anti-Soviet circles were broadcasting your writings over the radio.
DANIEL: You have no basis for that statement.
PROSECUTOR: Daniel, what prompted you to write slanderous anti-Soviet works maligning the political system of the USSR?
DANIEL: I refuse to reply to a question posed in that form.
JUDGE: This is no literary debate, and we don't need digressions into the history of literature.
DANIEL: I must insist on my right to draw literary analogies.   I am being accused of a political crime, and I am defending myself by drawing analogies.
SINYAVSKY (replying to a question from the Prosecutor): That is a thinly disguised sneer, and I shall not answer the question.[38]

The trial had worldwide repercussions (adverse) in addition to causing intellectual dismay within the Soviet Union.   Among Soviet writers, only three would testify against the two defendants at the trial, two of whom were virtual unknowns.   In 1966 a group of sixty-two Moscow writers petitioned the Twenty-third Party Congress for the release of Daniel and Sinyavsky.[39]   What is the meaning of all this for literature and the arts in the USSR?

Soviet literature, instead of serving mainly as a transmission belt for party policy, in Dunham's view, has more and more become the point at which the Soviet system is in the process of self-examination.[40]   The most popular contemporary Soviet poet describes it this way.   The press, radio, and television were quite obviously failing to keep up with rapid changes taking place in Soviet national life.   The country was "demanding the truth about itself from its writers."[41]   By the mid-1960's Soviet artists and writers were exhibiting greater independence from and resistance to tight party control over the arts.   Despite a few such events as the Daniel and Sinyavsky trial and the earlier arrest of Pasternak's friend Olga Ivinskaya, which are rather unusual since Stalin's time, the

[37] *On Trial, The Soviet State versus 'Abram Tertz' and 'Nikolai Arzhak'* trans. and ed. Max Hayward, (New York: Harper and Row, 1966), p. 144.   "In this fantastic, electrified atmosphere," Sinyavsky refers to the trial, "anybody who is 'different' may be regarded as an enemy . . .."   *Ibid.*, p. 148. Tertz and Arzhak are the pen names of the two writers under which they were published abroad.

[38] *Ibid.*, pp. 70, 71, 74, 134.

[39] *New York Times*, November 19, 1966.

[40] Vera Sandomirsky Dunham, "Insights from Soviet Literature," *Journal of Conflict Resolution*, Vol. 8 (1964), p. 408.

[41] Yevgeny Yevtushenko, *A Precocious Autobiography* (New York: E. P. Dutton, 1963), p. 96.

artistic literati in the USSR appear to be increasingly successful in forcing the party to satisfy their demands.

Education

As with literature and the arts, so is Soviet education closely watched over by the party apparatus. Both Lenin and Stalin viewed education chiefly as a weapon with which to further the development of communism. Their successors hold the same view. The whole system of education in the general "political-educational" sphere and in the particular realm of art, for Lenin, must be imbued with feelings for the class struggle of the proletariat, the abolition of exploitation, and the achievement of the aims of the dictatorship of the proletariat. The party, he continued, must actively lead in the entire activity of popular education.[42] A more recent Soviet author has written: "The Party regarded the school not as a self-inclosed educational institution, but as an educational center, disseminating Communist ideology and Communist morality...."[43] Somewhat less pointedly, the party has been depicted as raising the "ideological" level of teaching in all academic subjects and familiarizing young people with communist "construction." To the furtherance of this end, a new course was scheduled for the 1961–62 school year titled "Fundamentals of Political Knowledge"; it was taught at senior grades of general secondary schools.[44] The 1961 party program stated that public education would help mold "harmoniously developed members of communist society...."[45] This Communist Party control over education can be, of course, overstressed. Education in the Soviet Union, as elsewhere, contributes to political socialization, and it seeks also to train people to fill skilled and professional positions in society, to insure literacy throughout the nation, and to raise the general educational levels and attainments of Soviet citizens. Education, in brief, is not *solely* political in the USSR.

Organizationally, there are sections of the central committees, both nationally and in the republics, responsible for setting party policy and giving direction to the political aspects of school curricula. Sizable numbers of professors in Soviet universities are party members, hopefully to ensure execution of central party policy. In 1961 there were an estimated 400,000 Communist teachers in the USSR, and in the great majority

[42] V. I. Lenin, *Selected Works*, ed. J. Fineberg (New York: International Publishers, 1938), Vol. 9, p. 484.

[43] Cited in Counts, *op. cit.*, p. 264.

[44] A. Vlasenkova and Z. Demysheva, "Samyy blizkiy pomoshchnik partii v vospitanii novogo cheloveka," *Partiynaya Zhizn*, No. 2 (January, 1961), p. 36.

[45] Triska, *op. cit.*, p. 115.

of schools there were party organizers.[46]   At Moscow State University there are some 50,000 students, professors, instructors, and scientific workers, with a party organization of 5,000 members.   The main party committee for the university approximates 40, in addition to separate party committees in individual departments.[47]   Topics for the Communists to discuss at their meetings include the system and quality of instruction, lines of scientific research, and placing of cadres, although the Communists must not replace the regular administration of the university.[48]   The social science staff of the university, however, carries the main burden "in the ideological upbringing of the student body"; so here the party organization must be particularly attentive.[49]

A Western scientist who spent some time at the Leningrad Technical University reports that approximately half the scientists there were party members, who formed party cells in the departments, combining at the university level to form a party committee.

I gathered that the party committee and the party groups were the most powerful authorities at the university. If and when a party authority objected to a decision made by a prominent university official, this had the same effect as a court judgment. . . . Nor. . .did the party confine itself to supervisory functions; it took the initiative in working out directions and in conveying them in a binding form to the university staff. . . .I gathered that, everything else being equal, party members will be given preference in competition for university posts.[50]

The chief difficulty faced by the Communist Party in trying to guide Soviet culture is that culture is not easily manipulated nor safely stereotyped. It grows, evolves, develops, even changes slowly, but it does not respond quickly and surely to administrative fiat.   Moreover, the subtle nature of cultural patterns within a society makes it difficult for a dictatorship to prove to itself that it "controls" culture.   In education, too, results are not predictable with respect to popular acceptance of the doctrines and rationalizations of the ruling elite.   Recent studies indicate that the influence of education on political attitudes is more complicated, uncertain, and variable, to use Coleman's words, than it was thought to be earlier.   Education may reinforce or it may weaken prejudice; it may lead

[46] Vlasenkova and Demysheva, *op. cit.*, p. 36.

[47] B. Mochalov, "Partiynaya rabota v vuze," *Kommunist*, No. 10 (July, 1966), pp. 34–35. In the Politekhnical Institute "K. Marx" there are 533 Communists broken down into party organizations by faculty, each such organization containing 80 to 120 members, with an elected party buro of 5 to 11 people. A. Svinarenko, "Partorganizatsia vuza," *Partiynaya Zhizn*, No. 4 (February, 1965), p. 29.

[48] Mochalov, *op. cit.*, p. 36.

[49] *Ibid.*, p. 40.

[50] Hans Kuebler, "Exchange Scientist in Leningrad," *Survey* (July, 1964), pp. 67–68.

either to radicalism or conservatism.[51]

A homogeneously oriented and universally accepted culture has not been produced by Soviet education.[52]   Student opposition to political propaganda is not unknown in the USSR.   In 1956, a number of university students reportedly walked out on lectures which tried to rationalize Soviet troops being used to put down the Hungarian rebellion.   There are several categories of students on whom political socialization, as the regime has desired it, has been ineffective.   Azrael notes several types of disaffection and apathy, including political idealists, whe were disaffected because Soviet reality does not measure up to Soviet ideology.   Another group was politically apathetic and indifferent, wanting above all to escape from politics.   Finally, there was a group of political instrumentalists who felt their own political involvement to be a way of acquiring prestige and status.[53]   Nevertheless, the elite must continue to believe that it can positively shape Soviet culture and its related spheres of activity, for not to so believe might call into question some very basic assumptions about communism itself.

THE PARTY AND THE MILITARY

To gain power in 1917 the Bolsheviks needed, among other support, the active assistance of the bulk of the military forces.   Since gaining that support, the Communist leadership over the years has taken special pains, even some risk, to retain the unswerving loyalty of the military, security, and police forces—even at the cost of seriously decimating the trained officer class which has followed various purges.   In building the Red Army, with few trained professionals, Trotsky early faced the necessity of placing former tsarist officers in Red Guard units.   At the same time Trotsky's military system was based on discipline, centralized political control, and orthodoxy of doctrine.   More than that, the party leadership has stead-fastly insisted on its unquestioning supremacy over the military high command in all matters whatsoever.

The list of high military officers who were purged by Stalin in order for him to maintain his preeminent position has included such Communist notables as Trotsky (who was the creator of the Red Army and military leader both of the October Revolution and the Civil War), Antonov-Ovseenko (field commander of the October Revolution), Marshal Tukhachevskii (outstanding Civil War commander and later commander-

---

[51] James Coleman (ed.), *Education and Political Development* (Princeton, N. J.: Princeton University Press, 1965), pp. 19–20.

[52] See Jeremy R. Azrael, in Coleman, *op. cit.*, p. 248.

[53] *Ibid.*, pp. 256–57.

in-chief of the Army), Gamarnik (head of the Political Directorate of the Army), and Marshal Bluecher (commander-in-chief of the Far East in the 1920's). One estimate of the purges in the 1930's is that about one half of the total officer corps was purged, including 3 of the 5 marshals, 13 of the 15 army commanders, 57 of the 85 corps commanders, 110 of the 195 division commanders, 220 of the 406 brigade commanders, and all 11 vice commissars of war—in all 90 percent of the generals and 80 percent of the colonels.[54]

During the time of Kerensky's Provisional Government and just prior to the October Revolution, the institution of political commisars (then called "front commissars") was introduced in order to win soldier support for the policies of the government. Later, under the Bolshevik's early reign, the political-military commissars, functioning as party aides rather than professional military officials, came under the supervision of an All-Russian Bureau of Military Commissars. In 1919 the Political Administration of the Soviet Republic was established with subordinate political departments in fleets, armies, divisions, and military districts. The Political Administration on the national level at this time came directly under the Central Committee.

In a 1937 statute, military commissars were assigned the task of political direction over, and carrying out political work within, the military units. In addition to some responsibility placed in the regular unit commander in this respect, the military commissar was to educate military forces in devotion to the motherland and to the government, to ensure a high level of "political-moral" feeling within the unit, to protect the unit against penetration by spies, to observe military secrecy, and to assess the overall mood, needs, and desires of the military forces.[55] At times these political commissars enjoyed rather extensive powers, including that of sharing operational decisions with the regular commanders. The commissars could even countermand the orders of the commanders and have them arrested for counterrevolutionary activity.[56]

Following a period of confusion, mistrust, and indecision, the military commissar system which resulted in a two-headed military leadership was deemed to be militarily inefficient and subsequently abolished in 1940. Taking its place was the newer *zampolit* system in which each important unit had a deputy commander for political affairs (who was the *zampolit*).

---

[54] Raymond L. Garthoff, quoted in Schapiro, *op. cit.*, p. 420.

[55] Harold J. Berman and Miroslav Kerner, *Documents on Soviet Military Law and Administration* (Cambridge, Mass.: Harvard University Press, 1958), pp. 12–15.

[56] Zbigniew Brzezinski, "Party Controls in the Soviet Army," *Journal of Politics*, Vol. 14 (November, 1952), p. 566.

But again, in the early war years the military commissars were recreated at various levels of the armed forces; this was because party leaders doubted the loyalty to communism of military officers.   The necessities of rational military leadership, especially in wartime, however, became once more apparent to the regime and, in 1942, the military commissars again were abolished and military commanders were restored to their earlier positions and given full control over their respective units.   The *zampolit* system in each unit was later reintroduced to become a permanent feature of the organizational pattern of the armed forces.

Functioning at present under the Central Committee's Chief Political Directorate for the Armed Forces, there are subordinate political directorates within military units.   At each such unit the head of the party organization generally is the *zampolit*.   The *zampolit* is subordinate both to the regular commander of the respective unit and also to the *zampolit* of the next higher military unit who, in effect, appointed him.   The main tasks of a *zampolit* are politically to "educate" officers and troops in official propaganda and to get them to support the Soviet system.   The *zampolit*, according to one view, functions as a combination chaplain, information and education officer, special services officer, censor, and disciplinarian.[57]

Party organization and activities within the military sphere, as might be anticipated, differ somewhat from party actions outside of the armed forces.   Except for the lower echelons within the party hierarchy, the practice of election of party leaders is abandoned, and party organs are organized by military units rather than on a territorial basis.   Although party leaders form a part of the general military hierarchy, the tasks of party organs very definitely do not include control over "production" matters, that is over operational military rule by the authorized military commander.[58]

The first problem facing the Communist leadership following the Revolution arose because most Red Army commanders in the time of the Civil War were, of necessity, former tsarist officers.   Questions as to loyalty of these officers to the Communist Party were real and pressing.   By 1928, however, the party could have somewhat more faith in the military because by now most of the higher army officers were regular party members.   And yet, in the Great Purge, as noted, Stalin still felt obliged to eliminate many high-ranking officers in efforts to do away with all military opposition both

---

[57] Harold J. Berman and Miroslav Kerner, *Soviet Military Law and Administration* (Cambridge, Mass.: Harvard University Press, 1955), p. 134.

[58] *Ibid.*, p. 20.   The ranking *zampolit* within a given military district is, however, a member of the three-man military council which governs the district.   There is also a military district party commission subordinate directly to the Central Committee's Chief Political Directorate for the Armed Forces.

real and imagined to his rule. During World War II, however, Stalin was forced, for lack of any other choice, to rely very heavily on the support of the armed forces, and he could only hope they would be loyal to the regime. Since Stalin's death, only an occasional slight purge (such as the removal from top command of Marshall Zhukov in 1957) has been necessary to keep the military forces faithful to the communist system and to acquiesce in the party's dominant position within Soviet society. In 1965 the party's General Secretary, Brezhnev, commented to a graduating class from the armed forces academies that the party believes in one-man command of troops (by professional military officers), but built on a "party basis." In their work, he continued, military commanders must rely on party and *Komsomol* organizations for raising the preparedness of military units and vessels. Party political work "is an integral area of the activities of the Soviet officer."[59]

Whether or not the regime can always count on the undying and absolute loyalty of the military forces is not so certain, however. If, for example, the policies of the party—in a controversial, perhaps even risky cold war venture—are felt to endanger the nation, some military leaders might attempt a military coup. Or, if certain military leaders believe Soviet foreign policy to be too weak and vacillating and not sufficiently aggressive, a coup might be attempted. Since the Cuban missile crisis of 1962, perhaps, the military high command has acted a bit more like an interest group and has more successfully articulated its demands before the political elite. These demands are mainly those of adequate military preparedness and national security. What the military leadership wants is a greater voice in military matters (reminiscent of political-military squabbles in recent U.S. history) and less of a "political" influence. Soviet military leaders seem to object not to party supremacy as such, but to party intrusion into what are considered by many to be strictly military matters.[60] Khrushchev's removal in 1964 might have been helped along by military pressures which were known to be in opposition to some of Khrushchev's military-defense policies. In sum, however, the danger of a military coup in the USSR seems remote. The communist system of rule in the Soviet Union over the years has seemed no more conducive to military coups than is the case with the Western democracies. Militarism and professional military

---

[59] *Pravda*, July 4, 1965. The task of the primary party organization in a military unit is to help the commander in the "political part of the training and instruction of servicemen . . . ." A. I. Lukoyanov and B. M. Lazarev, *Sovetskoe Gosudarstvo i Obshchestvennye Organizatsii* (Moscow, 1960), p. 163.

[60] See the discussions by Thomas W. Wolfe in *Problems of Communism* (May–June, 1964), and in his *Soviet Strategy at the Crossroads* (Cambridge, Mass.: Harvard University Press, 1964).

cliques have not been serious problems for communist regimes either in the Soviet Union or in most other communist countries.

PARTY IN GOVERNMENT

The formal legal government in the Soviet Union, be it national, regional, or local, is never far removed from supervision and control by the Communist Party. From the establishment of overall top policy, through review of yearly and quarterly plans, down to periodic checking on routine operations and selection of key governmental officials, the party unit at each stratum of the organization serves both as cornerstone and general guide for all governmental actions of any importance. Party policy for decisions on matters of industry become governmental policy, party programs for agriculture become governmental programs, party assignments, whatever they may concern—such as education, culture, foreign policy, local industry—become, by definition, governmental responsibilities. This virtual merger of party and government is neither concealed nor rationalized by Soviet leaders. Rather, it is freely admitted and held up as a healthy example of the success and novelty of the Soviet political-governmental system. In fact, for many Soviet officials, especially those on the higher policy-forming levels, there is no practical difference between party and government. They function, when all is said and done, as one organ. Failure to grasp this intimate relationship, as Rigby suggests—that the party command structure is an integral part of the governmental administration—gives rise to much of the confusion over the nature of Soviet politics regarding crude dichotomies between party *apparatchiks* and governmental technocrats.[61]

In one sense, this close control over government can be considered as the single most important and most zealously guarded of all the functions of the party. At the national level three regular members of the Politburo occupied the three highest posts on the Council of Ministers in mid-1966, at the formation of the new government (Chairman and the two First Deputy Chairmen). At the same time, three regular and two candidate members of the Politburo were on the Presidium of the Supreme Soviet.

Party leadership of governmental ministries is exercised by way of the national and regional party central committees picking ministers and inspecting the work of the ministries.[62] Representatives of party committees within ministries meet on occasion, such as a four-day session of

---

[61] T. H. Rigby, "Traditional, Market, and Organizational Societies and the USSR," *World Politics*, Vol. XVI (July, 1964), p. 553.

[62] I. N. Ananov, *Ministerstva v SSSR* (Moscow, 1960), pp. 22–23.

secretaries of ministries, state committees, and departments of the USSR and RSFSR governments meeting with appropriate section heads of the Central Committee.[63] The following tasks were listed for party organizations of the Ministry of Instrument Building, Automation and Systematic Management:[64]

1. Raise the activity and responsibility of each worker for his assigned task.
2. Suggest production innovations and planning improvements.
3. Stimulate production increases.
4. Discuss industrial problems faced by ministries.
5. Improve labor discipline.

Apart from broad policy-setting roles of party organizations at the higher levels, the above items indicate more concretely what party organizations are expected to do. The most important "governmental" task, however, is to initiate legislation. As one Soviet source depicts it, the most important changes and additions to Soviet legislation belong to the sphere of the Central Committee; usually, however, the Committee works with the Council of Ministers in this activity.[65] Two such important laws, the 1957 reorganization of industrial management and restructuring the school system, are cited as examples of Central Committee initiation of laws.[66]

On the regional and local levels there is a similar, although not identical, interweaving of party and governmental leaders in the more responsible positions. Normally the heads of local governments at the same time are members of the guiding bureau of the respective local party committee, and first secretaries of the latter also are on the local government's executive committee. In addition, each governmental unit usually has a party cell, with its own elected secretary, which itself is subordinate to the party committee at the appropriate area level.

All down the administrative hierarchy the party's directing hand is apparent. The Central Committee of the CPSU even introduces some of its proposals (such as the 1957 economic decentralization) directly into the Supreme Soviet, thereby bypassing the government Council. Down through the middle and lower echelons, too, the pattern of party control is similar. One purpose of local party units, in addition to preparing slates of candidates for election to executive committees, is to plan for the work of local governments. It would not seem an exaggeration, in the words of

[63] *Pravda*, December 4, 1966.

[64] T. Vladimirov, "Zaboty Kommunistov ministerstva," *Partiynaya Zhizn*, No. 21 (November, 1966), pp. 29–31.

[65] A. I. Lepeshkin, *et al.*, *Kurs Sovetskogo Gosudarstvennogo Prava*, Vol. 2 (Moscow, 1962), p. 412.

[66] V. S. Osnovin, *Gosudarstvenno-Pravovye Otnosheniya* (Moscow, 1965), p. 101.

Churchward, to claim that it is the party committee in the *rayony* that really constitutes the agency of government at that level.[67]

Local party organizations control the leading appointments (such as chairman, vice-chairman and secretary) to the local governments, even to the extent of regulating the volunteer police units, the *druzhiny*.[68] Party committees in cities and *rayony* supposedly "study and generalize" the experience of local soviets and their executive committees, and help to overcome deficiencies and to perfect the methods of leadership.[69] And yet, lower party organs periodically are admonished not to interfere with the routine administrative actions of these governments, but instead are urged to inject into them loyalty, conscientiousness, and policy leadership. According to Politburo member Podgorny's criticism, there are cases in which party committees actually carry out the duties of local governments in many matters instead of aiding and raising the respect for these governments.[70]

The Soviet system has become an amalgamation of a single party and government, sharing in common their joint tasks, responsibilities, burdens, even leading personnel. When the workings and the successes of the system satisfy the nation's leadership, then both party and governmental officials up and down the hierarchy are given a nod of approval and are duly rewarded. When something goes wrong, no one associated with the problem escapes blame, and it makes little difference in the case whether the errant official is a party or government functionary.

PARTY DEMOCRACY

The problem of allowing lower party organs to exercise some democratic procedures while yet holding these organs strictly accountable to higher control has caused hope, expectation, frustration, and confusion among party units over the years. One member of a city party committee complained that in two "superfluous years" in which he sat on the committee he rarely was informed of the decisions reached by the committee's guiding bureau.[71] In elections held in a primary party organization containing

[67] L. G. Churchward, "Continuity and Change in Soviet Local Government, 1947–1957," *Soviet Studies*, Vol. 9 (January, 1958), p. 261.

[68] L. G. Churchward, "Soviet Government Today," *Soviet Studies* (April, 1966), p. 444.

[69] A. Tokarev, "Partiyne organizatssi i mestnye sovety," *Sovety Deputatov Trudyashchikhsya*, No. 8 (August, 1966), p. 10. Two *rayon* party bureaus, for example, recommended to local governments that they increase financial controls over local institutions. *Partiynaya Zhizn*, No. 3 (February, 1967), p. 33.

[70] *Pravda*, April 1, 1966.

[71] V. Vodyanov, "Povyshat otvetstvennost chlenov komiteta," *Partiynaya Zhizn*, No. 16 (August, 1956), p. 62.

100–150 Communists, one member protested that only a few people made the decisions for the whole group. In some elections, too, a candidate may receive more votes than even the secretary, but the former still is not elected to the bureau while the secretary is.[72] Still other objections concern the predominance of only a few party leaders. One party official, it was pointed out, simultaneously is a member of the party committee in his collective farm, a member of the bureau of the *raykom*, a member of the *obkom*, deputy to three different local units of government (*selskiy, rayon, oblast*), and a member of several commissions.[73] In the mechanics and math departments of Moscow State University for the past fifteen years the same twenty-five to thirty scientists have been elected to the departments' party *buros* over and over. As a result, party work becomes habitual, repetitive, and monotonous.[74] Complaints have been registered against bureaus of party committees which heavily dominate general sessions of the party committees; the illegal practice in some *rayon* and city party committees of co-opting new members into leadership circles has been singled out for condemnation.[75] Another member protested that because a party secretary failed to get reelected—since he received one to two negative votes—this resulted in a minority of one to two people imposing its will on the majority. The villain in the story is secret balloting and too many candidates on the election list which, the complainant notes, often result in losing "good party workers." Acknowledging the necessity for retaining the secret ballot, though, the writer continues, a way around the dilemma would be to have the superior party committee inform the lower group prior to the balloting as to which person "would best qualify for work in the party organ...."[76] In other words, "controlled" and pre-arranged elections are the practical solution to the philosophical dilemma of too much electoral freedom versus desired electoral results.

Representatives of higher party organs who attend and participate in election meetings, of course, bear responsibility for seeing that "good workers" are elected and, in short, for guiding the elections. The representative may "recommend" to the meeting the election of specific

---

[72] N. Piskunov, "Dva pisma o vyborakh v pervichnykh partorganizatsiyakh," *Partiynaya Zhizn*, No. 16 (August, 1956), p. 50.

[73] N. Fedulov and Uu. Vostrikov, "Chlen partiynogo komiteta," *Partiynaya Zhizn*, No's. 15–16 (August, 1961), p. 115.

[74] Mochalov, *op. cit.*, p. 36.

[75] A. Vodolazskiy, "Kollegialnost—vazhneyshee uslovie pravilnogo rukovodstva," *Partiynaya Zhizn*, No. 18 (September, 1961), pp. 37–39.

[76] "S otchetno-vybornykh partiynykh sobraniy," *Partiynaya Zhizn*, No. 19 (October, 1957), pp. 40–41.

candidates to the party bureau.[77]   His main task is to see that his recommendations are accepted.

Criticisms against violations of party democracy appeared to be on the increase after Khrushchev's demise, perhaps in response to high-level criticism of the nondemocratic ruling techniques of Khrushchev.   Complaints are recorded of secretary-dominated meetings ("The secretary designated the reporters, prepared resolutions by himself."),[78] of higher party organs failing to consult local party organs on local matters,[79] and of stuffed ballot boxes in party elections ("Of 458 persons eligible to vote for leading party agencies, 509 voted.").[80]   At a local election meeting an "approved" slate was presented by the old guard, followed by immediate attempts to shut off potential debate and to call for a vote.[81]   One flagrant case involved a primary party organization refusing to elect as a party secretary the recommendation of the higher *raykom*.   Instead, another person, a local favorite, was elected.   At several succeeding meetings the local communists still refused to change their votes and the *raykom* doggedly refused to verify the election.[82]

Obviously, freedom to criticize, supposedly guaranteed to Communists by the party rules, does not mean, from the party's standpoint, freedom to speak against party policy or to express views which are "antiparty" or which are alien to "Marxism-Leninism."   And yet, there are officials who complain about "undemocratic" procedures, however infrequently.   This suggests that some improvements both from below and from above aimed at improving democratic methods may yet be forthcoming in Communist Party procedures.   In 1956 the special representatives (party organizers) of the Central Committee which had been attached to important enterprises and organizations were withdrawn in favor of less national supervision and a bit more autonomy for the local party organs.   In another vein, a collective farmer prided himself on the fact that in his farm secret balloting prevails; there are even two or three candidates regularly nominated for the position of farm chairman.[83]   So far, these examples drawn from different spheres of party control are but straws in the wind.   They are

---

[77] V. Churaev, "Yedinstvo partii i vnutripartiynaya demokratiya," *Kommunist*, No. 17 (December, 1957), p. 37.

[78] *Kommunist*, No. 7 (May, 1965), p. 76.

[79] *Partiynaya Zhizn*, No. 12 (June, 1965), p. 27.

[80] *Pravda*, February 23, 1966.

[81] "Partiynaya demokratiya i partiynaya distsiplina", *Partiynaya Zhizn*, No. 23 (December, 1966), p. 5.

[82] *Kommunist*, No. 18 (December, 1965), p. 37.

[83] *Selskaya Zhizn*, May 20, 1961.

too few to indicate any definite trend. Nevertheless, they *may* have some bearing on future developments within the party's control system.

The pathway which Communist Party methods will take regarding genuine democratic techniques as they are applied to internal party rule is difficult to discern clearly. It might not be too presumptuous, however, to anticipate a growing pressure from lower party organs for just such changes in central political domination as more regularized habits of operation, a greater reliance on opinions and suggestions from below, and even more of a tendency toward viable party elections with a somewhat less dependence on the age-old process of co-optation.

The party's self-assumed responsibility for the function of controlling all operating parts of Soviet society is both ideologically motivated, to pursue the goal of communism, and practically oriented, to continue the party elite's hold on political power. Success in the latter objective, however, may obviate the necessity for ever finally achieving the former. The *retention* of simple power may have supplanted the *achievement* of complex communism, in the minds if not in the hearts of the elite. Fifty years' experience of the Soviet Union has meant fifty years of rule by the Communist Party elite. The fifty years have not yet, by concession of the elite itself, resulted in communism. It is proper to raise the question as to which goal is more important, and, furthermore, if the dynamism of one has rendered the other inert.

PART THREE

Rule Administering and

Adjudicating:

The State Apparatus

CHAPTER IX

Central Government: Structure and Functions

FOLLOWING the Communist Party's function of rule making and checking on the enforcement of those rules, the governmental apparatus as such administers the rules for the party. In fulfilling this assignment, an elaborate central governmental structure has been erected since Lenin which includes a very large, proliferated bureaucracy, with numerous organizations having interminable suborganizations, departments, sections, and offices, almost ad infinitum. From executing laws for a modern nation and administering the extensive socialist state system, to supervising regional and local governments, even to indirectly managing the economy—all fall within the purview of the state apparatus as directed by the central governmental institutions. This very broad, almost sweeping range of responsibilities and functions throws the government full force into the political, economic, cultural, even social life of the nation. It also firmly dedicates the government to promoting the Russian's "socialist" system.

SOVIET CONSTITUTIONALISM

The year 1936, in addition to seeing the start of the last phase of the Great Purge, marked the inauguration of a new constitution. It was referred to as the "Stalin Constitution" for Stalin headed a commission which wrote the document. Prior to this time there had been two earlier constitutions. The first, in 1918, established the "Russian Socialist Federated Republic," provided for a central governmental structure with a Council of People's Commissars (*Sovnarkom*) at the top, and authorized a system of elections to the All-Russian Congress of Soviets (the rough equivalent of a legislature). The elections, however, were not universal and were not direct. The first Constitution also called for such freedoms as those of speech, press, and assembly, and for the separation of church and state. The Constitution's purpose was to usher in the socialist society in the USSR and to promote the victory of socialism around the world.

The second Constitution in 1924 established the Union of Soviet Socialist Republics (USSR). No great changes appeared in this Constitution over the first. It did provide for secession from the Union by a member republic, legally if not practically, and the central governmental structure was elaborated. It assumed more its present form with a two-house Central Executive Committee (with a Council of the Union and a Council of Nationalities), and a description of the commissariats which made up the *Sovnarkom*. Suffrage remained indirect and not universal, and a Supreme Court and procurator-general (as the highest legal officer) were organized. As with the first Constitution, too, there was no mention of the Communist Party.

The third (1936) Constitution, for the first time, mentioned the Communist Party, depicting it as the vanguard of the working people and the vanguard of all organizations of the people, both public and state. Now the Communist Party is officially and constitutionally enthroned as the leading organization for all of Soviet society. There were electoral changes made with provision for universal suffrage which this time would be equal, direct, and secret. No longer were certain people excluded from elections because of their occupational classes, and voters now directly elected a national legislature, the new Supreme Soviet, which replaced the old Central Executive Committee. Of this Constitution, Stalin remarked that it was based on the fact that now there were no antagonistic classes in the USSR and as a result it is the only really democratic constitution in the world. Stalin proudly admitted that the new Constitution continues the dictatorship of the working class as it also continues unchanged the leading position of the Communist Party. In the 1936 Constitution there was also a more extensive description of governmental powers, duties, and responsibilities (see Appendix I for the text of the Constitution).

The 1936 Constitution begins with a claim that the USSR is a state of workers and peasants, a theme carried through several of its parts. Article 3, for example, states that all power in the country is vested in the working people. Socialism, another recurring theme in the Constitution, includes such features as opposition to capitalism and the provision for socialist (state, cooperative, or collective) ownership of property, natural wealth, industry, and agriculture. Private enterprise is permitted only in handicrafts (if the person works at it himself without hiring anyone else); citizens do have the right, however, to own personal property, a house, and sundry personal articles.

The federal structure as outlined in the Constitution assigns the bulk of state power to the central government which, in addition to such normal Western-type governmental functions of defense and foreign policy, also includes, among other functions, supervising foreign trade, establishing economic plans for the nation, managing industrial and agricultural enterprises assigned to the government, and defining basic principles for the guidance of education and public health. Powers assigned to the regional governmental level (union republics), according to the Constitution, include republic constitutional adoption and revision and governmental organization and reorganization, the exercise of general state authority within its sphere, and the "right" to engage in foreign relations (the Ukrainian and Belorussian Union Republics have seats in the United Nations General Assembly).

The major portion of the Constitution is taken up with a description of the structure and general procedures of government: legislative, executive, and judicial, with a listing of the powers and responsibilities which belong to the various branches. These are covered in some detail in later chapters.

Other parts of the Constitution refer to rights of citizens (rest, leisure, disability benefits, education, equality with other citizens and between the sexes, and freedom of speech, press, and assembly). In addition to these rights, the Constitution obliges citizens to abide by the Constitution and laws, to maintain labor "discipline," to perform public duties "honestly," to respect the rules of socialist society (including safeguarding public socialist property as the "sacred" foundation of the Soviet system), to fulfill one's military service, and to defend the country. Finally, procedures for elections to the representative organizations (soviets) are included, and provision is made for Constitutional amendments (by the national Supreme Soviet).

A constitutional commission was formed in 1962, headed by Khrushchev, to write a new constitution for the USSR. It was reconstituted in 1966, with the new party chief Brezhnev at its head and composed of 97 members, all deputies to the Supreme Soviet. Among the commission's members were the regular and candidate members of the Politburo, Central Committee Secretaries and a number of other top party and governmental leaders.[1] Although the commission had published no report of any of its proceedings up to 1967, the draft of a new constitution might well give expression to the concept, developed in the later years of Khrushchev's leadership, of referring to the current Soviet "state of all the people," connoting thereby more of an emphasis on popular sovereignty. In listing the nine basic principles of socialist constitutions, Ilinskiy includes these

---

[1] *Pravda*, December 20, 1966.

three: the unity of state power with the sovereignty of representative organs, the participation of workers in the decisions of state affairs, and the principle of people's sovereignty.[2] Osnovin, in commenting on development of the new Soviet constitution, writes that there is the assumption that the primary source of state power is the people, who hold sovereignty.[3]

Constitutions have the ostensible purpose of setting forth the governmental framework. In addition, they set the tone of political rule and list the powers (and, by implication, the responsibilities) of government. By indirection they constitute a limitation on government (by defining its functions and setting forth its boundaries). The Soviet Constitution only partly details the governing structure, chiefly because it does not portray (nor even outline) the vital role played in Soviet governmental affairs by the Communist Party. Moreover, the Constitution fails to reveal the great, unlimited power of the state apparatus and constitutes no barrier against the arbitrary dictatorships under which the Soviet Union has been ruled most of the time since 1917. Soviet constitutions have in no way limited the powers either of the government, the Communist Party, or the ruling elite.

Why bother, then, with a constitution at all? First, it has a legitimizing function, seeming to authorize and legalize the various governmental structures and processes, thereby legitimizing the ruling elite itself. The Constitution might reassure some citizens that the governmental edifice has been built for them because of its representative and democratic phraseology. Constitutional clauses incorporating such terms as workers' rule, equality, and rights are no doubt designed for popular appeal. Hopefully, the Constitution also will encourage a sense of citizen obedience to law and institutions and to the leaders. By setting forth the Constitution the leaders sought, in addition, to impress the West with the great "democratic" nature of the Soviet government.

It is conceivable that the promised new Soviet constitution will attempt to embrace somewhat more positively the concept of popular rule in the USSR. As this chapter points out with respect to the expanding influence of the subcommissions of the national legislature, there are a few governing innovations which may augur well for a slow, painful growth of Soviet representative institutions in the future.

Immediately we can raise an appropriate question. What kind of a large, central government must be required to carry out such a grandiose task as that indicated above? The precise organizational form and the

---

[2] I. I. Ilinskiy, "Ob osnovnykh chertakh i printsipakh sotsialisticheskikh konstitutsiy," *Sovetskoe Gosudarstvo i Pravo*, No. 1 (January, 1965), p. 28.

[3] V. S. Osnovin, *Gosudarstvenno-pravovye Otnosheniya* (Moscow, 1965), p. 143.

sphere of operation of the central government, in attempts to answer the question, undergo continuing reassessment by Soviet leaders. To date, they have not yet solved the problem to their own satisfaction. The organization which tries to carry out these objectives in the USSR is the Council of Ministers—popularly called the "government."

The constitution describes the Council of Ministers, USSR (*Sovet Ministrov*), as the highest executive and administrative organ in the nation. The Council is responsible for directing the work of the central managerial organizations (such as the ministries and state committees), overseeing the national economic plan and the budget, maintaining public order, conducting foreign relations, guiding the armed forces, and exercising general supervision and control over regional and local governments. The organization of the Council has changed from time to time because of rather frequent internal reorganizations growing out of domestic power struggles, but also because of conscious efforts of the regimes to improve their administrative structures.

DEVELOPMENT OF THE CENTRAL GOVERNMENTAL APPARATUS

Soviet governmental organization since 1917 has grown by fits and starts. Serious economic, political, and governmental problems arising in the years of 1921, 1928, 1932, 1939, 1953, 1957, and 1964 have all been met, in part, by reorganizations in the central governmental apparatus. Apart from the events of 1921 and 1957 (which resulted in a partial decentralization of some managerial authority), the other organizational changes have followed a rather consistent pattern of increasing and sharpening centralized control over the whole administrative system.

After gaining power in 1917 the Communists first moved to place all economic activity in the country under central control. Though not immediately successful in these first efforts, by 1919 all large-scale raw material development and manufacturing came under central supervision, and by 1921 small-scale industry was governmentally controlled, either directly or indirectly. The impact of these developments, from the administrative standpoint, was to plant the seeds for the large, centralized governmental apparatus in Moscow which was to come later and which, in turn, sought to organize and manage the entire country. For this purpose, the Supreme Council of National Economy was established; it embraced a proliferation of divisions, chief directorates, councils, commissions, and "centers." Although solid managerial experience was all too often limited in these early years, imaginative and ambitious schemes were in abundance.

The NEP of 1921–27, organizationally, was a partial and temporary withdrawal from over-centralization and from complete socialization of the economy. Small-scale industry was freed from central control and permitted to develop more or less privately. Medium-scale industry was leased to individuals and cooperatives and was given some freedom to engage in private manufacturing and trade. As for large-scale industry, factories producing similar commodities and those falling within specific geographic areas, these were grouped under special government trusts, the administration of which was decentralized and made quite autonomous. The trusts, at first only very loosely directed from Moscow, were drawn bit by bit under the Supreme Council of National Economy; in short, under more centralized control. In 1923, when the USSR was formally established, the Supreme Council was reorganized and made more simple; there were now two main divisions, one dealing broadly with nationwide economic problems and the other with specific branches of industry.

The chief effect of a 1927 reorganization of the Supreme Council of National Economy was to increase central planning. Branches of industry were regrouped under chief directorates and committees, each of which was made responsible for planning the output of a specific industry. The central chief directorates next extended their administrative jurisdiction over republic and local industry.

In early 1932 Soviet governmental organization began to assume the form, roughly, which it retained throughout the Stalin era. In that year the Supreme Council of National Economy was abolished and replaced by three commissariats—heavy industry, light industry, and the timber industry. The objectives were to increase specialization of production and administration while yet tying these two functions closer together. The pattern for administering industrial enterprises was determined by placing them in one of three categories: All-union (industries of nationwide importance), union-republic (those which could and should be administered at least partly through regional governments), and republic (industry of only local significance). It was during this period, too, continuing until shortly after Stalin's death, that the specialized chief directorates (glavki) functioned as the most important echelon of industrial management.

Increased administrative specialization continued intermittently until 1939, when the five basic divisions of industry—heavy, light, defense, timber, and machine building—were further split into eighteen separate commissariats. This reorganization, a war preparatory move, was followed in June, 1941, by creation of a supra-cabinet, the State Defense Committee. This latter five-member Committee, headed by Stalin, was responsible for the supreme direction of the war effort; it was abolished in 1945. Prior to

1946 the government cabinet was the Council of People's Commissariats.

In an adaptation of the Western style of cabinet terminology, which earlier had been the Russian version too from 1906–17, the Council of Commissariats was renamed the Council of Ministers. At this time individual commissariats were renamed ministries, and their commissars were now called ministers. These identical name changes were carried out in the regional governments.

Post-Stalin Changes

Immediately following Stalin's death, the Communist Party leaders, fearing a possible internal revolt, consolidated and tightened control over the governmental apparatus by drastically reducing from 62 to 30 the number of ministries, special committees, and chief directorates attached to the Council. Once the insecurity of the leaders passed, the ministries, committees, and chief directorates (by 1954) again were expanded to 54.

In 1953 the Soviet leadership took a long critical look at its governmental structure and concluded that some strong measures were sorely needed to improve the whole managerial system. Many shortcomings in administration, resulting from overcentralization and the proliferated bureaucracy which had flowered under Stalin, were becoming all too apparent. There was undue interference in industrial and agricultural management on the part of police and party officials on the middle and lower levels; there were many examples of unrealistic planning as well as frequent barriers to the cooperation needed among industrial units throughout the country; a demoralizing atmosphere arose in part because the limited power and authority of administrators throughout the country was nowhere commensurate with their heavy burden of assigned responsibilities. In 1955, for example, Chairman of the Council of Ministers Bulganin argued that outmoded and excessive bureaucratic procedures discouraged managerial initiative, thereby wasting both personnel and material resources.[4]

In the initial period of post-Stalin reform, emphasis was laid on streamlining the structure of the higher echelons of control. Multiple-stage organization, reflected in the burdensome pattern of ministry, chief directorates, regional directorates, and combines and trusts, was singled

---

[4] Report to the Central Committee Plenum in *Pravda*, July 17, 1955. See also the comments of A. G. Zverev, "Uluchshat i sovershenstvovat rabotu gosudarstvennogo apparata," *Kommunist*, No. 16 (November, 1954), pp. 29–40; and the article "Ukreplenie apparata sovetskoy gosudarstvennoy administratsii," *Sovetskoe Gosudarstvo i Pravo*, No. 5 (May, 1953), pp. 18–25.

out as a particular target for attack. An overabundance of sales and supply organizations at all levels of administration and bloated ministerial departments which directed construction and repair were especially criticized. By the end of 1954 officials were claiming that some improvements already had been achieved. In November, Finance Minister Zverev announced that some 200 chief directorates and divisions, 147 trusts, 898 supply organizations, and 4,500 other offices and small subdivisions had been consolidated or abolished in 46 ministries and departments. Zverev also claimed that administrative staffs of the central ministries and departments had been reduced by 20.6 percent during the period 1952–54. In late 1954 similar reorganizations were begun in regional ministries and directorates, in enterprises, and in local governmental and party organs. In his speech to the Supreme Soviet in December, 1955, Zverev announced that in the preceding two-year period (1954–55) the number of administrative employees in enterprises, establishments, and organizations had been reduced by 750,000; this reduction, reportedly, achieved an annual saving of more than 7.2 billion rubles.[5]

Since early 1954, a number of all-union ministries have been transformed into union-republic ones, thus decentralizing some of their functions and providing for branches of these ministries to be established in one or more of the union republics. All-union ministries, for example, were those of heavy, extractive, and defense industry. Union-republic ministries were those of more regional significance, such as Health or Trade. After 1957, however, most national ministries (all-union and union-republic) were abolished or severely reorganized so that the former distinction between the two types of ministries was of little significance. In addition, some ministries abolished at the national level were recreated at the union-republic level—such as the Ministry of Internal Affairs (MVD). The advantages which Soviet leaders anticipated from these changes were a reduction in the central bureaucracy, expansion of the authority of regional governments, and a general improvement in the efficiency of planning, financing, and administration.

Following Khrushchev's recommendation to the Central Committee Plenum in February, 1957, a resolution was adopted carrying out the most widespread reorganization of the central governmental structure in the past 25 years. This so-called decentralization, which took effect in May, 1957, had as one of its goals the abolition of all central ministries engaged in industry and construction (25 ministries) and transferring their

---

[5] Zverev, *op. cit.*, pp. 3, 34; *Pravda*, December 27, 1955.

functions to newly created regional councils of national economy (*sovety narodnogo khozyastva*, abbreviated *sovnarkhozy*).[6]

Several reasons for the extensive reorganization of 1957 were given by Khrushchev. Industrial ministries in Moscow were too powerful, arbitrary, semi-independent, and competitive among themselves for scarce resources. Overcentralization in management, the real evil, resulted in long delays in decision making, in an overgrowth of directorates, departments, sub-departments, and other managerial organs, all of which contributed to a sizable waste in resources and services and added to the overall cost of economic production.[7]   What Khrushchev only alluded to, however, was that these ministries, each with thousands of employees and each headed by a powerful and influential minister, constituted a potent managerial class which conceivably could become a political force in and of itself to challenge even the supremacy of the party apparatus.

The reorganization created 104 regional economic councils located throughout the country; they were made responsible for directing all economic activity within their respective areas.   Industrial enterprises and construction organizations, heretofore controlled by ministries in Moscow, were turned over to the jurisdiction of economic councils, or in some cases to local governments.   In Moscow, the old system of ministerial management which had been the heart of central government administration since the 1930's was gone.   In its place were a few remaining central ministries (such as Communications) now stripped of their former managerial functions and confined to long-range technical and scientific planning for their particular industry.   Several of the abolished ministries (such as Shipbuilding) were recreated as State Committees, retaining some planning and research but no directing functions.   The State Economic Commission (*Gosekonomkommissiya*) was abolished and *Gosplan* was revitalized and given a more influential role in the central administrative structure.   There were several marked effects of this drastic reorganization on the Soviet governmental system.

In the first place, in the breakup of the central ministerial bureaucracy, where industrial ministers exerted considerable influence over planning and management of the economy, the Communist Party apparatus both in the center and in the regions was able to reassert its former unchallenged role of dominance over the economy.   Secondly, the restructuring and streamlining in the central governmental agencies has resulted in more

---

[6] In the period 1917–31 there were regional councils of national economy subordinate to the Supreme Council of National Economy.

[7] *Pravda*, May 8, 1957.

rationality and increased efficiency in operation of the government. Thirdly, there has taken place a slight decentralization of minor decision-making powers to lower levels: central to regional, regional to local. *Sovnarkhozy* were given authority, for example, to fix preliminary wholesale prices on goods produced by their subordinate enterprises and to approve, within certain limits, wholesale prices. Fourthly, new problems of governmental administration were created as a result of the reorganization. In one instance, *sovnarkhozy*, supposedly given authority over production, lacked sufficient authority to allocate critical raw materials. Confusion arose, too, regarding actual subordination of *sovnarkhoz* sales organs. In 1960 the Astrakhan *Sovnarkhoz* was called to account for faults similar to those which existed under the old ministerial system: overstaffing in administrative offices, superfluous organizational units, and duplication of functions.[8]

In late 1962, following the November meeting of the party's Central Committee, there was a recentralizing of parts of the governmental apparatus. A Party-State Control Committee, guided jointly by the Central Committee and the Council of Ministers, was established to serve as a central auditing-inspection arm of the party and government. At this time several other state committees were formed and *Gosplan*, once again, was enlarged to assume the responsibilities of the State Economic Council (*Gosekonomsovet*), now abolished.

The 1957 decentralization and the accompanying creation of the burdensome *sovnarkhoz* structure were those of Khrushchev. On his removal from party leadership in 1964, his successors began dismantling the *sovnarkhoz* apparatus and returning to the pre-1957 ministerial system—in which ministries rather than *sovnarkhozy* direct the economy. After some reshuffling, eliminating smaller and creating larger *sovnarkhoz* units in late 1964 and early 1965, they were to be phased out, then eliminated by 1966. Their economic activity was divided among central economic ministries and regional and local governments, after the pre-1957 pattern. By mid-1966 the Council of Ministers, with many reconstituted ministries, bore a likeness more to the highly centralized Stalinist format than to that of Khrushchev's decentralizations.

It should not be surprising that the administrative system, frequently reorganized, has had difficulty functioning smoothly. Traditional methods of Communist administration (extreme centralization, inflated bureaucracy) are not easily modified. Meanwhile, the governmental apparatus is

---

[8] *Pravda*, August 25, 1960.

changed and changed once again in a never-ending search for that magical organizational combination which in and of itself will solve all other Soviet governmental problems, big and little. The combination so far has not yet been discovered by the Soviet leaders.

ORGANIZATION AND FUNCTIONS OF THE COUNCIL OF MINISTERS

As presently organized the Council of Ministers is headed by its chairman, who is referred to in the West as the "prime minister" or "premier." The chairman has the right to appoint all of the Council's remaining members—with perfunctory Supreme Soviet approval. There is a Presidium of the Council consisting of the Chairman, the First Deputy, and Deputy Chairmen. In August, 1966, on the reappointment of the government following the legislative elections, there were two First Deputy Chairmen and nine Deputy Chairmen; the number varies a bit from time to time. On occasion the Presidium establishes *ad hoc* commissions for specific tasks, such as the Commission for Transport.[9]

The Presidium prepares questions on the most important matters for Council action and decides problems of national significance, such as providing leadership for ministries and departments of the Council.[10] In July, 1964, the Presidium held a meeting to discuss the next five-year plan (1966–70). Attending this meeting were Secretaries of the Central Committee, chairmen and deputy chairmen of union-republic councils of ministers, as well as other key governmental officials.[11] Other reported Presidium meetings, for example, have considered post-*sovnarkhoz* reorganizations (in December, 1965), and new forms of economic incentives (February, 1965).[12] *Gosplan* Chairman Baybakov addressed the Presidium on the performance of industrial enterprises under the new system of planning and economic incentives. The Presidium then assigned a special commission to review results and performance of these enterprises and to draw up suitable measures for other enterprises to be transferred to the new system. The Presidium also directed *Gosplan* and ministries to attain greater precision in their plans for capital operations.[13]

---

[9] E. V. Shorina, *Kollegialnost i Yedinonachalie v Sovetskom Gosudarstvennom Upravlenii* (Moscow: Gosurizdat, 1959), p. 27.

[10] *Pravda*, May 11, 1962.

[11] *Pravda*, July 25, 1964.

[12] *Izvestiya*, January 1, 1966; February 27, 1966.

[13] *Ibid.*, October 30, 1966.

COUNCIL OF MINISTERS, USSR (1967)

Presidium

Chairman
First Deputy Chairmen
Deputy Chairmen

Administrative ——————————————————————— Secretariat
Affairs

All-Union Ministries

Aviation Industry
Motor Vehicle Industry
Foreign Trade
Gas Industry
Civil Aviation
Machine Building for Light
and Food Industries, and
Household Appliances
Merchant Marine
Defense Industry
General Machine Building
Instrument Building, Auto-
mation and Control Sys-
tems
Transportation (RR)
Radio Industry
Medium Machine Building
Machine Tool and Instru-
ment Industry
Machine Building for Con-
struction, Road Building
and Civil Engineering
Ship Construction Industry
Tractor and Agriculture
Machine Building
Transport Construction
Heavy, Power, and Trans-
port Machine Building
Chemical and Petroleum
Machine Building
Electronics Industry
Electrotechnical Industry

Union-Republic Ministries

Geology
Public Health
Foreign Affairs
Culture
Light Industry
Lumber, Pulp and Paper,
and Wood Processing In-
dustry
Land Reclamation and
Water Resources
Installation and Special
Construction Work
Meat and Dairy Industry
Oil Extracting Industry
Oil Refining and Oil Chem-
ical Industry
Defense
Defense of Public Order
Food Industry
Building Materials Indus-
try
Fish Industry
Communications
Agriculture
Trade (Internal)
Coal Industry
Finance
Chemical Industry
Nonferrous Metallurgy
Ferrous Metallurgy
Power and Electrification
Education
Higher and Middle Spec-
ialized Education

State Committees

Planning
Material-Technical Supply
Science and Technics
Construction Affairs
People's Control
Questions of Labor and
Wages
Professional-Technical Ed-
ucation
Procurement
Forestry
Foreign Economic Rela-
tions
State Security (KGB)

Other Organizations

All-Union Farm Machin-
ery Association
State Bank
Central Statistical Direc-
torate
Council for Religious
Affairs

Chairmen of the 15 Union Republic
Councils of Ministers

The chairman and his deputies in the Council Presidium constitute as an inner, top-level cabinet, the highest and most important policy-forming group of leaders in the governmental side of the Soviet system. An operative Council Presidium of perhaps 10 to 15 members may render unnecessary frequent meetings of what would be a large and unwieldy body—the full Council of Ministers. There are in the Council a number of ministers who head individual ministries. In addition to the chairmen of the state committees, the chief of the Central Statistical Directorate, the chairman of the Board of the State Bank, the chairman of the Committee for State Security, the chairman of *Gosplan* plus a few of his leading assistants and several other high officials of the government all sit on the Council. Finally, the heads of the governments of the 15 union republics sit on the Council, *ex officio*. Thus, there are approximately 80–90 members in all who can be referred to, in a body, as the functioning central government of the Soviet Union. Finally, there are administrative-housekeeping organs, such as the Secretariat and Bureau of Administrative Affairs of the Council. Attached to, but not members of, the Council are several organizations such as the Civil Service Commission, the Academy of Sciences, the State Arbitration Commission, and the Telegraph Agency of the Soviet Union (TASS).

The responsibility of the Council of Ministers includes "all important questions of state administration in all fields of the economic, cultural, and political life of the country.[14] This amounts, practically, to administering all national activity. Of its numerous tasks, perhaps the most important is its role in drawing up the annual and five-year economic plans and ensuring their fulfillment. It might be logical, in fact, to subsume under the broad classification of national economic planning virtually all detailed functions of the Council.

Laws or statutes (*zakony*) can be enacted only by the Supreme Soviet, but the Council is really the source of the laws (acting together with the Politburo of the party's Central Committee), and it is the Council which has been given the formal assignment, in Soviet terminology, of "legislative initiative."[15] Prior to sessions of the Supreme Soviet, for example, the Council submits to it preliminary drafts of the economic state plan.[16] Resolutions or decisions (*postanovleniya*) and orders (*rasporyazheniya*) of the Council have a "juridical form" and are binding on all institutions, organizations, officials, and citizens throughout the territory of the USSR. The actual power of the Council seems to equal its formal prescription of authority.

In a meeting of the Council in November, 1959, the chairman of *Gosplan* gave a progress report on fulfillment of the 1959 capital construction plan and on general "production capacities." Following proposals and critical

---

[14] A. I. Denisov and M. G. Kirichenko, *Sovetskoe Gosudarstvennoe Pravo* (Moscow, 1957), p. 194.

[15] *Ibid.*, p. 196.

[16] *Pravda*, October 17, 1959.

remarks of Chairman Khrushchev, the Council then adopted a decision "evaluating progress" in plan fulfillment and another for stepping up "initial operations" of productive capacities. At this same session the Council approved a draft law, for later submission to the Supreme Soviet, on land use in the USSR and the union republics. This draft law grants to the union republics more extensive rights in deciding questions of land use and defines the rights and duties of land users—*kolkhozy, sovkhozy,* industrial enterprises, other economic organizations, and individual citizens. And, in another Council meeting there were reports by a first deputy chairman, a deputy chairman and the minister of finance. Following these reports, the Council then approved the drafts of the state plan and state budget for the forthcoming year.[17]

Another significant function of the Council is to direct and supervise the work of all lower levels of government throughout the nation. This involves Council approval of yearly economic plans, budget proposals, and high level managerial decisions. Consequently, the Council passes down orders and instructions and reviews the work and the decisions of the regional and local governments. To assist the Council in these supervisory functions, each union republic has permanent representatives assigned as liaison contacts with the Council and with other central government offices.[18]

The executive-administrative burdens of the Council are indeed immense. From daily, perhaps hourly decision making on innumerable governmental questions, it directs the nation's military and civil programs and conducts its foreign relations. All of this is added to year-round planning for the economic and cultural life of all Soviet citizens and organizations. Despite the minute involvement of the number one leader, be he a Stalin or Khrushchev, in decision making, the sheer enormity of his job requires the active participation in policy formation of a number of his chief advisors in the Council. Thus it can be assumed that the half-dozen or so leading personalities in the Council (chiefly the deputy chairmen) divide among themselves responsibility for guiding specific functions of the government, such as foreign policy, heavy industry, defense, and agriculture. The top Soviet leader normally retains final veto over most proposals and decisions of his colleagues.

[17] *Pravda,* November 6, 1959; November 6, 1961. In official terminology, acts published by the Council of Ministers have, naturally, the force of acts of the government, and not the force of laws of the USSR. *Sovetskoe Gosudarstvo i Pravo,* No. 10 (October, 1965), p. 28.

[18] A. M. Krokhotkin, "Postoyannye predstavitelstva—organy svyazi sovetov ministrov souznykh respublik s sovetom ministrov SSSR," *Sovetskoe Gosudarstvo i Pravo,* No. 11 (November, 1962), pp. 93–94.

The Council of Ministers, as the functioning executive branch of the Soviet government, is a genuine decision making body. It not only issues binding orders and instructions to central, regional, and local governmental bodies, it also prepares laws which are put into force even before they are formally enacted by the "legislature," and occasionally publishes them (in "draft" form) even prior to their submission to the Supreme Soviet. In view of the rather innocuous role of the Supreme Soviet and of the contrary strong position of the chairman and deputies of the Council, it can be safely concluded that all decisions of the Council are adopted throughout the country and given automatic ratification by appropriate legislative and executive bodies.

The Council, it should be remembered, is the main rule-administering organization in the Soviet political system. Its powers and responsibilities, although extensive (such as guiding and directing the legislature) are limited as well as supervised by the top organs of the Communist Party (Politburo, Secretariat, Central Committee). The party still formulates policy, as the rule maker of the system. The governmental organs, from the national Council of Ministers down through the regional and local governments, are the executing arm, the handmaiden, of the Communist Party.

THE SUPREME SOVIET

The national legislature in the USSR is the bicameral Supreme Soviet (*Verkhovny Sovet*), popularly elected for a four-year term. Officially, the Soviet is more than merely a legislative body. It is an organ invoked by the "will" of the entire Soviet people to preserve and to protect the interests of the workers and to reinforce and defend "victorious socialism."[19] The two houses of the Supreme Soviet, enjoying equal power, are the Council of the Union (*Sovet Souza*) and Council of Nationalities (*Sovet Natsional–ostey*).

In the 1966 elections to the Supreme Soviet 1,517 deputies were elected with a breakdown of 761 deputies to the first council (Union), and 750 deputies to the second (Nationalities). Each deputy in the Council of the Union represents approximately 300,000 people. In the Council of Nationalities, there are 32 deputies from each of the 15 union republics, 11 from each of the 18 autonomous republics, 5 from each of the 10 autonomous provinces and 1 from each of the 10 national districts.

---

[19] Andrei Y. Vyshinsky (ed.), trans. Hugh W. Babb, *The Law of the Soviet State* (New York: The Macmillan Co., 1948), p. 309.

SUPREME SOVIET, USSR (1967)

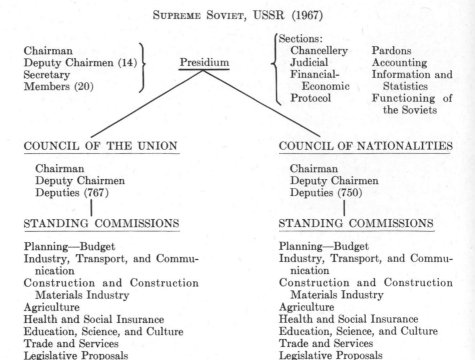

Chairman	Sections:
Deputy Chairmen (14)	Chancellery Pardons
Secretary	Judicial Accounting
Members (20)	Financial- Information and
Presidium	Economic Statistics
	Protocol Functioning of
	the Soviets

COUNCIL OF THE UNION

Chairman
Deputy Chairmen
Deputies (767)

STANDING COMMISSIONS

Planning—Budget
Industry, Transport, and Commu-
  nication
Construction and Construction
  Materials Industry
Agriculture
Health and Social Insurance
Education, Science, and Culture
Trade and Services
Legislative Proposals
Foreign Affairs
Mandate

COUNCIL OF NATIONALITIES

Chairman
Deputy Chairmen
Deputies (750)

STANDING COMMISSIONS

Planning—Budget
Industry, Transport, and Commu-
  nication
Construction and Construction
  Materials Industry
Agriculture
Health and Social Insurance
Education, Science, and Culture
Trade and Services
Legislative Proposals
Foreign Affairs
Mandate

The Council of the Union, then, represents the people nationwide, and the Council of Nationalities, to use Soviet words, "insures the independent representation of all nationalities—large and small," and protects their special national interests.[20]   Each of the two chambers has identical standing commissions to handle its legislative work.   There are also various *ad hoc* temporary commissions.

Presidium of the Supreme Soviet

The two houses, in joint session, elect a ruling Presidium to serve as the executive body of the entire Soviet.   The Presidium elected in March, 1966, had a chairman, 14 deputy chairmen, 1 secretary, and 20 regular members (15 of whom are the chairmen of the 15 union republic presidiums.) Organizationally, the Presidium normally has several sections, such as those for Accounting and Protocol.[21]

---

[20] *Osnovy Sovetskogo Gosudarstva i Prava* (Moscow: Gosurizdat, 1947), p. 157.
[21] T. B. Anisimova, *Vysshie Organy Gosudarstvennoy Vlasti SSSR, Souznykh i Avtonomnykh Respublik* (Moscow: Vysshaya Partiynaya Shkola, 1955), p. 33.

Article 49 of the Constitution gives to the Presidium a broad grant of power and responsibility. Its powers include the relatively unimportant convening of sessions of the Supreme Soviet, conducting nationwide referendums, exercising the right of pardon, awarding orders, medals, and titles of honor, and appointing and receiving diplomatic representatives. The powers also include the ostensibly significant issuing of decrees, interpreting laws, dissolving the Supreme Soviet and ordering new elections—given an impasse between the two houses—annulling illegal decisions of the Council of Ministers, appointing and removing the high command of the armed forces, proclaiming martial law, appointing and releasing members of the Council of Ministers when the Soviet is not in session (on the recommendation of the chairman of the Council), and declaring war under certain circumstances, ordering mobilization, and ratifying and denouncing international treaties.

Although created by the Supreme Soviet and legally accountable to it, the Presidium has been described by Soviet writers as the collegial president of the USSR, the "permanently functioning supreme organ" of state power. The Presidium has been depicted also as an independent organ of power, possessing its own distinctive character. It supposedly unifies the activity of the two houses of the Soviet and provides leadership, administration, and control.[22] In the Russian view, then, the Presidium is more than the mere creature of the Supreme Soviet; it is the body's year-around directing force, expressing through its leadership the designation applied to the whole Soviet—"supreme organ of state power." An interesting discussion took place in 1966 when a Soviet law instructor argued that the Supreme Soviet's standing commissions should not be responsible to the Presidium in the period between sessions of the Soviet (the current practice) because, he pointed out, the commissions really are the creation only of the entire Soviet. The point was an argument for greater independence for the commissions; in effect, for more independence for the Soviet.[23] This author's argument was answered and the preeminence of the Presidium in *all* Supreme Soviet matters defended by another Soviet writer.[24] The Presidium's role vis-à-vis the Supreme Soviet is reflected, also, in the decrees (*ukazy*) and resolutions (*postanoveleniya*) which the Presidium can issue between sessions of the Soviet. Although the Presidium is forbidden

---

[22] A. S. Fedoseeva (ed.), *Osnovy Sovetskogo Gosudarstva i Prava* (Moscow: Gosurizdat, 1958), pp. 74–75; Denisov and Kirichenko, *op, cit.*, pp. 178, 180. The Chairman of the Presidium is sometimes referred to in the West (but not in the USSR) as the Soviet "president."

[23] O. E. Kutafin in *Sovetskoe Gosudarstvo i Pravo*, No. 4 (April, 1966), p. 35.

[24] L. Mandelshtam in *Izvestiya*, July 30, 1966, p. 3.

to issue laws (*zakony*),[25] some of its decrees have stood for more than a year (on occasion even having the effect of amending the Constitution) prior to formal approval by the Soviet in the form of laws promulgated.[26]

From 1938 to 1960, one source lists 201 laws passed by the Supreme Soviet, 105 of which were *ukazy* issued by the Presidium in the interim between sessions of the Supreme Soviet. In the same period, the Supreme Soviet passed 212 resolutions, 125 of which were previously issued by the Presidium.[27] The table below lists the source of questions taken up by the Supreme Soviet for a twenty-two-year period.[28]

INITIATION OF QUESTIONS FOR SUPREME SOVIET, USSR
(1938–60)

Convocation (Term)	Number	Leadership of One House	Commissions of Supreme Soviet	Division of Deputies	Council of Elders	Presidium, Supreme Soviet	Council of Ministers	Council and Central Committee	Union Republics
1st.........	41	—	2	3	7	5	19	—	5
2d..........	22	—	3	—	8	6	5	—	—
3d..........	16	1	—	1	2	3	4	5	—
4th.........	33	1	5	—	6	7	12	1	1
5th (partial).	29	—	5	—	6	6	9	3	1
Total	141	2	15	4	29	27	49	9	7

As one might anticipate, most of the questions brought before the Soviet, at least as indicated by this table, come from the Council of Ministers. The Presidium of the Supreme Soviet competes with the group of senior-age deputies (Council of Elders) as the next most frequent initiating source. Although very few questions are raised by the union republics or by the leadership of one of the two houses of the Soviet, the table does indicate a growing importance of the commissions of the Supreme Soviet in this respect. What the table does not indicate, however, is the types of questions so initiated and whether they are important or meaningless items.

The Council of Ministers is the operating executive branch of government and there is no record of the Supreme Soviet or the Presidium of the

---

[25] *Sovetskoe Gosudarstvo i Pravo*, No. 7 (July, 1965), p. 4.

[26] Two decrees of 1941 established Comissariats (for Rubber Industry and for Machine Tool Building), but the decrees were not confirmed by law of the Supreme Soviet until its March, 1946, session. *Zasedaniya Verkhovnogo Soveta SSSR* (Pervaya Sessiya), Stenograficheskiy Otchet (Moscow, 1946), pp. 33–37.

[27] A. I. Lepeshkin *et al.*, *Kurs Sovetskogo Gosudarstvennogo Prava*, Vol. 2, (Moscow, 1962), pp. 418, 429.

[28] *Ibid.*, p. 411.

Supreme Soviet ever refusing to adopt a Council proposal. The Presidium of the Supreme Soviet seems to serve the purpose of having on hand a permanent organ of the duly elected legislature which can be readily available to give immediate legal approval to any and all decrees, resolutions, and draft laws issued by the party Central Committee and the Council of Ministers.

The Work of the Supreme Soviet

There are both regular and special sessions of the Supreme Soviet, any one session lasting only several days as a rule. Regular sessions are called by the Presidium twice a year (though only one session was held each year from 1946 to 1953), and special sessions are convened at the discretion of the Presidium or (the Constitution provides) on demand of one of the union republics.

The constitutional assignment of duties to the Supreme Soviet is both vague and broad. All legislative power, formally, rests with the Soviet, and that body theoretically exercises all rights of government as defined in Article 14 of the Constitution (e.g., resolving questions of war and peace, organization of defense, direction of the monetary system) *provided* these rights do not fall within the jurisdiction of the Presidium of the Supreme Soviet or of the Council of Ministers. This last stipulation is meant to restrict the Supreme Soviet's power, legally as well as practically. The Soviet is reponsible for exercising general jurisdiction over matters of war and peace, military organization, general governmental operation, the establishment of national economic plans, budget determination, changes in orders of administrative regions, setting the basis for criminal, civil, labor, and family law, and the use of land and natural resources.

Sessions of each house of the Soviet are opened by a senior member; the house then proceeds to elect its chairman and four deputy chairmen. Sessions usually run from 11:00 A.M. until 3:00 P.M. and from 6:00 P.M. until 10:00 P.M. each day, with speakers and commentators limited in their presentations of from three minutes to one hour, depending upon the nature of the remarks (whether they are presenting a motion or reading a report). Finally, each house appoints a Council of Elders, a group of senior-age deputies (representative of groups of deputies organized by province, territory, and republic) for preliminary arrangements regarding the organization and conduct of the session in that particular house.

Proceedings of the Supreme Soviet follow a rather standardized format of electing presiding officers and standing commissions, voting on the agenda for the session, and hearing governmental reports, such as those from the chairman of the Council of Ministers and from the minister of finance. "Debate" among deputies takes the form of laudatory speeches extolling plan fulfillment in the deputy's own republic or region, but it occasionally injects mild criticism of second or lower echelon administrators. Finally, the Supreme Soviet approves interim decrees of its Presidium and passes sundry other resolutions, such as those favoring world disarmament, or world peace. Voting at a session of the Soviet gives the impression of being perfunctory, even mechanical, always unanimously in favor of governmental proposals. In one such vote the presiding officer at a joint session of the two houses asked the members of each house in turn to vote by raising their hands. To each house his words were identical: "Those who are for adoption of the aforementioned law please raise their hands. Please lower them. Who is opposed? None opposed. Who abstains? No abstainers. The law has been adopted. . . ."[29] And so the law was passed with not an opposition vote nor an absention from any of the members of the entire Supreme Soviet.

In the January, 1960, proceedings of the Supreme Soviet a joint session of the two houses heard a report by N. S. Khrushchev titled "Disarmament Is the Road toward Strengthening Peace and Securing Friendship among Peoples." At the second joint session there was a discussion of items on the agenda. At this same meeting the two houses, acting separately, unanimously adopted a law on "New Extensive Reduction of the USSR Armed Forces" and unanimously adopted an "appeal" by the Supreme Soviet to the parliaments and governments of all states of the world. As for the agenda of the two sessions, the one for the May, 1960, meetings included three main items: (1) abolition of taxes for workers and employees, (2) measures for completing the change-over to a shortened workday for all workers and employees in 1960, (3) ratification of the decrees of the Presidium of the Supreme Soviet.[30]

This simple procedure is highlighted by a session of the Soviet in October, 1965, which was convened on the 1st and adjourned on the 2d. During this brief time the Soviet unanimously:

Appointed the deputy chairmen of the Council of Ministers, the chairmen of state committees, and ministers.
Confirmed *ukazy* of the Presidium.
Elected Brezhnev a member of the Presidium.
Adopted appropriate laws and decrees.[31]

---

[29] John N. Hazard and Isaac Shapiro, *The Soviet Legal System: Post-Stalin Documentation and Historical Commentary* (Dobbs Ferry, New York: Oceana, 1962), Part I, p. 31.

[30] *Pravda*, January 15, 1960; January 16, 1960; May 6, 1960.

[31] *Pravda*, October 1, 2, 3, 1965.

Apart from broad, noncommital resolutions, the chief functions of the Supreme Soviet are to appoint a government (Council of Ministers) and to ratify laws and decrees previously adopted by its Presidium. These laws, decrees, and resolutions include such matters as awarding medals and other honors to deserving citizens, approving personnel and organizational changes in the governmental apparatus, formally appointing the Council of Ministers and its chairman, electing the Presidium, electing a Supreme Court, and designating the Court's chief officer, the procurator-general, in addition to passing normal governmental laws. As for appointing a new government, Karpinsky notes (with apparent seriousness) that Stalin, as head of the "out-going" government in 1946, "surrendered" his powers to the newly elected Supreme Soviet. Thereupon the Soviet "unanimously commissioned" Stalin to propose a new government, which he did (with himself as head) at the next session of the Soviet. Following this proposal, the chairman of the Soviet declared that there was no objection to the new government, that "none of the deputies insisted on a roll-call vote." Stalin's proposed government, as anticipated, was voted on "as a whole and unanimously adopted amidst loud appause passing into an ovation in honour of *Comrade Stalin....*"[32] Neither objection nor dissent, just approval—unanimously—of whatever Comrade Stalin proposed. There is no indication that the process of forming a government today is any different than it was under Stalin.

On occasion, however, deputies ask questions and make requests in the Supreme Soviet discussions. A deputy from Leningrad noted that at recent sessions of the Supreme Soviet, deputies from Leningrad and other *oblasty* repeatedly introduced a proposal for integrated planning of capital investments for housing, and construction of cultural and everyday services. The request is so obvious that it receives no objections from anyone. And yet, he complained, nothing has been done about it.[33] In a 1965 session, a First Deputy Chairman of the Council of Ministers, Mazurov, called attention to deputies' speeches in which they criticized managerial shortcomings, suggested organizational changes in regional governments, called for improved planning techniques, and proposed methods for stimulating production. In response to these points, Mazurov replied that the Council will take under consideration for study the wishes

---

[32] V. Karpinsky, *The Social and State Structure of the U.S.S.R.* (Moscow: Foreign Languages Publishing House, 1951), pp. 123–24. At the ratification of the Council of Commissariats in 1938, criticism of specific individuals forced the dropping of several proposed commissars from the government list prior to final approval by the Supreme Soviet. See Julian Towster, *Political Power in the U.S.S.R., 1917–1947* (New York: Oxford University Press, 1948), p. 279.

[33] *Izvestiya*, December 11, 1964.

expressed by the deputies.[34]

Perhaps even more significantly, two authors frankly noted the weakness of the Supreme Soviet and called for its increased role in policy making. These authors revealed that prior to 1957 the Supreme Soviet, USSR, ratified only the state budget at its sessions, but beginning in 1957, simultaneously with the budget, the Supreme Soviet examined and ratified the yearly economic plans. However, up "to the present time, the Supreme Soviet USSR did not especially examine such accounts, although in discussions at the sessions on the execution of the state budget, many essential questions on the fulfillment of the national economic plan were brought up."[35] These authors then recommended that the Supreme Soviet should examine the reports of ministries and departments and important questions of deputies, that the deputies should see the budget earlier than the month prior to its execution, and that the Presidium of the Supreme Soviet should not have the right to issue *ukazy*, "since the Constitution and constitutional law does not permit the Supreme Soviet USSR to delegate its authority to issue laws."[36]

Role of the Standing Commissions

The work of the two houses of the Supreme Soviet is frequently handled through its standing and temporary commissions. The standing commissions are formed of regular deputies, with the membership of 31 per commission in 1966, slightly larger for the Industry (41 members) and Planning-Budget (51 members) commissions. Normally, there is a further breakdown into subcommissions. The Standing Commission on Legislative Proposals of each house, perhaps the most important of the commissions, was established for the preliminary examination and preparation of draft laws, prior to their ratification by the Supreme Soviet. These commissions supposedly meet in the intervals between Supreme Soviet sessions and at these times are subordinate to the Presidium. Each Legislative Proposals Commission has a staff secretariat, and occasionally the two commissions form one joint subcommission for both houses made up of deputies, mem-

---

[34] *Izvestiya*, September 3, 1965. In what appeared to be a procedural change pointing to slightly more legislative involvement in decision making, the session of the Supreme Soviet, USSR, of December, 1966, in addition to having normal joint sessions of both houses, had each house meet in separate sessions, not simultaneously, to hear reports and discuss items on the agenda. *Pravda*, December 16, 1966.

[35] S. G. Novikov and M. A. Shafir, "Voprosy organizatsii raboty verkhovnogo soveta SSSR na sovremennom etape," *Sovetskoe Gosudarstvo i Pravo*, No. 12 (December, 1966), p. 25.

[36] *Ibid.*, pp. 25–27.

bers of the Council of Trade Unions, the Central Committee of the Young Communist League (*Komsomol*), the Ministry of Social Insurance, and other ministries and departments.[37] This is a typical Soviet technique, to bring into an elected group some appointed officials—such as those from the ministries who are not deputies to the Soviet. The Russians, no doubt, think of this as a broadening, healthy influence. A Westerner, however, might consider it proof that the Russians violate the spirit of their own elective-representative system by allowing appointed officials an equal voice with elected officials.

In October, 1959, the Credentials Commission of the Council of the Union, responsible for examining and certifying election results, reported to the Council on the election of new deputies in four electoral districts to replace those deputies who for some reason were no longer members of the Soviet. Sessions of the Economic Commission of the Council of Nationalities, meeting July 7–12, 1960, heard reports on agriculture in the union republics, on new pension procedures, and on improving the planning of retail commodities in the union republics. At these sessions there were representatives of *Gosplan*, the Ministry of Finance, the Ministry of Agriculture, and directors of certain ministries and departments from the republics.[38]

At a joint session of the budget commissions of the two chambers of the Soviet, several subcommissions were formed to examine individual sections of the annual plan and budget. These subcommissions were: Basic Plan Indicators, State Income, Heavy Industry, Agriculture-Procurement and Trade, and Plans and Budgets for the Union Republics.[39] According to one report, the Ministry of Finance ordered all enterprise and other economic organizations to change the schedule of profit deductions in accordance with suggestions from the Budget Commission of the Council of the Union.[40]

Commissions have the right to require information and testimony from organizations and individuals. Decisions in a commission are reached by a simple majority vote, a quorum being two thirds of its membership. The

---

[37] M. Gedvilas and S. Novikov, "O Deyatelnosti komissii zakonodatelnykh predpolozheniy verkhovnogo soveta SSSR," *Sovetskoe Gosudarstvo i Pravo*, No. 9 (September, 1957), pp. 12–19.

[38] *Pravda*, October 28, 1959. In the Economic Commission there were subcommissions for industry, agriculture, trade, and one for culture, education, public health, and communal services. *Pravda*, November 16, 1962.

[39] *Pravda*, November 16, 1962.

[40] I. S. Senin, "Nekotorye voprosy deyatelnosti budzhetnoy komissii soveta souza verkhovnogo soveta SSSR," *Sovetskoe Gosudarstvo i Pravo*, No. 11 (November, 1962), p. 35.

commission chairmen organize and direct the work of the commissions and maintain contact with other deputies and with governmental offices. The temporary commissions, contrasted with the standing ones, are formed by the entire Supreme Soviet and are described as investigating and auditing bodies.

Soviet sources report that the standing commissions examine draft laws and make recommendations to central and regional governmental bodies.[41] These sources also report on the commission's work of drafting new laws and, even on occasion, of amending draft laws once submitted to them.[42] On closer inspection, however, the work of the commissions seems more to have consisted in superficially examining draft laws submitted to them by the Council of Ministers and proposing simple noncontroversial recommendations aimed at improving the efforts of the governmental agencies.[43]

The modest role of the commissions has been undergoing change, however. There are reports of two of the standing commissions meeting prior to regular sessions of the Supreme Soviet. The Soviet met in December, 1963, for example, but its budget commissions had been meeting since November, 1963, and the same pattern evidently continues.[44] The legislative proposal commissions meet, reportedly, no less than once every three months.[45] At the January 5 session of these legislative proposal commissions, the chairman read the draft of a mineral use bill. "Suddenly proposals, objections and amendments were made." The chairman asked that amendments be submitted in writing to the editorial group.[46] These stepped-up activities of the commissions illustrate changes that have been planned for several years.

In 1961, the party program called for an increase in the responsibilities of the commissions of supreme soviets, even to the extent of the commissions controlling the activities of ministries and contributing actively to implementing decisions of the soviets. For the carrying out of these new duties, deputies should be released, periodically, from their official tasks to

---

[41] For example, see D. Rasulov and S. Novikov, "Voprosy dalneyshego sovershenstvovaniya raboty komissii zakonodatelnykh predlozheniy soveta natsionalnostey verkhovnogo soveta SSSR," *Sovetskoe Gosudarstvo i Pravo*, No. 10 (October, 1961), pp. 68–70; A. E. Lunev, "O dalneyshem razvitii demokratii v sovetskom gosudarstvennom upravlenii," *Sovetskoe Gosudarstvo i Pravo*, No. 7 (July, 1962), p. 26; and *Pravda*, September 8, 1962, p. 2.

[42] See the discussions in *Izvestiya*, October 23, 1959, quoted in *Current Digest of the Soviet Press*, Vol. XI (November 25, 1959), p. 13; and Val. Ivanov, *Chelovek i Zakon* (Moscow: Tsk., VLKSM, 1960), p. 25.

[43] For example, see the comments by Rasulov and Novikov, *op. cit.*, p. 71.

[44] *Izvestiya*, November 26, 1963; *Pravda*, November 21, 1964.

[45] *Sbornik Zakonov SSSR* (Moscow, 1961), p. 127.

[46] *Izvestiya*, January 9, 1966.

permit full-time committee work.[47] Following this policy announcement, articles in the Soviet press criticized the weak position of the commissions in the past and recommended certain improvements. Prior to the 1966 reorganization of the commissions, only the draft national economic plans and the state budget were required to be considered by the commissions. Moreover, of 241 laws adopted by the sixth convocation of the Supreme Soviet (1962–66), only 53 underwent preliminary consideration by the standing commissions; the choice of whether to submit them to the commissions or not was left to the Presidium of the Supreme Soviet.[48] All acts within the sphere of the commission, Kutafin argued, should be, of course, submitted to the commissions, and instead of allowing the Council of Ministers to decide on adopting suggestions of the commissions as the Council chooses, perhaps the Supreme Soviet itself ought to decide such questions.[49] There are increasing indications, though, that suggestions and recommendations of the commissions are being acted on more frequently by governmental organs.

Budgetary changes, usually increases, initiated by the commissions are being acknowledged by the government. Newly appointed Chairman of the Council of Ministers Kosygin told a session of the Supreme Soviet in December, 1964, that in light of such budgetary suggestions, if the Supreme Soviet approves, "the necessary changes will be made in the national economic plan." Other proposals of deputies, Kosygin continued, will be considered by the government, and its agencies will seek to implement them.[50] At the December, 1965, session of the Supreme Soviet, on behalf of the Budget Commission of the Council of the Union, one deputy moved the approval of the national economic plan for 1966 with the proposal that the state revenues be increased 120,600,000 rubles and the additional money be allocated to the union republic budgets.[51] At the December, 1966 session, the Council of Ministers agreed to raise the budget for 1967,

---

[47] Jan F. Triska (ed.), *Soviet Communism: Programs and Rules* (San Francisco: Chandler Publishing Company, 1962), p. 100.

[48] Kutafin, *op. cit.*, pp. 36–37. The 241 laws exclude those initiated from the commissions themselves. At times the Presidium submits draft decrees and resolutions to the commissions which, after being adopted, are not submitted to the Supreme Soviet! *Ibid.*, p. 33.

[49] *Ibid.*, p. 39. In the 1960's the authority of the commissions was expanded and from 1963 some ministerial and departmental representatives have been appearing before the commissions to give reports. *Sovetskoe Gosudarstvo i Pravo*, No. 12 (December, 1966), p. 30.

[50] *Pravda*, December 12, 1964. At this session Minister of Finance Garbuzov said, of certain proposed budgetary increases, "I have been instructed to report that the Council of Ministers, USSR, examined these proposals and considers it advisable to accept them," while other proposals will be considered by the government.

[51] *Pravda*, December 9, 1965.

following requests of the Planning and Budget Commissions. Another deputy complained that the Ministry of Finance failed to satisfy certain requests of deputies.[52]

At the Twenty-third Congress of the CPSU, Politburo members Brezhnev and Podgorny called for more power and responsibility to be assigned to the Supreme Soviet. Brezhnev stated that reports of the Council of Ministers to the Supreme Soviet "should become more customary."[53] At the first session of the newly elected Supreme Soviet, Podgorny, who in addition to sitting on the Politburo was the Chairman of the Presidium of the Supreme Soviet (its highest office), stated that the new standing commissions will analyze budgetary and plan details, noting that heretofore deputies have had insufficient time to examine carefully the budget. He also called for a considerable expansion in the responsibility and tasks of the commissions. He noted that the Presidium of the Supreme Soviet should see that commission recommendations are implemented by ministries and departments, and that deputies should be released from their other responsibilities for a specific period to work on commissions. Documents, he concluded, must be presented to commissions early enough, and an end must be put "to the intolerable instances where certain officials ignore deputies' requests. A statute should soon be adopted to cover these and related points."[54] At this session, the standing commissions were reorganized, increased in number from nine to eighteen, and supplemented by new, enlarged subcommissions.

The Supreme Soviet as a Legislative Body

In comparison to legislative bodies in Western systems of government, the Supreme Soviet, its commissions, and its directing Presidium cannot yet be considered as influential organs in Soviet policy formation for several reasons. The Presidium is not staffed to be a policy-making organ. Moreover, there is no evidence available to indicate that the Presidium of the Supreme Soviet actually exercises any of its considerable rights (such as voiding decrees of the Council of Ministers), or, indeed, that it ever meets as a whole body in between sessions of the Supreme Soviet. We do know that it gives its approval to governmental decrees, as drawn up by the Council of Ministers. Even this approval, however, might involve

---

[52] *Izvestiya,* December 19, 20, 1966.

[53] *Pravda,* March 30, 1966; April 1, 1966. In December, 1966, the Ministry of Finance agreed to report promptly to the deputies on decisions relating to the 1967 budget. *Izvestiya,* December 20, 1966.

[54] *Izvestiya,* August 3, 1966.

only the chairman and the secretary, both of whom sign resolutions of the Supreme Soviet. No meetings of the Presidium, as a body, are reported in the Soviet press.

Sessions of the Supreme Soviet meet regularly only twice a year, for a total time of less than 10 days. The bulk of this time is taken up with hearing reports from the government and party leaders. Moreover, the Soviet passed only some 200 laws in the 20-year period, 1938–59. Modern governments in most other parts of the world, on the other hand, require the passage of literally hundreds of laws each year, all of which consume weeks if not months of legislative deliberation. Consequently, there must be numerous laws (or decrees having legal force) which are secretly passed by the Supreme Soviet or which are approved by party and governmental leaders without ever being referred to the Supreme Soviet. Of the two possibilities, the latter seems the more probable. Again, having on hand an interim Presidium which can approve laws—any laws, including constitutional amendments—while the parent Supreme Soviet is not in session is itself an act of disrespect for an elected legislature and can only testify to the emptiness of the Soviet legislature as a true law-making body.

From reports of Supreme Soviet meetings, one is struck by the remarkable absence of any normal, parliamentary type of debate and discord found in Western type governments. At the joint session of the two houses of the Supreme Soviet on May 6, 1960, for example, Deputy Demichev of the Moscow *Oblast* introduced a decree which would give approval to actions of the Council of Ministers in domestic and foreign policies. The suggestion, which was greeted with loud applause, in effect would give to the Council of Ministers legislative *carte blanche* to pursue any and all of its foreign and domestic policies—present and future—with neither detailed nor perfunctory legislative investigation and review. At the closing session of the Soviet on May 7, 1960, Khrushchev gave an address, after which the Soviet "passed laws and decrees," almost, it would appear, as an afterthought. With much applause and with unanimity the decree was passed giving full approval to the actions of the Council of Ministers in its domestic and foreign policies.[55] Thus, virtually at the end of the sessions of the Supreme Soviet, the nation's highest legislative body finally got around to legislating; laws and decrees were passed, simply, rapidly, smoothly, with applause and unanimity. Finally, there is no record, officially or otherwise, of any serious debate taking place in any of the sessions of the Soviet, or of dissent on the part of any deputy either to laws which are presented or to programs which are recommended by party and governmental leaders.

---

[55] *Izvestiya*, May 7, 1960; *Pravda*, May 8, 1960.

The foregoing analysis is only part of the picture, however. Despite the limitations on the power of the Supreme Soviet, relegated to a very subordinate role in the political system as compared with the Council of Ministers and the party's Central Committee, its position is being strengthened. Curbing some of the Presidium's arbitrary power vis-à-vis the whole Soviet and measurably enlarging the responsibility and duties of the standing commissions point up a long-term trend, beginning in the late 1950's, of enhancing the role of the Supreme Soviet. In the Supreme Soviet elected in 1962, only six of the thirty-three-member guiding Presidium were on the party's Central Committee. Among the 1966 Supreme Soviet's thirty-six-member Presidium, there were nineteen regular and three candidate members of the Central Committee—more than a threefold increase. This fact alone testifies to the growing importance which the political elite attaches to the Supreme Soviet's new role. Taking a broader view of the Supreme Soviet, the changes discussed above seem to indicate that this legislative body, through its deputies and standing commissions, is more effectively articulating and aggregating popular interests within the Soviet political system, somewhat in line with two other communist systems, those of Poland and Yugoslavia. That the political elite allows, even agrees to, a growth in the legislature's power in the USSR suggests that they believe it is not harmful to their position of dominance and that there are some positive advantages in this growth. It may well be, finally, that the growing functions of articulation and aggregation on the part of the legislature cannot really be prevented, so the elite increases its own representation in the legislature's control organs as a form of political insurance. To do away with a popularly elected legislature is out of the question, because it confers legitimacy on the entire political system, an effect which may be as desirable as it is necessary to a ruling elite.

THE ELECTORAL PROCESS

According to Soviet theory, elections in the USSR strengthen the power of working masses in both city and village and permit the people to create for themselves their own organs of state power. Yet, in practice this theory has carried with it certain proscriptions. Prior to 1937 many people were denied the vote (such as those of bourgeois background, clergy, former members of the tsar's police). Elections were indirect and were held for local government offices only; the electoral system was based on the realistic assumption that not everybody was in favor of the Soviet regime. After that date, class discrimination against voters was eased, elections were made direct and provision was made for a national legislature. The system now rested on the premise that everybody supported the regime.[56]

The constitution authorizes universal suffrage at age eighteen. The only disfranchised voters are the mentally infirm and those deprived of their vote by a court of law. By disclaiming any other suffrage requirements and by emphasizing the direct, secret, responsible, and representative nature of its elections, the Soviet Union has proclaimed its electoral process to be the most democratic in the world.

Nomination of candidates to the Supreme Soviet is done not by individuals, but by organized groups: Communist Party, trade unions, cooperatives, youth and cultural societies. In addition, workers at their factories, collective and state farmers at their farms, and soldiers and sailors in their military units can nominate candidates. Nominations are made at general meetings attended by interested persons who represent specific organizations.

At one nominating meeting held in a factory club, a fitter, in the name of her micrometer shop, nominated Tatyana Sovelieva to be a deputy to one of the local district councils. Tatyana was described as an active and helpful worker who "always paid attention to other people's ideas." Some workers at the meeting, reportedly, wanted commitments from Tatyana regarding better service facilities and a children's club. Tatyana won the nomination by her statement of things that ought to be done by the district council.[57] Although many nominations, if not most of them, may well be made in a shallow manner, a more searching pre-examination might occur, such as the above account, in which the prospective nominee is questioned on his work attitudes, political activity, and his moral views. Thus in a nomination meeting several years ago in the Ivanovsk factory which 400 people attended, 20 candidates were selected, but one was turned down because he supposedly failed to "pass on" his work experience to his fellow employees.[58] There should be no reason why workers, peasants, and employees cannot nominate their favorite co-workers for the local, regional, and national legislatures (soviets). So long as the nominees are sober, honest citizens, the party probably does not object to them being the "people's choice." After all, there are enough key local and regional party leaders elected to check any popular impetuosity in the various local, regional, and national soviets. Then too, the soviets, as legislatures, do not possess policy-setting authority, so nothing is really left to chance by the regime.

[56] George Barr Carson, Jr., *Electoral Practices in the U.S.S.R.* (New York: Frederick A. Praeger, Inc., 1955), p. 49.

[57] USSR, *Illustrated Monthly*, No. 10, 1957, p. 23.

[58] L. Churchward, "Some Aspects of Republican and Local Government before the Decentralization," *Soviet Studies*, Vol. IX (July, 1957), p. 88.

Nominees receive the approval of the Communist Party, although just how this is accomplished is not clear because it is not openly admitted, and relevant statutes and codes on the subject are silent. Kim writes that of several people nominated for one seat, the electors in a free discussion finally "crystallize on one candidate."[59] Closer to the mark, another writer notes that the local party committee "devotes special attention" to the nominating process so that "the most deserving, competent comrades" are selected.[60] Kim also confesses that the one half to two thirds of the electorate required for a nominating quorum, in a majority of cases fails to attend the nominating meetings.[61] From this and other information available on the preselection of candidates by occupational groupings, sex, and party affiliation,[62] we may safely conclude that the party does indeed screen all nominees before they are officially registered as candidates.

Local urban and rural governments throughout the country make up voters' lists which are then posted 30 days before elections. For deputies to the Supreme Soviet, single-member districts of roughly equal population are drawn up by the Presidium of the Supreme Soviet and announced at least two months prior to election time. Local governments, in turn, break the election districts down into precincts which vary in size from 50 voters (such as in mountain and nomad villages) up to as many as 3,000 voters in heavily populated areas. In addition to a territorial breakdown, percincts are formed in hospitals, in military units, on ships and boats, even on trains which are traveling on election day.

The "bloc of party and nonparty" candidates now campaigns on a common platform. Local campaign headquarters, called "agitation points" (*agitpunkti*), campaign for the "bloc's" nominees by use of posters, literature, press, radio, and armies of volunteer "agitators." Much of the campaigning, according to one Russian source, is done before candidates are even nominated.[63] This, of course, reveals the chief purpose of campaigning: something divorced from the specific candidates running for office. The campaigns are for the official "bloc" and, in reality, for the Communist system more than they are for the people nominated for office. Black depicts a Soviet campaign meeting in 1958 as a scene of half a dozen speakers extolling the candidate's merits; the candidate himself then

---

[59] A. I. Kim, *Sovetskoe Izbiratelnoe Pravo* (Moscow, 1965), p. 185.

[60] A. Shlyamin, First Secretary of the Petrozavod City Party Committee in *Partiynaya Zhizn*, No. 9 (May, 1966), p. 58. Mote reports conversations he held with Soviet citizens, explaining that the party informs local nominating meetings of how many candidates are to be suggested for nomination for each seat initially, and then the party is in on the final selection process. Max E. Mote, *Soviet Local and Republic Elections* (Stanford: Hoover Institution, 1965), pp. 26, 38.

[61] Kim, *op. cit.*, p. 174.

[62] See p. 230, below.

[63] *USSR, Illustrated Monthly*, No. 10, 1957, p. 23.

promises to work for higher production and better living conditions. The audience claps politely and the meeting ends with a concert or variety show.[64]

Administration of the elections is handled through numerous electoral commissions formed by trade union and cooperative societies, Communist Party, youth, cultural, scientific and other organizations. In the 1966 election to the Supreme Soviet, the commissions for all of the USSR had a membership of 1,300,000 workers. Commissions hear any voter complaint which might arise, supervise the balloting, count and certify the votes, and transmit the results to the respective houses of the Supreme Soviet. At the top, a Central Electoral Commission is selected from various public organizations.

In the election itself the voter, upon identifying himself, receives his ballot and, according to the regulations, goes into a booth or special room where he crosses out the names of all candidates except the one he chooses—leaving untouched this name on the ballot. Regulations to the contrary, in fact only one name appears for each office, so the voter upon receiving his ballot has merely to drop it untouched in the box—even by-passing the privacy of the voting booth if he wishes. If a voter so desires, he may vote against the single candidate by crossing out the candidate's name, an action of possible but not too frequent occurrence. If the candidate receives a majority of votes in a district in which at least 50 percent of the eligible voters cast their ballots, that candidate is elected. If no such majority is received, a new election is called for within two weeks for that particular district.

In each national election, a few voters do cross out the officially sponsored candidate and, occasionally, the candidate actually does not get the needed majority of votes and consequently fails to be elected. In the 1966 election to the Supreme Soviet, 345,643 voted against the officially endorsed candidates to the Council of the Union, and 289,298 voted against candidates to the Council of Nationalities. Affirmative votes for these candidates were 143,570,976 (99.76 percent of the vote) for the Council of the Union and 143,595,678 (99.80 percent) for the Council of Nationalities. With the utmost of confidence one can predict with a margin of error not exceeding 1 percent the outcome of Soviet elections. Nomination, practically without fail, is tantamount to election. By a series of pressures the regime assures itself of practically a 100 percent turnout of voters at elections. A party organizer, agitator—someone—will call on a voter who has not turned out by, say, noon on election day. Even the ill cannot escape, because they will have a sealed urn brought to their apartment for

---

[64] Cyril E. Black, "Soviet Political Life Today," *Foreign Affairs*, Vol. 36 (July, 1958), pp. 572–73.

voting.[65] To abstain from voting is widely interpreted in the USSR as a positive action taken against the political system.

Soviet voters have the right, by a simple majority vote, to recall deputies once elected. Although this right is very seldom taken advantage of, voters in the Ukraine recalled a deputy when, reportedly, they found him "incompetent" and "unsatisfactory." Similarly, a deputy to the Latvian supreme Soviet was recalled for failing to carry out the voter's "mandate." And a deputy to the Belorussian Supreme Soviet was recalled because of "dishonest" practices.[66]

The Supreme Soviet Deputy

Deputies to the Supreme Soviet receive no salary as such, but they do get a remuneration for clerical help (in addition to the use of a secretary), a per diem allowance when the Supreme Soviet is in session, and free public transportation. Deputies, who must be at least twenty-three years old, represent a variety of occupations. An occupational breakdown of the deputies elected to the Supreme Soviet 1958–1966 shows the distribution given in the table below.[67]

DEPUTIES ELECTED TO THE SUPREME SOVIET, USSR
(National Elections in 1958, 1962, and 1966)

	Number of Deputies			Percent of Total Deputies		
	1958	1962	1966	1958	1962	1966
Members and candidate members of the Communist Party	1048	—	1141	76.0	75.8*	75.2
Women deputies	366	390	425	26.5	27.0	28.0
Occupational breakdown:						
Full-time Communist Party officials	267	274	277	19	19	18
Full-time governmental officials	215	232	235	16	16	15
Manual workers	260	296	303	19	21	20
Farmers, peasants	202	219	263	15	15	17
Directors of state and collective farms	146	117	119	11	8	8
Military officers	54	63	67	4	4	4
Scientists, agronomists, technicians	42	24	26	3	2	2
Teachers, academicians	35	27	22	2	2	1
Artists, writers, composers	35	46	46	2	3	3
Directors of institutes, academic officials	33	58	53	2	4	3
Economic managers (factory directors, etc.)	24	15	39	2	1	3
Industrial, construction, drilling foremen	22	32	24	2	2	2
Others	43	40	43	3	3	3

* A. I. Kim, *Sovetskoe Izbiratelnoe Pravo* (Moscow, 1965), p. 128.

[65] Mote, *op. cit.*, pp. 77–78.

[66] *USSR, Illustrated Monthly*, No. 10, 1957, p. 22; *Pravda*, March 15, 1961. During the first six months of 1935, from 36,078 rural councils in the Russian Republic, 30,165

The election data reveal several interesting facets about the internal makeup of the Supreme Soviet, one of these being the extent of Communist Party dominance. Full-time party officials elected to the Soviet constituted 18 percent of the whole in 1966, with the number of Communist Party members and candidate members in all (full and part-time) numbering 1,141, or 75 percent of the total number of deputies. Moreover, the full-time party officials were representative of most sections of the country. Thus, the deputies were elected from 144 governmental units (15 union republics, 2 large cities, 6 *kray*, 104 *oblasty*, 17 autonomous republics). Of these 144 units, 135 included among their elected deputies their respective party first secretaries. Consequently, only 9 of 144 regional and local governmental units (6 percent) did not elect their respective top party official (first secretary) to the Supreme Soviet. Sixty-seven military officers were elected deputies, with the following breakdown:

Rank	*Total Elected*
Officers of flag rank (Marshalls, Generals, Admirals)	65
Colonels	2
Total	67

The election data for the three elections, 1958–66, display a remarkable similarity in percentage breakdown of the various categories. That the figures vary extremely little from one election to another, for example in the percent of Communist Party members, or women deputies, or full-time party officials, or governmental officials, can only mean that these percentages are predetermined before election time. Evidently the party presets quotas for nominees in both national and local elections,[68] quotas that the party no doubt believes reflect a desirable and "representative" legislative body. The data also reveal that the Supreme Soviet is dominated by "officialdom," 52 percent of the deputies representing party, governmental, and military officials and directors of farms, institutes, and factories. Although this figure does not seem unreasonably high in what has come to be a bureaucratic-managerial state, the regime still contends that it is a workers' and toilers' state—a group that is represented by only 37 percent of the national legislators.

---

deputies were recalled. See Vyshinsky, *op. cit.*, p. 720. It must be noted that this was on the eve of the Great Purge in the Soviet Union, so one must assume that many, if not all, of the "recalls" were demanded from high party circles. In 1965 more than 350 deputies were recalled from Soviets at all levels—national, regional, and local. *Pravda*, April 1, 1966.

[67] Compiled from *Pravda*, March 19, 1958; March 29, 1958; *Izvestiya*, March 21, 1962; TASS, Moscow, April 24, 1962; *Pravda*, June 15, 1966; August 4, 1966.

[68] See below, pp. 303–4, 317.

Responsibilities and duties of deputies include representing their constituents in the government. Deputies are expected to meet the "lawful" complaints, needs, and requests of those whom they represent. One deputy relates how he helped his constituents get land to build houses after the city council originally had refused their request. The voters also complained to this deputy of inadequate electricity, which he remedied by getting the Ministry of Power Stations (since abolished) to send a portable power station to his city.[69] One deputy of the Supreme Soviet has depicted his role as that of a connecting link between the local and the Supreme Soviet, where in the latter body he represents the interests of the local soviet. In the local area, the deputy in turn serves as a representative of the Supreme Soviet.[70] In addition, deputies are expected to be leaders in promoting and carrying out directives of the Communist Party: to be, in fact, the functional link between the regime and the people. The "rights" of deputies include those of participating in legislative review, such as it is, addressing inquiries to governmental officials, and enjoying immunity from arrest during sessions of the Supreme Soviet.

This condition may change, however, as the role of the Supreme Soviet and its standing commissions are scheduled to assume a greater responsibility for conducting governmental business. If this eventually takes place, especially in light of the 1966 reorganization, then perhaps deputies themselves will assume more of a responsible role within the Soviet political system.

Nature of the Electoral System

The theory of the Soviet electoral system is that it expresses unanimous popular ratification of the policies and actions of the regime. The nation as a body, through its elections, gives to Soviet leaders a legal mandate of approval and displays to both those at home and abroad the apparent unity and devotion which the Soviet people have for communism. The voting public—more than 99 percent of them—put themselves on record, formally, as approving and endorsing the Communist system. In the frank words of the government's leading newspaper, the 1958 elections to the Supreme Soviet expressed the people's "profound approval of the internal and foreign policies of the Communist Party and the Soviet government and demonstrated before all the world its firm solidarity, its

---

[69] V. Narbutovich, "How I Became a Legislator," *USSR, Illustrated Monthly*, No. 3, 1957, pp. 20–21.

[70] B. I. Samsonov, "Deputatskaya deyatelnost v izbiratelnom okruge," *Sovetskoe Gosudarstvo i Pravo*, No. 6 (June, 1961), p. 94.

supreme moral-political unity.'"[71]   This statement readily explains the way of Soviet elections; it shows the necessity for holding elections even when no contest for office exists, when no dissenting minority views of any sizable proportions emerge, when results of the election can be safely predicted before the event actually takes place, and when the occupational quotas for deputies seem to be preselected to achieve a certain desired percentage distribution.   Apart from popular endorsement, Soviet elections give many citizens in the USSR the feeling of participating, however remotely, in the overall governmental process.   And how is the Soviet voter to know that his electoral system is not the most democratic in the world?   Not from Russian history will he find this out, nor from the controlled press.   And why not hold elections, from the standpoint of the leaders of the regime?   Why not permit the people to nominate and elect some of their more popular fellow citizens so long as those nominated are loyal to the system and so long as the party watches over and guides all phases of the electoral process?   Such elections, despite their transparency, are not without meaning and importance to the Soviet political system.

---

[71] *Izvestiya*, March 19, 1958.

CHAPTER X

Economic Organization

MUCH OF what Soviet government and politics is about has to do with economics. The entire organization, administration, and functioning of the economy is very closely tied to and, in fact, is the reason for a great deal of the governmental and political apparatus. This close identification of politics with economics has several notable effects on both aspects of Soviet life.

Economic goals and policies are set, in broad scope, by the political leaders. Annual and long-term economic plans and a host of other policies such as the establishment of levels of production for certain commodities, choice of investments and determination of prices are political decisions as much if not more than economic ones. Economic decision making rests on a political base. The clearest expression of this reliance of economics on politics is in the foreign trade policies of the Soviet Union. By the same token, a reverse influence also occurs.

Political decision making under communism has an even greater economic orientation than is the case in capitalist nations. In the Soviet Union political leaders are concerned with and motivated by a multitude of problems such as raw material allocations, production scheduling, and retail distribution with which their counterparts in Western governments are involved only indirectly. Of course, the economy is run by specialists, but the political leaders provide overall administrative guidance.

CENTRAL ORGANIZATIONAL STRUCTURE

Institutionally, the Soviet economy is based on three main operational principles of (1) political control of the economy, (2) public (state) ownership of economic resources, both natural and manufactured, and (3) central planning for the entire economy. The organizational format followed in the USSR has sought to implement with some efficiency the above principles. At the top of the command structure for the economy is the Central Committee's Politburo and Secretariat, then the Council of Ministers, through economic ministries and finally down to the producing or enterprise level (by way of the union republic governments for certain enterprises. The main operational level of economic management is that of the ministries, which provide guidance in planning and financial matters and overall supervision of producing enterprises. Ministries were temporarily in eclipse during the Khrushchev era, but since 1966 they have been reinstituted in their former position of prominence.

ECONOMIC ORGANIZATION

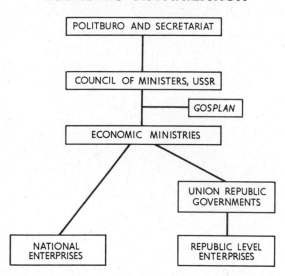

This multilevel hierarchy, though accurate enough, still is oversimplified and does not portray what frequently develops in practice, a myriad of conflicting, jurisdictional lines, duplicating operations, and confused, superfluous organizational units. This structure also includes, in practice, other administrative bodies, such as the *oblast* governments.

State Planning Committee

One of the most important economic organizations in the Soviet Union is the *Gosplan*. Formed originally in 1921 as the State Planning Commission (out of the old State Commission for Electrification—*Goelro*), *Gosplan* has gone through a number of structural changes and has even been the focus of a power struggle during the anti-Khrushchev reorganization of the planning apparatus in December, 1956.

Gosplan has an elaborate structure of coordinating divisions, such as the divisions of Finance, Capital Investment, Foreign Economic Relations, and Costs and Prices. These divisions study general economic problems and work out summary parts of the long-term plans. In addition, there are branch divisions for specific commodity planning, for example, Gas and Petroleum, Ferrous Metallurgy, Heavy Machine Building, Defense Industry, and the one for Agriculture, State Farms, and Procurement.[1] Subordinate to *Gosplan* is a wide network of research organs, such as the Central Ferrous Metals Research Institute and the Research Institute of Planning and Standardization. Following the general reorganization of 1957 and subsequent changes, *Gosplan* was enlarged, made more important and given additional assignments.

The functions of *Gosplan* are to draw up and approve plans for allocating materials such as fuel, electric power, and metals; distribute major goods; set wholesale and some retail prices, as well as rates for transport and related services; allocate capital investment; coordinate somewhat the economic plans of the USSR with other communist member nations of the international Council for Mutual Economic Assistance (CEMA); and perform a host of related duties such as examining plans for designing and survey work in the construction industry.[2] In addition, *Gosplan* has specific operational responsibilities, such as in supplying material-technical commodities to industry.[3]

Gosplan carries out its assignments through subordinate *gosplany* of the union republics, then, down through the planning organizations of the regional economic organizations and, finally, to the planning bodies of the basic production units such as the factories. *Gosplan* attempts, generally, to confine itself to broad problems of planning, assigning to the subordinate planning organs responsibility for drawing up and processing specific details of the plans. To accomplish these tasks, *Gosplan* apparently has the authority to issue binding orders on all lower planning bodies.

THE ECONOMIC ENTERPRISE

The primary industrial producing unit is the factory or plant, normally referred to in Soviet terminology as the enterprise. It is a business

---

[1] A. N. Yefimov, *Perestroyka Upravleniya Promyshlennostu i Stroitelstvom v SSSR* (Moscow: Gospolitizdat, 1957), p. 85. G. Mironov, *Ekonomicheskaya Gazeta*, No. 47 (November 23, 1963).

[2] I. A. Yevenko, Planning in the USSR (Moscow: Foreign Languages Publishing House, m.d.), pp. 36ff.

[3] V. V. Laptev, "Nekotorye organizatsionno-pravye problemy upravleniya promyshlennostu," *Sovetskoe Gosudarstvo i Pravo*, No. 8 (August, 1960), p. 33.

organization in that it not only produces goods or services, it purchases raw materials, sells its product, hires and fires its employees, and seeks to make a profit. Within this general format, the enterprise has a measure of choice in decision making and a certain amount of administrative flexibility, for example, in the use of its financial resources to achieve its assigned goals. On the other hand, the enterprise is not a "free" business agent. It must fulfill its plan, and its actions at all times are subject to the continuous review and supervision of local and central party, government, and economic agencies. It is subject to "control by the ruble"—the use of money as an accounting method to realize greater economies from investments.

The profits, although customarily limited and carefully prescribed from above, are intended to keep the enterprise on a financially self-sustaining basis. Profits (income left over after expenses and planned charges, not return on investments in a capitalist sense) are important sources of state revenue, constituting perhaps a fifth of the entire national budget. The enterprise director's fund also is taken from the profits. This fund is an important source of additional money available to the director for the purpose of covering enterprise losses, improving services and benefits to the worker, expanding production facilities, increasing capital, granting bonuses, and for other uses such as paying interest on loans.

The rights of the enterprise, to a very important degree, center around the rights of the director because he is the representative of and spokesman for the enterprise in all of its relationships with other organizations. Since 1955 the rights of directors, and hence of enterprises, have been on the increase. In that year directors were permitted to accept independent, above-plan orders for production of certain types of goods. Directors also were given the right to modify quarterly plans, with the consent of the customer.[4] Since then, bit by bit enterprise directors have been granted powers somewhat more commensurate with their burdensome responsibilities. They have, for instance, been freed from some of the more stifling restrictions under which they used to suffer at the hands of central party inspectors, police agents, and ministerial officials. The trend, as with industry as a whole, is to grant to competent lower-level managers more (though by no means all) of the personal authority they need to carry out their duties in a rational manner.

---

[4] V. A. Dozortsev, "Pravovoe polozhenie promyshlennogo predpriyatiya," *Sovetskoe Gosudarstvo i Pravo*, No. 8 (December, 1955), pp. 47, 51. Later, the director was granted authority to pay, under certain conditions, wage advances to workers and employees. L. Galinov, "Voprosy bankovskogo kontrolya za raskhodovanem fondov zarabotnoy platy," *Dengi i Kredit*, No. 9 (September, 1956), p. 27.

FARM ORGANIZATION

One of the major problems of the nineteenth and early twentieth century Russia resulted from the undeveloped state of agriculture. Even after serfdom finally was ended in 1861, the peasant was granted very little relief. As one result of this long suffering, the peasant by 1917 became opposed to government but in favor of a vague, idealized form of socialism. The Revolutions of 1917 gave the peasant hope and expectation for a new and improved life. By this time, too, the peasant had gained a measure of political power; he served, not unwillingly, as the backbone of the Bolshevik Revolution. But that is only a part of the picture. The communists in 1917 inherited all of the old unresolved peasant problems. In answer, they offered a bagful of grandiose promises and boasts, but few practical solutions. On one point the communists quickly reached a decision, however. Agriculture in Russia would not remain private and capitalistic.

A national Ministry of Agriculture, with numerous subordinate chief directorates, commissions and associations, oversees agriculture ministries in the union republics. In turn, below the republic ministries are *kray* and *oblast* and, sometimes, *rayon* governments which supervise the farms, both collective and state. Other national ministries related to agriculture are those of Tractor and Agriculture Machine Building and Meat and Milk Industry. The All-Union United Agricultural Technics Committee completes the central organization. Ministries of agriculture in the union and autonomous republics also supervise *kolkhozy* and *sovkhozy*, but only indirectly in matters of material-technical supply, electrification, leadership of higher training institutions, and mechanization of agriculture.[5]

The Collective Farm

The first collectivization drive was launched in 1926 and was aimed at getting most of the peasants into collectives as a preparatory move toward the eventual goal of setting up a series of nationwide, completely state-owned and state-operated farms. In a way, one purpose of collectivization was political. It sought to consolidate governmental power over peasants and to subject them more completely to party control.[6] A more primary objective, however, simply was to achieve greater agricultural production

---

[5] I. V. Pavlov, *Kolkhoznoe Pravo* (Moscow: Gosurizdat, 1960), pp. 69–70.

[6] This approach is forcefully made in Roy D. Laird, *Collective Farming in Russia: A Political Study of the Soviet Kolkhozy* (Lawrence, Kans.: University of Kansas, 1958), p. 65.

at a relatively low price. The regime hoped to channel much of the agricultural output into the cities with the hope of keeping down the costs of industrialization, by transferring the disposal of farm commodities from individual farmers to collective farms supervised by the government.

Because the collective farm (*kolkhoz*) is a "voluntary" union of peasants who pool their resources to work in and share benefits from the land collectively, the farm ostensibly is run by its general meeting of all members. The general meeting elects its own chairman and executive board, approves a budget, plans new construction, and agrees to an annual plan for the *kolkhoz*. In addition to the chairman and an executive board, there is a deputy chairman, an agronomist (in charge of planting), livestock managers and a chief accountant. An auditing commission is elected from the membership and is responsible for inspecting the financial transactions of the *kolkhoz*. This, at least, is the legal, official framework under which it functions. In practice, the *kolkhoz* is not nearly so independent. In fact, the *kolkhoz* must accept and abide by the government's national plan and most of the economic and political life of the *kolkhoz* is controlled, at least indirectly, by local party and government organs.

The individual collective farmer (*kolkhoznik*) may join or leave a *kolkhoz* only with the approval of its members. After joining, the *kolkhoznik* is assigned to one of the farm's basic producing units, a brigade. His income is from two sources. First, he gets a share of the return from the farm's output (usually part cash and part in kind—grain, vegetables, meat). Second, he keeps that money which he receives from the sale of produce grown on his own personal garden plot. More recently, the government has tried to reduce the *kolkhoznik* noncash income in favor of a more predictable cash stipend. This is more acceptable to the farmers, too, of course.

Kolkhozy are subject to the normal governmental and party control agencies, chief among these being the local party committee and government. The Machine Tractor Stations (MTS), which were created in the early years of collectivization as highly specialized units for supplying machinery to the *kolkhozy*, also had important political functions. Directly subordinate to the *obkom*, the MTS were used by the regime as instruments through which the party channeled its directives and policies to the peasants.

State Farms

Following early unsuccessful efforts to establish state farms (*sovkhozy*) under Lenin, the regime in the latter 1920's organized some large *sovkhozy* as well as a number of unified *sovkhozy-kolkhozy*. Both of these forms were very unpopular among peasants who could see only disadvantages in joining what looked like a new, government version of the old discredited landlord estate. Only gradually since then have *sovkhozy* been increased in number and accepted by some peasants. In 1952 Stalin stated that the desired changeover from *kolkhoz* to *sovkhoz* is necessary to achieve communism. Yet, by 1953 *sovkhoz* production still accounted for only $7\frac{1}{2}$ percent of total land sown to grain. In the past few years *sovkhozy* have been on the increase, approximating 10,078 in 1965. By late 1961 *sovkhozy* were cultivating 80 million hectares (197 million acres) of crops which equaled 43 percent of total grain production; they also produced 28 percent of the meat, 32 percent of the milk, and 31 percent of the wool.[7]

Long the ideal goal of Soviet agricultural policy, *sovkhozy* are the rough equivalent of industrial units. That is, peasants are employed by the state and are subject to rules similar to those of factory workers. Officials of the *sovkhozy* are government-appointed. In a concession to the permanent employees of *sovkhozy*, though, they now are provided with small, individual garden plots for their own use after the fashion of the *kolkhoz*.

There are, apart from *kolkhozy* and *sovkhozy*, some 60,000 independent or private peasant households which farm land plots of one quarter to two and one half acres each, totaling some 247,100 acres in all. These "free" household farms are tolerated by the state in certain areas of sparse population where formation of *kolkhozy* or *sovkhozy* is not economically feasible.[8] Although independent, these households fall under the general supervision of the appropriate agency of local government, of course.

POST-STALIN REORGANIZATIONS

In mid-1957 the Soviet economic structure was altered in the first of the large-scale post-Stalin reorganizations. Although the 1957 reorganization was more political than economic in its original cause, the latter consideration nevertheless was important.

By 1957 Soviet industry had grown out of its early childhood into greater maturity. The economy had achieved a number of technical advances, capital resources had been accumulating at a high rate, and the

---

[7] *Pravda*, October 18, 1962. For the entire Soviet Union in 1964 comparative figures show 110.8 million hectares (one hectare equals 2.47 acres) of sown acreage under the collectives versus 87.3 million hectares under the state farms, and 37 million head of cattle under the collectives versus 22.2 million head under the state farms. *Narodnoe Khozyaystvo SSSR v 1964 g* (Moscow, 1965), pp. 245, 253, 272.

[8] Vladimir Katkoff, *Soviet Economy, 1940–1965* (Baltimore: Dangary Publishing Co., 1961), p. 187.

labor force was increasing its proficiency. The last under-developed area of the economy was that of management, which still was being conducted too much in the obsolete Stalinist pattern. It now became apparent to the post-Stalin leaders that the high degree of administrative centralization in which not only major but minor decision making rested with Moscow had serious disadvantages. Problems of short and irregular shipments of supplies, poor coordination among factories, illogical transport schedules, and shoddy planning could be alleviated, it was believed, by reducing the size and functions of the central Moscow bureaucracy. In the process, it was hoped, a great deal of minor decision making would be relegated to the union republics and to the newly created councils of national economy (*sovnarkhozy*).

The establishment of *sovnarkhozy* in 1957 had an earlier precedent. In December, 1917, the new Bolshevik government created a Supreme Council of National Economy which, in turn, organized local *sovnarkhozy*. Following nationalization of industry in 1918, the *sovnarkhozy* were responsible for direct supervision of the newly nationalized enterprises, although the *sovnarkhozy* fell into disuse after the central commissariats were established in the early 1930's.

In 1957 individual *sovnarkhozy* were established in over 100 economic regions throughout the country; the region's borders coincided with the *oblast, kray,* or republic borders. In some cases (Ukraine, Kazakh, and Uzbek Republics) there were inter-*oblast sovnarkhozy*. Internal organization followed a general pattern based on the size and importance of the particular region. The ruling council, appointed by the council of ministers of the union republic, has a chairman, deputy chairmen, and heads of main divisions. When first organized the Sverdlovsk *Sovnarkhoz*, for example, had a ruling council, an advisory technical-economic council, and 13 functional subdivisions, such as those for Capital, Construction, Labor and Wages, Finance, and Transport. In addition, there were 14 branch directorates—such as Fuel Industry, Timber, Construction, Machine Building, and Sales.[9] These branch directorates were patterned after the old chief directorates (*glavki*) of the former economic ministries.

In large republics having a number of *sovnarkhozy*, unique problems of coordination and supervision arose so that, in late 1960, additional super-all-republic *sovnarkhozy* (one for each republic) were authorized for some republics as broad coordinating agencies. There has been established, too, a still larger, Central Asian *Sovnarkhoz*. Following creation of these super-*sovnarkhozy*, the *gosplan* of the respective republic was relieved of

---

[9] Yefimov, *op. cit.*, p. 65.

operational decision making for its subordinate economic institutions.[10] As we might anticipate, however, even with the super-*sovnarkhozy* all remaining problems involving the deconcentration of industry were not solved.

Shortcomings included the usual failings of Soviet organizations: overlapping administrative staffs, frequent delays in resolving problems, and confusing organizational patterns. The disease of "localism" (*mestnichestvo*) had broken out in a number of *sovnarkhozy*, where they attempted to improve their own capabilities irrespective of neighboring regions and when they concerned themselves more with local than with national economic problems. As a result, *sovnarkhozy* granted favorable treatment in the quality and the scheduling of goods supplied to their own as opposed to other regions. The constant recurring problems of insufficient supplies for industry, accompanied by delays in delivery, and the numerous conflicting and competing supply agencies plagued the *sovnarkhozy* no less than they plagued the former ministries which preceded them.

In 1961 the nation was divided into seventeen large economic regions for territorial planning (previously the planners vaguely thought in terms of thirteen large regions). The new breakdown called for ten regions in the RSFSR, three in the Ukraine, one in the Kazakh Republic, the three inter-republic regions: one for the three Baltic republics of Latvia, Lithuania, Estonia, one for the four Central Asian republics, and one for the Transcaucasus republics. In an organizational meeting of the Coordinating and Planning Council for the new Central Asian Economic Region, a Council membership of 40 people was appointed, 10 from each of the four republics forming the region (Kirghiz, Tadzhik, Turkmen, and Uzbek).[11]

Following this trend toward making economic units fewer and larger, in the reorganization of late 1962 the *sovnarkhozy*, originally numbering 103, were reduced to approximately 40. One national unit, the All-Union *Sovnarkhoz*, was authorized; it was headed by a deputy chairman of the Council of Ministers, USSR. This *Sovnarkhoz* was responsible for current, year-by-year economic planning for the country. Early in 1963 the Supreme Council of National Economy was established in what appears to have been a recentralizing trend. Also, in 1963 a broad, regional

---

[10] Laptev, *op. cit.*, pp. 32–36. All main sales offices were scheduled for transfer to the all-republic *sovnarkhozy* from the republic *gosplany*. *Izvestiya*, June 1, 1962, p. 3. The organization of the all-republic *sovnarkhoz* in the RSFSR followed somewhat the structure of *Gosplan*, RSFSR. *Ekonomicheskaya Gazeta*, December 25, 1961, p. 10.

[11] *Ekonomicheskaya Gazeta*, August 28, 1961.

organization was provided for—the Central Asian Economic Region which had responsibility for administration of the economy of the Central Asian republics. The Soviet penchant for reorganizing continues almost unabated, searching, always searching, for ever newer, more responsive, and more workable organizations. By 1966 the *sovnarkhoz* system had been practically eliminated in favor of a return to the former pattern of industrial ministries. This included elimination of all *sovnarkhozy*, from top to bottom, with their enterprises transferred to the appropriate ministries.

Following the economic reforms begun in 1963 (the so-called Liberman proposals, named for an economics professor who was one of several suggesting radical improvements in economic management), a number of enterprises were placed on a more independent basis in 1965. This changeover was authorized in a statute on the Socialist State Production Enterprise.[12] Among a large number of changes in enterprise management now permitted, a few might be singled out for mention. These include greater enterprise flexibility in managing available resources, such as leasing or selling surplus equipment and facilities by the enterprise and the disposal of its own internal resources; more leeway in dealing with other enterprises (negotiating contracts, acceptance of additional production orders, setting delivery dates); additional authority in price and wage setting and drafting of annual plans; and less supervision from higher administrative agencies.

The thrust of the reform on the enterprise level, in the Soviet view, is that the actual profit of the enterprise will become the incentive fund—the higher the profit, the greater the incentive fund to be used at the discretion of the enterprise management.[13] The result, hopefully, will be to enable the enterprises themselves to decide on their own productive capacities and the utilization of their own internal reserves in a more rational manner, so that the cost of production will be lowered simultaneously with its rise in quality.[14] Of ten enterprises in the Moscow *Oblast* shifted to this system, results in the first quarter of 1966, compared to the first quarter of 1965, showed a reduction in enterprise indebtedness from 5 million to 1.8 million rubles, and a drop in unsold stocks of finished output in the first quarter of 1966 from 3.4 million rubles to only 70,000 rubles.[15] The following

---

[12] Reprinted in *Current Digest of the Soviet Press*, XVII, No. 42, November 10, 1965.

[13] *Izvestiya*, December 26, 1964.

[14] Report of First Deputy Chairman, Council of Ministers, USSR, Mazurov. *Pravda*, October 2, 1965. Success of enterprises will depend more on quantity of goods sold than on gross output.

[15] *Kommunist*, No. 8 (May, 1966), pp. 95–96.

claim was made for the performance of the 670 enterprises operating under the new system by mid-1966.[16]

	Total for the Industry (Percent)	Total for Converted Enterprises (Percent)
Increase in volume of productivity in 1965	8.3	10
Labor productivity increase	5	8
Profits increase	10	20

The success of the new system is yet to be determined. Although the direction of the changes—greater enterprise independence—sounds promising, such an administrative change as this inevitably will conflict with numerous other restrictions of the highly centralized command economy which have not been altered. The fundamental dilemma for Soviet leaders is whether a piecemeal reform of their burdensome economic structure will be able to combat successfully natural bureaucratic inertia, the usual unenlightened and inefficient customs of Soviet administration, and the traditional planners' sovereignty instead of consumers' sovereignty in the economy.

Agricultural Reorganizations

Since 1953 Soviet agricultural problems have been getting increased attention because of serious defects which long have needed correction. As in other areas of Soviet life, the harsh effects of Stalinism have stunted agricultural growth; the results have been left to Stalin's successors to deal with. In giving too little attention to agriculture, as compared with industry, Stalin prevented farming from developing its own incentives, achieving technological improvements, and realizing new efficiencies. By 1953 agriculture had lost all power to stimulate and in turn to be stimulated by progress achieved in other branches of the economy.[17]

Unlike Stalin, the present leadership considers agriculture to be fully as important as industry, but the key problem is how to increase both capital investment and labor incentives in agriculture at a rapid rate while yet not inhibiting industrial growth. One step taken was to amalgamate small *kolkhozy* into fewer, but larger ones. Although this action was initiated

---

[16] *Izvestiya*, October 30, 1966.

[17] See the comments of Francis Seton, "The Soviet Economy in Transition," *Problems of Communism*, Vol. 10 (January–February, 1961), p. 36. In 1960 more than nine million sheep died from a lack of food and shelter. Arcadius Kahan, "Troubles in Soviet Agriculture," *Problems of Communism*, Vol. 10 (March–April, 1961), p. 63. Stalin, for example, allowed industry the dominant share of electric power to the detriment of agricultural modernization.

under Stalin, it was carried out more vigorously following his death. Where there were 254,000 relatively small *kolkhozy* in 1950, by 1959 *kolkhozy* numbered 54,600, and they were considerably larger in size.[18] Larger *kolkhozy*, it was thought, could more efficiently use available agricultural machinery which was in short supply. Other hoped-for advantages to be attained from amalgamation were a tightening of party control over agriculture and cutting down on "small-farm" individuality through creation of *kolkhoz* party units. Swollen administrative staffs, too, could be reduced.

In 1958, following several years of cautious experimentation, the government no longer required collective farmers to turn over to the state part of the foodstuffs produced on their private garden plots. While in 1952 these "obligatory deliveries" to the state of meat from private plots amounted to 23 percent and of milk to 31 percent of total state purchases of these commodities, in 1957 comparable figures had dropped to approximately 10 percent and 7 percent respectively.[19]

In 1958 almost all of the MTS were abolished and replaced by Repair and Technical Service Stations (RTS). These latter stations repaired agricultural machinery and, in cases of the financially weaker *kolkhozy*, rented equipment to them. First begun in 1928, the MTS were government operated and party controlled; the primary purpose which they served was to supply *kolkhozy* with agricultural machinery. The machinery was operated and serviced by non-farm workers employed by the MTS. The MTS numbered more than 8,900 in 1953; in 1957, their last full year of operation, there were approximately 8,000 MTS employing two and one half million people. By 1960, there were only 34 MTS remaining.[20] Another hallowed institution of the Stalin era had fallen by the wayside.

In his speech explaining their abolition, Khrushchev gave several reasons why the MTS were now an obsolete form of agricultural organization. With machinery owned and operated solely by the MTS, *kolkhozy* of varying sizes and differing needs often were poorly serviced. The *kolkhozy* simply lacked needed flexibility in not being masters of their own machinery. Administrative staffs in both *kolkhozy* and MTS, too, constituted an unnecessary and costly duplication. More importantly, the MTS had outlived their usefulness. Years ago they helped collectivize

---

[18] Andrew Rothstein (ed.), *History of the Communist Party of the Soviet Union* (Moscow: Foreign Languages Publishing House, 1960), p. 623. *Narodnoe Khozyaystvo SSSR v 1959 Godu* (Moscow: Gosstatizdat, 1960), p. 423.

[19] *Pravda*, July 5, 1957, p. 1. Cited in *Current Digest of the Soviet Press*, Vol. 9, No. 24 (July 24, 1957), p. 9.

[20] *Narodnoe Khozyaystvo, op. cit.*, pp. 307, 435.

agriculture; now the state of collectivization made this particular assignment superfluous. Finally, the MTS were used as political instruments by the party to indoctrinate and control the peasants. Here again the MTS have successfully completed this task; collective farmers, according to Khrushchev, now are politically informed and enthusiastic supporters of communism.[21]

Another trend in Soviet agricultural organization has been directed at a long-time objective of the leadership—to transform *kolkhozy* into the more ideally communistic *sovkhozy*. In 1954 there were 4,857 *sovkhozy* and 93,000 *kolkhozy* (the latter down from a figure of 236,900 in 1941). By 1960 these two types of farms numbered 6,496 and 54,600 respectively.[22] By 1958 the *sovkhozy* in the four-year period since 1954 absorbed almost 74 million hectares (182 million acres) of collective land, 6,233 *kolkhozy* and 670 MTS.[23] By 1963, however, all of the anticipated efficiencies from these transfers had not yet materialized.[24]

In still another attempt to concentrate the resources of high-level leadership to solve agricultural problems, there was established in 1962 an All-Union Committee for Agriculture staffed by important party and governmental officials and headed by a deputy chairman of the Council of Ministers, USSR. On lower administrative levels, party secretaries were placed at the head of regional and local agricultural committees, thus making party officials up and down the line more directly responsible for agricultural administration. Another maneuver in 1962 provided for joint production directorates, referred to as either *kolkhoz-sovkhoz* or *sovkhoz-kolkhoz* production directorates, depending upon which type of farm unit prevailed in a given area. By mid-1966 a reconstituting of the Ministry of Agriculture virtually eliminated Khrushchev's 1962 reorganizations, for example replacing the All-Union Committee for Agriculture with the Ministry.

THE ORGANIZATIONAL ORIENTATION

The Soviet economy is typified in its organization by a high degree of centralized control in all phases of planning and management. Shifts,

---

[21] Khrushchev's speech to the Supreme Soviet. *Pravda*, March 1, 1958.

[22] *Narodnoe Khozyaystvo, op. cit.*, p. 307.

[23] Allen B. Ballard, Jr., "An End to Collective Farms?" *Problems of Communism*, Vol. 10 (July–August, 1961), p. 12. The main brake on a more precipitous transfer of *kolkhozy* into *sovkhozy* has been economic rather than political considerations. *Ibid.*, p. 16.

[24] *Ekonomicheskaya Gazeta*, January 12, 1963.

adjustments, even simulated decentralizations may occur (such as in 1957) but the structure has been, is now, and no doubt long will remain highly centralized. It seems that any move toward a deconcentration of administration—governmental or economic—makes the party leadership so nervous that a return to the normal, accepted pattern of overcentralization is the natural and eventual outcome of all Soviet organizational experimentation.

Economic decisions are almost inseparable from political decisions, though the latter receives somewhat higher priority over what can be termed strictly economic considerations. Economic choice, therefore, falls almost exclusively within the province of the Communist Party leadership. It is to this political dominance that many writers attribute a number of shortcomings of the economy such as overcentralization, illogical decision making, lack of sufficient managerial and worker initiative, and frequent breakdowns in the supply mechanism.[25] It is because of a political basis of economic decision making, too, that the Soviet leadership assumes an extreme organizational orientation. If difficulties arise, politics cannot be at fault, nor can communist economics. The fault, by a process of communist elimination, must rest in the organizational forms.

The post-Stalin leaders have shown a cautious willingness to experiment with the economy by discarding a few of the prejudices of Marxism-Leninism-Stalinism. Decision making now is somewhat more rational, with innovations of limited decentralization, linear programming, credit purchases, increased quality and quantity of consumer goods, a slightly improved supply network, a bit more realistic pricing policy, and, in general, an increased desire to look at a few of the weaknesses a little more objectively.

The Liberman proposals, by seeking to transfer much administrative decision making to the enterprise level and to stimulate the enterprise to better performance by increasing incentives, suggest that additional organizational changes will be forthcoming. The approach of Liberman and his fellow economists is to much more realistically assess the weaknesses and shortcomings of Soviet economic organization and management.

Efforts at improvement have been limited in no small degree, however, to the built-in limitations of the planned economy itself. As a result, improvements over the years have tended to be piece-meal and centered around almost periodic, superficial reorganizations of the structural apparatus. Obviously, the nation's resources are under severe strain to

---

[25] For a discussion of these points see Alec Nove, *Communist Economic Strategy: Soviet Growth and Capabilities* (Washington, D.C.: National Planning Association, 1959), pp. 28–29.

continue a high rate of defense spending, ambitious capital investments, economic aid to nations both within the Communist Bloc and among the neutrals, and, in addition, an increase in both the quantity and quality of consumer goods and a satisfactory upsurge in agricultural output. None of these problems can be resolved through mere organizational shifts by the political leadership no matter how enthusiastically rationalized. Nevertheless, the regime has centralized its economic apparatus, partly decentralized it, recentralized it, and, in the early 1960's, almost continually reshuffled officials, organizations, and offices in a seemingly uncontrolled frenzy of reorganizational mania. The persistent delusion under which top Soviet leaders have lived since 1917 is that a simple structural reorganization will correct any and all of their economic weaknesses.

Even *Pravda* has commented that the idea still exists that it is possible to solve serious economic problems through administrative measures: all one has to do is to reorganize the apparatus, to merge two administrations into one or, on the contrary, to divide one trust into two, and everything will be fine.[26] This delusion may in part be deliberate, however, to avoid facing squarely some of the erroneous assumptions upon which the Soviet economy is based.

---

[26] *Pravda*, November 1, 1964.

CHAPTER XI

Economic Administration

By ACCENTING organizational structures, Soviet leaders always have assumed that efficient administration would follow automatically. That it has not, has given rise to the frustrated efforts to achieve managerial efficiency by shuffling personnel assignments and reorganizing the structures. Two of the very important ingredients of the Soviet economy are those of highly centralized financing, and planning for the economy. The bulk of state economic activity takes place because the state buys large quantities of goods and services on its own account and, through the direct operation of the banking system, sets the volume of credit and, thus, the money supply.[1]

FINANCING THE ECONOMY

The State Bank (*Gosbank*), with numerous branch offices throughout the nation, is the main financial agent of the government for both domestic and foreign operations. Acting as the national treasury, *Gosbank* receives and pays out money according to the national plan. It lends to state enterprises, handles financial transactions of the government, and maintains accounts for all Soviet institutions. In what amounts to a single banking system, including loaning money and paying interest on savings deposits, in addition to the usual central banking functions, *Gosbank* has a network of regional offices supervising local branches. *Gosbank* has become, in addition, a main source of information on how the economic plans are being carried out, particularly so because of *Gosbank's* responsibility for seeing to the execution of the budget.[2]

[1] See the discussion in Edward Ames, *Soviet Economic Processes* (Homewood, Ill.; Richard D. Irwin, Inc., 1965), p. 159.

[2] George Garvy outlines the Soviet banking system in "The Role of the State Bank in Soviet Planning," in Jane Degras and Alec Nove (eds.), *Soviet Planning* (London: Oxford University Press, 1964).

The Soviet budget forms a part of the annual plan (to become the financial plan) and sets forth in some detail the limits for capital investments, overall income, and expenditures. The budget, of course, is comparatively much larger than that of noncommunist nations because it includes a much greater part of national life. This all-inclusiveness of the budget, because of the absence of privately owned business, is one of its distinguishing features. In both its preparation and execution it is marked by a high degree of centralized control and supervision. When submitted by the Council of Ministers, the budget is not subject to any serious legislative alteration. The legislature debates the budget and makes occasional administrative but never policy changes. It never rejects it. Following a rather formal, perfunctory survey, the legislature adopts the budget almost entirely as submitted.

A leading instrument of the government for channeling investments, restricting consumer purchasing power and providing the largest single source of revenue, is the turnover tax. First authorized in 1930, this tax is collected on each item of finished or semifinished goods by the wholesale distributing organizations, by enterprises, and by procurement agencies. The tax rate varies among different goods with a range, for example, of from 16 to 85 percent of the price for synthetic fabrics.[3] Because of the high turnover tax, Soviet citizens pay for their consumer goods almost twice the cost of producing and distributing them (it is not unusual for other taxes, such as the one on movie tickets, to exceed the basic sale price of the commodity itself). The real advantage to the Soviet leadership in the turnover tax is its flexibility so that, for example, the citizen's purchasing power, if growing too rapidly, can be shunted off into capital investments simply by altering the schedules of the tax. One result is that inflation is more easily controlled. Another result is that a high investment rate contributes to rapid economic growth in the USSR. This growth is aided, too, by the regime's tight control over its resources and its ability to repress consumption.[4] Other important sources of revenue are taxes on income from cooperative organizations and collective farms, and certain payments into the treasury such as "deductions" from profits of state enterprises. Other taxes are imposed on income, entertainment, houses, ground "rent," transportation vehicles, cattle, and a sales tax on produce sold through *kolkhoz* farm markets.

[3] Vladimir Katkoff, *Soviet Economy, 1940–1965* (Baltimore: Dangary Publishing Co., 1961), p. 252.

[4] See Robert W. Campbell, *Soviet Economic Power: Its Organization, Growth, and Challenge* (Cambridge, Mass.: Houghton Mifflin Company, 1960), pp. 151–52.

The Soviet economy, although still growing at a considerable rate, has had difficulties on the other hand with inflation, devaluation of the ruble, black markets, speculation in consumer goods, rationing, even smuggling. More importantly, strict controls over the economy which emphasize capital investment in heavy industry have resulted in great personal sacrifices from Soviet citizens who have been denied adequate consumer goods. These citizens, on occasion, have had their savings virtually confiscated by ruble revaluations. They have not, in addition, enjoyed the Western advantage of wide consumer choice, not to mention anything resembling consumer sovereignty at the market place. Citizens have suffered with pitifully inadequate goods (such as very poor-quality shoes), greatly over-priced items (such as cars), and significant shortages of most of the desired—even necessary—household and personal items. Not all people suffer with equal pain, however. The favored class elite of party and government officials, highly paid artists, and certain other "key" citizens enjoy more than adequate incomes with an abundance of pre-requisites such as cars, summer homes, and fine food and clothing. A nationwide economic equality among all citizens certainly is unknown in the Soviet Union.

ECONOMIC PLANNING

Soviet communists, of course, invented their system of centralized governmental planning, even though a measure of state planning had evolved under the tsars. A nineteenth century commentator writes that a governmental mania for planning existed before the reign of Alexander II. At this early time in Russia no public building could be constructed without a plan being sent from the capital. No house could be erected having more than five windows "no matter in what region of the empire, without a permit given from Petersburgh in the autocrat's own name."[5] Nevertheless, modern planning in the Soviet period originated with Lenin and his *Goelro* and was further elaborated in a very detailed manner under Stalin and the Five-Year Plans.

Economic planning in the Soviet Union is complex, involved, and all-embracing. Obviously, a national plan which sets production control figures as well as operational targets for practically all economic activity throughout the nation is an undertaking of immense proportions involving untold man-hours and literally months of preparation. It is such a vast

---

[5] Anatole Leroy-Bealieu, *The Empire of the Tsars and the Russians*, trans. Z. A. Ragozin (New York: G. P. Putnam's Sons, 1898), Part I, p. 61.

project that even its achievements appear difficult for the top leadership to assess accurately.

The Planning Process

Planning begins in *Gosplan*, where broad "control" figures for specific amounts and types of commodities which are to be produced in the nation are arrived at after having the broad guidelines handed down from top party and governmental officials. Control figures include such items as gross industrial output, gross agricultural harvest, volume of freight to be hauled, amount of capital investment and construction, growth of labor productivity, volume of retail trade, and the number of people to be trained in various institutions. Since 1953 *Gosplan* has been confined to setting fewer detailed control figures itself, relegating this minor task to subordinate planning organizations. Thus in 1953 *Gosplan* set 5,000 specific control targets, but only 1,700 in the 1955 plan.[6] The total number of specific items for which control figures were set, by all national and regional agencies, for 1960 amounted to 11,000 for the plan year 1960.[7] Preliminary or "approximate estimates" of the targets are sent down to the central governmental ministries and departments and to the *gosplany* of the republics in late May or early June. These estimates, in turn, are broken down and further divided by production assignments among their various factories and other producing units. In formulating the draft Five-Year Plan (1966–70), the ministries and departments were to submit a draft, broken down by branches, union republics, and economic areas, to *Gosplan*, USSR, by July, 1966. Gosplan was then to submit the draft plan to the Council of Ministers by September 15, 1966.[8]

Meanwhile, factories have been submitting their estimated requirements for the next year up to the republic planning agencies while at the same time filling in the details of the preliminary plans sent down to them. Detailed estimates once again are sent back up to *Gosplan* for approval. The whole process of submitting preliminary estimates both up and down the chain of command and of altering and adjusting the estimates takes until the end of the year when, at least formally, the plan for the next calendar year is approved. During this phase of the planning process negotiation takes place between the various echelons of planners. The

---

[6] *Planovoye Khozyaystvo*, No. 5 (May, 1954), p. 80. R. W. Davies, "The Reappraisal of Industry," *Soviet Studies*, Vol. VII (January, 1956), p. 81.

[7] I. A. Yevenko, *Planning in the U.S.S.R.*, trans. Leo Lempert (Moscow: Foreign Languages Publishing House, n.d.), p. 81.

[8] *Izvestiya*, April 24, 1966.

higher planning officials seek to raise production targets while lower, say, republic *gosplan* officials, and particularly enterprise directors seek lower production targets so that they will have a better chance of fulfilling the plan and thereby qualifying for bonuses. The so-called new system of enterprise management, inaugurated for some firms in 1965, makes allowance for limited planning between producing and consuming enterprises, to be carried out without strict central supervision.

Long-term planning, another primary responsibility of *Gosplan*, involves Five-Year Plans and rough estimates for fifteen-year ones. Throughout the period of the long-term plan, annual adjustments are made depending in part on the results of each year's performance. The obvious purpose of such long-term planning is to introduce into annual planning a greater measure of continuity and focus.

Planning Weaknesses

Economic planning in the Soviet Union, it should be stressed, works. Goods are produced, commodities are sold, the plan is fulfilled (at least to a degree), the country is further industrialized, and the economy functions with a measure of success. To this extent, economic planning is effective and will no doubt continue to be practiced for the foreseeable future. It can even be argued that Soviet planning has been a source of strength for that nation—such as its contribution to rapid industrialization. Granted these certain achievements for economic planning, however, the process is not without its inefficiencies and shortcomings.

In an economy where plans become law, their fulfillment can be a source of frenzied activity on the part of harried administrators. Although penalties for nonfulfillment are not nearly so severe as they were during the Stalin period—the penalty now may simply mean loss of one's bonus—administrators are responsible and still can be held legally accountable for failing to meet the plan goals. An obvious maneuver that a beleaguered manager might fall back upon in the event of imminent plan failure is to falsify his production figures to indicate a higher output than was actually the case. This statistical chicanery, so often relied upon, has been a leading problem for Soviet leaders over the long years of national planning. In 1957 a railroad division regularly was underfulfilling its monthly plan until it hit upon a simple scheme to meet its quota of freight to be hauled. Empty tank cars were filled with water from a pipeline at one station; the water was then hauled by the cars to a second station where the water promptly was poured back into the same pipeline—to flow back to the first station. Thus, the plan for "hauling" was overfulfilled,

at least on the records of the railroad division.[9] This high-pressure drive
to fulfill the plan induces managers to make certain decisions not in the
interest of the system, such as production of unplanned products, conceal-
ment of production capacity, the falsification of reports, and lowered
quality.[10]

There are other shortcomings in the planning process itself which occur
both at the central and regional planning levels. Inefficient allocation of
plant and equipment is a rather common complaint registered against
planners. The Kazakh Republic *Gosplan* assigned to the Alma-Alta Heavy
Machine Building Plant the production of a part for a shearing machine.
It cost the plant almost double the part's list price to produce it, while at
the same time a specialized plant in another *oblast* which could easily have
produced the spare part had unused capacity.[11] In addition to poor use
of facilities and lack of adequate coordination among producing units, in
many instances plans are overly rigid, while in other cases they are too
frequently altered. One machine building plant had its production
schedule changed twelve times in a six-month period. The Leningrad
Sovnarkhoz in the one year of 1962 changed the plans of its subordinate
enterprises 70 times. In other cases, plans may be so delayed that final
confirmation of them comes long after their initial starting date, or a
plant, because of scheduling problems, must place its orders for raw
materials before it has received its own production plan. Some plan goals
are unrealistically high (the planning error occurring most often) and
occasionally target figures in one category (such as labor) conflict with
figures in another category (such as cost).[12]

Djilas has written that for the sake of economic independence communist
nations often build plants irrespective of availability of raw materials, and
they rarely if ever pay attention to world levels of price and production.
Some products are manufactured at a high cost when there is a world
market surplus available at lower cost. Then too, branches of industry
which could become efficient producers of given commodities are not
assigned the production of these commodities.[13] The Soviet experience

---

[9] *Current Digest of the Soviet Press*, Vol. 9, No. 28 (August 21, 1957), p. 25. In 1961
the government authorized prison terms of up to three years for those found guilty of
falsifying state reports. *Pravda*, May 25, 1961.

[10] See the discussion by Joseph Berliner in Morris Bornstein and Daniel R. Fusfeld
(eds.), *The Soviet Economy, A Book of Readings* (rev. ed.; Homewood, Ill.: Richard D.
Irwin, Inc., 1966), pp. 109–41.

[11] *Pravda*, June 8, 1959.

[12] *Pravda*, November 22, 1962; December 8, 1962. See also David Granick, *Management of the Industrial Firm in the USSR: A Study in Soviet Economic Planning* (New
York: Columbia University Press, 1954), chap. 5.

[13] Milovan Djilas, *The New Class* (New York: Frederick A. Praeger, Inc., 1957),
p. 121.

bears out this indictment. There are cases, too, in which plants become quite proficient in the manufacture of large numbers of items for which, it later develops, there is a very limited market.

One difficulty stems from too many planning agencies which plan for too many economic organizations. In the Sverdlovsk *Oblast* alone, an official of the *sovnarkhoz* complained of a confusion of local governments, the *sovnarkhoz*, the national ministries, ministries and departments of the Russian Republic, industrial cooperatives, and subordinate organs of the *sovnarkhozy* as well as units from other economic regions—all engaged in various phases of planning in Sverdlovsk.[14] Ending of the *sovnarkhoz* system may slightly improve this situation of multiple planning levels.

This matter of weaknesses and inefficiencies, in part, is one of choice. In fact, there is scarcely an economic problem faced by Soviet leaders today which did not preoccupy their predecessors for at least the past three decades.[15] They must be aware of most of the shortcomings of their system, some of which apparently are accepted willingly as a cost of communism. Political considerations direct the Soviet economy toward developing autarky, for example, when the leadership must have some inclination of the economic cost involved resulting from such a decision. The planned rapid buildup of one sector of the economy at the temporary expense of another sector is more a deliberate choice than a planning weakness in and of itself.

RETAIL TRADE

The magnitude of retail trade, as with all other forms of economic activity in the USSR, is included in the annual plan. With something more than 500,000 state-controlled retail outlets in 1958, approximately three fourths of these were permanent and the rest were classified as temporary, or seasonal. In addition, there are consumer cooperative stores, public catering establishments, repair and servicing units, and collective farm markets. Finally, there are a relatively few privately run, one-man operations such as those owned by carpenters and tailors.

One retail store, on an average, will serve perhaps several hundred customers daily.[16] The quality of retail stores varies from the well-supplied and efficiently serviced central department store in Moscow (GUM) with its more than 2,000 employees to the more numerous small, ill-equipped,

---

[14] *Izvestiya*, June 29, 1960.

[15] Gregory Grossman, "The Structure and Organization of the Soviet Economy," *Slavic Review*, Vol. 21 (June, 1962), p. 204.

[16] Katkoff, *op. cit.*, p. 355.

and poorly managed stores which all too frequently offer customers only limited quantities of shoddy, over-priced goods.

Consumer's cooperatives existed in tsarist Russia and were continued, in limited numbers, in rural areas after the communists came to power. Following an immediate post-World War II spread of cooperatives into the cities, more recently they are being restricted to rural areas, leaving urban citizens to be served by state retail stores. Membership in co-operatives is voluntary and while they are organized and maintained by citizens, their goods, services, prices, and wages are government controlled.

Local cooperatives serve certain villages through their network of stores. Cooperatives also purchase farm products for resale both to rural and urban customers and supply collective farms with some of their instruments and equipment. Above the local cooperatives, which are member-owned and managed (although government supervised), are the regional, republic-wide cooperatives. All of these, in turn, form part of the Central Union Cooperative (*Tsentrosoyuz*) which acts like an overall ministry for the consumer cooperative organizations and which has seven main wholesale directorates. Membership in the 21,000 cooperatives in 1958 numbered 35 million people.[17]

Kolkhoz ("free") markets were allowed to spring up in the early 1930's as a convenience both to peasants and the state. The markets, managed by collective farmers in their spare time, sell directly to consumers surplus food taken from the farmer's individual garden plots. The atmosphere is one of a free market operating under the rule of supply and demand, with prices determined by mutual bargaining between buyer and seller. Located in urban as well as rural centers, and such places as railroad stations, the market facilities are built and maintained by the government from fees charged the collective farmers for use of the facilities. In 1953 there were more than 8,000 *kolkhoz* markets retailing annually foodstuffs valued at tens of billions of rubles.[18] In 1956 the markets included 29,547 stands, 4,440 stores, 1,253 refrigerated warehouses, 1,031 storage units, 2,054 meat and 1,925 milk inspection points. Sales for all of these markets equaled approximately 6 percent of total turnover of agricultural products.[19]

Although prices in the markets are flexible and uncontrolled, the state can exert an influence on them by increasing or decreasing the amount of products offered for sale in competing state stores (which normally are lower priced). Constituting a bit of free enterprise in an otherwise in-

---

[17] *Ibid.*, p. 351.

[18] Harry Schwartz, *Russia's Soviet Economy* (2d ed.; New York: Prentice-Hall, Inc., 1958), p. 436.

[19] Katkoff, *op. cit.*, pp. 361–62.

hospitable system, *kolkhoz* markets are a convenience to the farmer as a source of supplementary income, to the consumer as a source of additional food, and to the state because they make available more agricultural commodities to the public, thereby compensating somewhat for the deficiencies of the regular system of state supply.

THE WORKER IN SOVIET INDUSTRY

In order to win full support from industrial workers prior to and during the Revolution, the Bolsheviks advocated worker's control over industry. Following the Revolution, workers actually were permitted some voice in ruling industry by the new Bolshevik government, though more out of practical necessity than from any sense of deep conviction. Strikes were even permitted in these early days, some 500 taking place in the years 1922–23.[20] This relative independence for workers and their accompanying influence in controlling industry was short-lived, however. Under Stalin's rule the worker became a nameless cog in the industrial machine; he enjoyed few rights and fewer prerogatives.

As early as 1919 a compulsory labor law was passed which covered all able-bodied citizens between the ages of sixteen and fifty. By late 1932 one day's absence from work without an excuse could bring dismissal from one's job and loss of housing. Labor books which included employment history, reasons for changing jobs, and such related matters, were required by 1939. A worker could be reprimanded or transferred to a less desirable job if he reported for work late, left early, or took an extended lunch period. By a 1940 decree workers could be imprisoned or have their wages cut for as little provocation as being more than 20 minutes late to work. For more serious violations of the rules workers could be exiled to forced labor camps. This period of Soviet history, falling under the general era of the "dictatorship of the proletariat," accented the dictatorship much more than rule by the proletariat.

Although the Stalinist period saw very harsh labor conditions, penalties for errant workers were not always forthcoming. Managers still had to hire and keep a reasonably proficient work force, so that a too rigid enforcement of the labor rules could, and often did, harm the efficiency of the enterprise. Skilled workers, always in demand, were too scarce and valuable a commodity from the standpoint of the factory director to be abused mercilessly. For well-qualified workers there were usually managers to be

---

[20] Maurice Dobb, *Soviet Economic Development since 1917* (London: Routledge & Kegan Paul, Ltd., 1947), p. 416.

found who would overlook minor discretions for the sake of gaining and keeping able personnel.

The post-Stalin era ended the most abusive practices followed earlier; since then there has been a serious, if limited, effort to improve working conditions. Moreover, a move has been made toward reinstituting the cencept of worker's rule of factories. Worker-appointees, meeting as plant labor-dispute commissions, have been granted some powers of consultation and decision making in factory matters.[21] The 1962 reorganization authorizes, additionally, worker's advisory committees in factories to confer with management on matters of planning, work quotas, and job assignments. So far, the regime has not yet been very explicit as to the precise powers which workers are to gain under this new plan, however. If all Soviet history is any criterion, it seems unlikely that the regime is going to rush into any full-scale, or even half-scale, plan giving workers control over industry. Of more immediate concern to workers has been the official reduction in hours of work in industry, to a national norm of seven hours per day (discounting extra "volunteer" work such as overtime and holiday labor) and providing workers with more fringe benefits, for example, better housing.

As if to prove the vacuity of official promises for better working conditions, though, the Soviet press has reported instances of excessive labor turnover. One Leningrad factory in 1961 hired 705 new workers while it lost 757 in the same year. During the first eight months of 1962, at a hydroelectric construction project in Siberia, 11,000 workers quit. In 1962 Kazakh construction enterprises hired 210,000 new workers while simultaneously 200,000 workers quit. Causes given for the high turnover are poor living and working conditions with a considerable shortage of housing and service facilities.[22] As the data in Chapter V indicated[23], wages, working and living conditions, and job locality were the main reasons for workers leaving their jobs. In Brown's study, dissatisfaction with the work itself and with working and living conditions are more important reasons for quitting than is the question of wages. Naturally, a number of workers left for such mundane reasons as leaving the area and for purposes of education.[24]

---

[21] Michael Kaser, "The Reorganization of Soviet Industry and its Effects on Decision Making," in Gregory Grossman (ed.) *Value and Plan: Economic Calculation and Organization in Eastern Europe* (Berkeley, Calif.: University of California Press, 1960), p. 214.

[22] *New York Times*, Western Edition, January 9, 1963.

[23] See page 111.

[24] Emily Clark Brown, *Soviet Trade Unions and Labor Relations* (Cambridge, Mass.: Harvard University Press, 1966), pp. 35–37.

Collective Agreements

A collective agreement (*kollektivnyy dogovor*) setting forth mutual obligations of workers and managers has been a part of the Soviet labor scene for a number of years. As early as July, 1918, in fact, the government issued a decree calling for collective agreements which would cover such matters as appointments and dismissals, working hours and wage rates.

In modern Soviet life, collective agreements are signed in factory and farm, retail outlet and construction site—wherever there are more than 100 workers employed. The agreements are drawn up in the basic work unit, such as the factory, supposedly by management and workers cooperating to write the document. A general workers's meeting adopts the agreement which is signed by the factory director and the chairman of the local trade-union committee. The agreement then is "registered" (ratified) at the next higher administrative echelon. Registration serves to settle any differences remaining between management and workers and ensures that the agreement coincides with the annual plan and with existing labor law.[25] At various times throughout the year the agreement is checked to ensure its fulfillment. Failure on this account, as happened in one instance with a chief engineer who neglected to improve ventilation in his Moscow plant, may bring dismissal from one's post.[26]

Although collective agreements include benefits for the workers, the real emphasis is on the mutual duties of all concerned toward the more important objective of fulfilling the annual plan of work. The first section of an agreement specifies obligations of both management and labor in fulfilling *and* overfulfilling the plan, in increasing labor productivity, in using equipment in a more rational manner, and in raising the quality of products as well as cutting the cost of production. The agreements include other clauses which call for technological improvements and which list the obligations of management (for example, in promoting qualified workers to more responsible positions). They also provide for worker's technical training and embody a "Cultural Service" clause authorizing worker's recreational activities, certain wage rates, vacations, and medical facilities.

Wage rates are covered in the collective agreement, but only as a formality. A government decree in 1947 expressly forbade inclusion in collective agreements of any wage rate not *previously* approved by the

---

[25] V. S. Korotkhov, *The Collective Agreement in the USSR* (Moscow: Profizdat, 1960), p. 28.

[26] *Ibid.*, pp. 31–32.

government.[27] The basic wage payment system is that of piece-rate, of
which there are several types. In the *straight* piece-rate plan, each unit is
paid for according to an identical rate. Thus, the more units a worker
produces, the more money he receives. In the *progressive* piece-rate
workers are paid at a fixed rate for fulfilling their norms, and at a higher
rate for overfulfilling them. Under the *premium* piece-rate bonuses are
given for certain achievements, such as reducing waste or fuel consumption.
A *simple time-rate* system of pay differentiates among workers, depending
upon duration of work and the worker's skills.[28] In addition to the set
wage rate, workers frequently earn bonuses which, on occasion, equal their
gross wage. The majority of production workers (60 percent at present)
are paid under a piece-rate system, only about 5 percent on paid-time
rates, and the remainder on time rate plus bonuses.[29] Wage differentials
among branches of industry, in fact, resemble fairly closely the differentials in free market economies. Thus, the Soviet economy has been
subjected to many of the same competitive forces which operate in market
economies, including considerations of demand and supply.[30] The new
system of enterprise management partially inaugurated in 1965 seeks
greater managerial flexibility in matters of wage setting and bonus payments at the factory level.

Collective agreements between management and labor differ from
similar agreements in Western countries in one major respect. Soviet
agreements are not drawn up, agreed upon, and signed as a result of
settling wages or working conditions, except in a very minor scope. They
certainly are not the outcome of a struggle between labor and management.
The important decisions concerning wage rates and the mutual obligations
of workers and management are decided upon by the government regardless
of any collective agreements. What the agreements do provide is an
explicit statement of the duties of both workers and managers to fulfill
the annual plan as quickly and economically as possible. They are broad
statements of lofty principles, not firm guarantees of managerial performance.

Trade Unions

The source of strength of trade unions as well as their authority in the
Soviet Union stems not from their sizable membership but from the

[27] See I. L. O., *Trade Union Rights in the U.S.S.R.*, New Series, No. 49 (Geneva:
International Labour Office, 1959), p. 9.

[28] *Politicheskaya Ekonomiya* (Moscow: Gosizpolit, Akademia Nauk, SSSR, 1954),
pp. 455–57.

[29] Gertrude Schroeder, "Industrial Wage Differentials in the USSR," *Soviet Studies*,
Vol. XVII (January, 1966), p. 304.

[30] *Ibid.*, pp. 312, 313.

Communist Party, according to a Soviet statement in 1949.[31] This claim sets the tone and establishes a general framework in which trade unions live and function. The framework is one that has been carefully worked out by the regime since 1917.

In the turbulent revolutionary period factory committees made up of workers had exercised considerable power and no little amount of independence and self-rule. They were in a position, in fact, to challenge even national authority. Acting cautiously at first, the Bolsheviks encouraged the growth of trade unions hoping they would act as a counter to the independent power of the factory committees. Following an All-Russian Congress of Trade Unions in early 1918, the factory committees gradually were brought under the unions which, in turn, were controlled by the government.

Some of the early activities of Soviet trade unions were to administer social insurance programs and to recruit for the Red Army in the Civil War. By early 1919 the Communist Party called on trade unions to concentrate in their hands the administration of the entire national economy. This broad prescription of responsibility for unions was expedient for the party to write in 1919 when it sought to win support for its minority cause, but necessary to abandon shortly thereafter so that the party could retain for itself full political power. At the Tenth Party Congress in 1921 unions were singled out as merely "auxiliary organs" of the worker's state and as "schools" for communism. At the same time the party was designated the ideological as well as administrative supervisor of the unions. By late 1921 the party congress was directed to steer into positions of responsibility within the unions only experienced party members of long standing and of "clean" political background. Still, the party had not yet won full control. In 1921 the "Worker's Opposition" advocated greater freedoms for trade unions, arguing that unions should have a strong voice in planning and controlling the economy. The head of the Central Trade Union Council, taking a more conservative approach, thought that unions should represent their members first and should strive for higher production second. These views, however, defied the goal and the trend of communist power. They were soon put down and the Worker's Opposition was defeated. Since that time, Soviet trade unions have been placed in the "auxiliary" role called for at the Tenth Party Congress.

Organized on an industry-wide basis, all workers employed in a given industry have their own trade union. Below the All-Union Central Council of Trade Unions are, in descending order, republican, regional, and town unions. On the lower level, there are factory trade union

---

[31] Cited in I. L. O., *op. cit.*, p. 6.

committees (*zavkomy*) and, below that, the shop committees. With a membership of more than 80 million members in 1966, the unions include production workers, specialists, white-collar employees, and managers.

The several functions of trade unions include administering worker's social insurance systems, managing rest homes of workers as well as their factory farms, providing sanatoriums and vacation places, promoting cultural and entertainment facilities, "supervising" worker's housing, protecting labor's "interests" (such as inspecting working conditions), and taking part in paramilitary activities. Trade unions do have a legal right to request that the management of a given enterprise be replaced if Soviet labor law has been violated.[32] In addition, most labor legislation is drafted either by the Central Council of Trade Unions or with its participation.[33] More importantly, from the standpoint of the regime, unions educate workers in the duties of communist labor and in the responsibilities of socialist discipline and, as noted, aid in fulfilling the annual plan.

For individual workers there are certain advantages in union membership such as greater sick benefits and more opportunity to use rest homes and children's camps. Under union auspices there are labor disputes boards set up in each plant formed of management representatives and trade union members. The boards handle disputes arising out of wage payments, dismissals, and work norms. Appeals go to the plant trade union organization, then to the courts. Collectively, and this is a more unique feature of Soviet trade unions, workers gain little advantage from union membership. Soviet unions are dominated completely by, and remain loyal to, the policies, programs, and views of the regime. Instead of serving as a counterweight against managerial power, their normal posture in the West, unions in the USRR constitute an auxiliary arm of managerial power whose over-riding purpose is to support the party and government. It most assuredly is not the function of unions to oppose in any way management, which by definition is Soviet state management.

Whether slight changes in trade union practices, slowly developing in recent years, will alter their typically modest role cannot yet be determined.[34] It should be noted, though, that a 1958 decree increased the responsibility of unions in assisting factory managers and required the

[32] For an elaborated treatment see Isaac Deutscher, *Soviet Trade Unions: Their Place in Soviet Labour Policy* (London: Royal Institute of International Affairs, 1950), pp. 117–19; and G. Shitarev, "Rukovoditel i rukovodimye," *Kommunist*, No. 13 (September, 1960), p. 48.

[33] Brown, *op. cit.*, p. 82.

[34] See the discussions in Anne Kahl, "The Worker," *Problems of Communism* (March–April), 1965), and the statute in *Current Digest of the Soviet Press*, Vol. XVII, No. 42 (November 10, 1965).

factory *zavkom's* consent to the ordering of overtime work, dismissing workers, and hiring workers under age sixteen.   In 1962 the All-Union Central Council of Trade Unions adopted a resolution condemning illegal managerial demands for overtime in factories and on construction sites. In 1965, the statute on state enterprises listed the following managerial decisions which require the agreement of the local trade union prior to taking effect.

> Discharge workers.
> Establish regulations for internal labor order.
> Make bonus payments.
> Allocate housing that is at the enterprise's disposal.
> Call production technical and economic conferences.

Apparently, the item about discharging workers without the consent of the factory's trade union committee is, in some cases as least, taken seriously.   According to a member of the USSR Supreme Court, in a series of cases brought to court on the complaints of workers, the following data is pertinent.[35]

> In 90 of the 250 cases on employment reinstatement before people's courts in the Kirghiz Republic, workers were dismissed without the consent of the trade union committee.
> In Uzbek, every third case was found unjustified for the same reason.
> In nine months in 1964, Georgian and Uzbek courts redressed approximately 70 percent of employment reinstatement lawsuits; courts in Azerbaijan, Kirghiz, Tadzhik, and Armenia redressed more than 60 percent of such claims.

Unions increasingly are being recognized by workers as articulators of their several interests.   Accordingly, workers are demanding better union representatives and more vigorous union support for their interests.   More and more workers seem to be using unions as hearing boards for their grievances and aggregators of their demands.[36]

ADMINISTRATIVE POLICY

Economic management always has been a main problem area for Soviet politics from the earliest nationalization efforts to the present day.   The sheer enormity of the managerial task undertaken in a communist economy would present very challenging problems if no other difficulties existed. In the overall problem of economic control, industry has been the favored economic sector in the USSR.

---

[35] *Pravda*, March 12, 1965.
[36] Brown, *op. cit.*, pp. 170–171, 174, 317.

Industrial Policy

Because of the theory of communism, which is based largely on the plight of the industrial worker, Lenin and Stalin thought chiefly of and planned more for the development of the industrial system which would be the foundation, as it were, for the proletarian state. Moreover, the early goals which Lenin and Stalin sought (industrialization and militarization) emphasized, even required all efforts to be bent toward building a strong industrial base for the USSR. Consequently, industry was favored overwhelmingly over agriculture and services in the amount of state investment, establishment of workers' training schools, employment of skilled workers, and concentration of managerial talent. Heavy industry, the so-called "commanding heights," was given distinct priority over light industry. The base for an industry—producers' goods—as a result has always enjoyed a distinct preference over consumer goods in the USSR. It still does, although its absolute priority appears to be slipping. This point needs emphasis. The Soviet economy *can* produce quality goods, as it does, for example, in earth-satellite instrumentation. The shoddy consumer goods for which Soviet industry has become well known are based in part on a conscious choice by the leadership to stress the priority regarding investments of time, money, raw materials, and equipment for heavy industrial, producers' goods. Finally, for reasons similar to the above, there has been over the years considerably greater Communist Party involvement in, help toward, and interference with industry than with the other sectors of the economy.

By the 1960's, several decades of official concentration on building a heavy industry showed certain positive effects. A large modern industry had been erected so that the USSR now could be classified as an industrialized nation. Rather extensive technological developments, although confined chiefly to heavy industry, were another feature which contributed to the building of a modern and powerful war machine. From the standpoint of the bureaucracy, too, successful managerial careers were to be found in industry rather than in the other sectors. All of this official attention given to industry, as might be expected, has had adverse effects on the growth of agriculture.

Agricultural Policy

Agriculture has been the stepchild of the Soviet economy and generally has had to shift for itself in attempting to compete with industry for capital investment. At the same time peasants were forbidden to change over into any form of private farming. Half-hearted and misguided efforts by the regime to increase farm output too often have taken the form of merely setting high production targets and periodically reorganizing the state apparatus concerned with agriculture.

Early in the Soviet era the great hopes entertained for the *sovkhozy* met with considerable peasant resentment. In addition, forced collectivization had near disastrous results, again because of extreme peasant opposition. Other organs, such as the joint *sovkhoz-kolkhoz*, the MTS and the RTS, have enjoyed only limited success. Apart from these organizational hybrids, there occurred almost semiannual reorganizations of the national and republic ministries of agriculture—now splitting them, now joining them, now altering their forms. These intermittent and haphazard efforts, and particularly that of collectivization, continued and added to the pre-communist tradition among peasants of antigovernment attitudes; it also caused the peasants to resist political controls over farming. And yet, conversely, another tradition created by these government measures was that of establishing firm political control over farming.

In recent years the leadership has devoted much time and energy to resolving agricultural problems. Apparently their successes in improving farming have been minimal so far. The main trouble, apart from normal Soviet managerial weaknesses, seems to be in the areas of investment, rationality, and incentives. The previous law rate of state investment in agriculture may be partially corrected under the newer approach in which investment in agriculture for 1963 was increased 30 percent over 1962. The 1963 organizational format emphasized a new type of agricultural administrative board, special rural governmental committees and separate party organs—all established for the exclusive task of helping manage agriculture. By mid-1966 still another reorganization unified once again local party organs and reestablished the Ministry of Agriculture at the national level. As with industry, so with agriculture, party leaders have fooled themselves into believing that simple maneuvers such as reorganizing agricultural ministries or firing large numbers of local party secretaries could alleviate their problems. Instead much too optimistic plans for greatly increased output have resulted in plan failures which in turn give rise to frustration on all levels. But, there have been other weaknesses, too.

Incentives, personal and tangible, for individual peasant farmers throughout Soviet history have been woefully inadequate. Of all the deficiencies in Soviet agriculture, the failure to offer peasants adequate compensation has stood out most starkly and has done more than anything to depress agricultural growth. Russian peasants simply have failed to become enthusiastic state collectivists. Insufficiently high prices for meat, milk, and grain products explains another failure of Soviet agriculture to meet its targets for meat and milk during the first years of the now abandoned Seven-Year Plan (1959–65).[37] Unless and until the regime faces some of these problems with a great deal more realism than has been employed heretofore, the outlook for early improvements in farm output is not bright. Even the plans drawn up in 1965 to add to the incentives for collective farmers, such as a guaranteed monthly wage and social security benefits, are but slight improvements in an area which will require many more to reasonably satisfy farmer demands on the political system.

In the past few years the regime has become more lenient toward the private plots of the collective farmers. Obviously, there is an advantage to the state in subsidizing (by loaning the land for the plots) this area of "private enterprise" in farming. In 1960–64 collective farmers produced 66 percent of the total gross output of meat in one *oblast*, 55 percent of its milk, and 90 percent of its eggs on their private plots. During this period, the volume of production on these plots increased 1.8 times more than the production on the collective farms themselves.[38] The problem for the regime over the years has been what to do with an embarrassing private area within an otherwise public sector of agriculture. Can the regime afford to do away with these private plots? Obviously not, so the decision apparently has been taken to allow them to continue, perhaps even to flourish. It may be that the regime no longer overly worries about the private nature of the plots so long as they are productive and measurably help to feed the population.

BUREAUCRACY AND THE ADMINISTRATOR

A continuing objective of management in the Soviet Union has been to combine key central direction and control with decentralized operations in decision making on lower administrative levels. Toward the fulfillment of this rather difficult goal, the leadership has enjoyed a measure of success. It has suffered in the process, however, through no small amount of frustration and failure. One problem has always been how to motivate middle- and lower-level administrators within the managerial hierarchy,

---

[37] Morris Bornstein, "The Soviet Price System," in Morris Bornstein and Daniel R. Fusfeld, *The Soviet Economy, A Book of Readings* (Homewood, Ill.: Richard D. Irwin, Inc., 1962), p. 141. On June 1, 1962, the purchase price for beef and poultry was raised an average of 35 percent. *Partiynaya Zhizn*, No. 11 (June, 1962), p. 10.

[38] A. Kotechenkov, "Razvitie obshchestvennogo proizvodstva i lichnykh podsobnykh khozyaystvo," *Planovoe Khozyaystvo* No. 1 (January, 1966), p. 79. Men collective farmers in this *oblast* spent 15 percent of their working time in 1964 on their private plots, while the women farmers spent 37 percent of their working time on the plots.

while at the same time not curbing their initiative under the excessively top-heavy bureaucracy. Although Soviet leaders have experimented with administrative decentralization they look upon it with a good deal of suspicion. The possibility that intermediate or lower-level management might be given authority to establish and pursue goals that differ from those fixed by central authority is not seriously considered. What is contemplated, on the other hand, is that lower managerial organs shall be granted a bit more discretionary authority to determine just how resources under their immediate control can best be used to achieve the predetermined goals set by the state. What the Soviet leadership strives for, of course, is to speed up decision making from the field to the center and to reduce the heavy supervisorial load of the central government by permitting local administrators to decide more of the minutiae of daily management. The 1965 reforms which grant to factory directors more independence from higher administrative agencies is designed to help meet this need. In no case, however, is central direction and control of the economy to be short-circuited.

Soviet leaders apparently have been successful in encouraging a reasonable degree of such managerial initiative by allowing administrators to offer suggestions on matters of production, to make specific application of general assignments, and to initiate new techniques and methods.[39] Obviously, the need for a great abundance of managerial talent is very considerable in such a "managed" system, and the characteristics and qualifications of administrators become doubly important for Soviet economic success. The newly emerging managerial elite is more politically self-confident and not beset by the fears and insecurities which plagued former managers.[40]

American visitors to Soviet industries report that the typically successful Soviet administrator, or "organization man," has worked as a laborer, received some technical training to qualify himself as a technician or engineer, is a member of the Communist Party, and is politically loyal to the regime. He is tough, resourceful, and very capable. As one moves up the managerial hierarchy, a more specialized knowledge of budgeting, planning, statistics, and research are called for in the administrator's training and experience. Of 200 members of *Gosplan* in 1960, Bond

---

[39] Granick, *op. cit.*, p. 129. Material rewards offered high-quality managerial ability have been adequate to attract such talent while yet forcing managers to perform to get the rewards. In recent years managerial personnel have received handsome personal bonuses for overfulfilling the plan. Campbell, *op. cit.*, pp. 121, 133–34.

[40] Jeremy R. Azrael, *Managerial Power and Soviet Politics* (Cambridge: Harvard University Press, 1966), p. 167.

counted one half as engineers and one half as economists.[41]

The great size of the governmental administrative machine which is called upon to run the entire Soviet economy immediately suggests a huge, unwieldly, and expensive bureaucracy. It is just that, too. At the Thirteenth Party Congress in 1924 Stalin acknowledged that the state apparatus, already full of defects, was cumbersome, expensive, and mostly "bureaucratic."[42] And yet, we can say that the Soviet bureaucracy is within tolerable limits, if by that description we mean that it is able to function at all. In comparing administrative behavior, Armstrong notes many general similarities, although some differences, between Soviet and Western European administrators.[43]

Since Stalin's death in 1953, Soviet leaders have introduced three general managerial reforms that have been applied on an economy-wide rather than a regional or spot basis. These are: (1) simplification and reduction of administrative structures, (2) partial deconcentration of planning, and (3) limited decentralization of operational supervision and control. By the 1960's the bureaucracy still was excessively large and awkward, though, having grown in size even from Stalin's "bureaucratic" state in 1924. Khrushchev, in 1961, objected to the superfluous organizations and state employees ("white-collar" personnel) for the new *Tselinnyy Kray* which included the following:

Organizations		Employees
Kray headquarters............................	1	515
Oblasty......................................	5	1,421
Rayony......................................	67	3,128
State farm trusts.............................	54	1,248
State farms...................................	642	. . .
Collective farms..............................	104	. . .
Totals..................................	873	6,312

The employee figure of 6,312 as noted, excludes those working on state and collective farms.[44] Another example of bureaucratic congestion comes from the offices of the Ministry of Trade of the Russian Republic which, in a ten-month period in 1961, sent to outlying districts 143,000 letters, telegrams, instructions and orders, and received approximately that many

---

[41] Floyd A. Bond, "The USSR's Organization Man," *Saturday Review*, Vol. 44 (January 21, 1961), pp. 31–32. For a more extended treatment of the Soviet manager, see David Granick, *The Red Executive: A Study of the Organization Man in Russian Industry* (Garden City, N. Y.: Doubleday & Company, Inc., 1960).

[42] J. V. Stalin, *Works* (Moscow: Foreign Languages Publishing House, 1952), Vol. 6, p. 261.

[43] John A. Armstrong, "Sources of Administrative Behavior: Some Soviet and Western European Comparisons." *American Political Science Review* (September, 1965).

[44] Khrushchev in *Pravda*, November 24, 1961.

in answer.[45]   For the year 1964 and the first five months of 1965 in the Tadzhik Republic, the following figures reflect a measure of the problem:[46]

16,000 letters and orders (two tons of paper) were sent from the Tadzhik Consumers' Cooperative Union to lower echelons, and it received in return roughly as many.

16,000 different documents were sent from the Tadzhik Agricultural Equipment Association, and 12,400 were received.

27,000 papers, coming and going, were processed by the staff of the Ministry of Construction of the Tadzhik Republic.

A sizable, even measurable part of the Soviet bureaucratic difficulty, as we can see, stems from the elaborate and horribly complex organizational structure which proliferates throughout the entire economy.   Added to this is the extensive party hierarchy which can only contribute more confusion.   The dilemma, of course, is apparent.   How can the vast, modern economy of the Soviet Union be successfully guided and directed from the center without giving rise to an extremely burdensome administrative apparatus?   The regime recognizes the predicament, but it has been unable so far to solve it to any satisfactory degree.

----

[45] P. Voronina, "Sovershenstvovat deyatelnost apparata upravleniya," *Partiynaya Zhizn*, No. 2 (January, 1962), p. 11.

[46] *Kommunist Tadzhikistana*, July 30, 1965.   Even under the "new system" of enterprise management there are complaints of bureaucratic growth.   In one chemical plant, for example, the growth in numbers of workers and employees in recent years was 10 percent, but the accompanying growth in the administrative staff was 36 percent. Two enterprises had a 1966 planned increase in administrative expenses of 25–30 percent.   *Pravda*, September 25, 1966.

CHAPTER XII

Law and the Courts

LAW IN old Russia differed from that which grew up in the West in part because early Russian law, which was 500 years behind the West in its evolution, had always been ill-defined, arbitrary, class conscious, and more collectivistic than individualistic.[1] Russian law, so typical of other governmental and social institutions, was too closely identified with tsarism to be either enlightened or highly developed. Law in old Russia was given serious attention only when sporadic efforts were directed at its codification; here too, reforms, even piecemeal, were the exception rather than the rule. Normally law was but a personal appendage as well as an exclusive prerogative of the tsar. It was thought of chiefly as a support of and protection, not for individual citizens, but rather for state institutions.

With this tsarist heritage of a restricted, specialized, and very poorly developed legal system, the Communists found this framework to be readily adaptable to the needs of the Soviet period in terms of both a philosophy and an apparatus. Although occasionally there were early Soviet decrees relating somewhat vaguely to anti-state actions, no general criminal code was adopted until two years after the Revolution. The Communists did, however, abandon features of tsarist law which were odious to them, such as the professional bar and the formal apparatus of prosecution.

In late 1919 a governmental act instructed local judges, who were now to be elected by the soviets, in how to deal with certain law violators. It urged judges to call upon their "revolutionary consciousness" in their judicial determinations. Still, no specific crimes were defined.[2] And yet,

---

[1] Harold J. Berman, *Justice in Russia: An Interpretation of Soviet Law* (Cambridge, Mass.: Harvard University Press, 1950), pp. 126, 161.

[2] John N. Hazard, *Law and Social Change in the U.S.S.R.* (London: Stevens and Sons, Limited, 1953), pp. 85–86.

people's courts were established, also in 1919, by local governmental organs.[3]

At first there were two types of Soviet courts. One was set up to handle normal cases, criminal and civil. The other and more unique type was designated "revolutionary tribunals" to prosecute those people who harbored anti-Bolshevik and antiregime tendencies. A Judiciary Act of 1922 introduced a court structure somewhat resembling that of old Russia, although without certain tsarist features such as the jury. This was the time, too, when Soviet law was being codified and a criminal law was slowly taking form in the Soviet republics.[4]

The second Soviet Constitution, ratified in 1924, provided for a Supreme Court to carry out "revolutionary legality" throughout the country. At the same time there was established within the Supreme Court an office of Procurator-General (chief prosecutor) which had among other duties, that of watching over the activities of the secret police (Organization of State Political Administration—OGPU) with an eye to its legality. Both the Court and the Procurator's office were appointed by the inner Presidium of the Central Executive Committee of the USSR. Lower courts were appointed by the local soviets.

Under the third Constitution in 1936 members of the Supreme Court, USSR were elected by the Supreme Soviet, USSR with union republic supreme soviets electing union republic supreme courts. Local judges were elected by voters.[5]

Vyshinsky, Stalin's chief prosecutor during the Great Purge trials, has depicted Soviet law as being directed in its entirety against exploitation and exploiters; this fits the dogma of Marxism. Soviet law, he continues, struggles with the foes of socialism and with those who obstruct the building of a socialist society.[6] This statement typifies the early Soviet approach to law, one which considered law to be but one of several instruments in the hands of the leadership to assist it in constructing the new Soviet system. Such a broad prescription of responsibility for the law made it easy enough to include within the legal format such innovations

---

[3] *People's Court of the Russian Socialistic Federal Soviet Republic* (Petrograd: Commissariat of Justice, 1919), Article I.

[4] John N. Hazard, "The Courts and the Legal System," in Cyril E. Black (ed.), *The Transformation of Russian Society: Aspects of Social Change Since 1861* (Cambridge, Mass.: Harvard University Press, 1960), p. 152. And Hazard, *Law and Social Change in the U.S.S.R.*, p. 87.

[5] Although, according to John N. Hazard, *The Soviet System of Government* (rev. ed.; Chicago: University of Chicago Press, 1960), p. 164, no such local elections were held prior to 1949.

[6] Andrei Y. Vyshinsky (ed.), *The Law of the Soviet State*, trans. Hugh W. Babb (New York: The Macmillan Co., 1948), p. 50.

as the law of "analogy" by which judges could penalize a person for committing a "dangerous" act which might be interpreted as close (analogous) to a crime as defined by the code—even though the first act has not been specified as a crime. The law of analogy highlighted a period of Soviet rule under Stalin which was characterized by legal—even extralegal—protections for the state and the regime, but very few meaningful protections for the citizens. Subjected to deprivations of the police, arbitrary actions of governmental officials, and to the harsh terror emanating from the entire totalitarian structure, the citizen was scarcely protected by the law. With the death of Stalin, though, the relationship between the citizen and the law was to undergo something of a change.

THEORY OF SOVIET LAW

Soviet legal philosophy is all-embracing in its approach to society. Law performs a necessary integrating role in modern communism. Consequently, the legal distinction between public and private law as practiced in the West does not exist in the USSR; all law is public. It is more; it is all encompassing. Law, in the official Soviet view, is not some negative barrier against which a citizen on occasions runs afoul. Rather it is a positive, yet amorphous training ground for Soviet citizens. There are prescribed crimes and penalties to be sure, but there is much more. Soviet law is educational, instructive, and a general guide for society. The citizen, as a subject under the law, is a child, a youth to be trained, disciplined, even protected. The society is a family, or an organized club in which courts are the protecting, yet firm teacher, parent, guardian.[7]

Such a concept of the law might well explain one of the contradictions in the Soviet legal system. It is at one and the same time very permissive and yet unduly harsh. It sets an absolute maximum prison term for even serious crimes at but a mere 15 years. The law violator is like an errant child to be disciplined with firmness, but also with considerable leniency. On the other hand, Soviet law, rather petulant, vindictive, and arbitrary, can invoke the death penalty for embezzlement or for repeated falsification of governmental reports. Lawbreaking, then, is not the fault of the kind, tolerant parent, but of an intractable child. Similarly, Soviet legal theory holds that neither "socialism" nor its principles and foundations give rise to law violations. Such violations are nothing more than a hangover, a remnant of the old, "nonsocialist" views, customs, and beliefs of people who have not yet freely accepted the new "socialist" system.[8] No matter that the "socialist" system has been in operation since 1917, and that

---

[7] Berman, *op. cit.*, pp. 205, 273.

[8] I. S. Samoshchenko, *Okhrana Rezhima Zakonnosti Sovetskim Gosudarstvom* (Moscow: Gosurizdat, 1960), pp. 56–57.

many law violators are youthful persons who were born, raised, and educated only under communism.

Purpose of Soviet Law

As approved in late 1958 by the Supreme Soviet, the purpose of justice in the USSR is to protect the following: (1) the social and state system of the USSR; (2) the political, labor, residential, and other personal and property rights of citizens; (3) the rights of state institutions, enterprises, collective farms, cooperative and other public organizations.[9] In the above three-fold breakdown, as might be expected, preservation of the social and state system of the USSR is given higher priority than is protection of the individual rights of citizens. Another way to describe this priority is to note that Soviet law, not only in its principles but also in its detail, corresponds to the "political requirements of the building of communism."[10] Law thus becomes a regulator of various economic, political, and ideological relationships for the purpose of preserving, strengthening, and perfecting state and public "construction."[11]

The Soviet legal system does seek to preserve, for example, the rights of an accused in criminal cases and to be the source of impartial justice. At the same time, the system consciously and explicitly uses the normal legal safeguards, such as a court trial, as instruments to carry out the political goals of the state.[12] The Criminal Code of the RSFSR for 1961 contains a long list of individual rights, civil and political, which are protected by law. A citizen, for example, may not be interfered with in his voting, and forgery of electoral documents or miscounting votes is prohibited. Citizens enjoy such other rights as secrecy of correspondence, protection against illegal search or eviction, unfair court procedures, extraction of false confessions from accused persons, illegal arrest or detention, and the giving of false testimony. It is even illegal to hinder the performance of a religious service.[13] The whole concept of illegality, of course, is tied to the definitions of crime.

---

[9] *Fundamentals of Soviet Criminal Legislation, the Judicial System and Criminal Court Procedure: Official Texts and Commentaries* (Moscow: Foreign Language Publishing House, 1960), p. 40.

[10] Samoshchenko, *op. cit.*, p. 104.

[11] S. N. Bratus (ed.), *Voprosy Obshchey Teorii Sovetskogo Prava* (Moscow: Gosurizdat, 1960), p. 59.

[12] Harold J. Berman, "Introductory Comment," to *The Trial of the U 2: Exclusive Authorized Account of the Court Proceedings of the Case of Francis Gary Powers Heard Before the Military Division of the Supreme Court of the USSR, August 17, 18, 19, 1960* (Chicago: Translation World Publishers, 1960), p. xii.

[13] John N. Hazard and Isaac Shapiro, *The Soviet Legal System: Post-Stalin Documentation and Historical Commentary* (Dobbs Ferry, N. Y.: Oceana Publications, 1962), Part I, pp. 67, 87–88.

The Nature of Crime in the USSR

The 1961 party program contains the following general statements on crime.

There should be no room for law breakers and criminals in a society building communism. But as long as there are criminal offenses, it is necessary to punish those who commit crimes dangerous to society, violate the rules of the socialist community and refuse to live by honest labour. Attention should be mainly focussed on crime prevention.

Higher standards of living and culture, and greater social consciousness of the people, will pave the way to the abolition of crime and the ultimate replacement of judicial punishment by measures of public influence and education. Under socialism, anyone who has strayed from the path of the working man can return to useful activity.[14]

Despite this statement alluding to the cause of crime (in the practices of capitalism, not communism), one report cites the following results of an investigation into the causes of "anti-social behavior."[15]

Of minors convicted of hooliganism in the 1950's, 68 percent had lost one or both parents.

80 percent of the crimes committed by minors are related to a lack of supervision.

More than 40 percent of the thefts of state and public property are committed under conditions where control is lacking and proper accounting is absent.

Sociological research shows that lawbreaking is done primarily by juveniles who are not in school or working.

A crime, in Soviet words, is a "socially dangerous act or the omission of an act" prescribed by law which transgresses against the Soviet "socialist" system, or against the person and his rights.[16] Criminal codes in the USSR classify crimes into several principal groups. These include crimes against the state, against socialist property, crimes against persons and their rights and property, economic crimes, crimes committed by public officials, crimes against justice, administration, state security, law and order, public health, and military crimes.

Economic crimes include such matters as falsifying government reports and "speculation" (purchase and resale of goods or commodities for personal gain). One director of a shoe factory was convicted of breaking

---

[14] Jan Triska (ed.), *Soviet Communism, Program and Rules* (San Francisco: Chandler, 1962), p. 102.

[15] "Antiobshchestvennye yavleniya ikh prichiny i sredstva borby s nimi," *Kommunist*, No. 12 (August, 1966), pp. 62–64. Another source noted that 81% of first degree (deliberate) murders, 67% of the rapes, 57% of the bodily injuries and 96% of hooligan acts involved drunkenness *Sovetskoe Gosudarstvo i Pravo* No. 1 (January, 1967), p. 34.

[16] *Fundamentals of Soviet Criminal Legislation*, p. 7.

a main law of "socialist production" because he produced poor quality shoes. His crime resulted in material losses to his customers and a "moral loss" to the state. His sentence was six months of corrective labor with a deduction of 15 percent of his wages and, of course, removal as director of his factory.[17] In 1964 two workers were sentenced to one year of corrective labor, with deduction of 20 percent of their earnings and a 500 ruble fine, for shipping defective goods (quilted jackets and trousers, and overalls) from their sewing factory to clothing stores.[18] In a half-year period nearly thirty criminal proceedings were brought against "plunderers" in the Vilnyus trade network. Certain trade officials were guilty of misweighing, cheating customers and hiding goods which were in short supply behind counters.[19] An employee or official may even commit an economic crime simply by taking certain risks in production. Pointing out the ridiculous feature of this particular crime, one commentator notes that Soviet legal science largely ignores this important question of risk taking.[20] Of course, if a "risk" turns out satisfactorily, say by achieving a saving in the cost of production, or raising output, one need not anticipate prosecution. If the "risk," on the other hand, fails, perhaps causing damage to state property, then prosecution becomes more probable.

Crimes which can be considered to be crimes the world over, such as disturbing the peace, crimes of physical violence, and ordinary theft are classified, of course, as crimes in the USSR too. These are referred to as crimes against public security and they include, in addition, crimes of "rowdyism" (rudely violating law and order with disrespect for society), "hooliganism" (petty crimes), and taking the law into one's own hands.

There are, moreover, a series of crimes which are not typically categorized as such by Western nations. These crimes, at least some of them, relate to the peculiarities and prejudices of communism. They include the individual purchase or sale of land (title to land is always held by the government, and it is loaned at a low tax rate to individuals, for example, to build private houses), speculation and individual profit-making, procrastination and careless or unconscientious work attitudes of public employees, and religious instruction given in schools.[21] Establishing a private business is illegal in the Soviet Union; a case in Leningrad occurred

---

[17] *Izvestiya*, August 27, 1961.

[18] *Pravda*, March 9, 1965.

[19] *Ibid.*, August 15, 1966.

[20] *Izvestiya*, May 13. 1960, in *Current Digest of the Soviet Press*, Vol. XII (June 15, 1960), p. 37.

[21] Dudley Collard, "Soviet Criminal Law and Procedure," *Soviet Legal Bulletin* (London), Vol. 2 (March, 1955), pp. 8–9.

in which the "partners" in this "firm" manufactured and sold personal stamps to newly graduated medical students.[22]

The theory of Soviet law is characterized by its broad, all-encompassing nature which seeks to educate and retrain as much as it tries to discipline and punish. To a considerable degree, Soviet law is more subjective and personalized than is Western law; by the same token, it tends to be both more arbitrary and more indulgent toward lawbreakers. Soviet legal theory assumes a primary objective, if not indeed the chief purpose of the law, to be the protection of the social-state system in the USSR. This basic purpose takes precedence over even the protection of the citizen's individual civil and political rights. The social-state system is protected to no small degree by the list of economic crimes, unusual crimes, and by the fact that the first, sweeping definition of crime is that it involves any "socially dangerous" act. Under such a wide compass as "socially dangerous," almost any action by a citizen who might find himself in momentary disfavor with the ruling authorities of the country could be held illegal.

There is yet another connection of Soviet law to that of old Russia. In the former peasant *mir* and village, crimes against the "collective," such as stealing, often endangered many lives, where starvation frequently threatened. The resultant punishment was severe, even cruel. Thus, when Soviet officials severely punish offenders against collective, Soviet society, the practice may not seem so bad to Soviet as to Western citizens. Feifer cites several cases to illustrate the severity of Soviet law: theft of three rolls of tar paper—three years; a drunk stole a mirror from a school on election day—two years; theft of a car's windshield wipers and mirror— one year; a waitress stealing a bit of wine from each glass served—two years. A Soviet judge argues "every single violation must be uncovered and punished. With no exceptions. Everyone must know for certain that it is futile to break the law—that he has *no* chance of getting away with it. . . . Every living person must be made to understand that society is *his*, that to rob his neighbor is to rob himself."[23]

CRIMINAL PENALTIES AND PUNISHMENTS

Soviet criminal law provides a range of punishment from mere public censure and such other light penalties as fines and disqualification for a specific office or activity, to more severe punishments involving restricted residence (excluded from living in certain areas), corrective labor without

---

[22] *Leningradskaya Pravda*, June 1, 1965.

[23] George Feifer, *Justice in Moscow* (New York: Simon and Schuster, 1964), pp. 68, 330.

imprisonment, and sending of members of the armed forces to disciplinary detachments. Finally, there are the penalties of confiscation of property, imprisonment, and death by execution (shooting).[24]

A great deal of Soviet criminal law, particularly in dealing with first offenders, follows mild prescriptions of reprimand, censure, and fines. It is in just this area of minor crime (for example, petty theft) where Soviet law seems to be most paternal, educational, and lenient. With the exception of those few crimes calling for the death penalty, 10 years is a normal maximum prison sentence with a special maximum for certain exceptionally grave crimes or especially dangerous habitual criminals set at 15 years. In a 1959 plenary meeting, the national Supreme Court called for an easing of the severity of criminal punishment by the courts and recommended that noncourt, public organizations assume more of the responsibility for taking care of persons charged with or convicted of minor crimes.[25] The Chairman of the USSR Supreme Court stated that criminal cases heard outside of court, at farms and enterprises, amounted to 25 percent of all criminal cases in 1960 and 21 percent in 1961.[26] A court may, if it believes the circumstances warrant it, pass a sentence which is less than even the minimum prescribed by law. Some of the mitigating circumstances which a court may rely upon in imposing lighter sentences include: (1) prevention of harmful "circumstances" and voluntary recompense; (2) grave personal or family circumstances; (3) commission of crime under duress (threats, compulsion); (4) powerful mental excitation; (5) defensive action against another crime; (6) minor committing a crime; (7) pregnant women committing a crime; and (8) sincere admission of guilt or voluntary surrender.[27] For other crimes, however, such as political crimes (labeled "crimes against the state") it is almost as if an entirely new set of laws, calling for much more severe penalties, is invoked.

Labor Camps

By statute, corrective labor camps were set up in 1930 for the stated purpose of protecting society from "socially dangerous" violators of law. The theory was to isolate such persons and give them socially useful employment. Only persons sentenced by a court for at least three years

---

[24] P. S. Romashkin (ed.), *Fundamentals of Soviet Law* (Moscow: Foreign Languages Publishing House, n.d.), pp. 414–17.

[25] *Sotsialisticheskaya Zakonnost*, No. 9 (September, 1959), pp. 13–15, in *Current Digest of the Soviet Press*, Vol. XI (November 11, 1959), p. 14.

[26] A. F. Gorkin, "Zadachi sotsialisticheskogo pravosudiya v sovremennykh usloviyakh," *Sovetskoe Gosudarstvo i Pravo* No. 8 (August, 1962), p. 9.

[27] *Fundamentals of Soviet Criminal Legislation*, pp. 17–18.

imprisonment or those convicted by a special resolution of the OGPU were subject to confinement in labor camps.[28] These camps, so euphemistically labeled "corrective labor," were the infamous slave-labor concentration camps of the Stalinist period. There is another use of the term "corrective labor," referring to a person penalized only at his regular place of employment, part of his salary being confiscated. Before this, however, there had been concentration camps in the 1920's for certain prisoners; not all of these were under the QGPU, though. Corrective-labor camps were directed by the police apparatus over the years of their existence and were primarily for political prisoners, although some ordinary criminals wound up there.

The number of political-economic prisoners, those accused of opposing the regime or frustrating its plans and policies in carrying out the first and second Five-Year Plans, grew into the hundreds of thousands in the 1930's. A former inmate of one of the largest camps portrayed the OGPU in the 1930's as constituting a state within a state, with its own troops, its own navy, millions of its own subjects in the form of prisoners, its own territory where normal Soviet law and authority did not function, its own industry and stores, even its own currency.[29] The OGPU, later transformed into the People's Commissariat of Internal Affairs (NKVD) in 1934, became a vast penal organization, economically, legally, almost politically independent of the normal state apparatus.

Since the death of Stalin thousands of former prisoners, both Soviet citizens and foreigners, have been released from the corrective-labor camps in several post-Stalin amnesties. Various spokesmen for the regime, among them Khrushchev, have claimed an end to "political" prisoners and have stated that many changes have occurred in the camps. Some of the regime's spokesmen have implied that the whole collective-labor, concentration camp system has been practically ended. From 1953 until 1957 improvements evidently were made in alleviating sickness in the camps, reducing the number of prisoners and easing the stiff camp regulations. The secret police, too, were stripped of their control over the camps in this reform period. It is possible that conditions in these camps will continue to improve. We can imagine without too much difficulty that penal conditions in the Soviet Union are not nearly so bad as they were under Stalin, and that the corrective-labor camps have undergone

[28] Statute of April 6, 1930, in "Statute on the Corrective Labor Camps, USSR: Comments and Translation" (Cambridge, Mass.: M.I.T., Center for International Studies, July 7, 1955, mimeographed), p. 4.

[29] Vladimir V. Tchernavin, "Slave Labor and Big Business," in Julien Steinberg (ed.), *Verdict of Three Decades: From the Literature of Individual Revolt Against Soviet Communism: 1917–1950* (New York: Duell, Sloan & Pearce, Inc., 1950), p. 262.

some reforms. Other available evidence, though, strongly suggests that changes in corrective-labor camps have been limited and the camps are not at all on the way out, at least not in the near future. A 1960 Soviet publication on correctional labor camps listed the following figures for the camps in the USSR for the years 1952–54:[30]

Year	Percent of Total Number of Persons Convicted Who Were Sent to Correctional Labor Camps
1952	40.
1953	34.4
1954	38.4

These figures, as of 1955, in numbers of people sent to the camps do not reveal any great change over the last full year of Stalinism, 1952.[31] The conditions in the camps since de-Stalinization have changed, though. Feifer points out that in labor camps (colonies) the lot of prisoners supposedly approaches the level of ordinary backwoods life; men living in barracks receive wages for their work and are visited by their wives overnight (for the "general" colonies).[32] There are more severe categories of colonies; "enforced," "strict" and "special."

There are political prisoners still in the Soviet Union. One flagrant case is that of Olga Ivinskaya, close confidant of Boris Pasternak. After Pasternak's death and after the overt Soviet opposition to his novel *Doctor Zhivago* died down, Ivinskaya was arrested and tried for "crimes against the state" and sentenced to eight years imprisonment in Siberia— probably in one of the camps. No doubt this woman, who for a long time collaborated with Pasternak, is being penalized for the anti-Soviet flavor of *Doctor Zhivago*. In another example, a Leningrad Jewish notable by the name of Pershersky was convicted in 1961 as an "agent of a foreign power" and sentenced to twelve years imprisonment. His crime was to seek reestablishment in Leningrad of kosher butcher shops; he advocated other goals for the Jewish community, such as reopening the synagogue.[33] In the recent trial of the writers Sinyavsky and Daniel for publishing novels abroad under pseudonyms, the question of "political" crimes was again at issue. The government interpreted their novels as being against communist ideology and the leading role of the party, as containing hatred for everything Soviet, malicious attacks on the theoretical tenets of Marxism-Leninism, all in violation of the Criminal Code of the RSFSR

---

[30] Quoted in Hazard and Shapiro, *op. cit.*, p. 141.

[31] For a discussion of changes in the system and an evaluation of the changes, see Paul Barton, "An End to Concentration Camps?" *Problems of Communism*, Vol. XI (March–April, 1962).

[32] Feifer, *op. cit.*, pp. 68, 351.

[33] Barton, *op. cit.*, p. 41.

which prohibits propaganda which seeks to undermine or weaken the Soviet regime or to discredit the Soviet state and social system.[34]   Their trial (which was only semipublic) was held early in 1966, following a six months' detention.   Their penalties, following the inevitable conviction, given the accusations against them, were seven years at hard labor for Sinyavsky and five years for Daniel.

Capital Punishment

Capital punishment was, for a time following Stalin's death, on its way out in the Soviet Union.   The regime's leadership prided itself on the advanced and enlightened state of Soviet law under which the death penalty would soon be dispensed with.   Nevertheless, according to the 1958 Fundamental Law the death penalty is called for in cases of treason, espionage, premeditated murder under aggravated circumstances, banditry and terroristic acts.   To these fairly well-defined crimes (assuming plausible definitions of treason and espionage), the death penalty is permissible for a more loosely worded and vague category which includes "wrecking" and "particularly grave crimes" as provided for by law.[35]   In efforts to wipe out certain other crimes, the death penalty was extended in 1960 to cover large-scale embezzlement, violence by prisoners in their places of confinement, and counterfeiters.   Executions have been ordered for such crimes as illegal transactions in gold, as well as hoarding it, currency speculation, counterfeiting, forging official documents, embezzlement, swindling, theft of raw materials and speculation with goods and foodstuffs.   These crimes fit a pattern.   They are those which the elite interprets as anti-regime, or anti-political system; they are far more heinous in the eyes of the elite than crimes of, say, murder or personal attack.   The capital punishment crimes are considered dangerous crimes because they are directed against the idea, not to mention the practice, of communism.

COURT STRUCTURE AND OPERATION

The several levels of Soviet courts are the Supreme Court of the USSR, the supreme courts of the union and autonomous republics, courts at the *kray*, *oblast*, and city levels, those for autonomous *oblast* and national area (*okrug*), and local people's courts in the *rayon* and city.   Finally there are military tribunals.   All of these above the level of people's courts serve both as courts of first instance in specified cases and also as appeals courts.

---

[34] *Izvestiya*, February 11, 1966.
[35] *Fundamentals of Soviet Criminal Legislation*, Article 22.

Judges are elected for five-year terms by their respective soviet. People's courts are elected directly by the voters.

Supreme Court

The internal structure of the Supreme Court of the USSR includes three divisions—civil, criminal, and military—with a chairman, vice-chairmen, members, and a number of people's assessors. Sitting *ex officio* on the Court are the 15 chairmen of the supreme courts of the respective union republics. Plenary sessions of the Supreme Court not only try cases, the great majority of which are on appeal,[36] but also hear complaints from the procurator-general, concern themselves with general matters of law and legislation dealing with law per se and, in addition, they have the legal right to initiate legislation. In this latter instance, the plenary sessions can serve as a legal arm of the national Supreme Soviet.

Middle-Level Courts

The supreme court of a union republic includes a chairman, deputy chairmen, members and people's assessors. Having both civil and

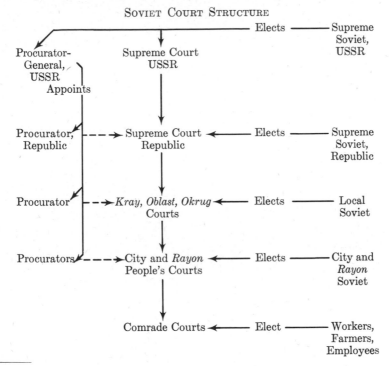

SOVIET COURT STRUCTURE

---

[36] *Nedelya*, No. 2 (January 3–9, 1965), p. 4.

criminal divisions, these courts serve primarily as appeals courts for their respective republics. In certain important criminal and civil cases, republic supreme courts have original jurisdiction. Similar organizations and functions (including both original and appellate jurisdiction) are assigned to the *kray, oblast, okrug,* and city courts. Criminal codes, differing from fundamental legal principles or basic laws, are enacted only by the union republics, not by the national government; thus original jurisdiction over most crimes is in the republican courts. Supreme courts of the union republics pass final verdicts, not subject to appeal to the Supreme Court USSR (except when the Chairman of the Supreme Court USSR or the Procurator General protests a given verdict).

Lower Courts

The primary, first-level courts in the legal hierarchy are the people's courts which exercise original jurisdiction in both criminal and civil matters. Each case coming before a people's court is heard by a panel of one professional judge and two lay judges (people's assessors). The professional judges are nominated by public organizations in general meetings and popularly elected for five-year terms. The lay judges are popularly elected for two-year terms. The three-member court examines the evidence, questions defendants and witnesses, votes a decision, and imposes a penalty or agrees to an acquittal in each case. The Soviet judge (the majority probably are party members), following his French rather than American counterpart, is an active player in court cases, questioning, examining, lecturing, remonstrating with defendants about their lack of morality, decency, communist character, and Soviet responsibility.[37]

All of the above courts are authorized by the national and republic constitutions. There are, apart from these courts, what are known as "comrade courts," acting under the general jurisdiction of the people's courts, which serve as factory, street, or neighborhood tribunals. Comrade courts first arose in the early period of "War Communism," having as their purpose an increase in labor discipline. The courts are set up (elected) in such places as enterprises, institutions, collective farms, and apartment buildings. Jurisdiction of these "courts" is optional on their part, and their range of actions might include imposing admonitions, reprimands, small fines, or a recommendation of dismissal of the accused from his work. There were more than 200,000 comrade courts in 1964.[38] The purpose

[37] Feifer, *op. cit.,* pp. 18, 84.
[38] *Izvestiya,* December 5, 1964.

of these "courts" is to sharpen and make more effective labor discipline, to keep workers from slacking off on their production, and to eliminate loafers, thieves, and other undesirables from the general population.[39] The range of jurisdiction of comrade courts includes such minor law infractions as slander, violations of labor discipline, drunkenness, debauchery, cursing, petty cheats, small-scale property quarrels, sloppy work, spoilage, minor damage to public property such as trees, and related activities. The comrade courts include no judges, public prosecutors, nor defense attorneys. They are, in Hazard's view, little more than organized institutions for simple mob rule.[40] And yet, Feifer argues that the sanctions at the disposal of the comrade courts simply are too insignificant to warrant indignation over departures from traditional procedures.[41]

Another semiofficial group of law enforcers or "crime fighters," known as *druzhiny*, are the unpaid, volunteer citizens who patrol streets, parks, and certain other areas as an adjunct to the regular militia. On occasion, the *druzhiny* apprehend and bring to trial petty criminals. At other times, however, the *druzhiny* have functioned as irresponsible vigilantes who have more often than not actually disturbed the peace of law-abiding citizens.[42] By 1961 in the city of Moscow alone there were 1,726 *druzhiny* units containing 89,176 volunteers. At this time there may have been upwards of 80,000 units and two and one-half million members nationwide. The *druzhiny* are heavily staffed by and operate directly under the party; in fact, they are a staff arm of the party. On balance, however, with inadequate training, vague jurisdiction, and arbitrary powers, the *druzhiny* apparently are of only limited effectiveness.[43]

Procurator

The Procurator's Office serves as the public prosecutor within the legal system. It was first established in 1922 for the general purpose of helping usher in a feeling of responsibility toward legal relations and toward the law. It is also the government's prosecuting arm. The Procurator's Office maintains supervision over: (1) execution of laws by all ministries, departments, institutions, public officials, and citizens; (2) legality of

---

[39] Glenn G. Morgan, "People's Justice: The Anti-Parasite Laws, People's Volunteer Militia, and Comrades' Courts," *Law in Eastern Europe*, Vol. VII, pp. 58, 70–71.

[40] John N. Hazard, "Soviet Codifiers Release the First Drafts," *The American Journal of Comparative Law*, Vol. 8 (Winter, 1959), pp. 75–76.

[41] Feifer, *op. cit.*, p. 128.

[42] A. Morris, "Hooliganism—and How (Not) to Deal with It," *Problems of Communism*, Vol. XI (July–August, 1962), pp. 55–57.

[43] Morgan, *op. cit.*, pp. 65, 69.

organs and procedures of inquiry and preliminary investigations; (3) legality of sentences, decisions, and judgments of court organs; (4) legality of the executions of sentences; and (5) legality of treatment of prisoners.[44] One of the more important functions of the Procurator's Office, of course, is that of prosecuting persons for violations of law. Another very important function of the Procurator's Office is to carry out the preliminary investigation of crimes.

The nation's top prosecutor, the procurator-general of the USSR, is appointed for a seven-year term by the Supreme Soviet, USSR. The Procurator-general, in turn, appoints for five-year terms procurators for the republic, *kray*, *oblast*, and autonomous *oblast* levels. He also must approve of appointments of all lower procurators, such as those in the *rayony* and cities.

The Legal Profession

Lawyers, though not actually prohibited immediately following the Revolution, were largely ignored. Communists considered lawyers to be merely an unneeded appendage of the capitalistic system of old Russia. Shortly thereafter, however, a measure of regularity was reintroduced into the legal profession in 1918 by the establishment of a College of Defenders, Accusers, and Representatives who were to handle civil suits—all on salaried employment as governmental civil servants. After several alterations, the lawyers (*advokaty*) were separated into colleges according to function and taken off regular salaries in favor of a fee system. As a result, private practice was squeezed out.

The two types of lawyers are advocate and jurisconsult, the first normally handling cases for individuals and appearing in court, the second mainly occupied as legal advisors to state institutions. In 1962 there were approximately 40,000 jurisconsults, at the least, and 17,000 advocates in the USSR, with 53 percent of the advocates in the RSFSR as members and candidate members of the Communist Party in 1961.[45] With respect to jurisconsults, it is a fairly common practice for enterprises and organizations to retain attorneys to handle their legal affairs on a contractual basis, paying them generous fees. One Kuibyshev attorney reportedly

[44] A. I. Denisov and M. G. Kirichenko, *Sovetskoe Gosudarstvennoe Pravo* (Moscow: Gosurizdat, 1957), p. 243. For an excellent brief history of one function of the office of the Procuracy, see the discussion in Glenn G. Morgan, "The Soviet Procuracy's 'General Supervision' Function," *Soviet Studies*, Vol. 11 (October, 1959).

[45] Harold J. Berman, *Soviet Criminal Law and Procedures, The RSFSR Codes* (Cambridge, Mass.: Harvard University Press, 1966), pp. 119, 123.

was under contract to four different enterprises.[46] Although a 125 ruble per month salary is about average for a lawyer, successful ones receive "extra" (unreported) fees to earn easily twice that amount.[47]

Colleges of advocates, to which lawyers are admitted after satisfying examination and other requirements, are set up in the republics. The colleges of advocates grant admission to new lawyers, set fees, regulate training of lawyers, and provide the disciplinary rules for members. Offices of the colleges of advocates are headed by a manager (elected by the lawyers) and operate on a generally agreed upon fee basis. Fees cover office expenses and include an amount for the lawyer who works on a given case. A lawyer is somewhat free to accept or reject a client, and he may even waive a fee in a hardship case.

COURT PROCEDURES

The overall purpose of Soviet court procedures, apart from the mechanical administration of legal relationships, is to inculcate in all citizens loyalty toward the USSR and communism, instill in them a sense of responsibility for obedience to the law as well as an attitude of concern toward socialist property, and to develop a general sympathy for order, for the rights of all citizens, and for the rules of socialist life.[48]

Arrest and Inquiry

Arrest of a person may be by militiamen (local police or troops), secret police, or even by the more unofficial, volunteer *druzhiny*. Although the laws on court procedure restrict arrest to an order of a court, or at least with the sanction of the procurator, and arraignment only as prescribed by law, there apparently are exceptions to the rule. The *druzhiny* may arrest, discipline, or haul before an *ad hoc* comrade court any citizen for committing an act defined by the *druzhiny* as a crime or as "socially dangerous."

The Soviet Union, thanks largely to the Stalinist purges, has earned a reputation for gross abuse of any procedural rights which defendants might otherwise have enjoyed by the iniquitous and terroristic pretrial actions of police, jailers, and prosecutors. Threats and torture, even though as much psychological as physical, were never far from the surface in Soviet

---

[46] Andreas Bilinsky, "The Lawyer and Soviet Society," *Problems of Communism* (March–April), 1965), p. 71.

[47] Feifer, *op. cit.*, pp. 233–35.

[48] *Fundamentals of Soviet Criminal Legislation*, p. 41.

courts during the height of Stalin's reign. In its efforts to rid the country of the more odious features of Stalinism, the regime since 1953 has attempted, among other innovations, to improve standards of legality. Pretrial inquiries, for example, now form a regular part of the new procedures.

Inquiries by the Procurator's Office, the militia, military commanders, or certain other agencies, such as the state security organs, are required before a case can be brought to court. The permissible organs of inquiry include the following: (1) organs of militia; (2) organs of fire protection; (3) organs of paramilitary protection of enterprises and construction sites; (4) organs of finance, sanatoria, technical institutes, trade inspection, and the inspection of labor affairs; (5) government institutions and public officials handling illegal actions of subordinate officials; and (6) commanders and chiefs of military units.[49] Results of the inquiry are given to the procurator if it is believed that a crime has been committed. Serious crimes (such as espionage, sabotage, or mass disorders) require a full-fledged preliminary investigation. In any case, an accused may not be detained more than three days prior to an inquiry without the specific approval of a procurator. As if to prove the value of preliminary careful investigation, total convictions reportedly dropped 19.6 percent in the period from 1958 to 1961.[50]

In a number of respects Soviet court precedure resembles that of American practice. Inquiries (similar to grand jury investigations) are made, public hearings are provided for accompanied by oral testimony, confrontation of witnesses is allowed, appeals are recorded and parties may be represented by lawyers. In other aspects, though, Soviet practice differs from the American. In the pretrial period, the life of the accused person is carefully examined. Information on his background, war record, mental condition, and personal economic situation is collected. The purpose in such a complete profile being drawn of the defendant is that the whole person, as an integral part of society, is placed on trial. In this way the Soviet paternalistic approach to its citizens can shine through. Extenuating circumstances (physical and psychological) form an acknowledged part of the regular legal process. In a criminal case, too, if the accused refuses a lawyer, the prosecution cannot be represented either and the case is conducted by the court alone. In addition to that, whereas in American law a guilty plea does away with the necessity for a trial, Soviet law follows the general continental European practice in which a

---

[49] V. M. Savitskiy, *Prokurorskiy Nadzor za Sobludeniem Zakonnosti v Deyatelnosti Organov Doznaniya i Predvaritelnogo Sledstviya* (Moscow: Gosurizdat, 1959), p. 101.

[50] *Sovetskoe Gosudarstvo i Pravo*, No. 8 (August, 1962), p. 4.

plea of guilty does not relieve the prosecution of having to prove its case against the accused, thus providing some safeguard against a false confession. One *oblast* court was criticized and its officials reprimanded for allowing "impermissible" methods of investigation which included a false confession from a defendant. On appeal, the RSFSR Supreme Court acquitted the defendant in the case.[51]

Procurator's Role

The procurator's role in a judicial proceeding, as the government's prosecuting arm, is a more ubiquitous one than is the case with his American counterpart, the prosecuting attorney. In addition to ordering an arrest and giving his approval for detention of the accused, the prosecutor can enter a given case on either side, he can appeal any civil or criminal case below the level of the national Supreme Court, and he must give his own opinion in a case on appeal before the appellate court can issue its decision. In a case reported in 1960, the Deputy Procurator-General of the USSR protested a sentence of the Supreme Court of the Armenian Republic because two defendants were tried and convicted on the basis of dubious testimony of witnesses, only circumstantial evidence, and in violation of the law requiring that an accused has a right to a defense lawyer. The national Supreme Court sustained the Procurator's protest, set aside the conviction and remanded the case for a retrial and called for a new investigation.[52]

The Procurator-General is, in Feifer's words, the commissar of the Soviet judicial system, who sanctions arrests, supervises the investigation, must be heard by every appellate court, may open a case at any time, may prosecute the case, executes the sentence, and supervises the place of detention.[53]

Defense Procedure

The rights of an accused to a defense in a Soviet trial include several steps. The accused must be informed of the charges brought against him and have a right to comment on them, to submit petitions in his behalf, to have a defense lawyer, to take part in the trial, to challenge the court

---

[51] *Izvestiya*, April 17, 1960, p. 2, cited in *Current Digest of the Soviet Press*, Vol. XII (May 18, 1960), p. 21. On Soviet Court procedures, see the discussion in Berman, *Justice in Russia* and Berman, "Introductory Comment," to *The Trial of the U 2.*

[52] Hazard and Shapiro, *op. cit.*, pp. 94–95.

[53] Feifer, *op. cit.*, pp. 130–32.

and appeal the decision. Differing from American practice, however, the accused has the right, before the trial begins, of examining all of the evidence gathered against him which has been compiled from the procurator's investigation. The accused, or his defense lawyer, may sift through such evidence and may make notes on any of the data, all in the interest of preparing an adequate defense. Defense lawyers, on occasion, take part in the preliminary investigation of some cases. In 1960, for example, defense lawyers took part in the investigations in 40 percent of the criminal cases in the Ukraine and 59 percent of such cases in Latvia.[54] Following the general theory of Soviet law, defense lawyers serve the functions of protecting the rights and legal interests of citizens, of contributing to the strengthening of socialist law, and of educating the Soviet people.

There is even criticism of defense lawyers not adequately defending their clients against illegal or ill-founded court punishments.[55] Such criticism is quite rare, however, in view of the shaky position of defense lawyers in the Soviet system. One newspaper ran a series of articles on the role which defense lawyers do play and should play in Soviet courts. The series revealed that one local prosecutor's office complained of defense lawyers who relied on all sorts of methods to protect known criminals. Three such lawyers in a ten-month period asked light sentences or partial and even complete acquittal for a number of their clients. The article concluded that, contrary to the wishes of the prosecutors, defense lawyers should in fact truly defend their clients, even to the extent of asking for their acquittal, in some cases.[56] Soviet citizens, too, often select the better lawyers to defend them, and the same author asks if the practice of siphoning off surplus earnings of successful and popular defense lawyers to give to the unsuccessful ones contributes to the growth of a higher quality of legal defense for the citizens.[57]

While defending their clients, however, defense lawyers are admonished not to forget the interests of the state. The areas in which a lawyer has the most freedom to develop a defense rests in nonpolitical cases. Where the state is involved, for example when a person is accused of an "antirevolutionary" or antistate crime, then the entire role of the defense lawyer is seriously circumscribed. Consequently, the defense lawyer must remember the "political significance" of the Soviet legal process. In the

---

[54] E. A. Shein, "Zashchitnik na predvaritelnom sledstvii v sovetskom ugolovnom protsesse," *Sovetskoe Gosudarstvo i Pravo*, No. 6 (June, 1962), p. 119.

[55] *Sovetskoe Gosudarstvo i Pravo*, No. 10 (October, 1964), p. 6.

[56] N. Chetunova, "Pravo na zashchitu," *Literaturnaya Gazeta*, September 20, 1966.

[57] *Ibid.*, September 22, 1966.

lawyer's main speech in defense of his client, a textbook for defense lawyers points out, there must be included appropriate political ideas and, finally, the legal interests of the client must be defended "from the point of view of the interests of the state."[58] In sum, no defense of a client, then, should in any way impugn communism, the state, or any of its instrumentalities or procedures. A defense lawyer operating under such a proscription obviously is handicapped in working up a thoroughgoing defense if, by challenging any statement of the prosecution, he indirectly challenges the state's case and, in effect challenges the logic, reason, and propriety of the state's prosecution. Clearly, a Soviet defense lawyer must proceed with great caution in any case having political overtones. In the famous Powers espionage trial of 1960, the defense lawyer for Powers began his defense by stating, first of all, that "the defense challenges neither facts of the charges preferred against Powers nor the assessment of the crime given by the State Prosecutor ... it is beyond doubt that the man in the dock is indeed guilty of the crime and that the crime itself has been committed as set forth in the indictment."[59] The defense lawyer immediately placed himself, his "client," and virtually the entire case of the defense in direct support of the prosecutor (who in this instance was the Procurator-General of the USSR) and the case for the prosecution.

Appeals and Sentences

In cases under appeal to a higher court the panel of three professional judges decides by majority vote. The appellate court is not restricted in its review of the facts presented, but actually is responsible for reviewing the whole case.[60] Appeals may be called for in any court case except those cases decided by the national Supreme Court. A court hearing a case on appeal may leave the original sentence unchanged, send the case back for a new trial, dismiss the case and annul the sentence, or make changes in the sentence (by lowering, but not increasing it) as prescribed by law.[61] Reasons given for setting aside or modifying sentences heard on appeal to the Criminal Division of the Supreme Court, USSR, in 1963 included code violations (punishment, for example, may not cause physical suffering

---

[58] A. M. Levin, P. A. Ognev, V. L. Rossel, *Zashchitnik v Sovetskom Sude* (Moscow: Gosurizdat, 1960), pp. 7, 171.

[59] *The Trial of the U 2*, p. 138.

[60] Collard, *op. cit.*, pp. 23–24.

[61] Romashkin, *op. cit.*, pp. 478–79.

or lowering of human dignity), incomplete preliminary investigation of cases, and improper definition of the criminal act originally committed.[62]

On occasion, people's courts have shown a leniency and softening toward the law. In some instances these courts are rebuked by higher authority for possessing liberal tendencies.[63] One Soviet judge, reporting on 70 cases he had heard regarding suits against railroads, noted that in 63 of the cases, judgment was for the plaintiff.[64] Following shortly after Stalin's death, a general amnesty released from prison all those serving sentences of up to five years, those convicted of economic or military crimes, pregnant women and women with small children, women over fifty, juveniles under eighteen, men over fifty-five, and those suffering from incurable diseases. For those serving sentences over five years, their sentences were cut in half—except for certain serious crimes.[65] The 1958 Fundamentals of Criminal Law, as approved by the government, continued this liberalizing tendency by laying greater emphasis on imposing lighter sentences; conditional releases and pardons were made easier too. The following table is the result of a study made of errors in criminal court cases.

ANALYSIS OF ERRORS FOUND IN 842 CRIMINAL COURT CASES[66]

Types of Errors by Categories	Number of Errors in Category	Percent of Total Cases in Category
A. One-sided or incomplete preliminary or court investigation		
1. No interrogation of the person whose testimony had importance to the case..........................	98	32.5
2. No investigation of the circumstances, required by court order, for additional investigation or a new court examination...................................	74	24.0
3. Insufficiently complete data on the personality of the accused..	62	20.5
4. No demand for documents having an essential bearing on the case....................................	33	10.8
5. No finding from an examination when, according to law, it was obligatory or necessary.....................	31	10.2
6. No demand for material evidence which had an essential bearing on the case.............................	6	2.0
	304	100.0

---

[62] *Biulleten Verkhovnogo Suda SSSR*, November 5, 1964, translated in *Soviet Law and Government*, Spring, 1965, pp. 6–7.

[63] Berman, *Justice in Russia, op. cit.*, p. 193.

[64] *Ibid.*, p. 207.

[65] Collard, *op. cit.*, pp. 7–8.

[66] V. E. Chugunov and G. F. Gorskiy, "Primenenie kiberneticheskikh ustroystv dlya analiza oshibok v sudebnoy i sledstvennoy praktike," *Sovetskoe Gosudarstvo i Pravo*, No. 11 (November, 1966), pp. 41–43.

ANALYSIS OF ERRORS FOUND IN 842 CRIMINAL COURT CASES
(Continued)

Types of Errors by Categories	Number of Errors in Category	Percent of Total Cases in Category
B. Discrepancy in court inference, summary of the sentence, or facts of the case		
1. Contradiction in the inference of the court influencing the degree of punishment......................	259	26.9
2. Court failed to account for important circumstances in the case................................	231	25.0
3. Incorrect court conclusions *in re* the application of criminal law..................................	157	17.0
4. Contradiction in conclusions of the court influencing decision in the case.............................	111	13.0
5. Conclusions of the court unconfirmed by the evidence examined in the court session....................	83	9.0
6. Contradiction in conclusions of the court influencing the question of innocence of accused.................	25	2.7
7. Contradiction in conclusions of the court influencing the question of guilt or innocence...................	17	1.8
	883*	95.4
C. Important violations of the law on criminal processes		
1. No discontinuance of case in the absence of a criminal act..	16	36.9
2. No reading of the changes in the conditions of the case when the act ceased to be a public danger...........	5	11.5
3. No discontinuance of the case in the absence of the occurrence of a crime..........................	4	9.0
4. Unfounded discontinuance of the case after the guilty was placed on bail.............................	4	9.0
5. Absence of court protocol in the case..............	4	9.0
6. No discontinuance of case because date of prescription expired..	2	4.5
7. Unfounded discontinuance of case with its transferral to a comrades' court............................	2	4.5
8. Unfounded discontinuance of case with its transferral to commission for affairs of minorities.............	2	4.5
9. Sentence carried out illegally by court..............	2	4.5
10. No discontinuance of case because accused was a minor.	1	2.2
11. No reading of the changes in the conditions of the case when the person ceased to be a public danger........	1	2.2
12. Case was examined in the absence of a defense lawyer when his participation was required...............	1	2.2
	44	100.0

Analysis of Errors Found in 842 Criminal Court Cases
(Continued)

Types of Errors by Categories	Number of Errors in Category	Percent of Total Cases in Category
D. Incorrect application of criminal law		
1. Application of an inapplicable law.................	120	53.3
2. Nonapplication of an applicable law...............	66	30.0
3. Interpretation of a law contrary to its meaning.......	38	16.7
	224	100.0
E. Incorrect punishment by the court		
1. Discrepancy in punishment set by the court due to the weight of the crime		
a. Sentence was too severe........................	262	37.1
b. Sentence was too light........................	106	15.1
2. Discrepancy in punishment set by the court due to the personality of the convicted		
a. Sentence was too severe........................	295	41.8
b. Sentence was too light........................	42	6.0
	705	100.0

* Forty-one cases unaccounted for in table, but cited in total for this category of cases.

The final disposition of the cases heard on appeal to a higher court (740 out of the 842 cases) included 57.2 percent in which the higher court changed the sentence, 30 percent returned for additional investigation or a new trial, 7.7 percent which were left unchanged, and 5.1 percent in which the sentences were set aside. Several conclusions can be drawn from the table of cases. The courts were found to be lacking in some procedures: inadequate pretrial investigation, incorrect court inferences from the evidence presented, wrongly continuing or discontinuing a case, incorrect application of the law, illegal procedures, and disproportionate punishment meted out to the convicted persons. The table also reveals, overwhelmingly, that most of the "errors" of the courts were errors in failing to provide adequately for the rights of the accused. In the last category of cases, for example, more than twice the total number of errors were found to be in court punishment which was too severe rather than too light. Thus, the discovery of errors favored the defendants in most of the cases. The table does show instances in which court "leniency" (or illegalities) that favored the defendant was discovered by reviewing authorities, but again, these formed only a minority of the total errors cited. Although we lack comparable data on other court errors, nevertheless, if this table at all reflects the normal instance of court error in the USSR, than it testifies to the growing sense of Soviet legality in the protection of the rights of citizens who are brought to trial.

NONCRIMINAL LAW

There are other sides of Soviet law, apart from the criminal; these can be designated as labor, administrative, and civil law. Under these categories come such legal relations as sales contracts (for example, between state organizations), mortages, housing leases and sales, copyrights, and patents.[67] A case involving a property dispute may occur, for example, when two owners of a given house disagree on the use of the land on which the house is located, or when one owner, without the consent of the co-owner, sells a house. Cases even occur dealing with civil suits arising from distribution of an inheritance,[68] and in one case, the editors of a local newspaper were summoned to a people's court, accused of harming an individual's honor and dignity.[69]

A considerable part of Soviet law has to do with labor relations. The main instruments of labor law are the labor contract and the collective agreement; the latter covers general working conditions and is signed between a trade union (in the name of the workers of a specific plant) and the management.[70] In the settlement of labor disputes, the first level of jurisdiction is that of the labor dispute board which is made up of an equal number of representatives from trade unions and management meeting at working sites, such as factories. In the event of an unsatisfactory settlement by a labor dispute board, the case may be referred to a people's court.[71] In these court cases the rights of workers more often than not are jealously guarded.[72]

The Chairman of the USSR Supreme Court's Civil Division has reported that 85 percent of all court cases are civil, with 86 percent of the suits brought in the courts settled in favor of the plaintiff. Further breakdowns (although incomplete) of these civil cases include the following data:[73]

---

[67] Romashkin, op. cit., p. 226.

[68] M. Tsunts, I. Furman, and S. Yezerskaya, Personal Property in the Soviet Union (Moscow: Foreign Languages Publishing House, 1960), pp. 30, 35, 59–60. For other examples of cases in civil, administrative, and criminal law see Hazard and Shapiro, op. cit.

[69] Izvestiya, April 28, 1964.

[70] See Chapter X for a discussion of the collective agreement.

[71] E. I. Filippov, Sudebnaya Zashchita Trudovykh Prav Grazhdan SSSR (Moscow: Gosurizdat, 1958), pp. 7–8.

[72] Berman, Justice in Russia, p. 265.

[73] Nedelya, No. 2 (January 3–9, 1965), p. 5.

	Percent of Civil Cases
Disputes between citizens.............................	71.0
Disputes between citizens and organizations.............	25.0
Disputes by category:	
Labor disputes.....................................	5.6
Housing disputes...................................	8.0
Property losses....................................	9.0
Divorce...	13.7
Alimony for children...............................	20.0

Cases involving administrative law can be handled either by the regular courts or by the state arbitration system (*Gosarbitrazh*). A decree in 1959 transferred to the jurisdiction of state arbitration bodies all disputes between state, cooperative (except collective farms), and mass organizations, enterprises, and establishments formerly supervised by the courts.[74] The range of disputes falling under the arbitration system includes contract and performance controversies in industry, agriculture, transport of all types, and communication, and even matters involving state insurance.[75]

THE RULE OF LAW IN THE USSR

There is a basic dilemma facing not only law but legal relations, courts lawyers, and the regime itself in the Soviet Union. On the one hand the communist leadership sees the necessity for having a rather fully developed legal system and yet, in the final analysis, these communists simply do not possess a fundamental faith and belief in established law. The dilemma points up one obvious characteristic of a communist dictatorship; in reality it trusts no one but itself and certainly no instrumentality but that of its own peculiar party apparatus. As a result, no movement toward reasonableness in the law and toward greater legal safeguards for the citizenry proceeds very far before it is checked by a disbelieving leader. Certain aspects of Soviet society, such as politics and policymaking, are beyond the sphere of ordinary law. The regime has also relied on force, violence, faith in the system, and a hoped-for sense of moral unity.[76] The

---

[74] Romashkin, *op. cit.*, p. 127.

[75] I. T. Gavrilenko and I. G. Pobirchenko, "Strukturu Gosudarstvennogo arbitrazha na uroven zadach novoy khozyaystvennoy reformy," *Sovetskoe Gosudarstvo i Pravo*, No. 6 (June, 1966), p. 45. In an effort to raise the concept of legality in administrative law, the number of agencies having the right to set administrative fines was reduced in 1962, while the right of ministries, bureaus, and local soviets to set administrative rules punishable by fine was eliminated. *Sovetskoe Gosudarstvo i Pravo*, No. 3 (March, 1963), pp. 59, 61.

[76] Berman, *Justice in Russia*, *op. cit.*, p. 193. Soviet law, differing from the Anglo-American system, differs too in that court decisions, as precedents, do not constitute a significant source of law. Instead, the state organs are the source of law. M. A. Arzhanov, *Gosudarstvo i Pravo v ikh Sootnoshenii* (Moscow: Akademia Nauk, SSSR, 1960), p. 48.

dilemma continues to frustrate the leaders in their efforts to construct a firm, solid, humane, and just system of law. It may well be, on the other hand, that the regime appreciates the problem but is simply unwilling to share any measurable degree of its power with something resembling a "reign of law."

Trends in Soviet law, particularly after Stalin, have moved along two general paths. The first has been to introduce more legality into judicial proceedings. This is illustrated by a Soviet author who was writing at the tail-end of the post-Stalin reform period, and arguing (perhaps it was pleading) that the stability of criminal law would be infringed if one erroneously contrasted a juridical with a political interpretation of the law.[77] A growing sense of heightened legality in the USSR has seen the abandonment of the discredited law of analogy, a declaration that newly established crimes cannot be made retroactive, a rise in the age of criminal responsibility, dropping of the applicability of complicity in crimes of negligence, reduction in the length of maximum prison sentences (from 25 to 15 years), easing of the rules for conditional release and pardons, and providing the accused with a more viable defense. Moreover, as Berman contends, the procurator in the average case normally performs his "protest" function (protesting violations of lawful procedures) rather honestly and impartially.[78] This trend was capped by the new Fundamentals of Soviet Criminal Law enacted at the end of 1958. When the antiparasite laws were being drawn up, calling for the extralegal comrade courts and the *druzhiny*, successful moves by the legal profession watered down somewhat the kangaroo court features of the original acts and helped establish greater procedural regularity.[79] In 1965 the Antiparasite Law of the RSFSR was amended to exclude some types of violations, remove some ambiguities in the original version, and soften punishments. This amendment, thus, is toward greater legality.[80] The 1960 espionage trial of the American pilot Gary Powers seemed calculated, in its elaborately drawn processes, to convince the West and the remainder of the world that, despite Stalinist deprivations, the Soviet legal system could conduct a trial openly and fairly and with a feeling for leniency. Powers could have

---

[77] A. S. Shlyapochnikov, "O stabilnosti sovetskogo ugolovnogo zakona," *Sovetskoe Gosudarstvo i Pravo*, No. 12 (December, 1957), p. 21.

[78] Berman, *Justice in Russia*, p. 170. For the most complete study in English of the procurator-general's supervisory role see Glenn G. Morgan, *Soviet Administrative Legality: The Role of the Attorney General's Office* (Stanford, Calif.: Stanford University Press, 1962).

[79] Morgan, "People's Justice," *op. cit.*, pp. 50–51.

[80] See the discussion of R. Berman in *Soviet Studies*, Vol. XVII (January, 1966), pp. 387–88.

received the death penalty for his crime, fully in accordance with Soviet law. Instead he was given a mild seven-year sentence, part of which later was commuted.

Other trends include militiamen being dismissed for "unworthy conduct" (beating a youth), arbitrariness, and lawlessness, and of being arrested and convicted (with four years in a corrective labor colony) for detaining a citizen illegally and beating him.[81] There have also been criticisms of judges for abridging legal procedures and for not acting independently of other officials, as well as for sloppy conduct of court cases. One listing of court errors included the following:

> Judges failing to explain to the parties their right to turn to comrade courts.
> Judicial broadening of interpretation as to when a judge may refuse to accept petitions.
> Courts not distinguishing between questions of competence and of jurisdiction.
> Judges who hold that preparation for trial is not an obligatory stage in the proceedings.
> Judges issuing commissions "off the bench."
> Inadequate minutes being taken of court sessions (with sentences and words being inserted that were never offered, things being deleted, etc.).
> Signatures of plaintiff, respondent, or parties in the court being at court discretion, instead of by law.
> Courts failing to verify the legality of out-of-court settlements—particularly labor disputes, which are susceptible to being inadequately supervised where management illegally dismisses workers.
> Failure of judges to oversee prompt execution of court decisions.[82]

The second trend in post-Stalin developments in Soviet law has been in the opposite direction, having the effect of cancelling out some of the advances listed above, or at least of modifying them. The expansion of the death penalty to include, for example, such crimes as gold hoarding and large-scale embezzlement point up this movement. The other development in this direction was taken in 1959 when the comrade courts and the *druzhiny* was established. In effect, the latter change removed a number of petty crimes from normal court jurisdiction and permitted nongovernmental, almost mob or vigilante forms of arrest and prosecution. The reversal of direction, from early post-Stalin liberalization to later reaction, came in part as an aftermath of 1956 following the downgrading of Stalin and the anticommunist revolution in Hungary. The regime has decided also to move against people committing economic crimes in attempts to hold up as horrible examples those who would carry out such anticommunist actions as embezzlement of state funds. In a partial

---

[81] *Sovetskaya Rossiya*, March 13, 1966; *Izvestiya*, December 28, 1965; *Pravda*, January 7, 1966.

[82] *Sovetskaya Iustitsiya*, No. 2, 1965, pp. 3–6.

downgrading of the court system, chiefs of militia recently were given the right to impose fines independently for petty hooliganism, without first appealing to a court.[83]

The former corrective-labor camps now designated as labor "colonies" have not been eliminated nor have they even been measurably reduced in size, according to one student of the problem.[84] Even in the matter of more rights for an accused to an adequate defense, these rights are still marginal if existent at all when a case involves a political crime. The Powers case is an example of an extremely passive and vapid defense of the accused. One is moved to suggest that the light sentence of Powers was calculated to win friends for the USSR by drawing attention to a judicial system which Russians claim to be fair, equitable, and lenient. Nevertheless, as Grzybowski notes, the Powers trial points up the fact that the 1958 Fundamentals of Criminal Law provide no machinery by which the otherwise well-equipped courts can individualize criminal cases.[85]

The Soviet Union has not yet embraced a consistent legal philosophy in which individuals are given binding protections for their civil and political rights. What is quite consistent and unchanging in the Soviet legal system, however, is its vacillation and weakness in the face of the prevailing political climate and its complete and repeated subordination to the momentary whims and desires of the Communist Party leadership. This is a universal characteristic of law under communism whether it be of the Russian, Hungarian, Yugoslavian or Chinese variety.

In the Soviet Union, law is the servant of the party; the law's main purpose is to educate and propagandize for communism and for the announced goals of the political elite. Stalin used the law to campaign against the West, to help him defeat his political opponents and to compel obedience to his schemes and policies. Consequently, Soviet law has reflected totalitarian undertones, has been mistrusted by many citizens, and has had only brief, sporadic periods of defending citizen rights. As a result, its image is tarnished in the minds of many people in the USSR.

The question now facing the Soviet political system is which way will Soviet law go, toward greater regularity and "legality," toward more

---

[83] By *Ukaz* of the Presidium of the Supreme Soviet, July, 1966. *Pravda,* July 27, 1966.

[84] See Barton, *op. cit.*

[85] Kazimierz Grzybowski, "The Powers Trial and the 1958 Reform of Soviet Criminal Law," *The American Journal of Comparative Law,* Vol. 9 (Summer, 1960), p. 437. Soviet citizens, Lipson argues, probably cannot believe that the legal system imposed from above is "their" system, nor can they really be assured that there will not be future violations of legality such as have occurred in the past. Leon Lipson, "Socialist Legality: The Mountain Has Labored," *Problems of Communism,* Vol. VIII (March–April, 1959), p. 19.

protection of citizen rights—even in the face of arbitrary governmental actions? Is there to be a "rule of law" in the Soviet Union, or will there be a retrogression into former Stalinist patterns of gross misuse of law and of legal institutions? The question really may be which way *can* Soviet law go? Can a communist political system allow the growth of anything like a legal apparatus and legal customs which do not depend on the Communist Party? In order for a "democratic" law to develop, must there be a commensurate, step-by-step development of related democratic institutions and procedures? What, in the final analysis, will Soviet citizens demand of the Soviet legal system? Will the citizens demand that the regime's legal system become *their* legal system?

CHAPTER XIII

Regional and Local Government

OVER THE course of Soviet history, units of government below that of the national level have been stunted in their growth, precluded from policy making, and prevented from developing any measure of autonomy which might serve as a counter against the power of the center. These limitations on regional and local government have contributed to nationalizing and centralizing all important functions of Soviet government in the hands of the leaders in Moscow. In the second half of the twentieth century these leaders now face the problem of mixed advantages and disadvantages arising from earlier policies of extreme centralization.

REGIONAL GOVERNMENT

Regional government in the Soviet Union includes the 15 union republics and the 20 autonomous republics. All other units from the territory (*kray*) and province (*oblast*) on down can be classified, as they are by the Russians, local governments. The most important of all these units is that which constitutes a rather important part of the Soviet system of government—the union republic. The present status of this echelon of government is a result to no small degree of Soviet history.

The collapse of the tsarist regime in 1917 left certain borderland groups in Russia relatively free to exercise latent nationalistic feelings, even to seek independence. The October Revolution of 1917 and the disrupting Civil War which followed meant that central rule of the old empire, if reestablished, could be done so only slowly and with some difficulty. During this period a sense of nationalism grew among several ethnic groups such as the Kazakh-Kirghiz, Uzbek, and Azerbaijani. In the 1917–20 period some of them assumed the trappings of semi-independent republics. The Ukraine took part in negotiations at Brest-Litovsk, Belorussia negotiated with Germany and Poland, and the Transcaucasus republics signed treaties with Turkey.

These borderland areas of the old empire in their economic, military, communications, and financial affairs as well as in their foreign relations came under the control of the new Soviet regime by the end of 1922. The Communists, following their military occupation of these areas, attempted to legalize their dominance over them simply by proclaiming that laws published by the new Russian Soviet Federative Socialist Republic (RSFSR) in Moscow were applicable throughout the territory of the old empire. Toward strengthening this rather loose and dubious relationship, the RSFSR signed bilateral treaties with each of the republics in question. And yet, in its efforts to win over the reluctant support of these peoples, most of whom were not enthusiastic over the possible return of Russian domination, the Soviet regime designated them as "independent" republics within the overall Soviet system. This led to a distinction in Soviet law (which remains to this day) between inland areas populated largely by non-Russians, and those territories on the fringes of the country which border directly on foreign nations. The inland areas were given the status of autonomous regions and republics, while the outlying ones were made into union republics—the latter being treated constitutionally, though not practically, as independent states having even a right to secede from the Soviet Union.[1]

In 1923 the Union of Soviet Socialist Republics (USSR) was organized; it was composed of the Russian (RSFSR), Ukrainian, Belorussian, and Transcaucasian Republics. To this union were added additional republics: the Turkmen and the Uzbek in 1925, Tadzhik in 1929, Kazakh and Kirghiz in 1936. Also, in 1936, the Transcaucasian Federated Republic was broken up into three separate republics: Azerbaijan, Armenian, and Georgian. Two other republics were created in World War II: Moldavia and Karelo-Finnish. The three Baltic states of Estoniya, Latvia, and Lithuania were incorporated into the USSR as union republics. When the Karelo-Finnish Union Republic was downgraded to the status of an autonomous republic in 1956, there remained 15 union republics.[2]

No doubt Soviet federalism since 1918, as witnessed by the increase in union republics, has made it easier and less painful to incorporate under one central government diverse nationalities which have harbored independent and secessionist tendencies. There were other reasons, however, for the peculiar development which Soviet federalism took. Formal

---

[1] For an extended treatment of this subject, see Richard Pipes, *The Formation of the Soviet Union: Communism and Nationalism, 1917–1923* (Cambridge, Mass.: Harvard University Press, 1954), pp. 190–91, 245–54.

[2] Slavic republics: Russian, Ukrainian, Belorussian; other European republics: Estoniya, Latvia, Lithuania, Moldavia; Caucasus republics: Armenia, Azerbaijan, Georgia; Central Asian republics: Kazakh, Kirghiz, Tadzhik, Turkmen, Uzbek.

establishment of union republics, having at least a semblance of legal sovereignty, were used by the regime as instruments for territorial expansion into Europe and Asia. The Karelo-Finnish Union Republic, before

REGIONAL AND LOCAL GOVERNMENT

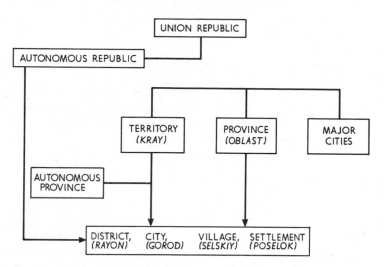

its demise, was to be the excuse for incorporating Finland into the USSR. The Kazakh and Kirghiz Republics in Central Asia, created at the time when the Chinese Communist Party under Mao Tse-tung won independence from Moscow, were to be jumping off places for Soviet expansion into Asia.[3] United Nations membership for the Ukrainian and Belorussian Republics, thereby giving to the Soviet Union three "memberships" in that organization, points up a rather successful diplomatic employment of Soviet federalism.

Union Republics: Structure and Operation

The special features of a union republic marking it as an important and "independent" level of government, at least in Soviet legal theory, is that it borders on a foreign state, has a compact majority of the nationality whose name it bears, and has a population of at least one million so that, in Soviet rationale, its separate existence will be guaranteed "in case it secedes from the USSR."[4]

---

[3] Vernon V. Aspaturian, *The Union Republics in Soviet Diplomacy: A Study of Soviet Federalism in the Service of Soviet Foreign Policy* (Geneva: Librairie E. Droz, 1960), pp. 82–84.

[4] *Osnovy Sovetskogo Gosudarstva i Prava* (Moscow: Gosurizdat, 1947), pp. 65–66. As of 1960 in two republics (Kazakh and Kirghiz), however, these respective native peoples did not constitute a majority within their own republics.

The Soviet Constitution gives to the supreme soviet of a union republic authority to adopt and amend its own constitution, to approve a national plan as well as a budget, and to have a voice in the republic's judicial procedures, international relations, and military "formations." Apart from these, the union republics have other rights which include those of secession from the USSR (none have tried, probably because it would be construed as traitorous action), sanctity of its borders, guarantee of republican citizenship, and special representation in the Council of Nationalities of the Supreme Soviet. The union republics can suspend decisions (*postanovleniya*) and orders (*rasporyazheniya*) of autonomous republics and amend those of subordinate local governments. In addition, several union republics have a minor part to play in Soviet foreign policy. The Ukrainian and Belorussian Republics legally are separate members of the United Nations, although, of course, they function simply as adjuncts of Soviet foreign policy. In recent years the chairmen of union republic legislatures have served as Soviet delegates abroad and as hosts for chiefs of state visiting their republics. Sh. Rashidov, formerly head of the Uzbek legislature in Central Asia, has been used from time to time to entertain representatives of Asian-African nations.[5] There are certain cultural rights of the union republics, such as teaching the native language (in addition to, not instead of Russian), cultivating native dances, plays and songs.

Despite the imposing list of rights and powers, the position of the union republic vis-à-vis the national government throughout Soviet history has been less than impressive. The republics were created to win the sympathy of the several ethnic groups for the Communist regime; they have been retained for the same purpose as well as for the administrative and diplomatic convenience of the Communist Party leadership. A measurable degree of genuine self-government for the republics, at least until the end of the Stalin reign, however, has been conspicuous by its almost complete absence.

The legislature of a union republic is its one-house supreme soviet which, in turn, has a smaller guiding presidium that meets in the intervals between sessions of the soviet. A presidium of a union republic's supreme soviet is formed of a chairman, usually two deputy chairmen (three in Uzbek and twelve in RSFSR), a secretary and from five to fifteen members.[6] Agendas for presidium meetings include such matters as road construction and repair, development of the educational system, improvement of

---

[5] Aspaturian, *op. cit.*, pp. 162–63.

[6] T. B. Anisimova, *Vysshie Organy Gosudarstvennoy Vlasti SSSR, Souznykh i Avtonomnykh Respublik* (Moscow: 1955), p. 40.

medical services, preservation of natural resources, internal border changes, state pensions and improving the work of local government. Each supreme soviet creates its own standing and special commissions, the standing ones being credentials, budget, legislative proposals, and foreign affairs. Standing commissions serve as auxiliary organs to the supreme soviet with a legal, if not actual right to look into the activities of all organs of administration within the republic which are subordinate to the supreme soviet. Similar to the increased functions of national legislative commissions, the report of the Budget Commission of the Kazakh Supreme Soviet pointed out unused coal reserves and revealed planning weaknesses on the republic level.[7] And yet, the legislatures are very limited in relation to their councils of ministers, the latter recently being criticized for ignoring "requests" from elected deputies.[8]

The soviet is elected to a four-year term and is made up of several hundred deputies; the pattern of representation varies from republic to republic. Each deputy in the RSFSR Supreme Soviet represents 150,000 electors, but in the Uzbek and Georgian Supreme Soviets the ratio is one deputy for each 15,000 electors. Supreme soviet elections follow rather closely the national model: they are secret, there is one candidate per vacancy, candidates are endorsed by party and government, and a very high percentage of voters turn out to vote for the officially sponsored candidates. The following table gives a breakdown of the various supreme soviets following the 1967 elections:[9]

COMPOSITION OF UNION REPUBLIC SUPREME SOVIETS
Following the 1963 and 1967 Elections (in Percent)

Union Republic	Total Deputies	Women Deputies	Worker and Collective Farm Deputies	Party Member Deputies	Newly Elected Deputies (1967)
RSFSR					
1963......884		33%	47%	67%	
1967......884		34	48	67	75%
Ukraine					
1963......469		34	51	68	
1967......469		34	52	68	52
Belorussia					
1963......421		36	46	69	
1967......421		36	47	69	80

---

[7] M. A. Binder and M. A. Sharif, "Verkhovnyy Sovet souznoy respubliki i rukovodstvo narodnym khozyaystvom," *Sovetskoe Gosudarstvo i Pravo* No. 11 (November, 1965), p. 11.

[8] *Ibid.*, p. 16.

[9] Data compiled from *Izvestiya*, March 16, 1967; March 23, 1967.

Composition of Union Republic Supreme Soviets
Following the 1963 and 1967 Elections (in Percent)
(Continued)

Union Republic	Total Deputies	Women Deputies	Worker and Collective Farm Deputies	Party Member Deputies	Newly Elected Deputies (1967)
Uzbek					
1963......458		30	47	72	
1967......458		31	46	72	59
Kazakh					
1963......473		33	49	66	
1967......473		34	49	66	79
Moldavian					
1963......312		38	61	64	
1967......315		38	56	64	67
Latvian					
1963......310		33	49	63	
1967......310		32	47	64	69
Tadzhik					
1963......300		33	48	69	
1967......315		33	48	70	56
Turkmen					
1963......282		35	50	67	
1967......285		35	50	67	62
Georgian					
1963......400		31	47	71	
1967......399		32	47	71	70
Azerbaijan					
1963......345		32	47	78	
1967......380		32	48	78	69
Lithuanian					
1963......290		33	54	65	
1967......290		32	51	67	69
Kirgiz					
1963......339		35	52	67	
1967......339		35	52	67	65
Armenian					
1963......300		32	44	68	
1967......310		33	45	67	69
Estonian					
1963......178		34	47	65	
1967......178		35	48	67	69

Several conclusions can be drawn from the above figures. In all but 5 of the 15 republics, workers and collective farmers together constitute less than half of the elected deputies, with most of the republics averaging 46–48 percent. Women deputies range from a low of 31 percent in the Uzbek Republic to a high of 38 percent in the Moldavian Republic, but with most of the republics averaging 32–35 percent. The percentage of party members averages in the upper 60 percentile. As with elections to the national legislature, it appears that the republican election "quotas" are predetermined, so that each republic includes among its elected deputies certain desired percentages of women, workers and collective farmers, and Communist Party members; even newly elected deputies.

The agendas for sessions of supreme soviets—the latter infrequently held—cover such varied topics as educational reform, road construction and repair, budgets for local governments, and confirmation of earlier decrees of their presidiums. As with the national Supreme Soviet, union republic soviets serve as simple ratifying instruments for the plans and policies of the national party and governmental leadership.

Routine governmental activity for a union republic is carried out through a council of ministers patterned after the format of the national council. Councils of ministers of union as well as autonomous republics are guided by their inner presidiums which serve a directing function. The former Bureau of the Estonian Council frequently invited enterprise leaders to its sessions to present their needs. Conflicts often arise at these sessions, usually over arguments between the enterprise leaders and representatives of the republic's *gosplan* regarding material and financial resources.[10] A typical republic council includes ministries for finance, trade, health, defense of public order, agriculture, state farms, construction, higher education, local industry and water resources. Each republic has a committee for state security (KGB), a central statistical directorate, and chief directorates for highways and for vocational and technical education, and a state planning committee (*gosplan*). Each republic also has additional administrative organs for reasons peculiar to that republic—such as the Ministry of Oil Industry in the oil-rich Azerbaijan Republic.

The ministries of justice at the union republic level have been abolished and the administration of the courts (formerly the responsibility of these ministries) has been transferred to the respective supreme court within the republic. Judicial commissions have been formed in the republics to assume the planning functions which previously had been the responsibility of the abolished ministry. In 1960 there was established in each republic a single directorate to sell tractors, agricultural machinery, and spare parts. Finally, in 1962 union republics began abolishing their ministries of internal affairs (MVD) and, in their place, creating ministries for defense of public order. This move, no doubt, was one to eliminate remnants of the secret police of Stalin's day, which persisted—at least in name—in the ministries of internal affairs.

Union republic governments are responsible for the planning and operating of agriculture and industry within their boundaries and also are

---

[10] *Izvestiya*, May 13, 1962.

held accountable for general supervision over all local government in their republics.   In recent years, union republic governments have been holding planning and informational conferences for officials from their subordinate local governments.

Despite the authority and rather broad functions of union republic governments, they are restricted on all sides (legislative, budgetary, planning, political) by the close confines of the national administration as well as by established policies and detailed instructions sent down through the ranks of the Communist Party.   The federal system in the USSR, in contrast to the American tradition, is much more unitary and centralized than federative and cooperative.   Of course, it is not meant to be a system which could draw to itself clearcut powers which might be used to defy the national government—or the party apparatus.   There can be no "rights" of regional governments which in any way oppose the interests, desires, and policies of the center.   And yet, by virtue of their wide sweep of formal, legal responsibilities which cover most phases of life within their borders, union republic governments possess a measurable and growing degree of administrative authority.

The recognition of practical necessity caused the national government to lean more heavily for assistance in ruling such a vast country as the USSR on the most accessible, logical, and oldest level of regional government available—that of the union republics.   Since 1954 Soviet leaders have been cautiously experimenting by granting to this level of administration somewhat greater rights and powers in the overall governmental scheme.   Since the death of Stalin, authoritative voices in the Soviet Union have called for greater power to be given to the union republics in order to make regional governmental operations more rational, meaningful, and more capable of fulfilling their assigned responsibilities.   In 1954 union republics were granted wider judicial powers; these were further expanded in 1956 and 1957.   In 1955 and 1956 their financial authority was extended and additional responsibility for administering enterprises was assigned to them; thousands of enterprises were subsequently transferred from national to republic subordination.

By a law of February, 1957, union republics were given additional legislative controls over criminal and civil codes, over the structure of courts and also greater jurisdiction in the field of general legal procedure. Beginning in 1957 the supreme soviets in the republics were granted the right to take part in setting up certain governmental and judicial bodies such as *oblast* and *kray* governments, and in issuing yearly laws on state economic plans of the republic.   In another move apparently intended to strengthen the role of republican legislatures (supreme soviets), these bodies were assigned certain functions previously handled by their respective councils of ministers, such as those concerning pensions and medical supplies.[11] The Central Committee and the Council of Ministers, USSR decreed additional budgetary and planning powers to union republics in 1965, to include limited redistribution of capital investments and to more closely supervise plans and enterprises within their territory.[12]

There are, surprisingly, occasional reports of union republic agencies objecting to actions of central governmental organs. To guard against problems of central versus regional disparity such as this, however, the chairmen of union republic councils of ministers now sit, *ex officio*, on the national Council. All of these developments which have aimed at enhancing the position of the union republics may be interpreted as potential accretions in power at this level. They have reflected so far, however, more a tendency toward administrative convenience, in the form of limited decentralization, rather than any significant shift in political authority from central to regional government. Under the Soviet version of communism, regional government cannot yet be described as vital or even significant government, though such might be the case in the future.

Autonomous Republics

Sixteen of the twenty autonomous republics (ASSR's) are in the RSFSR' two are in the Georgian Republic and one each is in the Uzbek and the Azerbaijan Republics. In the course of Soviet history several autonomous republics have been upgraded to union republics (Moldavian, Kazakh, Kirghiz, and Tadzhik), and one, the Turkestan, was reformed into two union republics (Turkmen and Uzbek)'

Autonomous republics are subordinate directly to their parent union republic in the establishment and interpretation of their constitutions, in economic planning, and budgetary management. Autonomous republics are to administer regional government within their areas, including supervision of local government, and to provide distinct groups of non-Russian Soviet citizens (such as Bashkirs, Udmurts, Tatars, Buryats) with at least a modicum of local autonomy. In Soviet words, the autonomous republic is one of several "state-legal" forms which embody the "sovereignty of

---

[11] V. Kotok, "Osnovnye tendentsii razvitiya sovetskoy predstavitelnoy sistemy v period razvernutogo stroitelstva kommunizma," *Sovetskoe Gosudarstvo i Pravo*, No. 7 (July, 1961), pp. 17, 20. By the 1960's the standing commissions of the supreme soviets were beginning to examine the work of republican ministries and departments. *Sovetskoe Gosudarstvo i Pravo*, No. 12 (December, 1966), p. 31.

[12] *Pravda*, October 2, 1965.

the nation."[13]   Nevertheless, the table of deputies below reveals the sizable membership of ethnic Russians in these three "native" assemblies.[14]

DEPUTIES ELECTED TO SUPREME SOVIETS
OF THREE AUTONOMOUS REPUBLICS, 1959

Autonomous Republic	Native (Ethnic) Deputies	Russian Deputies
Mordov.	52 (42.2%)	68 (53.1%)
Tatar.	108 (55.7%)	70 (36.1%)
Yakut.	102 (61.8%)	47 (28.5%)

These republics do have a measure of authority over primary and intermediate education, health, social security, housing, and municipal economy. In addition they have certain responsibilities for other selected activities, such as road maintenance, transportation, local communications, and local industry.[15]

Similar to the national and union republic models, autonomous republics have constitutions, elective supreme soviets (four-year terms) with their own presidiums, and a governing council of ministers. These councils include a chairman, deputy chairmen, and ministers for such functions as health, culture, education, agriculture, trade and finance. There are, too, planning commissions, state security committees, and chief directorates for such activities as construction and architecture, auto transport and highways, building materials, and fuel industry. Deputies to the supreme soviets of the republics vary in their representational proportions: one deputy, for example, represents 4,000 people in the Komi ASSR, whereas one deputy represents 20,000 people in the Tatar ASSR.

As the union republics are strictly limited in their powers and authority, the lesser autonomous republics are even more hindered in their managerial actions. They are regional governments, but like their superior union republics, they serve much more the function of area administrative offices of the national government, than as autonomous governing units.

LOCAL GOVERNMENT

In old Russia a semblance of local government arose in the eleventh, twelfth and thirteenth centuries in which a popular assembly (*veche*) of

---

[13] D. L. Zlatopolskiy, *Gosudarstvennoe Ustroystvo SSSR* (Moscow: Gosurizdat, 1960), pp. 216–17.

[14] A. I. Lepeshkin, *et al.*, *Kurs Sovetskogo Gosudarstvennogo Prava* (Moscow, 1962), Vol. 2, p. 505.

[15] The Constitution of the Bashkir ASSR, for example, lists a wide scope of responsibilities including, among others, health, economic, agricultural, trade, and cultural affairs. See *Konstitutsiya SSSR, Konstitutsii Souznykh i Avtonomnykh Sovetskikh Sotsialisticheskikh Respublik* (Moscow: Gosurizdat, 1960), p. 69.

adult males in a town discussed current affairs, arrived at some decisions and chose its own rulers (providing they were of the Rurik dynasty). The *Veche* House in ancient Novgorod was a permanent assembly with rather complete responsibility over matters of local government.

Under serfdom, local autonomy, such as had developed, was pruned back and replaced by centrally appointed regional governors who exercised rather extensive power over local affairs. Russia then was divided into 10 regional governing provinces (*gubernii*) with a governor, or governor-general, at the head of each one. The *gubernii* were further divided into districts (*uyezdy*) and smaller provinces (*provintsii*). Later, Catherine II partitioned the empire into 50 provinces and into numerous lesser districts. Catherine also attempted a revitalization of town government—even making provision for town councils (*dumy*). The councils, however, labored under rather heavy burdens, such as very limited financial powers.

During the nineteenth century there were increasing demands for liberal reforms, some of which called for a strengthening of local government. In a limited response to these demands, district and provincial elective councils (*zemstva*) were created in 33 provinces; these local units were given authority over raising revenues, roads, hospitals, education, and general public welfare, but not over police. The *zemstva*, as noted earlier, became in the latter part of the nineteenth century the rallying point around which native liberal forces grew. The period of *zemstvo* dynamism was short-lived, however; its vitality, and more importantly its hope, faded shortly after the accession of Nicholas II to the throne. Russian local government was to re-emerge again only briefly during and shortly after the Revolutions of 1917.

Early under Communist rule local government was given strong backing chiefly because of the vital supporting role played in the Revolution by local organizations then in existence, that of the soldiers and workers councils—the soviets. The first Soviet Constitution in 1918, in fact, was ratified by the Fifth Congress of Soviets in the summer of 1918. This constitution stated that *all* authority within the nation is derived from local, elected soviets. During the period of the Revolution and the Civil War, too, weak central government under the nascent communist regime left room for the growth of varying degrees of local autonomy. During these early years, however, the Communists paid lip service to local autonomy more out of necessity than of choice, for the essence of Lenin's theory of communist rule was to be that of very strong, centralized government.

From 1923, when the USSR was brought into being, local government, now somewhat more in tune with communist theory, came more and more under the close supervision of the union republics. The period of the 1920's was one of a steady cutting down of the powers and authority of local units of government, particularly in the rural areas.[16] Now the rights of the republics, too, were being restricted, and gradually, but steadily, the great bulk of governmental power throughout the country was being centralized in the hands of the national party and governmental apparatus in Moscow.

The Soviet Constitution lists several levels and types of local governments (soviets). They include territory (kray), province (oblast), autonomous province (avtonomnyy oblast), district (rayon), national region (okrug), city (gorod), village (selskiy), and settlement (poselok) soviets. On the rural local level, also, there are units called apilinkov in Lithuania, aul in the Kazakh, and ail in the Kirghiz Republics.

In 1964 the units of local government were as follows:[17]

UNITS OF LOCAL GOVERNMENT BY UNION REPUBLIC, 1964

Republic	Kray	Oblast	Avtonomnyy Oblast	Rayon Rural	Rayon City	Poselok	Gorod	Okrug	Selskiy
RSFSR.......	7	105	8	2638	394	3399	1802	10	39597
Ukraine......		25		394	83	846	365		8539
Belorussia....		6		100	13	125	74		1521
Uzbek........		9		86	6	78	37		786
Kazakh......	1	15		152	8	163	59		1802
Georgia......			1	62	7	54	44		897
Azerbaijan....			1	60	9	115	45		818
Lithuania.....				44	7	25	89		653
Moldavia.....				26	3	23	19		604
Latvia.......				21	5	34	54		564
Kirghiz.......		1		29	3	31	15		350
Tadzhik......			1	35	3	32	15		266
Armenia......				33	5	27	23		431
Turkmen.....				28	2	64	14		211
Estoniya.....				15	5	24	33		239
	8	161	11	3723	553	5040	2688	10	57278

In the 1957 elections, local soviets were grouped under three categories. The first included territories, provinces, autonomous provinces, national regions, and large cities, that is, those units directly subordinate to union republic governments. The second category of local government, districts, medium-sized towns, and city boroughs, was subordinate to autonomous republics, territories, or provinces. The third tier of villages, settlements, and small towns was subordinate to districts.[18]

[16] Julian Towster, Political Power in the U.S.S.R., 1917–1947 (New York: Oxford University Press, 1948), pp. 200–201.

[17] SSSR Administrativno-territorialnoe Delenie Souznykh Respublik (Moscow, 1965).

[18] L. Churchward, "Continuity and Change in Soviet Local Government, 1947–1957," Soviet Studies, Vol. IX (January, 1958), p. 256.

Functions of Local Government

The general functions of local soviets include the maintenance of public order and the direction of economic and cultural affairs within their borders. Above all, the soviets are to carry out decisions and orders of the higher units of party and government. In performing the latter function, soviets serve as subadministrative agencies for the central and regional organs of power. Even certain departments and directorates of local soviets (such as finance, trade, culture, health, and police) mirror union republic and national governmental bodies in the similarity of tasks performed.[19]

Local soviets have specific powers and functions—all in pursuit of their broad assignment of responsibilities for administering state activities within their respective territorial confines. Soviets, reportedly, "develop" quarterly and yearly economic plans, guide local industrial and small enterprises, oversee fulfillment of the plan for agriculture, participate in town planning and road construction, and develop educational and cultural facilities. At sessions of the soviets the chairman, or his deputy, normally reports on measures adopted and decisions reached by the soviet's executive committee, the latter having met in the interim between sessions of the soviet.[20] City soviets are responsible for directing the activity of numerous industrial and smaller enterprises, organizations and institutions within the city. Other functions of city soviets, according to official explanation, are to allocate land parcels for construction of enterprises, supervise local trade, and check on educational, medical, and cultural institutions.[21]

Within cities of 100,000 or more there may be created subordinate boroughs to assist in local administration. These boroughs are concerned with very limited budget-financial matters, social security, and housing services. Some city boroughs have subdivisions similar to those of the parent city government. In the city of Moscow the 17 boroughs, with 200–250 deputies in all, direct enterprises, institutions, and organizations of borough importance (schools, kindergartens).[22] In recent years one trend in Soviet local government has been to reduce the number of city boroughs through amalgamation, even abolition, in some cases, because they are considered too often to be superfluous, having a tendency thereby

---

[19] An extensive list of these functions can be found in *Sovetskoe Gosudarstvo i Pravo*, No. 4 (April, 1964), p. 26.

[20] N. Organov, "Mestnye sovety na novom etape," *Partiynaya Zhizn*, No. 21 (November, 1960), p. 10.

[21] A. V. Luzhin, *Gorodskiye Sovety Deputatov Trudyashchikhsya* (Moscow: Gosuzyulit, 1954), p. 69. G. V. Nechitaylo, *Organizatsionno-massovaya Rabota Gorodskikh Sovetov Kazakhstana* (Alma Ata: Akademia Nauk, 1957), pp. 74, 79.

[22] V. Kotok, "Some Data on the Local Organs of State Power in the USSR," *Quarterly Journal of Local Self-Government* (Bombay), Vol. XXIX (January, 1959), p. 394.

to weaken the overall effectiveness of city government. In the city of Gorki in 1956, 6 new city boroughs replaced 11 old ones; as a result of this amalgamation there was a claimed saving of 925,000 rubles in one year.[23]

Village and settlement soviets have few powers, although they are charged with some responsibilities. They have the right to "discuss" collective farm activities and to watch over the "observance" of the farm charter, but they may not take any "direct" action. In some cases, on the other hand, executive committees of village soviets have failed to exercise their right and duty of controlling the collective farms. Instead, strong farm chairmen have ruled their domains with the passive approval of relatively weak executive committee heads. There are even examples in which the collective farms work out their own production plans, later to be confirmed by the district executive committees—in the process they by-passed the village executive committee.[24]

In a 1957 law on the status of village soviets within the RSFSR, there were included several "rights." These were to supervise public services for workers and employees and local institutions and hospitals, watch over fulfillment of agriculture plans, guide the work of local industry as well as trade in stores and shops, and to lend general assistance to state and collective farms, to industry and construction activities. The statute also calls for sessions of village soviets to be held at least six times yearly and to elect a chairman and a secretary, pass decisions by simple majority vote, and to appoint permanent commissions for budget and finance, agriculture, culture, and public services, as well as to carry out the actual work assigned to the soviet itself.[25] The discussions held at one village soviet included the following:[26]

June 27, 1963—Results of the school year, presented by the chairman of the soviet, the director of the schools, and the director of the *sovkhoz*.
August 29, 1963—Work of the savings bank, presented by the chairman of the soviet and the director of the *sovkhoz*.
November 19, 1963—Report of the executive committee of the soviet, presented by the engineer of the *sovkhoz* and a division manager of the *sovkhoz*.
December 28, 1963—Budget, presented by one of the deputies.
April 9, 1964—Work of the public amateur organizations, presented by the director of the *sovkhoz*, the director of schools, and the secretary of the party committee of the *sovkhoz*.

---

[23] Yu. Tikhomirov, "Nekotorye voprosy organizatsii i deyatelnosti rayonnykh sovetov v gorodakh," *Sovetskoe Gosudarstvo i Pravo*, No. 9 (September, 1957), p. 63. In Kaunas, city boroughs were practically useless; they simply adopted resolutions and wrote memoranda to the Kaunas City Council. See *Izvestiya*, July 19, 1956.

[24] *Izvestiya*, June 28, 1961.

[25] *Vedomosti Verkhovnogo Soveta RSFSR*, No. 1 (October 22, 1957), pp. 10–18.

[26] M. A. Shafir, "Aktualnye voprosy polozheniya selskikh sovetov i metody ikh izucheniya," *Sovetskoe Gosudarstvo i Pravo*, No. 10 (October, 1964), p. 27.

Some champions of the villages have called for more real powers for these soviets particularly in budgetary and general administrative matters. Reflecting a change carried out to a limited degree on the union republic level, local soviets have been assigned certain functions which previously had been carried out by their guiding executive committees, such as supervision over school construction, hospitals, stores, and movie theaters. In some areas, however, village soviets have been consolidated, others abolished.

Organization of Local Government

Local soviets form volunteer, auxiliary standing commissions; there were 1.5 million deputies active on the commissions in 1964, aided by 2.4 million volunteer "activists."[27] The purpose of the standing commissions is to assist in the work of the respective local soviet by making use of the time and talents both of deputies and private individuals in the work of local government. The Standing Commission for Industry of the Moscow City Soviet discussed, in June, 1960, a question related to development of the knitted goods industry in the Seven-Year Plan.[28] The commissions have the "right" to examine the work of the executive committee as well as that of local enterprises and institutions and offer suggestions to the soviet for improvement in local management. The commissions can be established for various purposes, such as local industry, municipal services, road construction and communications, agriculture and procurement, health, education, culture, budget and finance. One chief function of the standing commissions is to prepare questions and to draft appropriate decisions of local import for submission to sessions of the soviets and to their respective executive committees, rather than to exercise any measurable degree of governmental power.[29] Some local soviets have been turning over more functions of management to their commissions, such as staffing boarding schools, children's homes and gardens, distribution of the general fund, and planning capital repairs of homes.[30] In a work plan for one local rural soviet for April–September, 1965, thirteen items were introduced for the soviet and its executive

---

[27] *Partiynaya Zhizn*, No. 1 (January, 1965), p. 40.

[28] Organov, *op. cit.*, p. 11.

[29] V. Sorokin, "Nekotorye voprosy raboty selskikh sovetov," *Partiynaya Zhizn*, No. 2 (January, 1957), p. 23.

[30] V. Vasilev, "Sovety—vlast narodnaya," *Kommunist*, No. 2 (January, 1965), p. 15. Although, he adds, in some cases standing commissions exist, unfortunately, only on paper.

committee. Various commissions of the soviet took over responsibility for carrying out eight of the items.[31]

There are also rather amorphous bodies attached to some local soviets which are referred to as mass organizations. Electing a chairman and a secretary, these organizations hold meetings of citizens to discuss local problems and to recommend programs to local government. Again, the main purpose appears to be that of enlisting masses of citizens into unpaid activities in support of the work of local government. The Karaganda city government organized 382 women in a mass organization to help out with matters of sanitation, culture, and education.[32]

Effective administrative work of local soviets and the actual power of local government is exercised through the inner, directing body—the executive committee (*ispolkom*). These are the local equivalent of regional councils of ministers. The executive committee, meeting in the interim between sessions of the full soviet (the latter, rarely held in some areas), is elected by the soviet and normally includes a chairman, a deputy, a secretary, and from 6 to 15 members. The committee is held accountable for all of its actions, including those of its departments as well, both to its parent soviet and to the next higher executive committee within the soviet hierarchy.

The executive committees act in the name of the local soviets. The Leningrad *Oblast* Executive Committee, holding two to three sessions monthly in 1955, discussed leadership and work activity of subordinate executive committees (district and village) and made a decision relating to repair time of tractors and agricultural machinery.[33] In one 11-month period in 1956, the Leningrad City Executive Committee met 16 times; its inner Presidium, meeting 29 times in the same period, dealt with 30 to 60 questions at each meeting. When decisions are taken on any question, they are done so by simple majority vote and signed by the chairman and the secretary of the executive committee.[34] The Penovskiy *Rayon* Executive Committee has dealt with such matters as tax assessments for agriculture, the granting of honorary awards to mothers, establishing grants-in-aid, and removing certain quarantines. A member of this Committee complained that these matters and a great deal more minutiae which could and should be resolved by the departments of the Committee,

---

[31] *Sovety Deputatov Trudyashchikhsya*, No. 5 (May, 1965), pp. 33–34.

[32] Nechitaylo, *op. cit.*, p. 201.

[33] G. Petrov, "Nekotorye voprosy rukovodyashchey deyatelnosti ispolkomov mestnykh sovetov," *Sovetskoe Gosudarstvo i Pravo*, No. 8 (August, 1955), pp. 23–25.

[34] E. V. Shorina, *Kollegialnost i Yedinonachalie v Sovetskom Gosudarstvennom Upravlenii* (Moscow: Gosurizdat, 1959), pp. 66, 71.

were by law referred to the full Committee for solution.[35] In another vein, however, the Moscow City Executive Committee has been given additional authorization to approve certain expenditures for capital construction not to exceed 25 million rubles, to grant supplementary production quotas (up to 10 percent of the city plan) for local industrial plants, to retain 50 percent of industrial goods from local and cooperative production, to authorize new construction and repair facilities and to enjoy greater flexibility in the disposition of above-plan income.[36] This largest of the city governments (Moscow) has thirty departments, with a regular staff of several thousand people. The executive committee is made up of a chairman, eight deputy chairmen, a secretary, and fifteen members. The committee meets weekly for a session lasting several hours.[37]

Executive committees exercise some supervision over local court procedures. The committees, at least city ones, publish decisions stipulating responsibility in libel cases as well as determining sanctions for violations of law. Local soviets too, in conjunction with local party organs, may create public (obshchestvennyye) courts in villages to handle minor law violations.[38]

The general organization of the executive committees is to have divisions (upravleniya) serving as local administrative offices of central organs (such as those for trade, agriculture, transport, industry, culture). These departments are subordinate and responsible not only to the executive committee itself but to the corresponding departments at the next higher level executive committee. There are, as well, departments (otdely) for strictly local or specialized activities (municipal services, social insurance, health). There is also a planning commission and a personnel office, both attached to the office of the chairman. This organizational format, though much of it is standardized, varies somewhat depending upon the size, importance, and locale of the soviet. The Moscow Oblast Executive Committee is important enough to have main divisions for local industry, building materials, construction, sales and supply, and auto transport, as well as a number of other subadministrative units.[39] The Chelyabinsk

[35] Sovetskoe Gosudarstvo i Pravo, No. 10 (October, 1960), p. 43.

[36] Luzhin, op. cit., p. 74.

[37] Soviet Life, November, 1964, pp. 20, 24.

[38] A. N. Yefimov, Perestroyka Upravleniya Promyshlennostu i Stroitelstvom v SSSR (Moscow: Gospolitizdat, 1957), p. 50. The executive committees of Moscow and Leningrad cities have smaller guiding presidiums, composed of the committee's chairman, deputy chairmen, and secretary. The authority of the presidiums is equal to that of the executive committees themselves. See Shorina, op. cit., pp. 65–66.

[39] Sovetskoe Gosudarstvo i Pravo, No. 8 (August, 1960), p. 126. Executive committees of city soviets usually have a planning commission and divisions for: finance, health insurance, education, militia, culture, social insurance, and communal economy. Sovety Deputatov Trudyashchikhsya, No. 11 (November, 1965), p. 18.

Oblast Executive Committee was reported to have, in its departments and divisions, 703 employees, with 95 of them in the Finance Division.[40] Lesser soviets have smaller organizations. The Sverdlovsk "October" *Rayon* Executive Committee had some 19 departments and divisions in 1960.[41] Executive committees of small rural soviets are responsible to the higher (such as city) executive committees.

ORGANIZATION OF AN EXECUTIVE COMMITTEE OF A LOCAL SOVIET

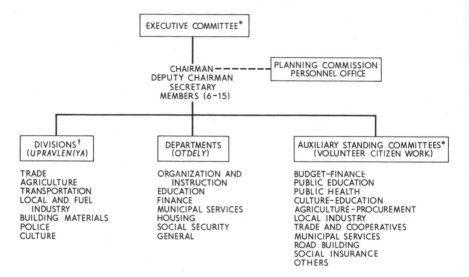

* These organs are elected by the whole soviet.

** Divisions normally are subordinate both to the Executive Committee and to the appropriate divisions of the next higher governmental unit.

The number and types of divisions and departments varies with the size and importance of the particular unit of government.

Local Elections

Elections for deputies to local soviets since 1936 were to have been held every two years. Prior to 1953, however, such elections were irregular. Election procedures—rules and mechanics—follow rather closely the national pattern. There are in local elections formal nominating meetings, marked influence of the Communist Party, a single candidate running for each seat, all-out voter participation, and predictable results. The number of deputies nominated and elected to each soviet depends upon the level of government (the higher the unit of government, the more deputies) and

---

[40] Organov, *op. cit.*, p. 13.

[41] Luzhin, *op. cit.*, p. 86.

the population of the territory involved. In 1957 the RSFSR election code provided for the following schedule of representation:[42]

Unit	Population	Deputies Authorized
Kray..............	11,000–15,000	1
Oblast............	8,000–30,000	1
Rayon............	Up to 35,000	35
	More than 35,000—for each 1,000	1
	(Maximum of 60 deputies)	
Gorod............	12,000–100,000—for each 350	1
	(Maximum of 250 deputies)	
	100,000–150,000—for each 400	1
	(Maximum of 300 deputies)	
	Less than 12,000	35
	Moscow and Leningrad—for each 6,000	1
Selskiy and poselok..	More than 1,500—for each 100	1
	(Maximum of 35 deputies)	
	Less than 1,500	15

The election machinery itself includes a great number of people who take part in nominating candidates, "agitating" for the official list of candidates during the campaign, getting out the voters on election day (or going to them, such as in hospitals), supervising the balloting, and counting and recording the results. In the 1961 local elections there were some eight million election workers throughout the nation taking care of the voting. Each union republic established its electoral commissions, which frequently are headed by members of the local party apparatus and supervised by the appropriate soviet executive committee. Election laws provide also for an appeal procedure for any voter who believes that he may be barred unjustifiably from voting.[43]

In the 1967 elections 2,045,277 deputies were elected to serve on local soviets throughout the country. The table below shows certain percentages of deputies elected by categories in five successive local elections. The percentage figures over the years appear remarkably similar, too much so

SOVIET LOCAL ELECTIONS[44]

	1957	1961	1963	1965	1967
Deputies elected.............	—	1,821,772	1,958,136	2,010,303	2,045,277
Communist Party Deputies (percent).................	46	45.5	43.3	45.1	45.4
Worker and Collective Farm Deputies (percent).........	58	61.8	62.4	62.2	62.5
Women Deputies (percent)....	36	40.7	41.6	42.6	43.8

[42] A. I. Denisov and M. G. Kirichenko, *Sovetskoe Gosudarstvennoe Pravo* (Moscow: Gosurizdat, 1957), p. 217. An excellent study of local elections is that of Max E. Mote, *Soviet Local and Republic Elections* (Stanford, Calif.: Hoover Institution, 1965).

[43] Howard R. Swearer, "The Functions of Soviet Local Elections," *Midwest Journal of Political Science*, Vol. V (May, 1961), pp. 130–31.

[44] Computed from *Pravda*, March 8, 9, 15, 16, 22, 1957; March 8, 22, 1963; *Izvestiya*, March 14, 25, 1961; March 14, 28, 1965; *Izvestiya*, March 17, 24, 1967.

to be accidental. These data, as in the case with national and regional elections, confirm other information indicating that the regime sets specific percentages of various types of deputies who are to be elected to local governments. The affixing of specific percentage figures has been admitted by several Soviet experts.[45] And, as with national elections, almost all eligible voters cast their ballots; more than 99 percent of eligible voters vote in the local elections.

Problems of Local Government

From time to time local soviets, and particularly their governing executive committees, are critized in the Soviet press for violations of either the letter or spirit of the law. Chairmen of executive committees have been accused of violating the principle of collective leadership by arbitrarily deciding questions themselves. Some executive committees exceed their authority and, in violation of law, fail to have many of their decisions ratified by the parent body, the soviet. During Stalin's reign the committees frequently neglected their soviets, completely failing not only to consult them but not bothering even to call sessions of the full soviet from year to year. Two executive committees in Kazakhstan failed to report to their parent soviet once during a 10-year period. In other instances, sessions of executive committees are attended by only a few members, occasionally only by the chairman, the deputy chairmen, and the secretary.[46] It should not be surprising, however, given the rather strict hierarchical nature of Soviet governmental operation, that the executive committee tends to usurp powers legally belonging to the whole soviet, and that some members of the committee feel apathetic toward attending meetings called by the ruling faction of chairman, deputy chairmen, and secretary. Executive committees also are blamed for tolerating inefficient work methods and poor office organization, for issuing illegal orders in violation of law, and for not responding to the complaints of workers. One deputy to a local soviet claimed he was never allowed to speak at sessions of the soviet, being ignored in favor of officially selected speakers,[47] while another complaint criticized a local executive committee for always delaying action until a local party organ takes the initiative and points the way.[48]

One Soviet journal asked its readers who also were deputies to soviets to answer three questions:

[45] L. G. Churchward, "Soviet Local Government Today," *Soviet Studies* (April, 1966), p. 451.

[46] Nechitaylo, *op. cit.*, pp. 145, 148, 153–54.

[47] *Izvestiya*, January 19, 1965.

[48] *Izvestiya*, December 19, 1964.

1. Do you have sufficient time for the business of deputies?

2. Do you carry out the mandate of your voters?

3. Are you satisfied, as a deputy, with the help given to you by executive committees?

Of the 300 replies received by the journal, the results were summarized in these figures.[49]

Question No. 1—69 percent answered yes.

Question No. 2—24 percent answered yes.
        —57 percent answered not always.
        —19 percent answered no.

Question No. 3—49 percent answered yes.
        —26 percent answered no.

Thus, while most deputies responding felt they had adequate time for their duties as a deputy, a significant proportion believed themselves to be inadequately fulfilling their voter's mandate. Perhaps the dominance of the executive committee over local government is reflected in the approximately one quarter of the responses criticizing the executive committees for failing to give proper assistance to the deputies of the soviets.

At all levels of Soviet government there is recurring confusion among administrative bodies as to jurisdictional lines of authority. Within an *oblast* there usually exist several organs administering similar (at times identical) enterprises. Sharply defined chains of command often are nonexistent because of a large number of departments of national and republican ministries and of regional economic councils—all functioning within the boundary of a single *oblast*. The chairman of the Novosibirsk *Oblast* Executive Committee complained of a lack of authority over enterprises because many of the enterprises were outside of his jurisdiction; they were subordinate instead to national or republican departments, or to the regional economic council. And yet, the executive committee nevertheless is responsible for the success or failure of these very enterprises. Various administrative organs are concerned with garment making in Novosibirsk *Oblast*—national and republican ministries, the Novosibirsk Economic Council, and local soviets. Still, there is a continuing shortage of garments being produced in the *oblast*. Although the RSFSR *Gosplan* and the All-Russian Economic Council normally submit a plan first to their subordinate Novosibirsk Economic Council, the plan belatedly is sent to the *Oblast* Executive Committee only after it already has been agreed upon. All too often, the chairman of the Committee concluded, industrial management in Novosibirsk is poorly planned, uncoordinated, and does not achieve satisfactory results.[50] Beginning in 1959, however,

---

[49] *Sovety Deputatov Trudyashchikhsya*, No. 10 (October, 1966), pp. 41–44.

[50] *Izvestiya*, August 6, 1961.

local soviets were given authority to participate actively in formulating the long-range economic plan, and the 1965 abolition of the *sovnarkhozy* should reduce somewhat the administrative confusion.

Trends in Soviet Local Government

In recent years the regime has emphasized the necessity for more citizens to become involved in the work of local government on a part-time, nonpaid basis. By the end of the 1950's there may have been as many as two million of these part-time "activists" serving on more than one-quarter million standing commissions of local governments, and more than four million people working on election committees. A counterpart tendency has seen a decrease in the number of full-time paid employees working in local government. These developments simply point up a rather typical characteristic of Soviet local government—that it depends less on skilled specialists and more on masses of amateurs than is the case with such governments in the West.[51] In the RSFSR alone, there were more than 6,000 nonstaff (unpaid) departments in 1963,[52] utilizing almost ten million people, most of them unpaid.[53]

While the scope of local government has widened by involving it more directly in administration of certain economic enterprises and giving to it greater powers over such matters as housing and finance, there has taken place a reduction in numbers of overall units of government. The following table lists increases and reductions in these units by category from 1955 to 1961.[54]

CHANGES IN NUMBER OF LOCAL GOVERNMENTAL UNITS

Year	Increases					Reductions				Net Change
	Kray	Gorod	Rural Rayon	City Rayon	Selskiy	Oblast	Rural Rayon	City Rayon	Selskiy	
1955......		23	9	2	52	3	45	14	119	— 95
1956......		57	7	6	216	2	178	66	459	— 419
1957......		31	15	3	276	5	121	18	834	— 653
1958......		31	5	4	306	..	78	24	1347	— 1103
1959......		14	9	1	169	6	457	37	5141	— 5448
1960......	1	14	..	..	201	4	90	22	2496	— 2399
Total .	1	170	45	16	1220	20	969	181	10396	—10114

[51] Churchward, *op. cit.*, 1958, p. 260.

[52] *Sovetskoe Gosudarstvo i Pravo*, No. 2 (February, 1964), p. 100.

[53] Churchward, *op. cit.*, 1966, pp. 440–441.

[54] R. Pavlovskiy and M. Shafir, "O nekotorykh voprosakh sovetskogo administra-tivno-territorialnogo ustroystva," *Sovetskoe Gosudarstvo i Pravo*, No. 5 (May, 1961), p. 41. In 1962, two additional *krai* were formed in the Kazakh Republic (the Western Kazakh and the Southern Kazakh *Krai*).

The table reveals a rather normal tendency for a vast, semiurbanized country to show a steady growth in the number of cities. It also displays a marked reduction in the units of local government in rural areas. Soviet press accounts have referred to the necessity for amalgamating and abolishing certain units of local government to eliminate superfluous and duplicated administrative functions. There may be other reasons for such reductions, such as increased centralization of government upwards toward the union republic level with a less felt need on the part of Soviet leaders for local government—at least for rural local government. Reasons for this change in attitude of the leadership, if such is the case, may result from growing party supervision over local administration and the assumption of some local powers and responsibilities by regional economic councils; both developments have occurred since mid-1957.

Since the Twenty-first Party Congress a greater emphasis on "socialist legality" has affected local government operations. Administrators now govern with somewhat more responsibility and less arbitrarily than formerly. Deputies to local soviets have been urged to report back to their respective electors on a more routine basis. There has been, also, more regularity in holding meetings of local soviets. Illegalities on the part of officials of local governmental and economic agencies have resulted in protests from divisions of the Procurator's Office.[55]

Still another facet of present-day local government has been a formalization of the concept of "groups of deputies" based on territorial lines. Although first appearing as early as 1929, these groups have been brought back since the death of Stalin. The groups are made up of deputies from certain areas—such as specific rural localities or city election districts. These deputies supposedly share common interests and needs and thereby assist one another in carrying out their tasks and assignments. Meetings of the deputy groups are to be conducted at least once every two months. In all cases, however, the deputies individually are still responsible to their respective local soviets.[56]

The assumption by local governments of increased functions as well as responsibilities can be seen in growing administrative supervision over subordinate organizations, evidenced in part by greater use of decision making on that level.[57] The growth in budgeted expenditures of rural soviets, for example, has expanded from 240 million rubles in 1946 to 548

---

[55] Churchward, *op. cit.*, 1958, pp. 271–73.

[56] R. Safarov, "Territorialnye deputatskie gruppy mestnykh sovetov," *Sovetskoe Gosudarstvo i Pravo*, No. 6 (June, 1961), pp. 97–100.

[57] See the discussion in V. F. Kotok, *et al.*, "Ob odnom iz putey povysheniya roli sovetov," *Sovetskoe Gosudarstvo i Pravo*, No. 9 (September, 1966), p. 125.

million rubles in 1955 and to 1,112 million rubles in 1965.[58] The added functions taken on by the standing commissions of local soviets (mirroring the recent developments in the national Supreme Soviet) include the power to adopt decisions which are binding on administrative organs.[59] Deputies of local soviets reportedly believe that rights of these commissions should be expanded to include more precise direction over the actions of comrade courts.[60]

As with regional government, so local government in the USSR, particularly since the Stalin period, has been gaining experience and proficiency. In Churchward's analysis, local government is less official, more voluntary, less bureaucratic, and more broadly based.[61] These accretions in administrative skill serve to point up for Soviet leadership the desirability of, if not necessity for, entrusting local units of government with even more powers and responsibilities. Whether this trend will contribute in the long run toward a genuine grass-roots movement for greater local autonomy aimed at evolving some "inherent" right of local government in the Soviet Union, a right which might become a bulwark against too much centralized rule, cannot be foreseen at this time. It might well be anticipated, though, that the prominent attention given local governmental organization and procedure by Soviet leaders will have the effect of facilitating the growth of more responsible administration on this level. If local governments are laid out in detail and with locally elected officials exercising some authoritative power throughout urban and rural areas of the nation, even where they may not be vitally needed, apathy toward local government on the part of citizens may result. Perhaps, though, a *sense* of governmental participation will more and more infuse the people, and, coupled with the growth of mass organizations and amateur participation, local autonomy will be increased rather than decreased. In the official view, local soviets are a "school of administration for hundreds, thousands, and millions of workers."[62] Toward the fulfillment

---

[58] N. Shirkevich, "Selskiy budzhet. Kak ego ukrepit," *Sovety Deputatov Trudyashchikhsya*, No. 11 (November, 1966), pp. 68–69.

[59] *Soviet Studies*, Information Supplement (January, 1966), p. 9. But these decisions must not alter the plan or the budget as adopted by the respective soviets.

[60] A. Vader, "Nuzhna stroynaya sistema," *Sovety Deputatov Trudyashchikhsya*, No. 12 (December, 1966), p. 64.

[61] Churchward, *op. cit.*, 1966, p. 452.

[62] *Kommunist*, No. 2 (January, 1965), p. 15. Although bringing volunteers into management of local affairs should not, in Wesson's view, be equated with democratization, since many are already local party and governmental officials. "The more completely citizens can be brought to share in a programme the less are they likely to oppose its purposes." Robert G. Wesson, "Volunteers and Soviets," *Soviet Studies*, Vol. XV (January, 1964), pp. 248–49.

of this optimistic view of local government, however, the Russians certainly have a long way to go.

As Soviet government in general is the handmaiden of high Communist Party leaders, so regional and local governments, in reality, are servants of the national government in duties, assignments, authority, and responsibilities.

PART FOUR

Patterns of Soviet Politics

CHAPTER XIV

Patterns and Trends of Soviet Politics

IT MIGHT be appropriate to begin this summarization of Soviet politics by quoting passages from two well-known writers. The first, a life-long communist and former high functionary within the Yugoslav communist movement, was subsequently removed from positions of authority and responsibility within his country.

> The heroic era of Communism is past. The epoch of its great leaders has ended. The epoch of practical men has set in. The new class has been created. It is at the height of its power and wealth, but it is without new ideas. It has nothing more to tell the people. The only thing that remains is for it to justify itself.[1]

The second quote is from the most well-known contemporary Soviet poet.

> The first mistake made by Western students of the Russian Revolution is to judge the revolutionary idea not by those who are genuinely loyal to it, but by those who betray it.
> Their other mistake is that they still regard the idea of communism as something imposed by force on the Russian people, without realizing that by now it is a part of the Russian people's flesh and blood.[2]

Of the two authors, which is the more accurate, the more perceptive in viewing contemporary Soviet society? In several respects both are useful in our interpretations and evaluations of the Soviet political system. Certainly the revolutionary fervor and era of dramatic, new ideas has been left behind in the USSR at its present stage of development, as Djilas indicated. Practical men rather than revolutionaries do govern the Soviet Union. Yevtushenko, on the other hand, all too vividly portrays a great deal of writing in the West about the Soviet Union which has long

---

[1] Milovan Djilas, *The New Class* (New York: Frederick A. Praeger, Inc., 1957), pp. 53–54.

[2] Yevgeny Yevtushenko, *A Precocious Autobiography* (New York: E. P. Dutton, 1963), p. 39.

emphasized the failings, weaknesses, and shortcomings of Soviet communism. There are many westerners who view modern communism as if it were unchanged, to any degree, from the heyday of Stalinist terror. Our analysis of the Soviet system will be more fruitful if we steer clear of emotional and sweeping observations about the Soviet Union and communism, and rely more heavily on the structural-functional approach.

The similarity in functions found in various political systems, Western and Soviet, as seen, for example, in the articulation and aggregation of interests and in the issuance of authoritative outputs, attests to the similarity of responsibilities, tasks, and problems faced by all modern societies. There may well be, in fact, more fundamental differences in political patterns between developing and modern political systems (say, Indonesia versus the USSR), than there are between some communist and noncommunist systems (such as the US and the USSR). There are differences between the latter two, of course, in such matters as whose demands are being satisfied. In the Soviet Union demands from workers and writers are not fulfilled to the extent they are in, say, Great Britain. Conversely, demands of the political elite are satisfied to a considerably higher degree in the Soviet Union than in the United States. More precise differences, in addition to a number of similarities, as suggested in the introduction to this book, relate to the manner in which political functions are carried out in given political systems.

The several leading patterns of Soviet politics might be arranged under three general headings which, taken as a whole, can more broadly characterize the Soviet political system, both in its past and in its present forms. The first of these leading patterns can be labeled *Ideological-Revolutionary.* Leninism was the time for the foundation building of the modern Soviet political system, and it was during the early years after 1917 that the philosophical base was solidified and the Communist Party dictatorship was established, when the first elements of national planning were organized and the techniques of routine political management were worked out under Lenin's guidance. The social, or public, aspect of the system was set up and included national ownership, or control, over land, farming, industry, and cultural and educational institutions. Soviet society was dedicated by its leaders to the concept of economic and social egalitarianism, led and guided by the Communist Party. All citizens within the nation were to benefit from this new, supposedly more humanitarian, equal, and just form of structuring and operating society.[3]

---

[3] "Now our country is at such a stage of its development that the satisfaction of the growing material and spiritual requirements of man must be advanced to first place in working out the perspective plan of development of our economy." Statement of Presidium of the Council of Ministers, USSR. *Pravda*, October 2, 1964.

Leninism and Stalinism russified the original doctrines of Marx; the result was Soviet Communism which throughout its history has defended vehemently its fidelity to a glorified and idealized theory of Marxism. This ideological mold for Soviet politics has continued into the 1960's, when official homage still is frequently paid to the Marxian image. The tendency to interpret governmental policies and actions in theoretical terms continues to be adhered to in such tenets as the withering away of the state, although modern Soviet Communists have added new variations to Leninism, such as the nonexportability of revolution and the doctrine of permanent peaceful coexistence. The modern Soviet system is portrayed by its ideologues as socialist-communist in its goals, humanitarian in outlook, and revolutionary in procedures; it precludes the development of capitalism at home while promoting the goal of a broadly-based, proletarian-led scientific and egalitarian society. The consciously articulated official ideology is a widely shared symbolic value among Soviet citizens, and if the majority of these people still object to the idea of Stalinist-type terror, they do accept the idealistic goal of communism for their society. A remaining question is, to what extent have successive Soviet regimes achieved this communist goal of an abundant, just, and humane life for their citizens? Although Soviet spokesmen claim much in this respect, Western analysts have remained skeptical.

The second main pattern is the *Dynamic-Developmental* one. In this, an outgrowth of the first pattern, Soviet politics can be viewed as mobilizing and mass-oriented. Soviet society thus reflects such achievements as overall modernization, rapid industrialization accompanying considerable economic growth, measurable expansion in publicly sponsored educational and cultural opportunities, development of a modern nation-state which effectively functions in the international arena, and building a common political society in which everyone is to share both in the responsible tasks to be performed as well as in the advantages to be obtained. Optimism is a feature of this category, which is associated with modernization. The latter concept, in Apter's words, is a special kind of hope. The modernization revolution is epic in scale, he contends, and moral in significance.[4]

The Soviet political elite from Lenin on has looked on the Revolution as dynamic, mobilizing, modernizing and capable of almost any accomplishment. There is, in Soviet history, a revolutionary mystique, similar to that which formerly existed in the United States and which continues to persist in the Mexican political system. It seems fair to ask at this point

---

[4] David E. Apter, *The Politics of Modernization* (Chicago: University of Chicago Press, 1965), p. 1.

whether rapid development and change in class proportions within society, such as a doubling in size of the Soviet intelligentsia in the twenty years 1939–59, according to one view,[5] will be to the advantage or disadvantage of the political elite. If the more alienated peasant-farmer class declines while the more politically socialized intelligentsia increases under speeded-up modernization, will the overall support level for the system increase proportionately? What Soviet experience does reveal, at least since Stalin's time, is that greater accretions of education among citizens in general and a growth in the size of the intellectual class specifically give rise to more demands being presented to the political elite. Political socialization in the USSR, if it is to continue to be communist and elite directed, will no doubt reflect the speed with which the elite can satisfy the rapidly growing demands of the various social groups.

The third main pattern of Soviet politics is *Conservative-Elitist*. Both in its organizational format and its operating customs, Soviet politics are highly centralized. They are center-directed and they are dictatorial and authoritarian in procedures. Soviet politics are shaped and controlled by the Communist Party, which always has been elite-oriented in its personnel, policies, and programs. In effect, this is a party-state system where at the highest, most centralized levels, the merger of party and government leaders is practically complete. Illustrations for this are found in the monopoly of high governmental offices (within the Council of Ministers and the Supreme Soviet) held by the 400-plus party members of the Central Committee Group. It is this group which predominates over and sets policy and supervises its execution for government, science, culture, education, and the economic and military aspects of organized Soviet society. In practice the leadership works through small ruling groups; the Politburo had eleven regular members in mid-1966 while simultaneously the Presidium of the Council of Ministers had twelve members. The three highest officials in this Presidium (Chairman and two First Deputy Chairmen) at the same time were three of the most important members of the eleven-man Politburo. Thus, the Soviet political system is a classical illustration of a party-state system in action.

Soviet politics tend, decade by decade, to become conservative and less revolutionary, and in the process more bureaucratic in that they are protective of the position of the elite in society and opposed to the rise of liberal, pluralized political movements. Operating goals of the elite center around fiscal soundness, rational economic investment and growth, increases in the amount of material benefits for society, advances in

---

[5] See Chapter V, p. 105.

educational and scientific achievements and, above all the enhancement of political stability. These goals involve a far greater concentration of ruling talents and energy in the USSR at the present time than do any thoughts or hopes of stirring up revolutions abroad. In foreign policy, too, conservative Soviet politics have been more cautious and defensive than they have been aggressive and aggrandizing, at least as the world is seen from Moscow. Following from these three leading patterns of Soviet politics, *Ideological-Revolutionary*, *Dynamic-Developmental*, and *Conservative-Elitist*, we can now discuss certain functional trends as illustrative of some changes in several minor patterns of Soviet politics.

The first such change is that of widening and more intensified articulation and aggregation of popular demands into the total political system. The Communist Party's jealous prerogative as *the* articulator and aggregator for social pressures has by design limited, if not virtually prevented, other societal groups and organizations from performing these functions in anything more than a very crude and inadequate fashion. One result has been poor articulation and aggregation of most of the demands of citizens, except, of course, those of the elite itself. That this is changing, either by crediting nonparty groups more highly (such as trade unions), or by the party itself becoming more of a channel for these functions, may in any case result from forces which the party simply cannot hold in check. In art, for example, the well-known editor of the literary journal, *Novy Mir*, voiced deeply felt artistic desires for more creativity by calling on artists to use more artistry and less "schematized" portrayals of Soviet life.[6] In another vein, Khrushchev had been countered somewhat in his military policies by cautiously voiced opposition from military leaders in what amounted to a stress on professional self-management of the military.[7] The party, in the view of some of these military leaders, had not been an effective enough spokesman for the demands of the military. More recently, there have been attempts to broaden and deepen the study of the social sciences and to allow these disciplines to escape some of the rigidity of past party strictures and ideological blinders. Soviet academicians have recommended setting up new disciplines of political science and sociology, in part "to pose questions for the first time for which answers are not already known."[8] At several different times (1962,

---

[6] *New York Times*, April 14, 1966.

[7] See the discussions in Curt Gasteyger, "Modern Warfare and Soviet Strategy," *Survey* (October, 1965), p. 50, and Z. Brzezinski, "The Soviet Political System," *Problems of Communism* (January–February, 1966), p. 12.

[8] *Sovetskoe Gosudarstvo i Pravo*, No. 2 (February, 1966), pp. 135–50. At the Twenty-third CPSU Congress in 1966 Brezhnev called for upgrading the social sciences, since they are as important as the natural sciences, and ridiculed some cadres who think that social sciences have only a propaganda value. *Pravda*, March 30, 1966.

1963, 1965) the Central Committee announced that it and other party organs should not interfere in purely scientific matters, for example in the choice of medical techniques or in problems of theoretical science.

Does all this mean that new interest groups, perhaps those of scholars, youth, or scientists, are coming to the fore in order to articulate their demands, irrespective of the party's historical role of domination? This has already occurred, Brzezinski argues, since many of Khrushchev's actions were in the form of mediating the demands of key institutions such as the army and industrial managers.[9]   More directly, Skilling believes that during Khrushchev's period of rule, specialized elites voiced their interests and to a degree influenced the outputs of the political system in such areas as education, military strategy, industrial management, legal reforms, science, art, and literature.[10]   It seems reasonable to assume that rapidly growing demands, such as those of the artistic community, the military, and the academic-educational, will seek, perhaps require, expression in the form of interest groups now in the budding stage or yet to be created.   Two such present groups are trade unions and legislative representatives, groups which are measurably increasing the articulation and aggregation of their demands.   A budding interest group is that of the artistic-literary community which is unofficially organizing pressure to bring to bear within the political system.

Apart from specific interest groups which assume a responsibility for promoting certain demands, individual classes within society might do the same.   The artistic-literary community, a significant part of the intelligentsia class, has on a number of occasions since 1962 sought new art forms (especially after official approval was given for the publication of Solzhenitsyn's novel, *One Day in the Life of Ivan Denisovich*) by writing and submitting many new stories and novels which were not always complimentary about Soviet life.   There have been pleas from artists to the party for more tolerance, even protest petitions to the Central Committee with respect to crackdowns on the artists.[11]   If to these are added scientists and academicians, then the intelligentsia class, for one, might well intrude itself into the system as an increasingly potent interest group, involving itself into the heretofore closed province of the party.   Other classes, such as workers and farmers, may not be so fortunate.   Although the level of "welfare" of workers has increased slightly since Stalin's time,

---

[9] Brzezinski, *op. cit.*, p. 8.

[10] H. Gordon Skilling, "Interest Groups and Communist Politics," *World Politics*, (April, 1966), p. 445.

[11] See the discussion in Priscilla Johnson, *Khrushchev and the Arts, The Politics of Soviet Culture, 1962–1964* (Cambridge, Mass.: M.I.T. Press, 1965).

this class has not won many new benefits from the regime. One exception to this general pattern is in the rise in influence of trade unions. Here is a nonparty organization (although party supervised, of course) which is more and more serving as spokesman for workers' interests.

A second, although related, pattern change in Soviet politics concerns the party within the conversion mechanism (the decision making apparatus) of the political system. As discussed in other chapters, there has been a partial decrease, perhaps an erosion, in the party's absolute dominance over all features of the system. Although this development has not downgraded the party in theory (unlike Tito's deemphasis of the Communist Party of Yugoslavia), this might be one of the results, intended or not, which will be brought about in practice. Following the demise of Khrushchev, collegial rule once again replaced one-man rule (this happened also after the death of Lenin in 1924 and of Stalin in 1953). Thus, de-Stalinization, attacks on the "cult of personality" associated with Stalin and Khrushchev, the general decline in the post-Khrushchev era of flamboyant praise of and personal tributes paid to individual leaders, all serve to indicate a weakening of the previous Soviet pattern of one-man dictatorship and conceivably even that of party dictatorship itself. The party continues in its historical roles as protector of the faith in arts and literature, guide and leader in education, ruler of the military and the governmental bureaucracy, and stimulator of the economy. It does so, though, in the face of growing restiveness among such citizens as writers, students, farmers, and a number of other consumers in general. How will, or how can the party respond to these rising pressures is an important question not only for the party apparatus, but for the political system itself.

The added importance of the legislatures, national, regional, and local, vis-à-vis the party and executive apparatus of government points to a new trend in Soviet politics. The enlarged number and expanded level of activity of the standing commissions of the legislatures, particularly those of the national Supreme Soviet, added to their newly assigned duties and responsibilities, eventually may prove to be a change of real significance. This development in effect opens up for Soviet citizens, by way of their elected legislative representatives, what could become a new channel of access and influence into the conversion mechanism of the political system. Coincidentally, the number of high party officials (members of the Central Committee Group) placed on the national legislature's guiding Presidium was more than tripled in the years 1962–64. Perhaps the party leadership is now aware of the growing political importance of the legislature and, as a result, is taking extra measures to preserve its own position of preeminence within this increasingly important political structure—the legislature and its Presidium. It is noteworthy, in this connection, that some Soviet specialists in government and law are calling for greater independence of the elected legislature from the close domination by the Council of Ministers and even from the Supreme Soviet's own inner Presidium. This development is probably the most important single one in Soviet politics within the past few years. It begins to seem more and more feasible that the Soviet legislature might evolve into a considerably more autonomous and representative political force than has ever been the case in Soviet history. At least, this is the direction that this development currently is taking.[12]

The third change in one of the patterns of Soviet politics to be noted is that of a shifting emphasis in the outputs, or authoritative decisions, of the system. There has been in recent years a decrease in what may be termed ideological outputs. Perhaps the problem is, as Lowenthal suggests, that the erosion of ideological dynamism is far advanced and that the heirs to the Russian Revolution "are reduced to the conservative role of stabilizing its institutions and defending their oligarchic privileges."[13] Among the newer outputs there are decisions to raise the quality and quantity of consumer goods, promises of higher and more regular wages for collective farmers, and shorter working hours for the industrial labor force. Accompanying these decisions are those which point to cautious shifts away from the traditional command economy in favor of such changes as the Liberman proposals, including an increased decentralization of factory management and more of a catering to the demands of the consumer. There have been authoritative decisions in recent years favoring greater literary freedoms (for example, loosening the rigidity of censorship) and greater legal protections for citizens, such as more rigorous defense of clients in court cases. In all of this, one might ask what influence changing outputs have or are likely to have on other features of the system. Does more liberality in one area by itself force more liberality in another? In this connection, it might be suggested that some of the economic reforms appear to parallel several political reforms which have taken place within the past decade in the USSR. Are the two types closely interrelated? The following lists suggest such an interpretation, although acknowledging the fine line drawn between "economic" and "political," especially in the Soviet Union.

---

[12] The fundamental long-term trend, for Hough, is an increasing specialization in decision-making of specialized institutions. Jerry Hough, "The Soviet Elite: Groups and Individuals," *Problems of Communism* (January–February, 1967), p. 35.

[13] R. Lowenthal, "The Revolution Withers Away," *Problems of Communism* (January–February, 1965), p. 17.

Economic Reforms	Political Reforms
Managerial decentralization in industry	Increased powers of regional and local governments
Increased administrative autonomy and flexibility	Growing legislative autonomy
Greater emphasis on satisfaction of consumer desires	Better articulation and aggregation of citizen demands

The Soviet political system is one in the process of rapid transition. Elements of this transition include a scaling down of the dictatorship following the post-Stalin era with a reduction in terror until its virtual disappearance for Soviet citizens by the 1960's; an improving legal system which is highlighted by added protections for individual citizens; a quantitative and qualitative increase in consumer goods following a concerted effort to satisfy more and more popular demands; a rise in the number and effectiveness of organized interest groups operating within the system; and the cautious but measurable stirrings of a more independent and representative legislature. Will all of these changes help to move the Soviet political system toward more democracy? Brzezinski notes the difficulty of a political elite trying to maintain a doctrinaire dictatorship within a modernizing industrial society.[14] Apter has suggested that as the hierarchy in Yugoslavia and in the USSR is decentralized, information comes in from an increasing number of points so that the structural requisites reflect the change in the growth of accountability groups, with more people sharing in the decision making process. Can mobilization systems, he asks, transform themselves into reconciliation systems committed to a liberal framework?[15] To a considerable degree, the answer to these questions hinges on which way the CPSU is going, as far as the Soviet Union is concerned.

If the CPSU evolves into a more pluralistic organization, perhaps institutionalizing a chief executive officer so that it becomes a structure specializing in adjustment and compromise of the various aspirations of social groups, then its continued existence might be assured for the indefinite future.[16] But, in the process can the party allow apathy toward its leadership role, and can it tolerate the possible growth of a more open form of opposition? In 1963 at a meeting called by party ideologists to discipline artists and writers, Khrushchev made an off-hand comment in reaction to a plea of Yevtushenko's for official patience and more time for unpopular art forms to be "straightened out." Khrushchev interrupted

---

[14] Brzezinski, op. cit., p. 14. Can a totalitarian regime, Lichtheim asks, continue to function after it has exhausted its original purpose? George Lichtheim in Slavic Review (December, 1965), p. 608.

[15] Apter, op. cit., pp. 305, 394.

[16] Brzezinski, op. cit., pp. 12, 14–15.

with, "The grave straightens out the humpbacked." Yevtushenko's amazing reply directed at Khrushchev was, "Nikita Sergeyevich, we have come a long way since the time when only the grave straightens out humpbacks. Really, there are other ways." Then, Yevtushenko continued to lecture the party chief by observing that he really did not believe that Khrushchev could like the tastelessly drawn picture of "N. S. Khrushchev among the Workers."[17] Can the party tolerate such condescending insolence toward its top leader? In December, 1965, Soviet students engaged in a short demonstration in Moscow demanding a public trial for the writers Sinyavsky and Daniel, who had been under arrest for "political" crimes since that September. A leader of the demonstration was then assured by some official that there would be such a trial.[18] Accordingly, a semipublic trial (open by invitation only) was finally held early in 1966. If all this does not amount to opposition to the political elite, it does testify at least to a growing willingness on the part of some citizens to ask party leaders to account for their actions. In Khrushchev's transitional rule, then, doors may have been opened which cannot be closed again. De-Stalinization and its aftermath may effectively prevent the rise of another single, strong dictator. Where does all this leave the CPSU and its hallowed doctrines, such as absolute party supremacy in all matters of Soviet life and the concept and the practice of unchallenged party dominance?[19]

The growth of more effective interest groups, such as the military, cannot be viewed as constituting the rise of effective opposition to the Communist Party. Not yet, at least. There still is no political opposition in the form of parties, movements, or legislators in the USSR. Even potential opposition is restricted by the absence of developed channels and avenues for its expression, as well as by the Soviet tradition of no opposition to the party. Once citizens acquire knowledge and experience in forming and using interest groups, however, the party's role of near absolute control will probably then be placed in jeopardy. Even then, conceivably, a surprising degree of opposition may be tolerated by the party elite as long as the prevailing myth, or shared value, of party supremacy is honored

---

[17] Johnson, *op. cit.*, pp. 121–22. In response to an article criticizing Yevtushenko, the main Soviet youth newspaper received 1,200 letters in reply. *Komsomolskaya Pravda*, May 23, 1963. This testifies, in part, to the very great popularity of Yevtushenko with young people in the USSR.

[18] *New York Times*, January 13, 1966.

[19] In Meissner's view, the successors to Khrushchev could soften the conflict between the ruling elite and progressive forces within the intelligentsia only if the elite was prepared to curtail the permanent and absolute dictatorship of the party while emancipating large areas of social life from party control. Boris Meissner, "Totalitarian Rule and Social Change," *Problems of Communism* (November–December, 1966), p. 61.

in the form of continued legitimization of the CPSU within the political system. The party elite might then agree, reluctantly, to share actual decision making with other interest groups within society, if these groups in turn agree to continue the ostensible leadership of the CPSU.

Rules of the Communist Party of The Soviet Union*

I. Party Members, Their Duties and Rights

1. Membership of the CPSU is open to any citizen of the Soviet Union who accepts the Program and the Rules of the Party, takes an active part in communist construction, works in one of the Party organizations, carries out all Party decisions, and pays membership dues.

2. It is the duty of a Party member:

a) To work for the creation of the material and technical basis of communism; to serve as an example of the communist attitude towards labor; to raise labor productivity; to display the initiative in all that is new and progressive; to support and propagate advanced methods; to master techniques, to improve his skill; to protect and increase public socialist property, the mainstay of the might and prosperity of the Soviet country;

b) To put Party decisions firmly and steadfastly into effect; to explain the policy of the Party to the masses; to help strengthen and multiply the Party's bonds with the people; to be considerate and attentive to people; to respond promptly to the needs and requirements of the working people;

c) To take an active part in the political life of the country, in the administration of state affairs, and in economic and cultural development; to set an example in the fulfillment of his public duty; to assist in developing and strengthening communist social relations;

d) To master Marxist-Leninist theory, to improve his ideological knowledge, and to contribute to the molding and education of the man of communist society. To combat vigorously all manifestations of bourgeois ideology, remnants of a private-property psychology, religious prejudices, and other survivals of the past; to observe the principles of communist morality, and place public interests above his own;

e) To be an active proponent of the ideas of socialist internationalism and Soviet patriotism among the masses of the working people; to combat survivals of nationalism and chauvinism; to contribute by word and by deed to the consolidation of the friendship of the peoples of the USSR and the fraternal bonds linking the Soviet people with the peoples of the countries of the socialist camp, with the proletarians and other working people in all countries;

* Adopted by the Twenty-second Congress of the CPSU, as amended by the Twenty-third Congress in 1966.

f) To strengthen to the utmost the ideological and organizational unity of the Party; to safeguard the Party against the infiltration of people unworthy of the lofty name of Communist; to be truthful and honest with the Party and the people; to display vigilance, to guard Party and state secrets;

g) To develop criticism and self-criticism, boldly lay bare shortcomings and strive for their removal; to combat ostentation, conceit, complacency, and parochial tendencies; to rebuff firmly all attempts at suppressing criticism; to resist all actions injurious to the Party and the state, and to give information of them to Party bodies, up to and including the C.C. CPSU;

h) To implement undeviatingly the Party's policy with regard to the proper selection of personnel according to their political qualifications and personal qualities. To be uncompromising whenever the Leninist principles of the selection and education of personnel are infringed;

i) To observe Party and state discipline, which is equally binding on all Party members. The Party has one discipline, one law, for all Communists, irrespective of their past services or the positions they occupy;

j) To help, in every possible way, to strengthen the defense potential of the USSR; to wage an unflagging struggle for peace and friendship among nations;

3. A Party member has the right:

a) To elect and be elected to Party bodies;

b) To discuss freely questions of the Party's policies and practical activities at Party meetings, conferences and congresses, at the meetings of Party committees and in the Party press; to table motions; openly to express and uphold his opinion as long as the Party organization concerned has not adopted a decision;

c) To criticize any Communist, irrespective of the position he holds, at Party meetings, conferences and congresses, and at the plenary meetings of Party committees. Those who commit the offense of suppressing criticism or victimizing anyone for criticism are responsible to and will be penalized by the Party, to the point of expulsion from the CPSU;

d) To attend in person all Party meetings and all bureau and committee meetings that discuss his activities of conduct;

e) To address any question, statement or proposal to any Party body, up to and including the C.C. CPSU, and to demand an answer on the substance of his address

4. Applicants are admitted to Party membership only individually. Membership of the Party is open to politically conscious and active workers, peasants and representatives of the intelligentsia, devoted to the communist cause. New members are admitted from among the candidate members who have passed through the established probationary period.

Persons may join the Party on attaining the age of eighteen. Young people up to the age of twenty-three may join the Party only through the Leninist Young Communist League of the Soviet Union (YCL).

The procedure for the admission of candidate members to full Party membership is as follows:

a) Applicants for Party membership must submit recommendations from three members of the CPSU who have a Party standing of not less than five years and who know the applicants from having worked with them, professionally and socially, for not less than one year.

Note 1. Members of the YCL who join the party shall submit a recommendation of the district or city committee of the YCL, which is the equivalent of the recommendation of one party member.

Note 2. Members and alternate members of the C.C. CPSU shall refrain from giving recommendations.

b) Applications for Party membership are discussed and a decision is taken by the general meeting of the primary Party organization; the decision is considered adopted if voted by no less than two thirds of the party members at the meeting, and takes effect after endorsement by the district Party committee, or by the city Party committee in cities with no district divisions.

The presence of those who have recommended an applicant for Party membership at the discussion of the application concerned is optional;

c) Citizens of the USSR who formerly belonged to the Communist or Workers' Party of another country are admitted to membership of the Communist Party of the Soviet Union in conformity with the rules established by the C.C. CPSU.

Former members of other parties are admitted to membership of the CPSU in conformity with the regular procedure, except that their admission must be endorsed by a regional or territorial committee or the C.C. of the Communist Party of a Union Republic.

5. Communists recommending applicants for Party membership are responsible to Party organizations for the impartiality of their description of the moral qualities and professional and political qualifications of those they recommend.

6. The Party standing of those admitted to membership dates from the day when the general meeting of the primary Party organization decides to accept them as full members.

7. The procedure of registering members and candidate members of the Party, and their transfer from one organization to another is determined by the appropriate instructions of the C.C. CPSU.

8. If a Party member or candidate member fails to pay membership dues for three months in succession without sufficient reason, the matter shall be discussed by the primary Party organization. If it is revealed as a result that the Party member or candidate member in question has virtually lost contact with the Party organization, he shall be regarded as having ceased to be a member of the Party; the primary Party organization shall pass a decision thereon and submit it to the district or city committee of the Part for endorsement.

9. A Party member or candidate member who fails to fulfill his duties as laid down in the Rules, or commits other offenses, shall be called to account, and may be subjected to the penalty of admonition, reprimand (severe reprimand), or reprimand (severe reprimand) with entry in the registration card. The highest Party penalty is expulsion from the Party.

In the case of insignificant offenses, measures of Party education and influence should be applied—in the form of comradely criticism, Party censure, warning, or reproof.

When the question of expelling a member from the Party is discussed, the maximum attention must be shown, and the grounds for the charges preferred against him must be thoroughly investigated.

10. The decision to expel a Communist from the Party is made by the general meeting of a primary Party organization. The decision of the primary Party organization expelling a member is regarded as adopted if not less than two thirds of the Party members attending the meeting have voted for it, and takes effect after endorsement by the district or city Party committee.

Until such time as the decision to expel him is endorsed by a district or city Party committee, the Party member or candidate member retains his membership card and is entitled to attend closed Party meetings.

An expelled Party member retains the right to appeal, within the period of two months, to the higher Party bodies, up to and including the C.C. CPSU.

11. The question of calling a member or alternate member of the C.C. of the Communist Party of a Union Republic, of a territorial, regional, area, city or district

Party committee, as well as a member of an auditing commission, to account before the Party is discussed by primary Party organizations.

Party organizations pass decisions imposing penalties on members or alternate members of the said Party committees, or on members of auditing commissions, in conformity with the regular procedure.

A Party organization which proposes expelling a Communist from the CPSU communicates its proposal to the Party committee of which he is a member. A decision expelling from the Party a member or alternate member of the C.C. of the Communist Party of a Union Republic or a territorial, regional, area, city or district Party committee, or a member of an auditing commission, is taken at the plenary meeting of the committee concerned by a majority of two thirds of the membership.

The decision to expel from the Party a member or alternate member of the Central Committee of the CPSU, or a member of the Central Auditing Commission, is made by the Party congress, and in the interval between two congresses, by a plenary meeting of the Central Committee, by a majority of two thirds of its members.

12. Should a Party member commit an indictable offense, he shall be expelled from the Party and prosecuted in conformity with the law.

13. Appeals against expulsion from the Party or against the imposition of a penalty, as well as the decisions of Party organizations on expulsion from the Party shall be examined by the appropriate Party bodies within not more than one month from the date of their receipt.

II.   Candidate Members

14. All persons joining the Party must pass through a probationary period as candidate members in order to more thoroughly familiarize themselves with the Program and the Rules of the CPSU and prepare for admission to full membership of the Party.   Party organizations must assist candidates to prepare for admission to full membership of the Party, and test their personal qualities.

The period of probationary membership shall be one year.

15. The procedure for the admission of candidate members (individual admission, submission of recommendations, decision of the primary organization as to admission, and its endorsement) is identical with the procedure for the admission of Party members.

16. On the expiration of a candidate member's probationary period the primary Party organization discusses and passes a decision on his admission to full membership.   Should a candidate member fail, in the course of his probationary period, to prove his worthiness, and should his personal traits make it evident that he cannot be admitted to membership of the CPSU, the Party organization shall pass a decision rejecting his admission to membership of the Party; after endorsement of that decision by the district or city Party committee, he shall cease to be considered a candidate member of the CPSU.

17. Candidate members of the Party participate in all the activities of their Party organizations; they shall have a consultative voice at Party meetings.   They may not be elected to any leading Party body, nor may they be elected delegates to a Party conference or congress.

18. Candidate members of the CPSU pay membership dues at the same rate as full members.

III.   Organizational Structure of the Party.   Inner-Party Democracy

19. The guiding principle of the organizational structure of the Party is democratic centralism, which signifies:

a) Election of all leading Party bodies, from the lowest to the highest;

b) Periodical reports of Party bodies to their Party organizations and to higher bodies;

c) Strict Party discipline and subordination of the minority to the majority;

d) The decisions of higher bodies are obligatory for lower bodies.

20. The Party is built on the territorial-and-production principle: primary organizations are established wherever Communists are employed, and are associated territorially in district, city, etc., organizations. An organization serving a given area is higher than any Party organization serving part of that area.

21. All Party organizations are autonomous in the decision of local questions, unless their decisions conflict with Party policy.

22. The highest leading body of a Party organization is the general meeting (in the case of primary organizations), conference (in the case of district, city, area, regional or territorial organizations), or congress (in the case of the Communist Parties of the Union Republics and the Communist Party of the Soviet Union).

23. The general meeting, conference or congress, elects a bureau or committee which acts as its executive body and directs all the current work of the Party organization.

24. The election of Party bodies shall be effected by secret ballot. In an election, all Party members have the unlimited right to challenge candidates and to criticize them. Each candidate shall be voted upon separately. A candidate is considered elected if more than one half those attending the meeting, conference, or congress have voted for him. At elections of all party organs—from primary organizations to the Central Committee of the CPSU—the principle of systemative renewal of their staff and continuity of leadership will be observed.

26. A member or alternate member of the C.C. CPSU must by his entire activity justify the great trust placed in him by the Party. A member or alternate member of the C.C. CPSU who degrades his honor and dignity may not remain on the Central Committee. The question of the removal of a member or alternate member of the C.C. CPSU from that body shall be decided by a plenary meeting of the Central Committee by secret ballot. The decision is regarded as adopted if not less than two thirds of the membership of the C.C. CPSU vote for it.

The question of the removal of a member or alternate member of the C.C. of the Communist Party of a Union Republic, or of a territorial, regional, area, city or district Party committee from the Party body concerned is decided by a plenary meeting of that body. The decision is regarded as adopted if not less than two thirds of the membership of the committee in question vote for it by secret ballot.

A member of the Central Auditing Commission who does not justify the great trust placed in him by the Party shall be removed from that body. This question shall be decided by a meeting of the Central Auditing Commission. The decision is regarded as adopted if not less than two thirds of the membership of the Central Auditing Commission vote by secret ballot for the removal of the member concerned from that body.

The question of the removal of a member from the auditing commission of a republican, territorial, regional, area, city or district Party organization shall be decided by a meeting of the appropriate commission according to the procedure established for members and alternate members of Party committees.

27. The free and businesslike discussion of questions of Party policy in individual Party organizations or in the Party as a whole is the inalienable right of every Party member and an important principle of inner-Party democracy. Only on the basis of inner-Party democracy is it possible to develop criticism and self-criticism and to strengthen Party discipline, which must be conscious and not mechanical.

Discussion of controversial or insufficiently clear issues may be held within the framework of individual organizations or the Party as a whole.

Partywide discussion is necessary:

a) If the necessity is recognized by several Party organizations at regional or republican level;

b) If there is not a sufficiently solid majority in the Central Committee on major questions of Party policy;

c) If the C.C. CPSU considers it necessary to consult the Party as a whole on any particular question of policy.

Wide discussion, especially discussion on a countrywide scale, of questions of Party policy must be so held as to ensure for Party members the free expression of their views and preclude attempts to form factional groupings destroying Party unity, attempts to split the Party.

28. The supreme principle of Party leadership is collective leadership, which is an absolute requisite for the normal functioning of Party organizations, the proper education of cadres, and the promotion of the activity and initiative of Communists. The cult of the individual and the violations of inner-Party democracy resulting from it must not be tolerated in the Party; they are incompatible with the Leninist principles of Party life.

Collective leadership does not exempt individuals in office from personal responsibility for the job entrusted to them.

29. The Central Committees of the Communist Parties of the Union Republics, and territorial, regional, area, city and district Party committees shall systematically inform Party organizations of their work in the interim between congresses and conferences.

30. Meetings of the active of district, city, area, regional and territorial Party organizations and of the Communist Parties of the Union Republics shall be held to discuss major decisions of the Party and to work out measures for their execution, as well as to examine questions of local significance.

IV. Higher Party Organs

31. The supreme organ of the Communist Party of the Soviet Union is the Party Congress. Congresses are convened by the Central Committee at least once in four years. The convocation of a Party Congress and its agenda shall be announced at least six weeks before the Congress. Extraordinary congresses are convened by the Central Committee of the Party on its own initiative or on the demand of not less than one third of the total membership represented at the preceding Party Congress. Extraordinary congresses shall be convened within two months. A congress is considered properly constituted if not less than one half of the total Party membership is represented at it.

The rates of representation at a Party Congress are determined by the Central Committee.

32. Should the Central Committee of the Party fail to convene an extraordinary congress within the period specified in Article 31, the organizations which demanded it have the right to form an Organizing Committee which shall enjoy the powers of the Central Committee of the Party in respect of the convocation of the extraordinary congress.

33. The Congress:

a) Hears and approves the reports of the Central Committee, of the Central Auditing Commission, and of the other central organizations;

b) Reviews, amends and endorses the Program and the Rules of the Party;

c) Determines the line of the Party in matters of home and foreign policy, and examines and decides the most important questions of communist construction;

d) Elects the Central Committee and the Central Auditing Commission.

34. The number of members to be elected to the Central Committee and to the Central Auditing Commission is determined by the Congress. In the event of

vacancies occurring in the Central Committee, they are filled from among the alternate members of the C.C. CPSU elected by the Congress.

35. Between Congresses, the Central Committee of the Communist Party of the Soviet Union directs the activities of the Party, the local Party bodies, selects and appoints leading functionaries, directs the work of central government bodies and public organizations of working people through the Party groups in them, sets up various Party organs, institutions and enterprises and directs their activities, appoints the editors of the central newspapers and journals operating under its control, and distributes the funds of the Party budget and controls its execution.

The Central Committee represents the CPSU in its relations with other parties.

36. The C.C. CPSU shall keep the Party organizations regularly informed of its work.

37. The Central Auditing Commission of the CPSU supervises the expeditious and proper handling of affairs by the central bodies of the Party, and audits the accounts of the treasury and the enterprises of the Central Committee of the CPSU.

38. The C.C. CPSU shall hold not less than one plenary meeting every six months. Alternate members of the Central Committee shall attend its plenary meetings with consultative voice.

39. The Central Committee of the Communist Party of the Soviet Union elects a Politburo to direct the work of the Party between plenary meetings and a Secretariat to direct current work, chiefly the selection of cadres and the verification of the fulfillment of Party decisions. The Central Committee elects a General Secretary of the C.C. CPSU.

40. In the period between congresses of the party, the Central Committee of the CPSU may as necessary convene All-Union party conferences for discussion of urgent questions of party policy. The procedure for conducting an All-Union party conference is determined by the C.C. CPSU.

The Central Committee of the Communist Party of the Soviet Union organizes the Party Control Committee of the C.C.

The Party Control Committee of the C.C. CPSU:

a) Verifies the observance of Party discipline by members and candidate members of the CPSU, and takes action against Communists who violate the Program and the Rules of the Party and Party or state discipline, and against violators of Party ethics;

b) Considers appeals against decisions of Central Committees of the Communist Parties of the Union Republics or of territorial and regional Party committees to expel members from the Party or impose Party penalties upon them.

V. Republican, Territorial, Regional, Area, City and District Organizations of the Party

41. The republican, territorial, regional, area, city and district Party organizations and their committees take guidance in their activities from the Program and the Rules of the CPSU, conduct all work for the implementation of Party policy and organize the fulfillment of the directives of the C.C. CPSU within the republics, territories, regions, areas, cities and districts concerned.

42. The basic duties of republican, territorial, regional, area, city and district Party organizations, and of their leading bodies, are:

a) Political and organizational work among the masses, mobilization of the masses for the fulfillment of the tasks of communist construction, for the maximum development of industrial and agricultural production, for the fulfillment and overfulfillment of state plans; solicitude for the steady improvement of the material and cultural standards of the working people;

b) Organization of ideological work, propaganda of Marxism-Leninism, promotion of the communist awareness of the working people, guidance of the local press, radio and television, and control over the activities of cultural and educational institutions;

c) Guidance of Soviets, trade unions, the YCL, the cooperatives and other public organizations through the Party groups in them, and increasingly broader enlistment of working people in the activities of these organizations, development of the initiative and activity of the masses as an essential condition for the gradual transition from socialist statehood to public self-government under communism.

Party organizations must not act in place of government, trade union, co-operative or other public organizations of the working people; they must not allow either the merging of the functions of Party and other bodies or undue parallelism in work;

d) Selection and appointment of leading personnel, their education in the spirit of communist ideas, honesty and truthfulness, and a high sense of responsibility to the Party and the people for the work entrusted to them;

e) Large-scale enlistment of Communists in the conduct of Party activities as nonstaff workers, as a form of social work;

f) Organization of various institutions and enterprises of the Party within the bounds of their republic, territory, region, area, city or district, and guidance of their activities; distribution of Party funds within the given organization; systematic information of the higher Party body and accountability to it for their work.

Leading Bodies of Republican, Territorial and Regional Party Organizations

43. The highest body of regional, territorial and republican Party organizations is the respective regional or territorial Party conference or the congress of the Communist Party of the Union Republic, and in the interim between them the regional committee, territorial committee or the Central Committee of the Communist Party of the Union Republic.

44. Regular regional and territorial Party conferences are convened by the respective regional or territorial committees once every two years. Regular congresses of the Communist Parties of the Union Republics are convened by the C.C. of the Communist Party at least once in every four years. Extraordinary conferences and congresses are convened by decision of regional or territorial committees, or the C.C. of the Communist Parties of the Union Republics, or on the demand of one third of the total membership of the organizations belonging to the regional, territorial or republican Party organization.

The rates of representation at regional and territorial conferences and at congresses of the Communist Parties of the Union Republics are determined by the respective Party committees.

Regional and territorial conferences, and congresses of the Communist Parties of the Union Republics, hear the reports of the respective regional or territorial committees, or the Central Committee of the Communist Party of the Union Republic, and of the auditing commission; discuss at their own discretion other matters of Party, economic and cultural development, and elect the regional or territorial committee, the Central Committee of the Union Republic, the auditing commission and the delegates to the Congress of the CPSU.

In the period between congresses of the Communist Parties of the Union Republics, for discussion of important questions for action by the party organization, the C.C. of the Communist Party can as necessary convene republic Party conferences. The procedure for conducting republic Party conferences shall be determined by the C.C. of the Communist Party of the Union Republic.

45. The regional and territorial committees and the Central Committees of the Communist Parties of the Union Republics elect bureaus, which also include secretaries of the committees. The secretaries must have a Party standing of not less than five years. The plenary meetings of the committees also confirm the

chairmen of Party commissions, heads of departments of these committees, editors or Party newspapers and journals.

Regional and territorial committees and the Central Committees of the Communist Parties of the Union Republics may set up secretariats to examine current business and verify the execution of decisions.

46. The plenary meetings of regional and territorial committees and the Central Committees of the Communist Parties of the Union Republics shall be convened at least once every four months.

47. The regional and territorial committees and the Central Committees of the Communist Parties of the Union Republics direct the area, city and district Party organizations, inspect their work and regularly hear reports of area, city and district Party committees.

Party organizations in Autonomous Republics, and in autonomous and other regions forming part of a territory or a Union Republic, function under the guidance of the respective territorial committees or Central Committees of the Communist Parties of the Union Republics.

Leading Bodies of Area, City and District (Urban and Rural) Party Organizations

48. The highest body of an area, city or district Party organization is the area, city and district Party conference or the general meeting of Communists convened by the area, city or district committee at least once in two years, and the extraordinary conference convened by decision of the respective committee or on the demand of one third of the total membership of the Party organization concerned.

The area, city or district conference (general meeting) hears reports of the committee and auditing commission, discusses at its own discretion other questions of Party, economic and cultural development, and elects the area, city and district committee, the auditing commission and delegates to the regional and territorial conference or the congress of the Communist Party of the Union Republic.

The quota of representation to the area, city or district conference are established by the respective Party committee.

49. The area, city or district committee elects a bureau, including the committee secretaries, and confirms the appointment of heads of committee departments and newspaper editors. The secretaries of the area, city and district committees must have a Party standing of at least three years. The committee secretaries are confirmed by the respective regional or territorial committee, or the Central Committee of the Communist Party of the Union Republic.

50. The area, city and district committee organizes and confirms the primary Party organizations, directs their work, regularly hears reports concerning the work of Party organizations, and keeps a register of Communists.

51. The plenary meeting of the area, city and district committee is convened at least once in three months.

52. The area, city and district committee has nonstaff functionaries, sets up standing and *ad hoc* commissions on various aspects of Party work and uses other ways to draw Communists into the activities of the Party committee on social lines.

VI. Primary Party Organizations

53. The Primary Party organizations are the basis of the Party.

Primary Party organizations are formed at the places of work of Party members—in factories, state farms and other enterprises, collective farms, units of the Soviet Army, offices, educational establishments, etc., wherever there are not less than three Party members. Primary Party organizations may also be organized on the residential principle in villages and at house administrations.

54. At enterprises, collective farms and institutions with over 50 Party members and candidate members, shop, sectional, farm, team, departmental, etc., Party

organizations may be formed as units of the general primary Party organizations with the sanction of the district, city or area committee.

Within shop, sectional, etc., organizations, and also within primary Party organizations having less than 50 members and candidate members, Party groups may be formed in the teams and other production units.

55. The highest organ of the primary Party organization is the Party meeting, which is convened at least once a month. In Party organizations having shop organizations, a general Party meeting is conducted at least once every two months.

In large Party organizations with a membership of more than 300 Communists, a general Party meeting is convened when necessary at times fixed by the Party committee or on the demand of a number of shop or departmental Party organizations.

56. For the conduct of current business and primary, shop or departmental Party organizations elects a bureau for the term of one year. The number of its members is fixed by the Party meeting. Primary, shop and departmental Party organizations with less than 15 Party members do not elect a bureau. Instead, they elect a secretary and deputy secretary of the Party organization.

Secretaries of primary, shop and departmental Party organizations must have a Party standing of at least one year.

Primary Party organizations with less than 150 Party members shall have, as a rule, no salaried functionaries released from their regular work.

57. In large factories and offices with more than 300 members and candidate members of the Party, and in exceptional cases in factories and offices with over 100 Communists by virtue of special production conditions and territorial dispersion, subject to the approval of the regional committee, territorial committee or Central Committee of the Communist Party of the Union Republic, Party committees may be formed, the shop and departmental Party organizations at these factories and offices being granted the status of primary Party organizations.

The Party organizations of collective and state farms may set up Party committees if they have a minimum of 50 Communists.

The Party committees are elected for a term of one year. Their numerical composition is fixed by the general Party meeting or conference.

58. Party committees of primary organizations having more than 1,000 Communists, with the permission of the C.C. of the Union Republic Communist Party, may be granted the rights of a district Party committee regarding questions of acceptance into Party membership and on registering regular and candidate members and on examination of personal cases of Communists. Within these organizations, where necessary, Party committees might be created in the shops, while Party organizations of production sectors would be granted the rights of a primary Party organization.

Party committees which have been granted the rights of district Party committees are elected for a two-year term.

In its activities the primary Party organization takes guidance from the Program and the Rules of the CPSU. It conducts its work directly among the working people, rallies them around the Communist Party of the Soviet Union, organizes the masses to carry out the Party policy and to work for the building of communism.

The primary Party organization:

a) Admits new members to the CPSU;

b) Educates Communists in a spirit of loyalty to the Party cause, ideological staunchness and communist ethics;

c) Organizes the study by Communists of Marxist-Leninist theory in close connection with the practice of communist construction and opposes all attempts at revisionist distortions of Marxism-Leninism and its dogmatic interpretation;

d) Ensures the vanguard of Communists in the sphere of labor and in the sociopolitical and economic activities of enterprises, collective farms, institutions, educational establishments, etc.;

e) Acts as the organizer of the working people for the performance of the current tasks of communist construction, heads the socialist emulation movement for the fulfillment of state plans and undertakings of the working people, rallies the masses to disclose and make the best use of untapped resources at enterprises and collective farms, and to apply in production on a broad scale the achievements of science, engineering and the experience of front-rankers; works for the strengthening of labor discipline, the steady increase of labor productivity and improvement of the quality of production, and shows concern for the protection and increase of social wealth at enterprises, state farms and collective farms;

f) Conducts agitational and propaganda work among the masses, educates them in the communist spirit, helps the working people to acquire proficiency in administering state and social affairs;

g) On the basis of extensive criticism and self-criticism, combats cases of bureaucracy, parochialism, and violations of state discipline, thwarts attempts to deceive the state, acts against negligence, waste and extravagance at enterprises, collective farms and offices;

h) Assists the area, city and district committees in their activities and is accountable to them for its work.

The Party organization must see to it that every Communist should observe in his own life and cultivate among working people the moral principles set forth in the Program of the CPSU, in the moral code of the builder of communism:

Loyalty to the communist cause, love of his own socialist country, and of other socialist countries;

Conscientious labor for the benefit of society, for he who does not work, neither shall he eat;

Concern on everyone's part for the protection and increase of social wealth;

Lofty sense of public duty, intolerance of violations of public interests;

Collectivism and comradely mutual assistance: one for all, and all for one;

Humane relations and mutual respect among people; man is to man a friend, comrade and brother;

Honesty and truthfulness, moral purity, unpretentiousness and modesty in public and personal life;

Mutual respect in the family circle and concern for the upbringing of children;

Intolerance of injustice, parasitism, dishonesty, careerism and moneygrubbing;

Friendship and fraternity among all peoples of the USSR, intolerance of national and racial hostility;

Intolerance of the enemies of communism, the enemies of peace and those who oppose the freedom of the peoples;

Fraternal solidarity with the working people of all countries, with all peoples.

59. Primary Party organizations of industrial enterprises and trading establishments, state farms, collective farms and designing organizations, drafting offices and research institutes directly related to production, enjoy the right to control the work of the administration.

The Party organizations at Ministries, State Committees, economic councils and other central and local government or economic agencies and departments which do not have the function of controlling the administration, must actively promote improvement of the apparatus, cultivate among the personnel a high sense of responsibility for work entrusted to them, promote state discipline and the better servicing of the population, firmly combat bureaucracy and red tape, inform the appropriate Party bodies in good time on shortcomings in the work of the respective offices and individuals, regardless of what posts the latter may occupy.

VII.   The Party and the YCL

60. The Leninist Young Communist League of the Soviet Union is an independently acting social organization of young people, an active helper and reserve of the Party.   The YCL helps the Party educate the youth in the communist spirit, draw it into the work of building a new society, train a rising generation of harmoniously developed people who will live and work and administer public affairs under communism.

61. YCL organizations enjoy the right of broad initiative in discussing and submitting to the appropriate Party organizations questions related to the work of enterprises, collective farms and offices.   They must be active levers in the implementation of Party directives in all spheres of communist construction, especially where there are no primary Party organizations.

62. The YCL conducts its activities under the guidance of the Communist Party of the Soviet Union.   The work of the local YCL organizations is directed and controlled by the appropriate republican, territorial, regional, area, city and district Party organizations.

In their communist educational work among the youth, local Party bodies and primary Party organizations rely on the support of the YCL organizations, and uphold and promote their useful undertakings.

63. Members of the YCL who have been admitted into the CPSU cease to belong to the YCL the moment they join the Party, provided they do not hold leading posts in YCL organizations.

VIII.   Party Organizations in the Soviet Army

64. Party organizations in the Soviet Army take guidance in their work from the Program and the Rules of the CPSU and operate on the basis of instructions issued by the Central Committee.

The Party organizations of the Soviet Army carry through the policy of the Party in the Armed Forces, rally servicemen round the Communist Party, educate them in the spirit of Marxism-Leninism and boundless loyalty to the socialist homeland, actively further the unity of the army and the people, work for the strengthening of military discipline, rally servicemen to carry out the tasks of military and political training and acquire skill in the use of new technique and weapons, and to irreproachably perform their military duty and the orders and instructions of the command.

65. The guidance of Party work in the Armed Forces is exercised by the Central Committee of the CPSU through the Chief Political Administration of the Soviet Army and Navy, which functions as a department of the C.C. CPSU.

The chiefs of the political administrations of military areas and fleets, and chiefs of the political administrations of armies must be Party members of five years' standing, and the chiefs of political departments of military formations must be Party members of three years' standing.

66. The Party organizations and political bodies of the Soviet Army maintain close contact with local Party committees, and keep them informed about political work in the military units.   The secretaries of military Party organizations and chiefs of political bodies participate in the work of local Party committees.

IX.   Party Groups in Non-Party Organizations

67. At congresses, conferences and meetings and in the elective bodies of Soviets, trade unions, cooperatives and other mass organizations of the working people, having at least three Party members, Party groups are formed for the purpose of

strengthening the influence of the Party in every way and carrying out Party policy among non-Party people, strengthening Party and state discipline, combating bureaucracy, and verifying the fulfillment of Party and government directives.

68. The Party groups are subordinate to the appropriate Party bodies: the Central Committee of the Communist Party of the Soviet Union, the Central Committees of the Communist Parties of the Union Republics, territorial, regional, area, city or district Party committees.

In all matters the groups must strictly and unswervingly abide by decisions of the leading Party bodies.

X. Party Funds

69. The funds of the Party and its organizations are derived from membership dues, incomes from Party enterprises and other revenue.

70. The monthly membership dues for Party members and candidate members are as follows:

Monthly earnings	Dues	
up to 50 rubles	10 kopeks	
from 51 to 100 rubles	0.5%	of the
from 101 to 150 rubles	1.0	
from 151 to 200 rubles	1.5	monthly
from 201 to 250 rubles	2.0	
from 251 to 300 rubles	2.5	earnings
over 300 rubles	3.0	

71. An entrance fee of 2 percent of monthly earnings is paid on admission to the Party as a candidate member.

Constitution of the Union of Soviet Socialist Republics*

I. The Social Structure

Article 1. The Union of Soviet Socialist Republics is a socialist state of workers and peasants.

Article 2. The political foundation of the USSR is the Soviets of Working People's Deputies, which grew and became strong as a result of the overthrow of the power of the landlords and capitalists and the attainment of the dictatorship of the proletariat.

Article 3. All power in the USSR is vested in the working people of town and country as represented by the Soviets of Working People's Deputies.

Article 4. The economic foundation of the USSR is the socialist system of economy and the socialist ownership of the instruments and means of production, firmly established as a result of the abolition of the capitalist system of economy, private ownership of the instruments and means of production, and the exploitation of man by man.

Article 5. Socialist property in the USSR exists either in the form of state property (belonging to the whole people) or in the form of cooperative and collective-farm property (the property of collective farms or cooperative societies).

Article 6. The land, its mineral wealth, waters, forests, the factories and mines, rail, water and air transport facilities, the banks, means of communication, large state-organized agricultural enterprises (state farms, machine and tractor stations, etc.), as well as municipal enterprises and the bulk of the dwelling-houses in the cities and industrial localities, are state property, that is, belong to the whole people.

Article 7. The enterprises of the collective farms and cooperative organizations, with their livestock, buildings, implements, and output, are the common, socialist property of the collective farms and cooperative organizations.

Every collective-farm household, in addition to its basic income from the collective farm, has for its own use a small plot of land attached to the house and, as its own property, a dwelling-house, livestock, poultry, and minor agricultural implements—in conformity with the rules of the Agricultural Artel.

Article 8. The land occupied by the collective farms is made over to them for their free use for an unlimited time, that is, in perpetuity.

---

* As amended to January, 1967. A new Constitution is now under preparation.

Article 9. In addition to the socialist system of economy, which is the predominant form of economy in the USSR, the law permits the small private undertakings of individual peasants and handicraftsmen based on their own labor and precluding the exploitation of the labor of others.

Article 10. The right of citizens to own, as their personal property, income and savings derived from work, to own a dwelling-house and a supplementary husbandry, articles of household and articles of personal use and convenience, is protected by law, as is also the right of citizens to inherit personal property.

Article 11. The economic life of the USSR is determined and guided by the state economic plan for the purpose of increasing the wealth of society as a whole, steadily raising the material and cultural standards of the working people and strengthening the independence of the USSR and its capacity for defense.

Article 12. Work in the USSR is a duty and a matter of honor for every able-bodied citizen, in accordance with the principle: "He who does not work, neither shall he eat."

The principle applied in the USSR is that of socialism: "From each according to his ability, to each according to his work."

II. The State Structure

Article 13. The Union of Soviet Socialist Republics is a federal state, formed on the basis of a voluntary union of equal Soviet Socialist Republics, namely:

The Russian Soviet Federative Socialist Republic
The Ukrainian Soviet Socialist Republic
The Belorussian Soviet Socialist Republic
The Uzbek Soviet Socialist Republic
The Kazakh Soviet Socialist Republic
The Georgian Soviet Socialist Republic
The Azerbaijan Soviet Socialist Republic
The Lithuanian Soviet Socialist Republic
The Moldavian Soviet Socialist Republic
The Latvian Soviet Socialist Republic
The Kirghiz Soviet Socialist Republic
The Tadzhik Soviet Socialist Republic
The Armenian Soviet Socialist Republic
The Turkmen Soviet Socialist Republic
The Estonian Soviet Socialist Republic

Article 14. The jurisdiction of the Union of Soviet Socialist Republics, as represented by its higher organs of state power and organs of state administration, covers:

a) Representation of the USSR in international relations, conclusion, ratification and denunciation of treaties of the USSR with other states, establishment of general procedure governing the relations of the Union Republics with foreign states;

b) Questions of war and peace;

c) Admission of new republics into the USSR;

d) Control over the observance of the Constitution of the USSR, and ensuring conformity of the Constitutions of the Union Republics with the Constitution of the USSR;

e) Approval of changes to boundaries between Union Republics;

f) Approval of the formation of new Autonomous Republics and Autonomous Regions within Union Republics;

g) Organization of the defense of the USSR, direction of all the Armed Forces or the USSR, definition of guiding principles for the organization of the military formations of the Union Republics;

h) Foreign trade on the basis of state monopoly;

i) Safeguarding the security of the state;

j) Determination of the economic plans of the USSR;

k) Approval of the consolidated state budget of the USSR and of the report on its implementation; fixing taxes and revenues that go to the Union, Republican and local budgets;

l) Administration of banks, industrial and agricultural institutions and enterprises and trading enterprises under Union jurisdiction; general direction of industry and building under Union-Republican jurdisdiction;

m) Administration of transport and communications of all-Union importance;

n) Direction of the monetary and credit system;

o) Organization of state insurance;

p) Contracting and granting of loans;

q) Definition of the basic principles of land tenure and of the use of mineral wealth, forests and waters;

r) Definition of the basic principles in the spheres of education and public health;

s) Organization of a uniform system of economic statistics;

t) Definition of the fundamentals of labor legislation;

u) Definition of the fundamentals of legislation on the judicial system and judicial procedure and the fundamentals of criminal and civil legislation;

v) Legislation on Union citizenship; legislation on rights of foreigners;

w) Definition of the fundamentals of legislation on marriage and the family;

x) Promulgation of all-Union acts of amnesty.

Article 15. The sovereignty of the Union Republics is limited only in the spheres defined in Article 14 of the Constitution of the USSR. Outside of these spheres each Union Republic exercises state authority independently. The USSR protects the sovereign rights of the Union Republics.

Article 16. Each Union Republic has its own Constitution, which takes account of the specific features of the Republic and is drawn up in full conformity with the Constitution of the USSR.

Article 17. The right freely to secede from the USSR is reserved to every Union Republic.

Article 18. The territory of a Union Republic may not be altered without its consent.

Article 18a. Each Union Republic has the right to enter into direct relations with foreign states and to conclude agreements and exchange diplomatic and consular representatives with them.

Article 18b. Each Union Republic has its own Republican military formations.

Article 19. The laws of the USSR have the same force within the territory of every Union Republic.

Article 20. In the event of divergence between a law of a Union Republic and a law of the Union, the Union law shall prevail.

Article 21. Uniform Union citizenship is established for citizens of the USSR. Every citizen of a Union Republic is a citizen of the USSR.

Article 22. The Russian Soviet Federative Socialist Republic includes the Bashkirian, Buryat, Daghestan, Kabardinian-Balkar, Kalmyk, Karelian, Komi, Mari, Mordovian, North Ossetian, Tatar, Tuva, Udmurt, Checheno-Ingush, Chuvash and Yakut Autonomous Soviet Socialist Republics; and the Adygei, Gorny Altai, Jewish, Karachai-Cherkess and Khakass Autonomous Regions.

Article 23. Repealed.

Article 24. The Azerbaijan Soviet Socialist Republic includes the Nakhichevan Autonomous Soviet Socialist Republic and the Nagorny Karabakh Autonomous Region.

Article 25. The Georgian Soviet Socialist Republic includes the Abkhazian and Adzharian Autonomous Soviet Socialist Republics and the South Ossetian Autonomous Region.

Article 26. The Uzbek Soviet Socialist Republic includes the Kara-Kalpak Autonomous Soviet Socialist Republic.

Article 27. The Tadzhik Soviet Socialist Republic includes the Gorny Badakh-shan Autonomous Region.

Article 28. The settlement of questions pertaining to the regional or territorial administrative division of the Union Republics comes within the jurisdiction of the Union Republics.

Article 29. Repealed.

III. The Higher Organs of State Power in the Union of Soviet Socialist Republics

Article 30. The highest organ of state power in the USSR is the Supreme Soviet of the USSR.

Article 31. The Supreme Soviet of the USSR exercises all rights vested in the Union of Soviet Socialist Republics in accordance with Article 14 of the Constitution, in so far as they do not, by virtue of the Constitution, come within the jurisdiction of organs of the USSR that are accountable to the Supreme Soviet of the USSR, that is, the Presidium of the Supreme Soviet of the USSR, the Council of Ministers of the USSR, and the Ministries of the USSR.

Article 32. The legislative power of the USSR is exercised exclusively by the Supreme Soviet of the USSR.

Article 33. The Supreme Soviet of the USSR consists of two Chambers: the Soviet of the Union and the Soviet of Nationalities.

Article 34. The Soviet of the Union is elected by the citizens of the USSR voting by election districts on the basis of one deputy for every 300,000 of the population.

Article 35. The Soviet of Nationalities is elected by the citizens of the USSR voting by Union Republics, Autonomous Republics, Autonomous Regions, and National Areas on the basis of thirty-two deputies from each Union Republic, eleven deputies from each Autonomous Republic, five deputies from each Autonomous Region, and one deputy from each National Area.

Article 36. The Supreme Soviet of the USSR is elected for a term of four years.

Article 37. The two Chambers of the Supreme Soviet of the USSR, the Soviet of the Union and the Soviet of Nationalities, have equal rights.

Article 38. The Soviet of the Union and the Soviet of Nationalities have equal powers to initiate legislation.

Article 39. A law is considered adopted if passed by both Chambers of the Supreme Soviet of the USSR by a simple majority vote in each.

Article 40. Laws passed by the Supreme Soviet of the USSR are published in the languages of the Union Republics over the signatures of the President and Secretary of the Presidium of the Supreme Soviet of the USSR.

Article 41. Sessions of the Soviet of the Union and of the Soviet of Nationalities begin and terminate simultaneously.

Article 42. The Soviet of the Union elects a Chairman of the Soviet of the Union and four Vice-Chairmen.

Article 43. The Soviet of Nationalities elects a Chairman of the Soviet of Nationalities and four Vice-Chairmen.

Article 44. The Chairmen of the Soviet of the Union and the Soviet of Nationalities preside at the sittings of the respective Chambers and have charge of the conduct of their business and proceedings.

Article 45. Joint sittings of the two Chambers of the Supreme Soviet of the USSR are presided over alternately by the Chairman of the Soviet of the Union and the Chairman of the Soviet of Nationalities.

Article 46. Sessions of the Supreme Soviet of the USSR are convened by the Presidium of the Supreme Soviet of the USSR twice a year.

Extraordinary sessions are convened by the Presidium of the Supreme Soviet of the USSR at its discretion or on the demand of one of the Union Republics.

Article 47. In the event of disagreement between the Soviet of the Union and the Soviet of Nationalities, the question is referred for settlement to a conciliation commission formed by the Chambers on a parity basis. If the conciliation commission fails to arrive at an agreement or if its decision fails to satisfy one of the Chambers, the question is considered for a second time by the Chambers. Failing agreement between the two Chambers, the Presidium of the Supreme Soviet of the USSR dissolves the Supreme Soviet of the USSR and orders new elections.

Article 48. The Supreme Soviet of the USSR at a joint sitting of the two Chambers elects the Presidium of the Supreme Soviet of the USSR, consisting of a Chairman of the Presidium of the Supreme Soviet of the USSR, fifteen Vice-Chairmen—one from each Union Republic, a Secretary of the Presidium and twenty members of the Presidium of the Supreme Soviet of the USSR.

The Presidium of the Supreme Soviet of the USSR is accountable to the Supreme Soviet of the USSR for all its activities.

Article 49. The Presidium of the Supreme Soviet of the USSR:

a) Convenes the sessions of the Supreme Soviet of the USSR;

b) Issues decrees;

c) Interprets the laws of the USSR in operation;

d) Dissolves the Supreme Soviet of the USSR in conformity with Article 47 of the Constitution of the USSR and orders new elections;

e) Conducts nationwide polls (referendums) on its own initiative or on the demand of one of the Union Republics;

f) Annuls decisions and orders of the Council of Ministers of the USSR and of the Councils of Ministers of the Union Republics if they do not conform to law;

g) In the intervals between sessions of the Supreme Soviet of the USSR, releases and appoints Ministers of the USSR on the recommendation of the Chairman of the Council of Ministers of the USSR, subject to subsequent confirmation by the Supreme Soviet of the USSR;

h) Institutes decorations (Orders and Medals) and titles of honor of the USSR;

i) Awards Orders and Medals and confers titles of honor of the USSR;

j) Exercises the right of pardon;

k) Institutes military titles, diplomatic ranks and other special titles;

l) Appoints and removes the high command of the Armed Forces of the USSR;

m) In the intervals between sessions of the Supreme Soviet of the USSR, proclaims a state of war in the event of military attack on the USSR, or when necessary to fulfill international treaty obligations concerning mutual defense against aggression;

n) Orders general or partial mobilization;

o) Ratifies and denounces international treaties of the USSR;

p) Appoints and recalls plenipotentiary representatives of the USSR to foreign states;

q) Receives the letters of credence and recall of diplomatic representatives accredited to it by foreign states;

r) Proclaims martial law in separate localities or throughout the USSR in the interests of the defense of the USSR or of the maintenance of law and order and the security of the state.

Article 50. The Soviet of the Union and the Soviet of Nationalities elect Credentials Committees to verify the credentials of the members of the respective Chambers.

On the report of the Credentials Committees, the Chambers decide whether to recognize the credentials of deputies or to annul their election.

Article 51. The Supreme Soviet of the USSR, when it deems necessary, appoints commissions of investigation and audit on any matter.

It is the duty of all institutions and officials to comply with the demands of such commissions and to submit to them all necessary materials and documents.

Article 52. A member of the Supreme Soviet of the USSR may not be prosecuted or arrested without the consent of the Supreme Soviet of the USSR, or, when the Supreme Soviet of the USSR is not in session, without the consent of the Presidium of the Supreme Soviet of the USSR.

Article 53. On the expiration of the term of office of the Supreme Soviet of the USSR, or on its dissolution prior to the expiration of its term of office, the Presidium of the Supreme Soviet of the USSR retains its powers until the newly elected Supreme Soviet of the USSR shall have formed a new Presidium of the Supreme Soviet of the USSR.

Article 54. On the expiration of the term of office of the Supreme Soviet of the USSR, or in the event of its dissolution prior to the expiration of its term of office, the Presidium of the Supreme Soviet of the USSR orders new elections to be held within a period not exceeding two months from the date of expiration of the term of office or dissolution of the Supreme Court of the USSR.

Article 55. The newly elected Supreme Soviet of the USSR is convened by the outgoing Presidium of the Supreme Soviet of the USSR not later than three months after the elections.

Article 56. The Supreme Soviet of the USSR, at a joint sitting of the two Chambers, appoints the Government of the USSR, namely, the Council of Ministers of the USSR.

IV. The Higher Organs of State Power in the Union Republics

Article 57. The highest organ of state power in a Union Republic is the Supreme Soviet of the Union Republic.

Article 58. The Supreme Soviet of a Union Republic is elected by the citizens of the Republic for a term of four years.

The basis of representation is established by the Constitution of the Union Republic.

Article 59. The Supreme Soviet of a Union Republic is the sole legislative organ of the Republic.

Article 60. The Supreme Soviet of a Union Republic:

a) Adopts the Constitution of the Republic and amends it in conformity with Article 16 of the Constitution of the USSR;

b) Confirms the Constitutions of the Autonomous Republics forming part of it and defines the boundaries of their territories;

c) Approves the economic plan and the budget of the Republic;

d) Exercises the right of amnesty and pardon of citizens sentenced by the judicial organs of the Union Republic;

e) Decides questions of representation of the Union Republic in its international relations;

f) Determines the manner of organizing the Republic's military formations.

Article 61. The Supreme Soviet of a Union Republic elects the Chairman of the Supreme Soviet of the Union Republic, consisting of a Chairman of the Presidium of the Supreme Soviet of the Union Republic, Vice-Chairmen, a Secretary of the Presidium and members of the Presidium of the Supreme Soviet of the Union Republic.

The powers of the Presidium of the Supreme Soviet of a Union Republic are defined by the Constitution of the Union Republic.

Article 62. The Supreme Soviet of a Union Republic elects a Chairman and Vice-Chairmen to conduct its sittings.

Article 63. The Supreme Soviet of a Union Republic appoints the Government of the Union Republic, namely, the Council of Ministers of the Union Republic.

V. The Organs of State Administration of the Union of Soviet Socialist Republics

Article 64. The highest executive and administrative organ of the state power of the Union of Soviet Socialist Republics is the Council of Ministers of the USSR.

Article 65. The Council of Ministers of the USSR is responsible and accountable to the Supreme Soviet of the USSR, or, in the intervals between sessions of the Supreme Soviet, to the Presidium of the Supreme Soviet of the USSR.

Article 66. The Council of Ministers of the USSR issues decisions and orders on the basis and in pursuance of the laws in operation, and verifies their execution.

Article 67. Decisions and orders of the Council of Ministers of the USSR are binding throughout the territory of the USSR.

Article 68. The Council of Ministers of the USSR:

a) Coordinates and directs the work of the USSR Council of Ministers' state committees and of other institutions subordinate to them.

b) Adopts measures to carry out the economic plan and the state budget, and to strengthen the credit and monetary system;

c) Adopts measures for the maintenance of law and order, for the protection of the interests of the state, and for the safeguarding of the rights of citizens;

d) Exercises general guidance in the sphere of relations with foreign states;

e) Fixes the annual contingent of citizens to be called up for military service and directs the general organization of the Armed Forces of the country;

f) Sets up USSR state committees and whenever necessary, special Committees and Central Boards under the Council of Ministers of the USSR for economic and cultural affairs and defense.

Article 69. The Council of Ministers of the USSR has the right, in respect of those branches of administration and economy which come within the jurisdiction of the USSR, to suspend decisions and orders of the Councils of Ministers of the Union Republics and to annul orders and instructions of Ministers of the USSR, as well as acts of other institutions subordinate to them.

Article 70. The Council of Ministers of the USSR is appointed by the Supreme Soviet of the USSR and consists of:

The Chairman of the Council of Ministers of the USSR

The First Vice-Chairmen of the Council of Ministers of the USSR

The Vice-Chairmen of the Council of Ministers of the USSR

The Ministers of the USSR

The Chairman of the State Planning Committee of the Council of Ministers of the USSR

The Chairman of the State Committee for Construction Affairs, Council of Ministers of the USSR

The Chairman of the State Committee for Material and Technical Supply, Council of Ministers of the USSR

The Chairman of the People's Control Committee of the USSR

The Chairman of the State Committee for Questions of Labor and Wages, Council of Ministers of the USSR

The Chairman of the State Committee for Science and Technology, Council of Ministers of the USSR

The Chairman of the State Committee for Vocational-Technical Education, Council of Ministers of the USSR

The Chairman of the State Procurements Committee, Council of Ministers of the USSR

The Chairman of the State Committee for Forest Economy, Council of Ministers of the USSR

The Chairman of the State Committee for Foreign Economic Relations, Council of Ministers of the USSR

The Chairman of the State Security Committee under the Council of Ministers of the USSR

The Chairman of the All-Union Farm Machinery Association, Council of Ministers of the USSR

The Chairman of the Board of the USSR State Bank

The Director of the Central Statistical Administration under the Council of Ministers of the USSR

The Chairmen of the Councils of Ministers of the Union Republics shall be ex officio members of the Council of Ministers of the USSR.

Article 71. The Government of the USSR or a Minister of the USSR to whom a question of a member of the Supreme Soviet of the USSR is addressed must give a verbal or written reply in the respective Chamber within a period not exceeding three days.

Article 72. The Ministers of the USSR direct the branches of state administration which come within the jurisdiction of the USSR.

Article 73. The Ministers of the USSR, within the limits of the jurisdiction of their respective Ministries, issue orders and instructions on the basis and in pursuance of the laws in operation and also of decisions and orders of the Council of Ministers of the USSR, and verify their execution.

Article 74. The Ministries of the USSR are either all-Union or Union-Republican Ministries.

Article 75. Each all-Union Ministry directs the branch of state administration entrusted to it throughout the territory of the USSR either directly or through bodies appointed by it.

Article 76. The Union-Republican Ministries, as a rule, direct the branches of state administration entrusted to them through corresponding Ministries of the Union Republics; they administer directly only a definite and limited number of enterprises according to a list confirmed by the Presidium of the Supreme Soviet of the USSR.

Article 77. The following Ministries are all-Union Ministries:

Aviation Industry
Motor Vehicle Industry
Foreign Trade
Gas Industry
Civil Aviation
Machine Building for Light Industry and the Food Industry and of Household Appliances
Merchant Marine
Defense Industry
General Machine Building
Instrument Making, Means of Automation and Control Systems
Transportation (Railroad)
Radio Industry
Medium Machine Building
Machine Tool and Tool Industry
Machine Building for Construction, Road Building and Civil Engineering
Shipbuilding Industry
Tractor and Farm Machine Building
Transport Construction
Heavy, Power, and Transport Machine Building

Chemical and Petroleum Machine Building
Electronics Industry
Electrical Equipment Industry
Article 78. The following Ministries are Union-Republic Ministries:
Higher and Specialized Secondary Education
Geology
Public Health
Foreign Affairs
Culture
Light Industry
Lumber, Pulp, and Paper and Wood Processing Industry'
Land Reclamation and Water Resources
Installation and Specialized Construction Work
Meat and Dairy Industry
Petroleum Extracting Industry
Petroleum Refining and Petrochemical Industry
Defense
Defense of Public Order
Food Industry
Building Materials Industry
Education
Fish Industry
Communications
Agriculture
Trade
Coal Industry
Finance
Chemical Industry
Nonferrous Metallurgy
Ferrous Metallurgy
Power and Electrification

VI. The Organs of State Administration of the Union Republics

Article 79. The highest executive and administrative organ of the state power of a Union Republic is the Council of Ministers of the Union Republic.

Article 80. The Council of Ministers of a Union Republic is responsible and accountable to the Supreme Soviet of the Union Republic, or, in the intervals between sessions of the Supreme Soviet of the Union Republic, to the Presidium of the Supreme Soviet of the Union Republic.

Article 81. The Council of Ministers of a Union Republic issues decisions and orders on the basis and in pursuance of the laws in operation of the USSR and of the Union Republic, and of the decisions and orders of the Council of Ministers of the USSR, and verifies their execution.

Article 82. The Council of Ministers of a Union Republic has the right to suspend decisions and orders of the Councils of Ministers of its Autonomous Republics, and to annul decisions and orders of the Executive Committees of the Soviets of Working People's Deputies of its Territories, Regions, and Autonomous Regions.

Article 83. The Council of Ministers of a Union Republic is appointed by the Supreme Soviet of the Union Republic and consists of:
The Chairman of the Council of Ministers of the Union Republic
The Vice-Chairmen of the Council of Ministers
The Ministers

The Chairmen of State Committees, Commissions, and the heads of other departments of the Council of Ministers set up by the Supreme Soviet of the Union Republic in conformity with the Constitution of the Union Republic

Article 84. The Ministers of a Union Republic direct the branches of state administration which come within the jurisdiction of the Union Republic.

Article 85. The Ministers of a Union Republic, within the limits of the jurisdiction of their respective Ministries, issue orders and instructions on the basis and in pursuance of the laws of the USSR and of the Union Republic, of the decisions and orders of the Council of Ministers of the USSR and the Council of Ministers of the Union Republic, and of the orders and instructions of the Union-Republican Ministries of the USSR.

Article 86. The Ministries of a Union Republic are either Union-Republican or Republican Ministries.

Article 87. Each Union-Republican Ministry directs the branch of state administration entrusted to it, and is subordinated both to the Council of Ministers of the Union Republic and to the corresponding Union-Republican Ministry of the USSR.

Article 88. Each Republican Ministry directs the branch of state administration entrusted to it, and is directly subordinate to the Council of Ministers of the Union Republic.

VII. The Higher Organs of State Power in the Autonomous Soviet Socialist Republics

Article 89. The highest organ of state power in an Autonomous Republic is the Supreme Soviet of the Autonomous Republic.

Article 90. The supreme Soviet of an Autonomous Republic is elected by the citizens of the Republic for a term of four years on a basis of representation established by the Constitution of the Autonomous Republic.

Article 91. The Supreme Soviet of an Autonomous Republic is the sole legislative organ of the Autonomous Republic.

Article 92. Each Autonomous Republic has its own Constitution, which takes account of the specific features of the Autonomous Republic and is drawn up in full conformity with the Constitution of the Union Republic.

Article 93. The Supreme Soviet of an Autonomous Republic elects the Presidium of the Supreme Soviet of the Autonomous Republic and appoints the Council of Ministers of the Autonomous Republic, in accordance with its Constitution.

VIII. The Local Organs of State Power

Article 94. The organs of state power in Territories, Regions, Autonomous Regions, Areas, Districts, cities and rural localities (stanitsas, villages, hamlets, kishlaks, auls) are the Soviets of Working People's Deputies.

Article 95. The Soviets of Working People's Deputies of Territories, Regions, Autonomous Regions, Areas, Districts, cities and rural localities (stanitsas, villages, hamlets, kishlaks, auls) are elected by the working people of the respective Territories, Regions, Autonomous Regions, Areas, Districts, cities and rural localities for a term of two years.

Article 96. The basis of representation for Soviets of Working People's Deputies is determined by the Constitutions of the Union Republics.

Article 97. The Soviets of Working People's Deputies direct the work of the organs of administration subordinate to them, ensure the maintenance of law and order, the observance of the laws and the protection of the rights of citizens, direct local economic and cultural affairs and determine and approve local budgets.

Article 98. The Soviets of Working People's Deputies adopt decisions and issue orders within the limits of the powers vested in them by the laws of the USSR and of the Union Republic.

Article 99. The executive and administrative organ of the Soviet of Working People's Deputies of a Territory, Region, Autonomous Region, Area, District, city or rural locality is the Executive Committee elected by it, consisting of a Chairman, Vice-Chairman, a Secretary and members.

Article 100. The executive and administrative organ of the Soviet of Working People's Deputies in a small locality, in accordance with the Constitution of the Union Republic, is the Chairman, the Vice-Chairman and the Secretary elected by the Soviet of Working People's Deputies.

Article 101. The executive organs of the Soviets of Working People's Deputies are directly accountable both to the Soviets of Working People's Deputies which elected them and to the executive organ of the superior Soviet of Working People's Deputies.

IX. The Courts and the Procurator's Office

Article 102. In the USSR justice is administered by the Supreme Court of the USSR, the Supreme Courts of the Union Republics, the Courts of the Territories, Regions, Autonomous Republics, Autonomous Regions and Areas, the Special Courts of the USSR established by decision of the Supreme Soviet of the USSR, and the People's Courts.

Article 103. In all Courts cases are tried with the participation of People's Assessors, except in cases specially provided for by law.

Article 104. The Supreme Court of the USSR is the highest judicial organ. The Supreme Court of the USSR is charged with the supervision of the judicial activities of all the judicial organs of the USSR and of the Union Republics within the limits established by law.

Article 105. The Supreme Court of the USSR is elected by the Supreme Soviet of the USSR for a term of five years.

The Supreme Court of the USSR includes the Chairmen of the Supreme Courts of the Union Republics by virtue of their office.

Article 106. The Supreme Courts of the Union Republics are elected by the Supreme Soviets of the Union Republics for a term of five years.

Article 107. The Supreme Courts of the Autonomous Republics are elected by the Supreme Soviets of the Autonomous Republics for a term of five years.

Article 108. The Courts of Territories, Regions, Autonomous Regions and Areas are elected by the Soviets of Working People's Deputies of the respective Territories, Regions, Autonomous Regions or Areas for a term of five years.

Article 109. People's judges of District (City) People's Courts are elected by the citizens of the districts (cities) on the basis of universal, direct and equal suffrage by secret ballot for a term of five years.

People's Assessors of District (City) People's Courts are elected at general meetings of industrial, office and professional workers, and peasants in the place of their work or residence, and of servicemen in military units, for a term of two years.

Article 110. Judicial proceedings are conducted in the language of the Union Republic, Autonomous Republic or Autonomous Region, persons not knowing this language being guaranteed the opportunity of fully acquainting themselves with the material of the case through an interpreter and likewise the right to use their own language in court.

Article 111. In all Courts of the USSR cases are heard in public, unless otherwise provided for by law, and the accused is guaranteed the right to defense.

Article 112. Judges are independent and subject only to the law.

Article 113. Supreme supervisory power to ensure the strict observance of the law by all Ministries and institutions subordinated to them, as well as by people in office and citizens of the USSR generally, is vested in the Procurator-General of the USSR.

Article 114. The Procurator-General of the USSR is appointed by the Supreme Soviet of the USSR for a term of seven years.

Article 115. Procurators of Republics, Territories, Regions, Autonomous Republics and Autonomous Regions are appointed by the Procurator-General of the USSR for a term of five years.

Article 116. Area, district and city procurators are appointed by the Procurators of the Union Republics, subject to the approval of the Procurator-General of the USSR, for a term of five years.

Article 117. The organs of the Procurator's Office perform their functions independently of any local organs whatsoever, being subordinate solely to the Procurator-General of the USSR.

X. Fundamental Rights and Duties of Citizens

Article 118. Citizens of the USSR have the right to work, that is, the right to guaranteed employment and payment for their work in accordance with its quantity and quality.

The right to work is ensured by the socialist organization of the national economy, the steady growth of the productive forces of Soviet society, the elimination of the possibility of economic crises, and the abolition of unemployment.

Article 119. Citizens of the USSR have the right to rest and leisure.

The right to rest and leisure is ensured by the establishment of a seven-hour day for industrial, office, and professional workers, the reduction of the working day to six hours for arduous trades and to four hours in shops where conditions of work are particularly arduous; by the institution of annual vacations with full pay for industrial, office, and professional workers, and by the provision of a wide network of sanatoriums, holiday homes and clubs for the accommodation of the working people.

Article 120. Citizens of the USSR have the right to maintenance in old age and also in case of sickness or disability.

This right is ensured by the extensive development of social insurance of industrial, office, and professional workers at state expense, free medical service for the working people, and the provision of a wide network of health resorts for the use of the working people.

Article 121. Citizens of the USSR have the right to education.

This right is ensured by universal compulsory eight-year education; by extensive development of secondary polytechnical education, vocational-technical education, and secondary special and higher education based on close ties between the school, real life and production activities; by the utmost development of evening and extramural education; by free education in all schools; by a system of state grants; by instruction in schools in the native language, and by the organization of free vocational, technical and agronomic training for the working people in the factories, state farms, and collective farms.

Article 122. Women in the USSR are accorded all rights on an equal footing with men in all spheres of economic, government, cultural, political, and other social activity.

The possibility of exercising these rights is ensured by women being accorded the same rights as men to work, payment for work, rest and leisure, social insurance and education, and also by state protection of the interests of mother and child, state aid to mothers of large families and to unmarried mothers, maternity leave with full pay, and the provision of a wide network of maternity homes, nurseries and kindergartens.

Article 123. Equality of rights of citizens of the USSR, irrespective of their nationality or race, in all spheres of economic, government, cultural, political and other social activity, is an indefeasible law.

Any direct or indirect restriction of the rights of, or conversely, the establishment of any direct or indirect privileges for, citizens on account of their race or nationality, as well as any advocacy of racial or national exclusiveness or hatred and contempt, are punishable by law.

Article 124. In order to ensure to citizens freedom of conscience, the church in the USSR is separated from the state, and the school from the church. Freedom of religious worship and freedom of antireligious propaganda is recognized for all citizens.

Article 125. In conformity with the interests of the working people, and in order to strengthen the socialist system, the citizens of the USSR are guaranteed by law:

a) Freedom of speech;

b) Freedom of the press;

c) Freedom of assembly, including the holding of mass meetings;

d) Freedom of street processions and demonstrations.

These civil rights are ensured by placing at the disposal of the working people and their organizations printing presses, stocks of paper, public buildings, the streets, communications facilities and other material requisites for the exercise of these rights.

Article 126. In conformity with the interests of the working people, and in order to develop the organizational initiative and political activity of the masses of the people, citizens of the USSR are guaranteed the right to unite in public organizations: trade unions, cooperative societies, youth organizations, sport and defense organizations, cultural, technical and scientific societies; and the most active and politically conscious citizens in the ranks of the working class, working peasants and working intelligentsia voluntarily unite in the Communist Party of the Soviet Union, which is the vanguard of the working people in their struggle to build communist society and is the leading core of all organizations of the working people, both public and state.

Article 127. Citizens of the USSR are guaranteed inviolability of the person. No person may be placed under arrest except by decision of a court or with the sanction of a procurator.

Article 128. The inviolability of the homes of citizens and privacy of correspondence are protected by law.

Article 129. The USSR affords the right of asylum to foreign citizens persecuted for defending the interests of the working people, or for scientific activities, or for struggling for national liberation.

Article 130. It is the duty of every citizen of the USSR to abide by the Constitution of the Union of Soviet Socialist Republics, to observe the laws, to maintain labor discipline, honestly to perform public duties, and to respect the rules of socialist society.

Article 131. It is the duty of every citizen of the USSR to safeguard and fortify public, socialist property as the sacred and inviolable foundation of the Soviet system, as the source of the wealth and might of the country, as the source of the prosperity and culture of all the working people.

Persons committing offenses against public, socialist property are enemies of the people.

Article 132. Universal military service is law.

Military service in the Armed Forces of the USSR is the honorable duty of citizens of the USSR.

Article 133. To defend the country is the sacred duty of every citizen of the USSR. Treason to the Motherland—violation of the oath of allegiance, desertion to the enemy, impairing the military power of the state, espionage—is punishable with all the severity of the law as the most heinous of crimes.

XI. The Electoral System

Article 134. Members of all Soviets of Working People's Deputies—of the Supreme Soviet of the USSR, the Supreme Soviets of the Union Republics, the Soviets of Working People's Deputies of the Territories and Regions, the Supreme Soviets of the Autonomous Republics, the Soviets of Working People's Deputies of the Autonomous Regions, and the Area, District, city and rural (stanitsa, village, hamlet, kishlak, aul) Soviets of Working People's Deputies—are chosen by the electors on the basis of universal, equal and direct suffrage by secret ballot.

Article 135. Elections of deputies are universal: all citizens of the USSR who have reached the age of eighteen, irrespective of race or nationality, sex, religion, education, domicile, social orgin, property status or past activities, have the right to vote in the election of deputies, with the exception of persons who have been legally certified insane.

Every citizen of the USSR who has reached the age of twenty-three is eligible for election to the Supreme Soviet of the USSR, irrespective of race or nationality, sex, religion, education, domicile, social origin, property status or past activities.

Article 136. Elections of deputies are equal: each citizen has one vote; all citizens participate in elections on an equal footing.

Article 137. Women have the right to elect and be elected on equal terms with men.

Article 138. Citizens serving in the Armed Forces of the USSR have the right to elect and be elected on equal terms with all other citizens.

Article 139. Elections of deputies are direct: all Soviets of Working People's Deputies, from rural and city Soviets of Working People's Deputies to the Supreme Soviet of the USSR, are elected by the citizens by direct vote.

Article 140. Voting at elections of deputies is secret.

Article 141. Candidates are nominated for each constituency.

The right to nominate candidates is secured to public organizations and societies of the working people; Communist Party organizations, trade unions, cooperatives, youth organizations and cultural societies.

Article 142. It is the duty of every deputy to report to his electors on his work and on the work of his Soviet of Working People's Deputies, and he may be recalled at any time upon decision of a majority of the electors in the manner established by law.

XII. Arms, Flag, Capital

Article 143. The arms of the Union of Soviet Socialist Republics are a sickle and hammer against a globe depicted in the rays of the sun and surrounded by ears of grain, with the inscription "Workers of All Countries, Unite!" in the languages of the Union Republics. At the top of the arms is a five-pointed star.

Article 144. The state flag of the Union of Soviet Socialist Republics is of red cloth with the sickle and hammer depicted in gold in the upper corner near the staff and above them a five-pointed red star bordered in gold. The ratio of the width to the length is 1:2.

Article 145. The capital of the Union of Soviet Socialist Republics is the City of Moscow.

XIII. Procedure for Amending the Constitution

Article 146. The Constitution of the USSR may be amended only by decision of the Supreme Soviet of the USSR adopted by a majority of not less than two thirds of the votes in each of its Chambers.

Glossary

A

advokat. Lawyer.
Agitprop. Abbreviation for Agitation and Propaganda Section of the Central Committee, CPSU.
agitpunk. Abbreviation for agitation point.
ail. Unit of local government in certain republics.
apilinkov. Unit of local government in certain republics.
artel. A type of collective farm.
ASSR. Initials for autonomous soviet socialist republic.
aul. Unit of local government in certain republics.
avtonomnyy oblast. Autonomous province.

B

barin. Member of the upper class.
barshchina. Compulsory labor.

C

C.C. Initials for the Central Committee.
CEMA. Initials for the Council for Mutual Economic Assistance.
chernozem. The black soil in the steppe.
Cherny Peredel. "Black Redistribution."
chistka. Purge.
Cominform. Communist Information Bureau.
Comintern. Communist International.
CPSU. Initials for the Communist Party, Soviet Union.
CPUSA. Initials for the Communist Party, USA.

D

druzhiny. Semiofficial group of law enforcers or "crime fighters."
duma. Town council in old Russia. Also the elected legislatures under Nicholas II during the years 1906–17.

G

glavki. Abbreviation for chief directorates.
Goelro. Abbreviation for the State Commission for the Electrification of Russia.
gorkom. Abbreviation for the city party committee.
gorod. City.
gorodskaya duma. Town or city council.

Gosbank.   Abbreviation for State Bank.
Gosekonomkommissiya.   Abbreviation for State Economic Commission.
Gosekonomsovet.   Abbreviation for State Economic Council.
Gosplan.   Abbreviation for State Planning Committee.
Gosudarstvenny Sovet.   State Council.
gubernator.   Governor.
guberniya.   Province in old Russia.

I

ispolkom.   Abbreviation for executive committee.
ispravnik.   "Corrector" or police official.

K

KGB.   Initials of Committee for State Security.
khozhdenie v narod.   "Movement to the People."
kolkhoz.   Abbreviation for collective farm.
kolkhoznik.   Collective farmer.
kollektivnyy dogovor.   A collective agreement.
Komsomol.   Abbreviation for All-Union Leninist Communist League of Youth (Young Communist League).
kray.   Region or territory.
kraykom.   Abbreviation for territorial party committee.
kulak.   Propertied peasant.

M

mestnichestvo.   Localism.
mir.   Peasant's village commune.
MTS.   Initials for Machine-Tractor Station.
muzhik.   Peasant.
MVD.   Initials for Ministry of Internal Affairs.

N

nakaz.   Order, or instruction.
Narodnaya Volya.   "Will of the People."
Narodnichestvo.   Populism.
Narodnik.   Populist.
Narodnoe Pravo.   "Party of the People's Right."
NEP.   Initials for New Economic Policy.
Nepman.   Private trader during the NEP.
NKVD.   Initials for People's Commissariat of Internal Affairs.

O

obkom.   Abbreviation for province party committee.
oblast.   Province.
obrok.   Rent.
obshchestvennyy sud.   Public court.
OGPU.   Initials for the Organization of State Political Administration.   More popularly, secret police.
okrug.   Area or circuit.
Orgburo.   Abbreviation for Organization Bureau.
otdel.   Department.

P

podraykomy. Abbreviation for sub-*rayon* party committees.
Politburo. Abbreviation for Political Bureau.
poselok. Settlement.
postanovleniya. Decisions.
Prombank. Abbreviation for Investment Bank for Industry.
provintsiya. Province in old Russia.

R

rasporyazheniya. Orders.
raykom. Abbreviation for district party committee.
rayon. District.
RKK. Initials of *Ratsenochno-Konfliktnaya Kommissiya* (Rates and Disputes Commission).
RSDLP. Initials of Russian Social-Democratic Labor Party.
RSFSR. Initials of Russian Soviet Federative Socialist Republic.
RTS. Initials of Repair and Technical Station.

S

SD. Initials of Social Democrat.
Selkhozbank. Abbreviation for Investment Bank for Agriculture.
selskiy. Village.
sobor. An assembly.
Sovet Ministrov. Council of Ministers.
Sovet Natsionalnostey. Council of Nationalities of the Supreme Soviet, USSR.
Sovet Soyuza. Council of the Union of the Supreme Soviet, USSR.
Sovet Stareyshin. Council of Elders.
sovkhoz. Abbreviation for state farm.
sovnarkhozy. Abbreviation for *sovety narodnogo khozyastva* (regional councils of national economy).
Sovnarkom. Abbreviation for *Sovet Narodniykh Kommissarov* (Council of People's Commissars).
SR. Initials of Socialist Revolutionary.
starosta. Village elder.

T

TASS. Initials of Telegraph Agency of the Soviet Union.
Torgbank. Abbreviation for Trade Bank.
Tsekombank. Abbreviation for Investment Bank for Municipal Construction.
Tsentrosoyuz. Abbreviation for Central Union Cooperative.

U

upravlenie. Division, or directorate.
USSR. Initials of Union of Soviet Socialist Republics.
uyezd. District in old Russia.

V

veche. Popular assembly in old Russia.
Verkhovny Sovet. Supreme Soviet.
volost. Rural district assembly.
Vserossiyskiy Tsentralnyy Ispolnitelnyy Komitet or *"VTsIK."* All-Russian Central Executive Committee.
VSNX. Initials of Supreme Council of National Economy.

Z

zakon.   Statute.

zampolit.   Abbreviation for assistant commander for political affairs.

zavkom.   Abbreviation for factory trade union committee.

Zemlya i Volya.   "Land and Freedom."

zemsky nachalnik.   Land chief.

Zemsky Sobor.   "Land Assembly."

zemstvo.   Elected local council in old Russia.

Selected Bibliography

The following list of books is a selection of only a few of the large number of English language works on the Soviet political system.

RUSSIAN AND SOVIET HISTORY

CARR, EDWARD H. *A History of Soviet Russia: Socialism in One Country, 1924–1926.* New York: The Macmillan Co., 1958.
A thorough treatment of the early Stalin period.
———. *The Bolshevik Revolution: 1917–1923.* 3 vols. New York: The Macmillan Co., 1951–53.
A standard source of information on the October Revolution.
CHAMBERLIN, WILLIAM HENRY. *The Russian Revolution: 1917–1921.* 2 vols. New York: The Macmillan Co., 1935.
Extensive treatment of the October Revolution including the events leading up to it.
FLORINSKY, MICHAEL T. *Russia: A History and an Interpretation.* 2 vols. New York: The Macmillan Co., 1953.
A standard, general source from ancient Russia up through 1917.
HARCAVE, SIDNEY. *Russia, A History.* New York: J. B. Lippincott Co., 1956.
A fairly short, clear history from Russia's origins up to the 1950's. Helpful chronologies, maps, and charts.
KERENSKY, ALEXANDER. *Russia and History's Turning Point.* New York: Duell, Sloan and Pearce, 1965.
Personal account of the October Revolution by the then head of the Provisional Government in Russia.
KLUCHEVSKY, V. O. *A History of Russia.* 4 vols. New York: E. P. Dutton & Co., 1911–26.
A standard source by a famous nineteenth century Russian historian, covering the origins of Russia up to the Revolution of 1762.
LEROY-BEALIEU, ANATOLE. *The Empire of the Tsars and the Russians.* 3 parts. New York: G. P. Putnam's Sons, 1898.
An exhaustive, very detailed treatment of early Russian governmental institutions and their operation.
PARES, BERNARD. *A History of Russia.* New York: Alfred A. Knopf, Inc., 1953.
A standard source by one of the most well-known authorities.

PIPES, RICHARD. *The Formation of the Soviet Union: Communism and Nationalism, 1917–1923*. Rev. ed. Cambridge, Mass.: Harvard University Press, 1964.
An excellent study of the early formative period dealing with incorporating the republics into the union.

REED, JOHN. *Ten Days That Shook the World*. New York: International Publishers, 1919.
A pro-Bolshevik American reporter gives his day-by-day, eyewitness account of the October Revolution.

ROBINSON, GEROLD T. *Rural Russia under the Old Regime*. New York: The Macmillan Co., 1949.
Extensive treatment of peasants, serfdom, and emancipation.

SETON-WATSON, HUGH. *The Decline of Imperial Russia, 1855–1914*. London: Methuen & Co., 1952.
A detailed, thorough coverage of the downfall of the tsarist system and the important events leading up to the collapse.

———. *From Lenin to Khrushchev, the History of World Communism*. New York: Frederick A. Praeger, Inc., 1960.
A broad-scope history which includes, in addition to the Soviet Union, communism in Eastern Europe and Asia.

SUKHANOV, N. N. *The Russian Revolution 1917, A Personal Record*. Trans. from *Zapiski O Revolutsii*. New York: Oxford University Press, 1955.
An eyewitness account of the Revolution by a member of the Petrograd Soviet. Contains short biographical sketches of all the key people involved.

TROTSKY, LEON. *The History of the Russian Revolution*. 3 vols. New York: Simon and Schuster, 1932.
An exhaustive, well-written although highly opinionated account by one of the Bolshevik leaders of the Revolution.

VON RAUCH, GEORG. *A History of Soviet Russia*. New York: Frederick A. Praeger Inc., 1957.
Clearly written, fairly comprehensive.

WOLFE, BERTRAM. *Khrushchev and Stalin's Ghost*. New York: Frederick A Praeger, Inc., 1957.
Includes the text and a commentary on Khrushchev's secret speech at the Twentieth Congress, which led to de-Stalinization.

———. *Three Who Made a Revolution, A Biographical History*. New York: The Dial Press, Inc., 1948.
The best biographies of Lenin, Trotsky, and Stalin.

THE THEORETICAL BASE

ANDERSON, THORNTON. *Masters of Russian Marxism*. New York: Appleton-Century-Crofts, 1963.
Includes selections from Plekhanov, Lenin, Martov, Trotsky, Kollontai, Bukharin, Stalin and Khrushchev.

BERDYAEV, NICOLAS. *The Origin of Russian Communism*. London: Geoffrey Bles, 1948.
A helpful explanation of Russian political theories and early revolutionary movements.

MARCUSE, HERBERT. *Soviet Marxism: A Critical Analysis*. New York: Columbia University Press, 1958.
Discusses the impact Marxism has had on Soviet politics and some of the resultant effects.

MARX, KARL, AND ENGELS, FRIEDRICH. *Basic Writings on Politics and Philosophy.* Lewis S. Feuer. Garden City, N.Y.: Doubleday & Co., 1959.

MASARYK, THOMAS G. *The Spirit of Russia: Studies in History, Literature, and Philosophy.* 2d ed. London: George Allen and Unwin, 1955.
Outlines and discusses political theory in old Russia.

MEYER, ALFRED G. *Leninism.* Cambridge, Mass.: Harvard University Press, 1957.
Analysis of Leninist thought in relation to Leninist action.

TOMPKINS, STUART RAMSAY. *The Russian Mind: From Peter the Great through the Enlightenment.* Norman, Okla.: University of Oklahoma Press, 1953.
Russian political theory, including atmosphere under which intellectuals functioned in old Russia.

SOVIET SOCIETY

BACON, ELIZABETH E. *Central Asians under Russian Rule, A Study in Culture Change.* Ithaca, N.Y.: Cornell University Press, 1966.
An extended study of Central Asian culture, both before and after 1917, with a detailed analysis of Russification and its failure under Soviet rule.

BARGHOORN, FREDERICK C. *Soviet Russian Nationalism.* New York: Oxford University Press, 1956.
Discusses Soviet russification in the border areas, including its problems and successes.

BRUMBERG, ABRAHAM. *Russia under Khrushchev, An Anthology from Problems of Communism.* New York: Frederick A. Praeger, Inc., 1962.
Covers a very wide range of subjects on the USSR.

FITZSIMMONS, THOMAS, *et al. USSR: Its People, Its Society, Its Culture.* New Haven: HRAF Press, 1960.
Information from the Human Relations Area Files; especially helpful for understanding the degree of political socialization attained in the USSR.

INKELES, ALEX, AND GEIGER, KENT (eds.). *Soviet Society, A Book of Readings.* Boston: Houghton Mifflin Co., 1961.
Includes selections from Soviet and non-Soviet sources in articles on public opinion, education, welfare, the family, social stratification, and nationalities.

JOHNSON, PRISCILLA (ed.). *Khrushchev and the Arts: The Politics of Soviet Culture, 1962–1964.* Cambridge, Mass.: M.I.T. Press, 1965.
Fascinating accounts of recent controversies between party leaders and the Soviet literary community.

MEHNERT, KLAUS. *Soviet Man and His World.* New York: Frederick A. Praeger, Inc., 1962.
Personal observations by the author, interesting anecdotes relating to Russian ideas and reactions.

MILLER, WRIGHT. *Russians as People.* New York: E. P. Dutton, 1961.
Includes a discussion of classes in Soviet society.

PIPES, RICHARD (ed.). *The Russian Intelligentsia.* New York: Columbia University Press, 1961.
Defines and categorizes intelligentsia and discusses the impact of this class on Soviet society.

SHAFFER, HARRY G. (ed.). *The Soviet System in Theory and Practice, Selected Western and Soviet Views.* New York: Appleton-Century-Crofts, 1965.
Discussions of Soviet policies and accomplishments from both Western and communist viewpoints.

SWAYZE, HAROLD. *Political Control of Literature in the USSR, 1946–1959.* Cambridge, Mass.: Harvard University Press, 1962.
Historical record of literature and arts versus the regime.

POLITICS AND GOVERNMENT

ANDREWS, WILLIAM G. (ed.). *Soviet Institutions and Policies, Inside Views.* Princeton, N.J.: D. Van Nostrand, Inc., 1966.
A wide collection of readings, based solely on Soviet sources.

ARMSTRONG, JOHN A. *Ideology, Politics, and Government in the Soviet Union: An Introduction.* New York: Frederick A. Praeger, Inc., 1962.
A brief, introductory essay with an annotated bibliography at the end of each chapter.

————. *The Politics of Totalitarianism: The Communist Party of the Soviet Union from 1934 to the Present.* New York: Random House, Inc., 1961.
One of the more complete treatments of recent Communist Party history.

ASPATURIAN, VERNON V. *The Union Republics in Soviet Diplomacy: A Study of Soviet Federalism in the Service of Soviet Foreign Policy.* Geneva: Librairie E. Droz, 1960.
A specialized study, the most adequate for this aspect of union republics.

BARGHOORN, FREDERICK C. *Politics in the USSR.* Boston: Little, Brown, 1966.
Approaches Soviet politics within the framework of the newer comparative analysis; contains information not only on the political processes as such but also on their related environmental aspects.

BRAHAM, RANDOLPH L. (ed.). *Soviet Politics and Government, A Reader.* New York: Alfred A. Knopf, Inc., 1965.
A careful selection of Soviet sources followed by Western commentaries and analyses.

BRZEZINSKI, ZBIGNIEW K. *Ideology and Power in Soviet Politics.* New York: Frederick A. Praeger, Inc., 1962.
A broad-stroke theoretical analysis of the nature and the practices of power as followed in the Soviet system.

CARSON, GEORGE BARR, JR. *Electoral Practices in the U.S.S.R.* New York: Frederick A. Praeger, Inc., 1955.
A detailed treatment, one of the very few sources in English on Soviet elections.

DENISOV, A., AND M. KIRICHENKO. *Soviet State Law.* Moscow: Foreign Languages Publishing House, 1960.
An officially endorsed Soviet source on the governmental institutions.

FAINSOD, MERLE. *How Russia Is Ruled.* Rev. ed. Cambridge, Mass.: Harvard University Press, 1963.
A standard source for Western students, especially rich in its detailed history before and after the Revolution. Extensive bibliography.

HAZARD, JOHN N. *The Soviet System of Government.* 3d ed. Chicago: University of Chicago Press, 1964.
Well-organized, highlighted by its excellent treatment of law. Includes an annotated bibliography.

HENDEL, SAMUEL (ed.). *The Soviet Crucible, Soviet Government in Theory and Practice.* 2d ed. Princeton, N.J.: D. Van Nostrand, Inc., 1963.
A careful selection of both communist and noncommunist writings on numerous features of the Soviet political system.

KARPINSKY, V. *The Social and State Structure of the U.S.S.R.* Moscow: Foreign Languages Publishing House, 1951.
A formal, structural approach, by a Soviet author.

KULSKI, W. *The Soviet Regime.* 4th ed. Syracuse, N.Y.: Syracuse University Press, 1963.
A massive coverage of a wide spectrum of Soviet public and private life.

LINDEN, CARL A. *Khrushchev and the Soviet Leadership, 1957–1964.* Baltimore, Md.: Johns Hopkins Press, 1966.
A penetrating analysis of Soviet politics in the Khrushchev era; a study of Soviet politics based on close examination of various foreign and domestic policies.

McCLOSKY, HERBERT AND TURNER, JOHN E. *The Soviet Dictatorship.* New York: McGraw-Hill Book Co., Inc., 1960.
Broad in coverage in considerable detail; well-organized.

MEYER, ALFRED G. *The Soviet Political System, An Introduction.* New York: Random House, 1965.
A large analytical study with a modern comparative scope. Includes helpful sociological data which add to the author's keen analysis.

MOTE, MAX E. *Soviet Local and Republic Elections.* Stanford, Calif.: Hoover Institution, 1965.
A very useful introduction into local government from the approach of Soviet elections.

PETHYBRIDGE, ROGER. *A Key to Soviet Politics, the Crisis of the Anti-Party Group.* New York: Frederick A. Praeger, Inc., 1962.
An exhaustive study of the policies over which Soviet leaders fought and struggled, centering around the interparty fight of 1957.

RESHETAR, JOHN S., JR. *A Concise History of the Communist Party of the Soviet Union.* New York: Frederick A. Praeger, Inc., 1960.
A compact, well-written study containing much valuable information; includes an extensive reading list.

ROTHSTEIN, ANDREW (ed.). *History of the Communist Party of the Soviet Union.* Moscow: Foreign Languages Publishing House, 1960.
An officially endorsed history from the viewpoint of the Soviet regime.

RUSH, MYRON. *Political Succession in the USSR.* New York: Columbia University Press, 1965.
A well-known Kremlinologist highlights problems and procedures involved in Soviet political succession.

SCHAPIRO, LEONARD. *The Communist Party of the Soviet Union.* New York: Random House, 1960.
A companion volume to Armstrong's. Contains a wealth of information, particularly on the party's early history.

SCHUMAN, FREDERICK L. *Government in the Soviet Union.* New York: Thomas Y. Crowell, 1961.
Brief, highly interpretive introduction to Soviet foreign and domestic policies.

SCOTT, DEREK J. R. *Russian Political Institutions.* 2d ed. New York: Frederick A. Praeger, Inc., 1961.
Compact source of accurate data and judicious interpretations; annotated bibliography.

SWEARER, HOWARD R. *The Politics of Succession in the U.S.S.R., Materials on Khrushchev's Rise to Leadership.* Boston: Little, Brown, 1964.
A translation of original Soviet materials, accompanied by the author's clarifying annotation.

TRISKA, JAN (ed.). *Soviet Communism: Programs and Rules.* San Francisco: Chandler, 1962.
A helpful introduction interprets and precedes the official party programs of 1919 and 1961 and the party rules of 1952 and 1961.

TUCKER, ROBERT C. *The Soviet Political Mind, Studies in Stalinism and Post-Stalin Change.* New York: Frederick A. Praeger, Inc., 1963.
Historical as well as contemporary analysis of Soviet policies, both foreign and domestic.

THE ECONOMY

AMES, EDWARD. *Soviet Economic Processes.* Homewood, Ill.: Richard D. Irwin, Inc., 1965.
A brief survey of the essential structure of the Soviet economy.

BORNSTEIN, MORRIS, AND FUSFELD, DANIEL R. *The Soviet Economy, A Book of Readings.* Rev. ed. Homewood, Ill.: Richard D. Irwin, Inc., 1966.
A carefully chosen selection of informative articles covering a wide range of topics pertinent to the economy.

BROWN, EMILY CLARK. *Soviet Trade Unions and Labor Relations.* Cambridge Mass.: Harvard University Press, 1966.
The most complete recent study; includes penetrating observations on the role of unions in the Soviet system.

CAMPBELL, ROBERT W. *Soviet Economic Power: Its Organization, Growth, and Challenge.* Boston: Houghton Mifflin Co., 1960.
A very readable introduction to the Soviet economy.

GRANICK, DAVID. *The Red Executive, A Study of the Organization Man in Russian Industry.* Garden City, N.Y.: Doubleday & Co., Inc., 1960.
An extensive study of Soviet management and managerial problems.

KATKOFF, VLADIMIR. *Soviet Economy, 1940–1965.* Baltimore: Dangary, 1961.
Broad in scope and coverage, excellent on the fundamentals.

NOVE, ALEC. *The Soviet Economy, An Introduction.* Rev. ed. New York: Frederick A. Praeger, Inc., 1966.
Well-written basic description and a clear analysis of the economy.

SHAFFER, HARRY G. (ed.). *The Soviet Economy, A Collection of Western and Soviet Views.* New York: Appleton-Century-Crofts, 1963.
A juxtaposition of Western and Soviet writings on a wide range of subjects dealing with the economy.

LAW

BERMAN, HAROLD J. *Justice in Russia: An Interpretation of Soviet Law.* Cambridge, Mass.: Harvard University Press, 1950.
Objective approach to the study of Soviet law.

———. *Soviet Criminal Law and Procedures, the RSFSR Codes.* Cambridge, Mass.: Harvard University Press, 1966.
A long, careful introduction helps to clarify the translation of the RSFSR codes, the most important criminal laws in the Soviet Union.

FEIFER, GEORGE. *Justice in Moscow.* New York: Simon and Schuster, 1964.
A popularly written account of Soviet courts in operation. Incisive analysis of judicial interpretations and citizen views of the law, as well as of the Soviet political system.

GRAY, WHITMORE (ed.). *Soviet Civil Legislation.* Ann Arbor: University of Michigan Law School, 1965.
A translation of the Civil Code of the RSFSR.

HAYWARD, MAX (ed. and trans.). *On Trial, The Soviet State versus 'Abram Tertz' and 'Nikolai Arzhak.'* New York: Harper and Row, 1966.
Verbatim record, although unofficial, of the Sinyavsky and Daniel trial. Includes insight into current Soviet politics.

HAZARD, JOHN N. *Law and Social Change in the U.S.S.R.* London: Stevens & Sons, 1953.
Covers the essentials of Soviet law in a careful manner.

————, AND SHAPIRO, ISAAC. *The Soviet Legal System: Post-Stalin Documentation and Historical Commentary.* 3 parts. Dobbs Ferry, N.Y.: Oceana, 1962.
A follow-up to the above account, but larger in scope.

MORGAN, GLENN G. *Soviet Administrative Legality: The Role of the Attorney General's Office.* Stanford, Calif.: Stanford University Press, 1962.
A specialized, exhaustive treatment of a little-known subject. The only work on the subject.

ROMASHKIN, P. S. (ed.). *Fundamentals of Soviet Law.* Moscow: Foreign Languages Publishing House, n.d.
An official Soviet interpretation of the legal system.

Index

Index

A

Administration
post-Stalin changes, 205–9
purpose, 199
Administrator, 266–69
Agitprop, 180
Agricultural policy, 264–66
Agricultural reorganizations, 244–46
Alexander I, 12
Alexander II, 12, 16, 26
Alexander III, 12, 30
ASSR; *see* Autonomous republics
Autocracy, tsarist, 61–62
Autonomous republics, 307–8

B

Bank; *see* State Bank
Bolsheviks; *see also* Communist Party
election to Constituent Assembly, 50
growing strength in mid-July, 38–39
July Uprising, 40
Kornilov, and, 41
leaders of the October Revolution,
48–49
Lenin's Theses, 39
origin, 141–42
participation in Pre-Parliament, 43
propaganda in 1917, 44–45
reasons for success, 51–53
Brezhnev, Leonid, 99, 224
Bureaucracy, 266–69
under Peter the Great, 14
Bureaucrat; *see* Classes, white collar

C

Capital punishment, 280
Capitalism
Lenin on, 63, 65
Marx on, 55–57
in old Russia, 23–24
Catherine II, 11
Central Council of Trade Unions, 261

Central Executive Committee
All-Union (VTsIK), 37
of Petrograd Soviet, 40–41
Central Union Cooperative
(*Tsentrosoyuz*), 256
Cherny Peredel, 60
Chief Political Directorate for the
Armed Forces, 189
Church, Russian Orthodox
early influence, 14, 20–21
relation to tsarist government, 20–21
Citizen; *see also* Classes
average citizen, 116–18
demands of, 99–101, 117–18
through legislatures, 101
Civil War, 69–71
Class structure
modern, 102–14
under tsars, 18–20
Classes
elite, 104–5
farmer-peasant, 112–14
intelligentsia, 105–9
mobility of, 114–16
white-collar, 109–10
working, 110–12
Collective agreement, 259–60
Collective farm (*kolkhoz*), 238–39
markets, 256–57
Collectivization, 78–81
Committee
Central; *see* Communist Party
Central Executive, All-Union, 37
Central Executive, Petrograd
Soviet, 40–41
of Party-State Control; *see*
Communist Party
State Defense, 204
for State Security (KGB), 210
for Struggle with Counter
Revolution, 41
Commune, 22–23
Communism; *see also* Marxism;
Leninism; *and* Stalinism
defined in 1961, 89